The Reminiscences

of

Rear Admiral Arthur H. McCollum

U. S. Navy (Retired)

Volume I

U. S. Naval Institute
Annapolis, Maryland

1973.

Preface

This manuscript is the first volume in a two-volume collection of interviews with Rear Admiral Arthur H. McCollum, USN (Ret.). It embraces nine interviews obtained by John T. Mason, Jr., with Admiral McCollum at his apartment in Vinson Hall, McLean, Virginia, during the period from December 8, 1970 to March 17, 1971. The interviews were conducted as a part of the ongoing program of the Oral History Office in the U. S. Naval Institute.

Admiral McCollum has made some corrections and emendations to the original transcript. The reader is reminded as always with the Oral History interview that the transcript is indeed a record of the spoken word rather than the written word. An index is added for the convenience of the reader.

Admiral McCollum was head of the Far East Desk in the Office of Naval Intelligence at the time of the Japanese attack on Pearl Harbor and on the Kra Peninsula. Later he was asked to testify before the Joint Congressional Committee Investigating Pearl Harbor. His MS is invaluable to anyone interested in the background to the conflict with the Japanese in 1941-45. It is invaluable also for a picture of the U. S. Navy Department prior to that event.

An appendix has been added to this volume. It contains copies of the following documents:

A. McCollum's memo of December 1, 1941 to the Director of Naval Intelligence.

B. Correspondence pertaining to Admiral McCollum's review in the Saturday Review of RADM R. A. Theobald's book, The Final Secret of Pearl Harbor. The correspondence is dated June 7, 1954, et. seq.

BIOGRAPHY

REAR ADMIRAL ARTHUR H., McCOLLUM USN (Ret)

Name: Arthur Howard McCollum

Birth Place: Nagasaki, Japan. Date: 4, August 1898.

Father's Name: John William McCollum

Mother's Name: Drucilla Franklin Collins

Married: Margaret Lois Benninghoff. Date, 2 October 1925.

Children: Arthur Howard McCollum Jr. presently a Commander USN.

EDUCATION

Primary: Private tutors and public schools abroad and in the United States; latterly at the public school of Marion, Alabama and the Perry County (Ala.) High School.

Preparatory: Two years - 1915 to 1917 - Marion Institute at Marion, Alabama.

College: Four years, U. S. Naval Academy at Annapolis, Maryland; graduating on 3 June 1921 with degree of B. S. in Naval Science.

Post Graduate:
(a) Three years (1922 - 1925) study of the Japanese language, Oriental History and culture in Japan. Qualified Interpreter and Translator of the Japanese language. (I understand this qualification is the equivalent of a Doctorate in the American educational system)

(b) Six months (1925) study of submarine operations and command principles at the U.S. Naval Submarine School at New London Connecticut.

(c) Various technical courses in Gunnery, Torpedoes, Communications, Diesel Engineering, etc.

OFFICIAL TRANSCRIPT OF RECORD OF SERVICE

SHIPS AND STATIONS	FROM	TO
USS Arkansas (battleship)	Jul 1921	Dec 1921
USS Argonne (transport)	Jan 1922	Mar 1922
American Embassy, Tokyo, Japan (instr)	Mar 1922	Apr 1925
USS Chewink, Submarine Base, New London, Conn.	Jul 1925	Nov 1925
Submarine Division EIGHT (USS O-7)	Jan 1926	Jul 1927
USS O-7 - Commanding	Jul 1927	Apr 1928
USS S-11 - Executive Officer.	Apr 1928	Jul 1928
Office of CNO, Navy Department, Washington, D. C.	Aug 1928	Sep 1928

October 1966

American Embassy, Tokyo, Japan (Asst. Naval Attache)	Oct 1928	Jun 1930
USS WEST VIRGINIA	Sep 1930	Jun 1933
Office of CNO, Navy Department, Washington, D. C. (Head of the Far East Section of O.N.I.)	Aug 1933	Feb 1935
Branch Hydrographic Office, San Pedro, California. (Special Intelligence duties)	Feb 1935	Jun 1936
United States Fleet - Staff (Asst. Operations Officer and latterly acting Operations Officer and Fleet Intelligence Officer)	Jun 1936	Jan 1938
Office of the CNO, Navy Department, Washington, D. C.	Feb 1938	Apr 1938
USS JACOB JONES - Commanding - (a 4 pipe destroyer)	Apr 1938	Sep 1939
Office of CNO, Navy Department, Washington, D. C. - various duties in connection with intelligence matters - (During this period I was Head of the Far East Section of the Office of Naval Intelligence and because of my presumptive capabilities in relation to the Far East was frequently consulted on policy matters)	Nov 1939	Oct 1942
Southwest Pacific Force - Intelligence Officer, additional duty on staff with U. S. SEVENTH FLEET -	Nov 1942	Apr 1945
Bureau of Naval Personnel, Navy Department, Washington, D. C. - Intelligence matters - (this was a sort of waiting period)	May 1945	Jul 1945
Bethlehem Steel Company, Quincy Massachusetts - cfo USS Helena; CA-75	Jul 1945	Sep 1945
USS HELENA: CA-75 - Commanding	Sep 1945	Oct 1946
Naval Administrative Command, Central Intelligence Group, Washington, D. C.: (name later changed to Central Intelligence Agency)	May 1947	May 1948
Office of CNO, Navy Department, Washington,, D. C. -OP 21 (in connection with organizing the Central Intelligence Group)	Nov 1946	May 1947
Fleet Training Group and Underway Training Unit, Chesapeake Bay, USNS, Norfolk, Virginia - Commanding	May 1948	Sep 1949
Military Sea Transportation Service, Atlantic - Deputy Commander -	Sep 1949	Jan 1951
Military Sea Transportation Service, Atlantic - Commander - (Either Deputy Commander or Commander the job was the same only the title was changed) additional duty as OIC NCSO, New York	Jan 1951	May 1951
Central Intelligence Agency, Washington, D. C. - continued on duty as a retired officer from 30 Jun 1951.	May 1951	Oct 1953

Retired 31 October 1953

Medals and Decorations

LEGION OF MERIT combat "V"; Commendation Ribbon, SecNav.
World War I Victory Medal with Atlantic Fleet Clasp
American Defense Service Medal with Fleet Clasp
American Campaign Medal; Asiatic Pacific Campaign medal with 5 battle stars
World War II Victory Medal; Navy Occupation Service Medal with Europe Clasp; China Service Medal; National Defense Service Medal; Philippine Liberation Ribbon with 2 bronze stars.
Order of Rafidin - Class III - by Iraq. Also numerous letters of Commendation by the Secretary of the Navy and others.

HIGHLIGHTS OF CAREER

Career has been that of a LINE officer of the Regular Navy with accent on Command of Combat ships, higher staffs, Intelligence and International Relations. Promoted through all ranks to Captain USN. Retired in 1951 and promoted to Rear Admiral USN (Ret.). Immediately upon initial retirement, re-called to active duty and served as a Consultant with the Central Intelligence Agency. Re-retired on 31 October 1953 and engaged in the Real Estate and Insurance business in Northern Virginia until June 1964 and again retired.

Served in every type of naval ship except Air-Craft carriers. Commanded three single ships viz:- submarine U.S.S. O-7, 1927-1928; Deastroyer U.S.S. Jacob Jones, 1938 - 1939; Heavy Cruiser Helena, 1945 - 1946; and on many occasions commanded groups and squadrons of ships. Service has been principally in the Navy Department at Washington and abroad.

In 1922 specially selected by the Navy Department for a three year course of study in Japan. In the autumn of 1923 served as special liaison officer with the Commander in Chief U.S. Asiatic Fleet during relief operations incident to the Japanese earthquake of that year. 1924 served on board the U.S.S. John D. Ford as liaison officer with Japanese naval units in the Kurile Islands incident to the U.S. Army's around the world flight of that year. Qualified as Interpreter and Translator of the Japanese language. Subsequently served twice as Head of the Far East Section of the Office of Naval Intelligence and once as Assistant Naval Attache at the American Embassy in Tokyo, Japan. In this latter duty, as Acting Naval Attache, arranged for U. S. Naval participation in the ceremonies attendant upon the coronation of the present Japanese Emperor (Hirohito) in the late fall of 1928. In 1934 served as Naval Aide To H.I.H. Prince Kaya (Japanese) during his visit to Washington, D. C.

Command of the submarine O - 7 1927 - 1928; Assistant Naval Attache American Embassy Tokyo, Japan 1928 - 1930; Battleship West Virginia 1930 - 1933; Head of the Far East Section of O. N. I. 1933 - 1935; Special Intelligence duties on the West Coast of the United States 1935 - 1936; Assistant Operations Operations Officer and then Acting Operations Officer and concurrently Fleet Intelligence Officer on the Staff of the Commander in Chief of the U. S. Fleet (Admiral A.J. Hepburn) 1936-1938 (Feb); Command of the destroyer Jacob Jones 1938-1939 (Sept) operating in the Mediterranean where assisted in the evacuations of American nationals from Barcelona Spain prior to the capture of that place by General Franco; Head of the Far East Section of O.N.I. 1939-1942 (Oct); Special mission to the British Admiralty Aug-Oct 1941. Developed the concept Fleet Intelligence Centers and designed and assisted in the installation of the first one at Pearl Harbor in April-May 1942.

From November 1942 to May 1945 served on the Staff of the Commander Allied Naval Forces Southwest Pacific Area, and Commander of the U.S. 7th., Fleet (Vice Admiral Carpender and then Admiral T. C. Kinkaid) as Director of Allied Naval Intelligence Southwest Pacific and Assistant Chief of Staff-Intelligence- 7th., Fleet and concurrently Commanding Officer of the 7th., Fleet Intelligence Center. In this capacity starting with no assistants, developed an Intelligence organization that succeeded in providing adequate information for Naval campaigns in the northern Solomons, New Guinea, Bismarck Archipelago,

Philippine Islands, including the decisive naval battles of Leyte Gulf and Lingayan Gulf. At its peak the organization consisted of more than 250 Officers and Enlisted Men including numerous outlying reporting stations. This Organization worked in close collaboration with the Staff of General Mac Arthur and with our Australian, Philippine, Dutch, British and French allies. In addition to its strictly Naval aspects it conducted all naval functions of the successful development of guerilla forces in the Philippines and in southern Asia.

In May 1945 I was assigned to Special Duties in the Navy Department and during June served as U.S. Naval Aide to H.R.H. Abdul Illah, Prince Regent of Irak during his state visit to the United States.

Ordered to Command of the Heavy Cruiser Helena, supervised the final details of the construction of the ship and accepted her for the government and placed her in commission in September 1945. In early 1946 in command of the Helena and two destroyers proceeded to England where until May served as Flag Captain to the Commander in Chief U.S. Naval Forces Europe. (Admiral H. Kent Hewitt). In May-June 1946 took the Helena to the Far East via the Mediterranean Sea, Suez Canal, Red Sea and Indian Ocean making diplomatic calls at French, Italian, Greek, Ceylonese and British ports. From June to October 1946 served in command of the Helena on the China Coast as Flag Captain to Rear Admiral W.A. Kitts, III, USN.

Upon detachment from command of the Helena, returned to the United States and assigned to duty in the Central Intelligence Group, later the Central Intelligence Agency. In May 1948 ordered to sea as Commander of the Fleet Training Group and Underway Training Center, Chesapeake Bay with headquarters at Norfolk, Virginia. In this position was responsible for the first stage training of all types of ships of the Fleet as assigned and provision of suitable sea training facilities and equipment for all types and ships in the vicinity; i.e., from Atlantic City, N.J. to the South Carolina border.

In October 1949 ordered to New York City to organize the Atlantic Division of the newly created Military Sea Transportation Service, a merger of the Army Transport Service and the Naval Transportation Service. Starting in late October of 1949, assembled a headquarters staff, established operating and administrative policies, provided for the orderly transfer of personnel and materiel rrom the Army to the Navy and, on 1 March 1950 assumed full control and direction of the Organization as Commander M.S.T.S. Atlantic. The command consisted of some 45 large ships and more than 8,500 persons, principally civilian employees, with outlying stations at Norfolk, Va., New Orleans La., San Juan, Porto Rico and Balboa, Canal Zone. The first annual budget was $54,00,000.00

Upon retirement from active service in June 1951 I was immediately recalled to active duty and was assigned as a consultant to the Central Intelligence Agency. I re-retired from this position in the late fall of 1953; and until 1964 was engaged in the Real Estate and Insurance business in Northern Virginia. Whereupon I again retired

DECLARATION OF TRUST

The undersigned does hereby appoint and designate as his (her) Trustee herein, the Secretary-Treasurer and Publisher of the United States Naval Institute to perform and discharge the following duties, powers, and privileges in connection with the possession and use of a certain taped interview between the undersigned and the Oral History Department of the United States Naval Institute.

1. Classification of Transcript.

    (✓)a. If classified OPEN, the transcript(s) may be read or the recording(s) audited by the qualified personnel upon presentation of proper credentials, as determined by the Secretary-Treasurer of the U. S. Naval Institute.

    ( )b. If classified PERMISSION REQUIRED TO CITE OR QUOTE, the user will be required to obtain permission in writing from the interviewee prior to quoting or citing from either the transcript(s) or the recording(s).

    ( )c. If classified PERMISSION REQUIRED, permission must be obtained in writing from the interviewee before the transcribed interview(s) can be examined or the tape recording(s) audited.

    ( )d. If classified CLOSED, the transcribed interview(s) and the tape recording(s) will be sealed until a time specified by the interviewee. This may be until the death of the interviewee or for any specified number of years.

2. It is expressly understood that in giving this authorization, I am in no way precluded from placing such restrictions as I may desire upon use of the interview at any time during my lifetime, nor does this authorization in any way affect my rights to the copyright of my literary expressions that may be contained in the interview.

Witness my hand and seal this __6/k__ day of __April__ 19___.

3. Copy autho
    (a) Division of naval History
    (b) Special Collection Naval Academy Library

_____

I hereby accept and consent to the foregoing Declaration of Trust and the powers therein conferred upon me as Trustee:

_____

Interview No. 1 with Rear Admiral Arthur H. McCollum, U. S. Navy
(Retired)

Place: His apartment in Vinson Hall, McLean, Virginia

Date: Tuesday morning, 8 December 1970

Subject: Biography

By: John T. Mason, Jr.

Q: Admiral, it's a delight to see you this morning. I certainly have been looking forward to this series with you, this biographical series. You had a fascinating career and, most appropriately, the beginning was in the proper place. Will you tell me about the circumstances surrounding that and something about your family background, and then launch into your early education?

Adm. M.: I was born in Nagasaki, Japan, on 4 August 1898. My parents were Southern Baptist missionaries to Japan. My father was John William McCollum, born in Alabama near Selma, actually a place later called Marion Junction. My mother was Drucilla Franklin Collins born at Hedge Hill, which was the name of a farm, to Joseph Todd Collins and his wife Catherine Smith Davies Collins. Do you wish any more on the background of my parents?

Q: Tell me how did your father happen to be in Japan at the time?

Adm. A.: He was an ordained Baptist minister and he was the first Southern Baptist missionary to Japan.

Q: That was a rather tough assignment, wasn't it?

Adm. M.: Well, they went out to Japan right after they were married. That would be 1889. They were married in 1889 and went to Japan immediately, and he started the mission work in Japan, in Kyushu. Our home, (the home I remember), was in Fukuoka, which is part of a twin-city setup, the port city being Hakata. Fukuoka was the seat of the Daimyo of the province, meaning the lord, or governor, or what-have-you. There were very few non-Asiatic foreigners in Fukuoka and, as a young child, I remember no young children locally to play with at all, other than my family. I had two older brothers and two younger sisters.

Q: Were Christian missionaries rather suspect among the Japanese?

Adm. M.: Yes, they were. They were suspect because, as you know, for several hundred years Christianity was proscribed in Japan, so the Japanese government rather reluctantly permitted proselyting again, after the overthrow of the Shogunate. But still some of the old prejudice, as could be expected, hung on. But, little by little, that was overcome. Nagasaki was one of the what they called open ports, and the reason my mother went there to give birth was that the hospital or the medical facilities in Fukuoka were not as well favored as in Nagasaki and, of course, the cities are not very far apart. That is how I happened to be born there. My oldest brother was born in Kobe, I believe, which is another port. My middle brother was born in Kyoto, and my youngest sister, Ida, was born in Kobe. She is three or four years younger than I am, and my sister immediately following me, Phyllis, was also born, I believe, in Kyoto, but I'm not sure of that. So that's the rundown on the family. Now, there was an older sister whom I never knew who died in infancy, some say diphtheria and some say cholera. But my

McCollum #1 - 3

father was busy in those early years in setting up mission stations, I suppose you would call them, in northern Kyushu.

Q: Had he gone there with a knowledge of the Japanese language?

Adm. M.: No. He studied Japanese for a while shortly after he came there, and he was reputedly very good at it. I have heard him preach in Japanese, which he apparently did very glibly. But you see my father died in 1910, so I was only about eleven years old, so anything that I say as to his effectiveness in the language would be that of quite a small and impressionable child.

Q: Tell me about growing up in a missionary household in Japan in those early days.

Adm. M.: In a place like Fukuoka, the household had to be pretty well self-sustaining. For instance, we kept cows to furnish milk for the children because in those days there wasn't any milk or dairy furnished from outside. That came later. We also kept a small herd of goats, as I remember, to furnish flesh food, and my father, having been raised on a farm in Alabama, was very adept at running this thing more or less like a farmstead. We had, as I remember it, quite a good sized piece of ground which, of course, the mission could not buy. Foreigners were not permitted to own property outright in Japan, nor were they permitted to so own it right up until World War II. So these mission properties all had to be owned through what we would call in this country a straw, in other words, a corporation was set up in which the controlling interest of the corporation were all Japanese nationals. The money was put up by mission authorities but the mission, as such, owned nothing. These things, if I remember, in Japanese are called shadan, which in effect is a corporate structure. All of your mission properties in Japan at that time and later, right up to World War II, were, as far as I know, owned through or managed through these corporations, and in case the Japanese directors of the corporation decided to abscond, there was nothing under the law to stop them.

Q: It must have been difficult, the initial effort, to get the Japanese nationals to do this.

Adm. M.: That I don't know. I only got this later on because my father-in-law, Dr. Benninghoff, of the Northern Baptist missions, was in this thing in a big way - he was headquartered in Tokyo and operated a center at Waseda University called Hoshien. One of the ways to proseltyze the Japanese was to help students go through college and that was his main object. He ran dormitories for students and assisted them in their work and taught them English and so on. So that was one approach.

Q: But your father was the first Baptist missionary on the grounds?

Adm. M.: Well, you see, there are two kinds of Baptists, the Southern Baptists and Northern Baptists, and while on the mission field they consorted together very happily, they ran with completely different boards in this country. For instance, the Southern Baptist Missionary Society was headquartered in, I think it was, Richmond. The Northern Baptist Missionary Society, it seems to me, was either in New York or Philadelphia. I've forgotten which. Possibly

New York later, because the Northern Baptists were fortunate in acquiring the very heavy interest of John D. Rockefeller, the first. He was a very ardent Baptist, as was his wife, and as are his children who were, monetarily at least, very good. The Southern Baptists, so far as I know, did not have any individual person of any such distinguished material means.

Q: Well, your household had to be self-contained in many more ways than one.

Adm. M.: That's right. You see, there was five years difference between the brother next above me and myself, so the two older boys - my oldest brother was eight years older than I and his brother immediately following, who was three years younger than he was - tended to consort together and left me out to play with the little girls when they got big enough. So my only playmates, other than the rare occasions when my brothers would permit me to play with them, were Japanese children, and I did have a number of Japanese children playmates. For instance, one of my particularly good friends was the son of the minister of our little church there, named Masao Sato - Sato being the last name. He was a year or so older than I was and he frequently came over to play with me, but we didn't run around loose in the town. We played within you might say, the compound, which was fenced in. That was the way we lived. Of course, we had servants and so on. In other words, it was pretty much a self-contained household and had to be. My father was away a good deal because he was busy traveling around setting up other stations and encouraging the converts not to backslide and so on. He did not do too much educational work himself. He was more of an evangelical type, in other words, he was a preacher and an exhorter. Later on, that became somewhat out of fashion in favor of, you might say, the educational approach.

Q: What about your own education in the household?

Adm. M.: My mother taught us, the younger children, and the older boys were sent off one year to a boarding school in Chefoo, China, that was known as the China Inland Mission School. As I say, my education was largely at my mother's knee. You see, we left Japan in 1904 for home leave for my parents and I accompanied them, and we went to Alabama where we lived, mostly in Marion. My father had gone to Marion Institute, which at that time was called Howard College. I'm named after the college. The college has changed its name now to Sanford, I believe, and has moved from Marion to Birmingham. But at that time Howard College was located in Marion, and my father was a graduate of Howard College, and from there he went to the Southern Baptist Seminary which I believe was then in Louisville, as it is now. After he graduated from there he was selected for the mission field, married my mother, and off they went. I was only about six years old, so all I had was more or less primary stuff.

Q: And you came back to Alabama. How long did you stay?

Adm. M.: We came back to Alabama and stayed until early 1906, about a year or a year and a half. My father's health was commencing to fail, even at that time. He was still quite a young man, only in his early forties. He was born in 1865, I think, or something of that sort. He was subject to asthma and colds and that sort of thing, and the climate of Japan is not conducive to curing it, so he stayed a little bit longer than the normal, you might say, sabbatical leave for missionaries, and at that time we lived, first, with my maternal grandfather for half a year or so. Then we moved and lived among relatives and friends in Marion. That's where my paternal grandfather's business was located. He was a horse trader and ran a livery stable, was a director of the local bank, and that sort of thing. That grandfather I never knew, because he died before we came back. He died in the early 1900s, 1902 or thereabouts, and his first wife, my grandmother, had predeceased him by a year or so. He had been in business with one of his sons, my uncle Eugene, who took over, you might say, the family business there and, of course, he operated the local hotel. In those days, the big business in that kind of thing was traveling salesmen who came in on trains. They were met at the station, which was roughly a mile from the center of town, and driven in carriages to the hotel, and then they hired what they called rigs, in other words, horses and buggies and so on to cover about a 15-mile area, then they'd come back, and as long as that method of peddling goods existed, the business was pretty lucrative. But of course with the coming of the automobile and so on that gradually faded away.

Q: The whole picture changed!

Adm. M.: The whole picture changed, that's right. So we went back to Japan, all of us, and first we settled very briefly in Fukuoka, but new missionaries were coming out, and we then moved from Fukuoka to a place called Kumamoto in north central Kyushu

300,000. It was near one of the most spectacular active volcanoes in Kyushu called Aso, and, of course, like most of those towns, it was an old castle town, and in those towns the castles were all vacated by the feudal lords, of course, but they performed as barracks of the local military. For instance, in Fukuoka, the castle there was the headquarters of the 27th Infantry Regiment, and I remember seeing that regiment parade off to go to the Russo-Japanese War, quite an occasion. They marched right by our front gate and we were permitted to go and have friends to stand and wave the soldiers off to war. And Kumamoto was the site of the capital of the last rebellion against the imperial authority in Japan, headed by a man named Saigo Takamori, and his statue is there. He was defeated in battle and committed suicide, but he actually led the revolt against the newly established imperial government. This would be back in the 1860s or early 1870s. But he is still looked on in that part of Kyushu as a great national hero regardless of the fact that he was in actual opposition to the emperor.

So, we lived there and again we found ourselves bored. As far as I was concerned there were no non-Asiatic children to play with at all, and we had to live again very much self-contained. The house was a rather comfortable wooden house with a lawn and so on, and from our front yard you could look over there and see the volcano smoking off in the distance as it did at a great rate. The education of the children started getting beyond my mother and my father realized it, so we moved to Kobe, which is a port city on the main island of Japan. As you know, it's near Osaka and so on, largely to go to school. My father rented a house there which was then considered in the suburbs but now, I understand, pretty well grown up, and I went to school there. We were taught in an English-type school. I was in the third form. My sisters went to a female school, which was operated by an English lady, but the sexes were separated in quite a different school. I stayed in that school until we came back to the United States. My father's health failed completely and we came back in 1909, and we landed in Seattle, actually in Vancouver, and from Vancouver we came back on a Canadian Pacific steamer to Seattle. That's about as far as my father could go, so we settled there, you might say, momentarily.

Q: Reflecting back on this earlier experience in Japan, let me ask about your mastery of the Japanese language?

Adm. M.: I spoke Japanese before I spoke English. In other words, as usual, I had a nurse, an amah, as we called her. She was my nurse, governess and what-have-you, and she knew no English at all, so I spoke Japanese. I did speak English, but with some difficulty, and I remember once that my father told me that he had had a very flattering offer: a local prominent Japanese offered to buy me of the family, because he said a bilingual kid was wonderful to have, wonderful opportunities. My father had to explain to him that I wasn't quite for sale!

Q: Did your mother master the Japanese tongue, also?

Adm. M.: She talked some, enough to talk to the servants on household things and so on, but she was never too fluent at it, and she didn't study it. Now, for instance, my mother-in-law, Mrs. Benninghoff never could talk Japanese to amount to anything. She talked a kind of pidgin Japanese and she was always ashamed of it. Dr. Benninghoff again, like my father, was very fluent. He preached and talked and so on in Japanese, and extemporaneously, he'd been taught it that way and it was a wonderful thing to see him do it.

Q: Did you experience any difficulty, was there any problem involved in living in two cultures simultaneously?

Adm. M.: Sure there was. You see, in a place like Japan when a foreigner walked down the street he was followed by a troop of boys shouting at him. They usually shouted, "Igin, Igin," which means foreigner. Actually, its translation is "a different person," but it has a sort of derogatory connotation.

Q: I suppose the present-day counterpart would be, "Howard, go home"?

Adm. M.: No, no. They were just making fun of you for being a foreigner. It wasn't that they didn't want you, but anybody that was foreign was just a funny guy, an odd guy, and was shouted at just like you would shout and chase a dog through the streets. That was the idea. And I found myself joining with other Japanese children shouting "Igin" at other foreigners, which amused my family no end. You did have difficulty and the main thing was when you came back from there to a place like Alabama - by this time, of course, I had acquired what passed for an English accent and you were really foreign then when you lived in Alabama saying cahn't and carf, and so on.

Q: You really had no roots then!

Adm. M.: That's right, and when we came back my maternal grandmother first taught me to read and cipher and so on, she ran sort of a private school out in the country for children. The public sch school was not quite established yet, and my grandmother was my grandfather's second wife, not my true grandmother, she was my step-grandmother, but she had previously eked out an existence teaching the local children there and after she married my grandfather she continued to do so and most of the children from three or four miles around would ride in on horseback in those days and grandmother taught them in her sitting room. And she taught me too. I can remember I would sit on a footstool at her knee there and she would teach me the letters and read out of a primer and ciphering and so on, and when that was through I'd sit over in a corner until she called on me again.

From there we went to Marion and I went into public school there. I was in the first or second grade in our public school. Then when we came back - this was when we came from Fukuoka in the first instance - then we went back to Japan and that's when we eventually ended up in Kobe, where I went to this English-type school. From there, as I say, we landed back in Seattle and I promptly was put in public school there in the Green Lake section of Seattle where we lived. I went to school there and was in the fifth grade.

Q: And your father was very ill at that time?

Adm. M.: He wasn't very ill, but he was ailing, as we used to say. He died in January of 1910. He had pneumonia and, as frequently happened in those days, the heart was not adequate to look after the thing and he died. My mother took the body back to Alabama for burial and then when she came back she picked up the children. The two older boys were working, not going to school, they had to work to support the family, and I did what little chores I could do working around, raising chickens and selling eggs and that kind of thing, which wasn't very much, but, see, I was only eleven, going on twelve at that time.

We then went back to Alabama and lived for about six months or a year with my mother's father again. My mother had nothing and the two older boys promptly went to work. My oldest brother worked for my grandfather who operated a country store, and the other brother worked for one of our cousins. In Alabama everybody in that neighborhood was kin to one another. If they weren't, they were foreigners. So, I mean, those were the only people you could work for in country stores in those days. I was sent to the one-room school there. The teacher was a cousin, again, like they all were. Then my mother found employment with Judson College, which is a Baptist ladies' school. She had graduated from Judson College herself. She was employed there as matron. That meant the housekeeper and of the grounds and that sort of thing. She was given a room and her board and the two little girls were permitted to live with her in the dormitory and also got their food. She got in addition to that, I think, either $25 or $30 a month. I, being a male, was not allowed on the premises, although I was only about twelve or thirteen, so she had to find other means for me. I grew up then in this town of Marion which had a population of about 2,500 and I don't think it's increased much. But it is a rather pleasant place to live. As I say, there was a girls' school and then there was a boys' school, the Marion Institute. When Howard College moved out of Marion, the buildings and so on were acquired by a man named James T. Murphy. He had come down there at the close of the Civil War. he had marched the corps - he was commandant of cadets at the state university of Tuscaloosa - and he had marched the cadet corps down to oppose the Union Forces and to join General Forrest's forces in the defense of Selma, which was a relatively large town, and after their defeat, the cadet corps had been marched to Marion, where Colonel Murphy set up a school and it was called Howard College. It was a Baptist school. In other words, Baptist-supported and endowed and so on, like Judson. In other words, there were the twin schools, one for boys and one for girls, both of them supposed to be college grade at that time, but of course later on they were more or less prep schools. For instance, Judson College nowadays, you probably know, is I think what they would call a secondary college. In other words, they go through about two years of university. And Marion Institute, the boys' school, which has grown since I went there, grown quite a bit, is also a junior college, but it accents training for examination and entrance to the military and naval academies. They're very successful at it, too.

So I grew up in this little town and there I got my primary education. They had a high school there and I went to high school for about - well, I was a junior in high school when the high school opened. The primary school went through ten grades, and of course the high school would go through twelve, and when the high school was opened they called it Perry County High School. That is the county that Marion is the county seat of. I went there and I got to running with a crowd that was raising too much hell and I was too much trouble for my mother to keep track of, so I was invited to go to Marion Institute by the then-president, Hobson O. Murphy. He was the oldest son of James T. and he and his brother, Walter Murphy, operated the school. I didn't graduate from high school because my graduation year of high school was spent as my first year in Marion Institute. The latter part of that year, Colonel Murphy sent for me and asked if I wouldn't consider going to the Naval Academy or West Point. He was very kind. He knew that my mother was a widow and jobs in Alabama were hard to come by, and he went out of his way to assist me and my family. I've never forgotten it. I don't think he charged full tuition for me, although I don't know.

Q: This must have been an entirely new world suggested to you, to go to a military academy?

Adm. M.: That is quite true. Although, you see, in Japan I had always thought that I would like to be a soldier. In Japan when I was growing up as a small boy, the soldiers were very much looked up to, and I thought it was a grand thing to be a military officer. But as far as the Navy was concerned, I never considered it. But, as things turned out, I finally managed to, through the help of Colonel Murphy and two of the editors of our local Weekly newspaper, Mr. Greer and Mr. Pope. We had two newspapers in town in those days, and both of them were helpful in procuring an appointment for me, and I finally ended up at the Naval Academy by appointment of the then-Senator Bankhead, who was the father of all the Bankheads around and he was one of the last remaining Confederate veterans in the Congress. His two sons both came to Congress, one as a senator, and the other ended up as speaker of the House. So that's the way I happened to get to the Naval Academy, and I went there in 1917. I spent four years in the place and, as far as the place where I grew up, nobody quite knew where this Annapolis was. They thought it was Indianapolis and all other kinds of places. I remember a colored boy who I grew up with on the farm whose name was William McKinley Ruffin, but he was known as Blicket, and Blicket said, "Howard, is this Indianapolis, is that in the United States?" I assured him that it was, but I didn't know quite what I was talking about. So, that's the way I got there, and again a very kind thing was done for me. In those days, of course, you passed the mental examination okay, but you took your physical examination at the Naval Academy. So I had to undergo a physical examination. Well, I didn't know what it was, but I, like a sap, had gone camping down on one of the rivers and I was bitten up with what we call red bugs down there, which they call chiggers. So when I bared my chest for an examination before the doctors up here, I was red all over, and these fellows started looking at it and said, "What's the matter with you?" And I said, "I don't know. That's nothing but red bugs." And they said, well, they didn't know. They all shook their heads over this thing quite a bit and finally they said, "Well, I tell you, maybe you'd better stay out in town for two or three days until we see how this thing clears up." I was kind of down in the mouth, and finally the senior doctor, Captain A. M. D. McCormick, who was a very famous surgeon and doctor in the Navy, his son was Lyne McCormick, later an admiral, sent for me and started chatting with me very briefly and he asked me a little bit about my background, and, understand me, I only had the railroad fare to get there, I didn't have any extra money. He looked at me and he said, "Where are you staying, young fellow?" I said, "I'm staying at Carvel Hall." He said, "Well, you'll find it pretty expensive, don't you?" And I said, "Oh, no." He said, "Stick around a little while," and he would see if he couldn't place me to a little bit better advantage, because he had to drive by there on his way home, anyway, so he drove me to a boarding house - now, this is the head doctor on his luncheon period - there weren't very many cars in Annapolis or anywhere else in those days, but I went in his car, he personally took me in and introduced me to the lady who ran the place, and arranged to underwrite my expenses while I was there. I think that was one of the kindest things that's ever happened to me. I stayed there three days, as the rash paled off and they let me in.

Q: Tell me about your educational experience there.

Adm. M.: I was a normal student, I suppose. I just missed graduating with distinction or honor or whatever they call it. In other words, I ended up with a 2.9 or something average, and I think you have to have a 3.0 to get the distinction on the diploma. My son kids me about it all the time. He had a 3.0 or something, so he graduated with distinction and he says, you just graduated. My class was one of the war classes, and we were split in two. In other words, when the war in Europe ended in 1918, the Naval Academy was operating on a three-year curriculum, and they decided to go back to the four-year curriculum, and my class was the one that was caught in the middle, so that half of my class was graduated in three years, and the other half of it graduated in four years. I was in the four-year period, so that's the reason I graduated in 1921, and the other half of the class graduated in 1920.

I had good teachers there and I remember with particular affection a Dr. Smith, who was the head of the English department. He was an innovation. He was, as far as I know, the first civilian head of department at the Naval Academy, and he came from the University of Virginia, where he'd been full professor of literature or something of that sort. A very fine gentleman. He was the most fascinating speaker I've ever listened to. Physically, he was almost repulsive in appearance, but he dressed beautifully, presumably to counter his physical defects. But I saw that chap stand on a platform and I thought what a wonderful stunt it was, and he talked for over twenty minutes and held an audience of third class midshipmen completely fascinated. His subject was the origin and development of the Egyptian hieroglyphs, a subject calculated to elicit no enthusiasm from midshipmen at all. But it was terrific. It was a tour de force, and I've never forgotten it and I've always tried to learn to speak ever since Professor Smith showed off to us.

But we had good instructors there and they were very kind and always helpful. I never had any trouble with any of them, except from the disciplinary department. I seemed not to be able to stay out of trouble with those people, but other than that I got along fine.

Q: What did you excel in largely?

Adm. M.: I'd say I excelled in languages and history and English, and also did very well in ordnance and gunnery, and that sort of thing. Mathematics was awfully hard for me. I still don't understand how I ever struggled through calculus at all - **ever**. But I did, but I was on the ragged edge of that, and my manual dexterity

— we had to do quite a bit of drawing in those days, mechanical drawing, they called it, and my drawings were futuristic, at least.

Q: Obviously, your preparation in Marion was ample for the Academy.

Adm. M.: Yes and no. It was, but, you see, the last year that I spent at Marion was spent on drilling to pass the examination, so instead of being a broad-view education, it was narrowed down to the subjects that were going to be asked on the entrance examination, and the whole business was pointed to that. For instance, as far as languages were concerned, we didn't take that up. That wasn't a part of the entrance exam. Mathematics, two kinds, and English and history and so on. I forget what they were, but those were the ones and the Murphys excelled. They were the first people that I know who had done what they called spot the examinations. It wasn't wrong for them, they had acquired the papers or the questions of past examinations, and then by the exercise of the mathematical genius of Colonel H. O. Murphy - he was the head of the school - they would "spot" what they expected the examination to be. We all went down to Selma which is about 30 miles from Marion, we were taken down and quartered in the Albert Hotel there to take the examination. The examinations in those days were given by the postmaster, I think, and I never will forget each night, as we'd be going in to take the examination, about five subjects would be run over in about five days, Colonel Murphy would hold a night session, and he'd stand up before us and he'd say, "Now, gentlemen, when you go in to the examination tomorrow, the first question that you will see on your examination paper will be this," and he went right down the line, and he missed it very, very seldom.

McCollum #1 - 19

Q: That was a distinct advantage, wasn't it?

Adm. M.: Yes, very much so.

Q: Tell me about your athletic prowess at the Academy.

Adm. M.: Well, I didn't have any. In those days I weighed about 130-135 pounds and that didn't qualify me for much of anything. I tried out for boxing. There was a guy who was about the same weight that I was and he'd beat the face off of me all the time. I got tired of that, and tried wrestling and found that I couldn't make it either. So I didn't do very much of anything. I was qualified in sailing and that kind of thing. I did a lot of yelling as a fan and that's about it.

Q: What about the summer cruises? Was there anything significant?

Adm. M.: Our first summer cruise, of course, was during World War I. I was on the USS Ohio. There were three or four battleships of the Ohio class - the Maine, the Missouri, and the Ohio - that year were the cruise ships. That year the only class that went on those ships that was my class, which had just finished their freshman year. The other class, which became first class, the class of 1920, which graduated in 1919, they were split up and farmed out in groups of a dozen or so to all of the ships of the fleet. They acted as junior officers, whereas we went down and scrubbed decks and heaved coal and so on. I got to be quite a good coal-heaver, and I liked it, curiously.. I shoveled coal into those furnaces and learned to handle a slice bar and all that sort of business, and, believe it or not, I gained weight doing it. I got to the point that I was water tender no less on the midshipmen cruise and fired one of the boilers, of course, under the supervision of an enlisted man who was a boiler attendant. I never will forget that fellow. He was reputed never to have gone on deck for the last ten years. He had about twenty years' service, and he would get through being water tender during his watch, then he would go wash up and clean up in the washroom, and he would come out in the most beautiful white clothes you've ever seen. He'd come into the upper gratings where it was warm, and there he'd sit. I don't know his name now, but he certainly taught us, and he was right there when trouble broke out to take prompt action on it.

Q: You learn a lot on those summer cruises, don't you?

Adm. M.: You learn how the other half lives and so on. We did learn how to steal, of course, which is necessary. We would be loading stores, for instance, and it's easy enough, you load stores and in those days the food didn't have much variety because we had very little refrigeration or anything of that sort, and it was very easy to let a crate fall down a couple of ladders and break open and hopefully, before you could gather it up somebody would stash away two or three cans of pears, for instance, canned pears, which were a delicacy. I remember one night we had accumulated half a dozen of these things and thought how nice it's going to be and how disgusted we were and gave the fellow who had stashed them hell, when we opened them up and found they were sauerkraut.

Q: After the cessation of hostilities, did you get abroad on one of these summer cruises?

Adm. M.: Oh, yes. The first summer cruise, that would be in the summer of 1918. In 1919 we again went on a summer cruise, and this time I was on a battleship called the Kentucky. There were two classes on there. My class being the senior class, we were not seniors but we were juniors and sophomores together. We were on the Kentucky, and there were two or three other battleships, the Kentucky and the Wisconsin and the Alabama and Kearsarge. They were all coal-burning, of course. The Kentucky, I think, was next to the oldest in point of time of the battleships, or so-called battleships. We went through the whole business. We learned to operate the turrets and the guns and so on and so forth, and we had some rather amusing experiences on that. I remember one case - no, that would be on the next cruise. We did all right on that. You see, we learned to live the way they lived in those days. Fresh water was an item much in demand, and every morning we'd line up with a bucket and go over to the fresh-water tap and under the eagle eye of the chief master-at-arms we'd draw a quarter of a bucket of water, and that's what we bathed in, if we wanted fresh-water bathing, shaved in, washed our clothes in, and so on. That's all you got. The rest of it had to be in salt water. I remember once on my first cruise I discovered a wonderful thing, they gave us a cake of stuff they called "salt water soap," and it came in a bar maybe 18 inches long by about 2 inches square, and you shaved off what you wanted and you scrubbed, and it lathered beautifully. Of course, in salt water you don't get much of a lather with an ordinary soap. I thought I'd made a wonderful discovery, as did a number of my classmates. So we used this soap to scrub our hides with and it worked fine, but after about a week we noticed the hide got noticably tender. It started peeling off in a lot of places. Well, of course, the reason that the stuff lathers is that it's got a very high content of lye in it.

That cruise we went down to the Caribbean. We went to Guantanamo, of course, and then to the Virgin Islands, then to the Panama Canal, and as a big treat the ship was locked through to Gatun Lake and there we had a regular fine day because we pumped the fresh water from the lake and everybody took a fine bath and washed their clothes and so on. Then we came back out. The following year, which was my first class cruise, I was a new first-classman, we were on the battleship <u>Connecticut</u>, and we went then from Annapolis - about six of these ships - to the Hawaiian Islands. It was a most delightful cruise. Pretty dirty. We were all coal-burners, and the one big advantage from the midshipmen's point of view was that when we went through the Panama Canal on the way to the Hawaiian Islands, we did not have to shovel coal out of the barges. They had very fine mechanical coaling out there and the coal was shunted directly into the bunkers. The one hitch in that was that it was quite a long way from there to the Hawaiian Islands, so the ships all carried deck loads of coal. Coal just poured on the decks and battered around in various places, because the bunkering wasn't sufficient to carry them the distance to the Hawaiian Islands. So we went there on that basis, and that was quite a memorable cruise. The Hawaiian Islands were not as sophisticated as they probably are nowadays. It was the first time that any midshipmen had ever been there and the whole place went wild and we were treated royally, and we just had a wonderful time in that place. We were all sorry to leave it. Of course, there was a big band playing an aloha. I remember a

McCollum #1 - 23

classmate of mine who couldn't swim fell so enamored of a girl he was sitting up there looking at that big Hawaiian moon and he thought he could just get across anyway, so he hopped into the water and darned near drowned!

From there we went back to Seattle and again the same thing was repeated. The town people treated us royally. We had a parade in town. All the pretty girls were out, and we couldn't buy anything anywhere. It was really something.

Q: It was great being . . .

Adm. M.: Yes! Then from there we went down to San Francisco, and then from San Francisco to San Pedro, and from there back through the Panama Canal. And going through the canal the ship that I was on, the Connecticut, got one of the cables twisted around one of her propellers, and the Vice Admiral was a fellow named H. P. Jones, a very distinguished name in the Navy in those days, later commander-in-chief of the U. S. Fleet. And I thought, how silly, he'd been a bachelor all his life, but he was going to get married and this business of having his flagship, having so disabled, he couldn't take it. So we lashed the thing up together and he said, "My gracious, he was going to run her..." and finally he did run her as hard as he could and that screw fell off and so did the other one, about halfway to Cuba. So we were ignominiously towed in to Guantanamo by the collier Orion, and the midshipmen were transferred to other ships for passage back to Annapolis, which was made in good time. I went back on the South Dakota. But you had all kinds of curious things happen. The midshipmen this time were manning all the guns, and of course those old battleships had a variety of calibers of guns. For instance, the Connecticut had two 12-inch turrets fore and aft, and she had four 8-inch turrets on the side, and then she had on the gun deck about eight or nine 7-inch guns on each side, and on the spar deck above, she had 3-inch guns. It was a regular gunnery officer's nightmare. And the 7-inch guns - I don't think they have them in the Navy any more, I'm sure they haven't - were what they call case guns. In other words, you have a projectile that weighed, oh, 125 or 130 pounds, something like that, and you pushed the projectile in with a wooden rammer, and then behind this you'd come up with what amounts to a brass cartridge full of powder, and you pushed that in behind. The other guns of the bigger calibers, the 12-inch guns and the 8-inch guns, were what they called bag guns because the powder, of course, was in a bag. This was fine, but we had one fellow named Skeets Mercer who was the gun captain of one of the 7-inch guns. The only trouble with Skeets was he was a little bit of a short, lightweight fellow and was a trifle gunshy. He didn't like noise. His job was to pull the lanyard to make the gun go off. On one of these battle practices where we were firing all these guns, and of course the 3-inch guns were going off overhead, and the 8-inch guns were going off on the side, Skeets would turn his back to the gun and pull the lanyard. I never will forget, I was supposed to be a safety observer, and I was standing back there and Skeets would turn his head and pull the lanyard, the gun went off, and he would open the breech and so on, while somebody else was holding this can of powder. He pushed it in all right, and Skeets pulled the lanyard and nothing happened. So Skeets not knowing anything - he was supposed to watch the recoil of the gun, you know - he didn't know this, so he reached out and opened the breech block. Well, of course, that jumped the cartridge back out. Technically, they'd had a misfire, and the next thing you knew was everybody looked around and here was this fellow, whose name was McKee, holding this can of powder. And Skeets looked at him and saw this powder, and he crawled right out over the end of the gun! We finally prevailed on Mac to throw the thing in the water. I don't think it went off anyway.

That was the cruise when everybody got the yen to get tattooed, and some of them did get tattooed. I was on the point of getting tattooed but we decided we'd get more fun running a tattoo parlor on board ship, down in the paint locker, so we persuaded one guy that we had the captain of the paint locker down there, who was an enlisted man, was a tattoo master, and if he'd come down there we'd stand by and get him tattooed. I don't think he was too bright. He was bright enough in his studies, but he came down and placed himself in our hands and we painted him up striped like a barber pole all round his body, but it was paint. He got mad and finally went ashore at the next port of call and got himself tattooed anyway.

Q: Was that not illegal for a midshipman to be tattooed?

Adm. M.: Theoretically, but I don't think they paid too much attention to it. For instance, Admiral Halsey was tattooed, and most of them got it as midshipmen. You know the thing to do was to have your class crest tattooed on your upper arm. Some did. Theoretically it was frowned on, but I don't know of anybody getting kicked out of the Naval Academy for being tattooed.

McCollum #1 - 26

Q: Well, when your career there came to an end, what kind of an assignment were you hoping for?

Adm. M.: Well, we all having had this wonderful reception on the West Coast of the United States, everybody in the Naval Academy wanted to go to the West Coast. We were no exception. They ran a sort of a lottery to pick your selection of ships, the ships that you were going to be assigned and so on, and they held it up in Mmeorial Hall in Bancroft Hall, and we all went and we'd draw numbers, and you'd have a pick, and you could pick a ship. The ideal thing to do was to get a ship that was based on the West Coast, we'd had enough of shoveling coal, so we wanted an oil-burner. Those were the two things that stuck out in our minds. But also there was a group of us that had gotten to be very close friends at the Academy, and the idea was that we all wanted to go to the same ship, about a dozen or so. Well, of course, unfortunately, some of the fellows didn't draw high numbers, so we gradually percolated down until we hit the lowest common denominator, so that I was picked on that basis - I drew a pretty good number, and I picked the Mississippi, but by the time we got through trying to all stay together, we had graduated down to the Arkansas. Well, the Arkansas was on the West Coast all right, but the hitch was, she was a coal-burner. That was fine, but at that time most of the fleet was in the Pacific. There was very little in the Atlantic, that is, no battleships, anyway, that I remember. So that we promptly did that and we of course had a month's leave, and then from there we went to - at that time the Arkansas was at Bremerton. We went to Bremerton to board the Arkansas.

Q: This group of friends?

Adm. M.: Yes. We went around. A fellow named C. R. Bornw, he's a retired Admiral, an aviator, and so on, lives here in town. He comes from Tuscalooas. We cattycornered across the country, which we had been warned against, but we tried it anyway. We got stranded inall sorts of odd places, like Kansas City, and Billings, Montana, and so on, because we missed connections on the train. But we finally landed up in the place, and both of us reported for duty to the Arkansas. And then the Navy Department played a dirty trick on us, because about that time they decided to reorganize the fleet, which they did, and the Arkansas, along with her sister ship, the Wyoming, was ordered into the Atlantic. We promptly sailed in the Arkansas from Seattle and came down the West Coast and so on, went through the Panama Canal, where we got a new admiral, Admiral John D. MacDonald, who was the first commander of what they then called the Scouting Force. He didn't like the Arkansas because his flagship had been the Arizona, which was an oil-burning battleship and fairly clean. The Arkansas threw cinders out as big as the end of your thumb and caught the old man's collar. He didn't like that either. The navy was at pretty low ebb in personnel. Right after World War I the enlistment rate was not very high. It was announced that only those people who wanted to go to the East Coast had to stay aboard, all the rest of them, if they wanted to stay on the West Coast, could transfer. And they did. The result was that we were pulled way down. I was a junior officer in the first division on the Arkansas which, in those days, had turret 1, and the admiral's quarters were also located on that part of the ship. The officers' quarters in that type of ship were all forward, not aft, as they were in other ships. It was pretty grim going. In other words, the first division, even with a reduced complement, was supposed to have about 80 people in it, and I had 25. It didn't have enough people to man the guns, of course, not even to make a gun crew. You needed about a dozen to man each gun chamber, nothing other than that, and the housekeeping chores you couldn't keep up with it, all these people. We finally got a draft of new recruits. We came in to New York and got these recruits on board, and they were pretty sorry specimens. I think they were the sweepings of the waterfront of the whole northeast. They offered disciplinary problems and other things. They were slum kids and so on, and they needed a lot of training, and the training stations were such that they didn't get the full course. They were only there for about two or three weeks at a place like Newport and were shipped out as live bodies to the ships.

They posed a real problem in what you might call human relations on the part of the young officers and the few petty officers. For instance, in our division I had a chief turret captain who was a wonderful man, but he interfered very little with the operation of the division. His specialty was the turret, of course, and the man who ran the division was a first class bo'sun's mate named Reick, who had the amazing record in those days of having been in the Navy 16 years. The next petty officer was a third class petty officer, who had been in the Navy about two years and they rated him in the third class, but he was probably a year older than most of them. Other than Reick, for instance, Blaha, the chief turret captain, he ran the turret and that was it and helped out with whatever he could. Reick was supposed to run the division, and he did it. They were all just wonderful to me, those fellows. They saw that we were in a tough spot all the way around.

We came up there and we spent the winter of 1921 in New York. We had come up through Guantanamo, of course, and done the usual thing we went in to Yorktown where the admiral tried to discipline his new ships because the crews were not well trained. So we spent about three weeks in training, operating out of Yorktown, much to everybody's disgust. We thought we would go back to the fleshpots of New York. They weren't as good as Seattle. Then we proceeded to have a wonderful time in New York. We'd known a lot of girls from up there, and they and their parents were very kind. We liked to go out to Garden City. That seemed to be a favorite place. Two or three very nice-looking girls lived out there. The one trouble was that you'd take the girl home and you had to sit in a railroad station until next morning at four o'clock to catch the first commuter train back.

Q: That was the penalty, was it?

Adm. M.: That was the penalty.

Q: Did your units make any effort at recruitment in New York?

Adm. M.: No, there wasn't any effort so far as I know. I was just a junior officer in the first division and stood a junior officer's watch on the bridge and that sort of thing. Our captain was a fellow named Stanford E. Moses and, again, he befriended me. We had gone in to Newport, Rhode Island, and there the officers every morning went ashore to attend lectures at the War College. These lectures, or, at least, a good part of them were pointing out the dangers accruing from Japanese naval expansion and so on and so forth, and Captain Moses was quite disturbed about this because he thought it was an unbalanced presentation. He sent for me one day and he said, "McCollum, I see you were born in Japan." I said, "Yes, Sir," and didn't think much of it. I wondered what was coming next. Then he went on and he delivered a little lecture. He said he thought that we were getting a one-sided view at the War College, that he had been flag lieutenant to Admiral Beardsley, Lord knows how many years before, on the Asiatic Station and had found that the Japanese were very reasonable people. He did think that there should be a balance. Then he turned to me, and he said, "How would you like to be an attache at the American Embassy in Tokyo?" Well, a question like that posed to a 23-year-old kid who was getting darned sick and tired of having the Admiral's finger shaken under his nose because the dogs on his doors were not shined properly - there were 83 of them or something like that on his outside doors - why, it was wonderful. And he said, "Well, if you'd like to go, I think I can fix it up for you." I said, "Thank you, Captain," and with that I left. And that was the last I heard of this thing. And I was out at a dance at the Navy Yard and squiring the daughter of the chief naval constructor there, a very nice girl, and we were dancing around when some guy came up to me and said Lieutenant Commander Wentworth wants to see you. He was the flag secretary and was one of the discipline officers at the Naval Academy with whom I'd had some entanglements. I went to see him at this dance and he said, "Your orders are in." I looked at him blankly and said, "What orders?" "Oh," he said, "I don't know but you've got orders detaching you." I said, "What do I do now?" and he said, "Come in in the morning - of course, this was Saturday night - I'll be on board ship on Sunday and we'll go over them."

I went down and, sure enough, here was my order detaching me to go to Tokyo to be an attache at the Embassy. That was just wonderful. I had about a week. We really burned it up in New York, and then I went down to Philadelphia and got on the old Argonne which was a transport. It had been pulled out of the bone yard. In those days you worked your way. You were a passenger, but you also caught all the outside jobs like recorder of summary courts-martial, standing watch on deck, and all that sort of thing, and I stayed on that ship until we got to Manila...

Q: There was no indoctrination in Washington or...?

Adm. M.: No. I just had my orders in my hand. I didn't even have sense enough to get a passport. I took these orders and went down to the Argonne. She was in Philadelphia, and she was recruiting madly to get a crew on board that looked like they were competent to move her out. They did, and from there we went to Norfolk where we picked up some people, and went to Charleston, South Carolina, where more came. The Navy Department was broke, so they were sending officers and, presumably, enlisted men to the West Coast by this ship which was going. They didn't have money enough to pay the railroad fare - so they said. So you had a class of graduates coming up from Pensacola and they got as far as Norfolk, then they went on the ship. They spent about a couple of months getting around to San Diego. So we were pretty crowded, and I didn't have any place - I was the most junior person on the ship, and I had no place to sleep. This ship was not insulated. It was hotter than the hinges. I finally acquired a single room over the steam steering engine and that was even worse. I used to go up on the poop deck and sleep under one of the lifeboats till one of the lady passengers complained. I don't know why. She was up about 50 yards ahead of me somewhere.

So I applied for and got the job of assistant navigator. That entitled me to kick the chief quartermaster off the transom in the chart house where I could sleep.

Q: You were very enterprising, weren't you.?

Adm. M.: You had to be. The Argonne was quite a ship, rag-tag crew and all. She finally made it. We came in to San Diego and we went up to San Pedro and then very briefly in San Francisco, and across to the Hawaiian Islands, and from there to Guam, and from Guam in to Manila. I don't know what it is right now, but that stretch of water between Hawaii and Guam is probably the loneliest ocean in the world. There's no commercial traffic, nothing. We would sail there day after day, day after day, going to Guam, seeing nothing in the world but wide-open space, nothing.

One night, the quartermaster on watch with me on the bridge, sang out and he said, "Looks like the stern light of a ship up ahead." I said, "You're crazy. No ship's crazy enough to be out there." Sure enough, it looked like a little white light, just like a stern light of a ship. We went on and I thought, "Well, I won't report it to the Captain yet, because I don't believe any ship is out there." Then, all of a sudden, this thing started to grow and grow and grow and it went into a great big fireball, and the quartermaster yelled at me and he said, "We're going to hit it," and with that both of us fell flat on our tummies on the deck and this thing sailed overhead. It looked to me just about masthead high. It must have been a meteor of some sort because you could hear it sizzling like frying bacon. Then it disappeared over the horizon somewhere. But it's funny the reaction you have to these things. What good would falling flat on your tummy behind a canvas wind screen do anyone? And yet I had exactly the same reaction at the battle for Leyte Gulf. Our fleet surgeon, Dr. Walker, and I were standing on the bridge and we were getting one of these recurring Japanese air raids and it was dark. We weren't too much scared by the Japanese bombs that were coming down, but these darned ships of ours were shooting these 20-mm. caliber all over hell and high water, and these things started to look like they were coming right for us. Both Doc and I hit the deck and hid behind the canvas wind screen!

Q: Self-preservation is an instinct that's pretty strong. Well, were you apprehensive about this new assignment? Had you kept up with your Japanese?

Adm. M.: No. I had lost all Japanese. You see, when I was going to this English school in Kobe - well, to go back - when I left Japan in 1904 or 1905, or thereabouts, I knew probably more Japanese, but it was baby talk type of Japanese, like Papa and Mama, that kind of thing, but it was perfectly understandable. But I lost all that during the first year and a half that we were in this country, when I was between the ages of five to seven, and when we went back I never recovered it. And when we were in school in Kobe, most of the boys there could speak Japanese, but it was not the thing to do. We didn't speak Japanese. We only talked English.

Q: You were Anglo-Saxons?

Adm. M.: Well, the school was integrated. We had all nationalities in that school. I remember one class and our teacher was an Englishman, named Mr. Walker, I suppose he was in his twenties, and in this particular classroom we sat at desks that the lids opened up, but there were three or four in a row and a bench behind us. And when we'd stand up to move out to recess or something of that sort, Mr. Walker would call out the name of the boy on the aisle to lead the rest of us out. You've never seen such a polyglot group of names. He'd start off, "Song Chu Long, Avon, Paquito, Harry, Max." Song Chu Long was a Chinaman, Pauito was what they called in those days a Macao Portuguese, he was some sort of a half-breed from down there. Harry was a Eurasian with a British father and a Japanese mother. Max was a German. So you had all kinds in there. One house we lived in in Kobe our next door neighbor was the Dutch consul. I've forgotten the name. He had two boys, both about the same age as I. We used to play together. But the mother of these boys was a Spanish lady. So there was a pretty good mix, you might say.

Q: Yes, but you hadn't really kept up with your Japanese?

Adm. M.: No, not at all. I had none, and when I got to Japan finally - you see, we went to Manila, and from Manila we transshipped to the Army transport Thomas, which brought us up to a coal port in the southern end of Japan, the southern end of Kyushu, not too far from Nagasaki, called Miike, and from there we went ashore and took a train which brought us up as far as Shimonoseki, and at Shimonoseki we transferred to the express train which took us in to Tokyo. Traveling with me was Lieutenant Hulings, his wife, and two small children, and a French governess...

Q: Was he also going to the Embassy?

Adm. M.: He was going to Japan to be the assistant naval attache, and he came out by the same route that I did. We all went together, and I never will forget when we were sitting in this train on the way to Shimonoseki - I'd been trying to read up on Japan and I recognized what they were - a couple of these huge Japanese wrestlers came in to the little dining car they had there, attended by their satellite geishas and so on. Of course, their hair was dressed in the old-fashioned manner, and one of these little girls, Isabelle was her name, Isabelle Hulings, piped up in a loud voice, "Mama, look at those great big women."

We got to Tokyo finally on the 17th of March. We left - Hulings did, too - Philadelphia on about the 2nd of January, to show you how long it took on the <u>Argonne</u>. It took us about two months and a half to get there. Of course, there were stops en route and so on, and there was a day of waiting in Manila. An amusing thing happened. I had a lot of classmates who were serving on the Asiatic Fleet flagship, at that time, a ship called the <u>Huron</u>, an old armored cruiser, and we all went out on the town that night. They were showing me the sights and so on, mostly, I'm afraid, the bar of the Army and Navy Club, and I stayed in the Manila Hotel which is right on the waterfront. There's a little park between that and the Army and Navy Club in Manila. Next morning I came down to breakfast and, as I was checking out of the hotel and wondering how in the world to get down to the dock and having breakfast, and a fellow that I had known at the Naval Academy, a classmate of mine who graduated a year ahead of me, named Tommy Ryan came in, and said, "What are you doing here?" He was then serving on a destroyer called the Zane, and they'd been down in the southern islands, the Sulu Sea and that sort of thing, and I said rather grandly, "Why, Tommy, I'm going to Japan to be an attache at the embassy." His eyes got kind of big, and he said "Mac, how in the world did you ever get an assignment like that?" "Well," I said, "I put in for it," which I hadn't but I might as well make it look good, and he said, "What are you going to do now?" And I said, "I'm just waiting to go down, get a carametta or what have you, and see if I can get aboard this Army transport Thomas." And he said, "Well, be my guest," rubbing it on. He said, "I have a carriage outside."

Q: You were both doing a bit of bragging!

Adm. M.: Yes. So we went out and got in Tommy's carriage, which boasted two horses, these little Filipino horses, and a driver sitting up on a box. Tommy broke out a big pith helmet which impressed the pants off of me, and put it on his head. So we drove in style. Meantime, Tommy crossexamined me about this cushy assignment that I was having. So I laid it on a bit, not knowing anything about it. So we went down to the Thomas, and that was the last I heard about it. Six months later, I got a cable from Tommy which said, "I'm on my way to be an attache at the embassy." And a little while later after he got in to Japan he sent me another wire and said, "I will be in Tokyo station at such and such a time." I said that was just fine. I thought that he'd impressed me with a carriage and pair down there, so I would impress him a little bit. In those days in Tokyo, believe it or not, they didn't have such a thing as a taxi, but they had cars for hire. What you did was you went down to the garage and you hired a car and a chauffeur, and the chauffeur usually affected riding breeches and leather puttees and that kind of thing, and there was one particular outfit that I rather liked on the rare occasions when I could afford one to patronize, for the very simple reason that, in those days in Japan, there was one car color reserved for the imperial family. It was a beautiful cherry red, and theoretically nobody else could have a car of that color. Well, the fellow who had this garage had his cars painted as close as he could to that cherry red color. It was something that he managed to get away with it. I don't know who he bribed, but he did. And so I drove down in this car and had it wait outside. In those days, there wasn't any parking problem. And I went in to the Tokyo station which, as usual, was busy and noisy - wooden clogs on those concrete floors make an awful racket. And here came Tommy with a boat cloak flowing and looking around holding onto his baggage for fear somebody was going to steal it from him. Everybody trying to gather around, and finally he said, "I'm sure glad to see you." "Well, come on out. I've got a car waiting for you." We went out and he looked at this car. Here was the chauffeur standing holding the door open and saluting as we went in, you know. We got in the car and Tommy's head started swiveling, and we went driving down through town, and the car was close enough to the Imperial color that as we came by each police station the cops would stiffen to attention and salute, and Tommy said, "Hey, this is pretty hot."

At that time, again, a kind thing happened to me. I was taken in by a missionary family who had known my people, Mr. and Mrs. William Wynd, to live with them as a paying guest, we might call it, but very, very reasonable. Otherwise, I couldn't have stayed there. My pay wasn't sufficient. So we stayed for about a week. The Wynds kept Tommy, too. They offered kindly to keep him but Tommy thought that would be too much, so he got quarters elsewhere. At that time, for a non-Asiatic, Tokyo was probably one of the most expensive capitals in the world, just to live. You couldn't live without servants and that sort of thing, and the idea of living with a Japanese family didn't work out. Some of the people tried it for a while, and you were teaching them more English than they were teaching you Japanese. Financially, it was pretty rough.

Q: What were your duties?

Adm. M.: To study the Japanese language. There was no course, nothing set up at all. There were two officers out there...

Q: And this is something you didn't really realize when you went out?

Adm. M.: I didn't have any idea what I was getting into. I just went to Japan. The naval attache, who was a Captain Edward H. Watson - a very, very fine Kentucky gentleman. He had flowing mustaches and a goatee and so on and was perfectly charming. I went up, of course, and reported and, after two or three days of floundering - the other two fellows out there - this was in March of 1922 - who had preceded me, a fellow named Zacharias, who gained some fame in writing, E. M. Zacharias, and Hartwell C. Davis, both of them quite a bit senior to me. Zach was a lieutenant commander, and Davis, who was a class behind Zach, had reverted to a lieutenant, because everybody had had wartime temporary ranks and they were all being

McCollum #1 - 39

shaken down. Zach was the class of 1912, I think it was, and he managed to hold on to two and a half stripes, just barely. He was fairly well up, at the time. Garret Hulings, who was the new assistant naval attache, had been a lieutenant commander, but he had reverted to lieutenant, as had Hartwell Davis, who was the class of 1913. So that was the three of us out there. Zach very kindly took me in to live with him. He and the former assistant naval attache, a fellow named John W. McLaren had rented a house and acquired a couple of servants, a Japanese-style house, out in one of the then-suburbs of Tokyo, not too far from the Meiji Shrine area and there was a little colony of language students there. For instance, our next-door neighbor was Lieutenant Colonel and Mrs. Hazard of the Army, and next door to them were Major and Mrs. Whitsel. Whitsel ended his Army career as judge advocate general, I think it was. So there were about three houses there, very simple, Japanese-style houses, and Zach very kindly took me under his wing because I didn't know anything, and he said, "Well, now, the first thing we have to do with you is to get you a suit of clothes. Get you some proper clothes." I said, "What's the matter with this?" and he said, "Well, you need a dinner jacket, for one thing and you've got to have a set of white tie and tails." I said, "What for? If I ever go out at night I just wear these." He said, "Oh, no, you won't. Out here when you go to dinner anywhere after six o'clock at night, you wear a black tie a tux, as he called it - and if it's after eight o'clock, you put on a white tie and tails." That was the social thing, so we went down and Zach pawned his credit and I pawned mine and acquired this rig from a Chinese tailor in Yokohama.

But, as I said, when I reported to Captain Watson he was very cordial and very nice. After two or three days I went back up to the naval attache's office, which was a wing of his house actually, and finally after standing on one foot and then the other, I turned to the captain and said, "Captain, just how can you go about studying this Japanese? What books do you get? How do you go about it?" "Why," he said, "bless my soul, the country's full of it. They all speak Japanese. It's just full of it. All you've got to do is just go out and start talking to them." So we did. We acquired some books, the standard book of grammar of the Japanese language, one written by a German the other written by a Professor Chamberlain, an Englishman, very distinguished - Basil Hall Chamberlain. He wrote a lot of books on Japan. He was one of the early scholars of Japanese. He was the professor of philology at the Tokyo Imperial University. His introduction to Japanese writing, called the Mojino Shirube Introduction to the Study of Japanese Characters. An introduction, mind you. The technique was to sit down - the Navy Department gave us an allowance of $50 a month, out of which you had to pay for your books and any instruction and so on for which you had to send in receipts...

Q: There was no formal enrollment at any...

Adm. M.: No, no. What you did was you went out with one of the students that had been there before and if you could, you got one of their instructors - a tutor - and most of us would take about two hours a day with two different tutors. You had one come in the morning and one in the afternoon.

Q: To your residence?

Adm. M.: Yes, to your residence. They would come right to you. You didn't go to any school or anything of that sort. You set up a time with them and they came to your residence and gave you an hour, and you paid them so much a month or whatever it was. The only thing that we could have to study with to start with was a primary school reader, just like Japanese children used in Primary schools. Of course, it got very much more formalized later on, but that was what you did.

Q: And there was no actual supervision of what you were doing?

Adm. M.: No, but you had an examination to pass every six months.

Q: Given by whom?

Adm. M.: Given by the man in those days they called the Japanese secretary of the American Embassy. In other words, he was a Japanese-speaking official of the Embassy. In my case, most of the time, it was a fellow named Gene Dooman, and Gene Dooman was the son of missionaries and he had been educated in Japan, then came back to this country and was educated in schools in New England, where their family came from. He was a very highly educated person and a very nice fellow. He and I lived together. In other words, I messed with him, as we called it, later on. I got to have a very high regard for him. He was a very nice chap. Almost more Japanese in some ways than American. He'd spent so much of his early life out there, and he was very, very good and, believe you me, whether you lived with him or not, when you took an examination with Gene

McCollum #1 - 42

Dooman you'd had it. You went through the loops. He was a hard task master. And you had to make that every six months. As far as that's concerned, they didn't care how you made it, but that was it.

Q: And if you didn't make it?

Adm. M.: If you didn't make it, theoretically you were sent home.

Q: How many students were there, actually?

Adm. M.: On the Navy side, there were three. On the Army side there were, at that time, Hazard, Whitsel, Mashbir, Crane, and Martin. Later on, three or four others came.

Q: Were there State Department people, too?

Adm. M.: Yes. They called them student interpreters, and at that time there were two, and later on it was increased to three or four. their technique was to study the Japanese language just the same way that we did for about two years. The Navy course was three years and the Army course was four years, for some curious reason. These fellows spent two years in which they studied Japanese, and they also had the same types of examinations given by this Dooman character that we did. Then, after their two years, they would usually go to a consulate where they would be a vice consul. For instance, one of my close friends out there was a chap named Salisbury who was a student interpreter when I first arrived, and shortly after that he went down to be a vice consul in Yokohama. So another guy names Broomall, who was also a student interpreter, after his two years went down to Shimonoseki to be a vice consul. There was a fellow named Sturgeon who followed the same route. In other words, he spent two years - he was about finished with his two years when I arrived - he was a vice consul in Yokohama. We didn't have a consulate in Tokyo in those days. Later on the consulate general was set up. In those days there was a consul general, as they called him, in Yokohama - no, our man was a consul, I reckon. The British had a consul general. That's the way the thing was set up, and you got along pretty good. You didn't have too much social life. You understand that, in order to read a Japanese newspaper, just a common, ordinary Japanese newspaper, you have to have mastery of somewhere around 2,000 of these ideographs. The technique of mastering them is sheer memory. You just have to memorize it, that's all. I also did something that some of the rest of them didn't do so much and which Gene Dooman suggested to me. I read every book I could find on Japan, mostly by English writers who had written about the culture and the history and so on. Fellows like Sir George Satow.

Q: And Hearn?

Adm. M.: Lafcadio Hearn. His stuff was almost poetry. I've still got a set of his books and I read them just for the sheer beauty of the language. In most cases, you're really reading fairy stories to a degree. Some of these other guys were pretty much down to earth.

Q: You started to mention Momotaro.

Adm. M.: Yes, well, there are a great many such stories. Just like in any other country there are a great many fairy stories. In this country we have Snow White and the Seven Dwarfs and Little Red Riding Hood. And those things are alluded to in ordinary speech, and so on and so forth. If you want to talk about the god of war, for instance, the tutelary god, the son of the Empress Jingo, who probably never existed, a legendary character, who is reported to have held back the birth of this child by wearing a stone wrapped around her genitals so that he couldn't come out, while she went off and conquered Korea. That's where we get our word "Jingo," for instance, named after a legendary Japanese empress. Her son later became the emperor, Ojin, and he is worshipped all over Japan as Hachimas, the god of war, the biggest general of all. These are all things that are alluded to in ordinary speech, among other things, and one must have some knowledge of these sort of things, or else you don't get the feel of the country. The easiest way to get it was though books that you could read easily because in a great many cases, the Japanese books writing about these historical or semi-historical, mythical characters were very little used because they had to stick pretty closely to an official genealogy of the imperial family, which, according to Japanese chronology, started 2,500 to 3,000 years ago. So you had to follow that, and the result is that they had to go through all kinds of contortions to fit in to this artificial thing. Actually, I think the first historical date that can be historically verified as happening in Japan - and Japan obviously was in a very primitive state, but you get this from the Chinese - the Chinese, you know, are great record-keepers - is somewhere around the year 400 or 500 A.D. So you have a whole history to develop with these people.

This is a little book, not a very good history - it's a short one - by my friend Dr. Clement. He was a Northern Baptist missionary and he lists some of the things that are very useful. For instance, the first emperor was a fellow called Jimmu. Now this is an official thing, 660 to 585 B.C., so he ruled for 75 years, and so on all the way down the line. The first dozen or so of these guys, some of them ruled 210 years. It's just like the old patriarchs of the Bible, and a lot of this has been reconstructed - well, not reconstructed - but they had to have something to start with, so they put it down. You don't get any meaningful history - or didn't at the time I was out there - from native sources which are frequently highly suspect. But there were two good histories. One by a Dr. Murdock, who was an Englishman who was a teacher in Japanese schools. It's very dull reading and it's a very difficult book. The other one is by a fellow named Brinkley, who was a publicist and lived in Japan. Captain Brinkley was an early one out there, say, 1860 or 1870, and he was editor of the Japan Daily Mail, a subsidized English-language newspaper. If you read these things you got a feel for some of this stuff. A lot of it was told to these people by their Japanese friends or instructors and so on, and they screened it out and, being in English, why, the Japanese government permitted them to publish. They couldn't have published in Japanese.

Q: You were a very astute young man to have arrived at this conclusion, that by reading fairy tales and all the rest you began to get the background necessary!

Adm. M.: Well, of course, I was encouraged to do this by such fellows as Gene Dooman. You did have to have this, and I still read Lord Redesdale's <u>Tales of Old Japan</u>. He was at that time Second Secretary at the British Embassy, and he comes of a very distinguished literary English family.

Q: Mitford is his name?

Adm. M.: That's right. He had some daughters, I believe, who also are noted authors.

Q: And they were very fond of Mr. Hitler!

Adm. M.: Very likely.

I started in more or less under the tutelage and help of Zacharias who was very helpful. I was supposed to be sharing expenses with him, but I couldn't quite cut it and he knew that so he made allowances. I was staying at the Imperial Hotel. Not the Imperial Hotel that's just been destroyed, not this thing by Frank Lloyd Wright. That was building at that time, just starting to build. But the hotel that preceded it was a white frame Victorian type of place, heavy on red plush and gold fringes and so on. I was staying there and when I tried to inquire of Captain Watson couldn't I find a cheaper place to stay, he said, "Well, being an attache at the Embassy, you can't afford to stay anywhere else." So that was a real poser. I developed a little boil on my arm and I said to Zach I'd better have it cut out, and he said, "Why don't you go down to the naval hospital in Yokohama and have Dr. Spear take a look at it." I said, "Go down to the hospital for a little pimple, a little boil!" He said, "Sure, why not? It costs fifty sen to ride down on the inter-urban one way and fifty sen to come back. You can walk from the station, if you want to, or take a rickshaw. It doesn't cost too much." So, in those days we had a naval hospital in Yokohama, and the British had a naval hospital there set on one of the most desirable residential sections of town, called The Bluff. It was a great big wooden structure. So I went in to see him. They only had one doctor and he was a Captain doctor. In those days in the Navy, a Captain doctor was very senior. They didn't call them captains, he was a Medical Director. So I went in and Dr. Raymond Spear had been the executive officer of the naval hospital in Annapolis when I was a midshipman, and was reputed to be one of the finest surgeons in the Navy. In a sense, that hospital was a bit of a sinecure. I mean, he was out there, had very lovely living conditions, servants, and services, and so on, and he had two or three enlisted corpsmen, three or four nurses up there, and they had no patients!

I went down there to see him. Finally he sent for me and we had quite a chat. He was a very nice fellow and I said, "What do you do, Doc?" And he said, "I'm just making money out here hand over fist." I said, "What do you do?" and he said, "Well, I cut people's appendix out most of the time. Not in this hospital, but I do it in a hospital in town." I said, "What do you charge for that?" He said, "It depends on how far the guy came and what I think I can get. When I see a fellow come in here all the way from India for me to open his belly and take his appendix out, I don't think $25,000 is too little, do you?" He looked at my boil and lanced it and said, "That ought to fix that." Then we chatted a little more, and he said, "By the way, where are you living?" I said, "I'm living in the Imperial Hotel." He said, "Pretty expensive, isn't it?" And I said, "Well, no." He siad, "Well, do you have an outside income?" I said, "Oh, no, Sir, I don't have an outside income." "How much is an ensign's pay?" I said, "About $125 a month." He said, "Do you mean to tell me that you're living in the Imperial Hotel on $125 a month?" I said, "Why, sure." He said, "How long do you think you can last?" I said, "I don't know, but that's what I'm doing." He said, "Let me look at that thing again. You might have complications on that. I just think I'd better turn you in here." I said, "Doc, you won't turn me in for a little boil like this," and I remonstrated. Finally, he lost patience and he said, "Young man, you can stay here in SOQ - Sick Officers Quarters - for 50 cents a day and be waited on by servants around here. Now you get to hell up here and stay here till I tell you you can go." That's why I lived in the hospital there for about six weeks, food and everything, 50 cents a day.

Q: Checked out of the Imperial Hotel!

Adm. M.: Yes. That's another of the very kind things that happened. When I left the hospital, Zach invited me to come back and stay with him in his house.

Q: You didn't get overseas compensation?

Adm. M.: Oh, no, nothing of that sort. So that's where I stayed, and then as the spring and so on approached Zach decided to go off to a place called Zushi down on the bay, not too far from Kamakura. So I and a fellow named Jim Denby, who was Third Secretary of the Embassy, rented a house furnished from Captain and Mrs. Mashbir - he was an Army language officer in Tokyo - and we stayed there pretty much through the summer of 1922. This old Imperial Hotel, the wooden one, caught fire during an imperial garden party, the first one I ever attended. You know, they had one in the spring for the cherry blossoms and one in the fall to view the maple leaves and what have you. We were all out there, and Jim was living in this hotel, and I never will forget the sight when we went down there when we came back from the garden party and somebody said, "Oh, the Imperial's on fire." Of course, that didn't bother me. I wasn't staying there, but I never will forget going down to gawk at the fire and watching Jim Denby in striped pants and swallow-tail coat and a top hat stepping out of a window holding an armful of clothes.

Q: What were the highlights of your period of study there?

Adm. M.: In 1923 all of Yokohama and most of Tokyo were destroyed by an earthquake, and I functioned as a sort of liaison officer between the Embassy and the commander-in-chief of the Asiatic Fleet, who came up to render aid, at that time Admiral E. A. Anderson, in the Huron again. I ran back and forth. All my clothes and gear were destroyed. I had been living, as I said, with the Reverend and Mrs. Wynd, who had invited me to come and live with them. They lived in what had been the old international settlement in Tokyo, a section called Tsukiji, not very far from St. Luke's Hospital, which was a big Episcopalian missionary enterprise. There was not only a hospital but also there was St. Paul's School...

Q: University?

Adm. M.: University, some of them called it. We had been living there together. There again was a kindness that I had no way of paying back, so when summer came it was customary, in those days, for people to go away for the summer from out of Tokyo, if they could. They would go up to the mountains or to the seashore, or something like that, for a couple of months, and the Wynds invited me to come with them to such a resort at a place called Nojiri, which is in the central part of Japan, in a section nowadays known as the Japanese Alps. This was a pioneer summer colony, mostly missionaries and their teachers. They put up these little houses, summer cottages. This place started by them and is a little bit farther from Tokyo, and did not have quite the elevation that Karuizawa did, but it does have the benefit of a rather pretty lake, and we were there on September the first when the earthquake struck.

I made my way back to Tokyo. It took about two or three days to get there, largely because of the refugee trains and the whole transportation business was disrupted. But I did get through and learned enough to know that all my gear had been destroyed, and the house in Tsukiji was burned completely to the ground; wiped out.

Q: The houses were rather flimsy, weren't they?

Adm. M.: No, these were foreign-style houses. They were all wooden, more or less Victorian type things. The Japanese houses, yes. They're built on quite a different scheme of architecture than we have. Actually, it's what we nowadays call a cantilever type. In other words, you have a central pole and the thing hangs around it. It's the latest thing in architecture. The Japanese house can withstand an earthquake because it gives and sways and so on, but they are very vulnerable to fire, always have been. They're regular match boxes. The only thing that is fireproof on them are the very heavy tiled roof, mud tiles, which is characteristic of the city houses. In the country that, of course, is thatch, reed or straw or what-have-you, and that is pretty inflammable, too. So that once a fire gets started in a Japanese area, there isn't very much you can do about it, except do what you do in forest fires, blow up all the houses in the way and hope that it will die out because there's nothing for it to feed on.

My friend Tommy Ryan that I mentioned earlier won the Congressional Medal of Honor in that earthquake. He was sitting in a barber's chair in the Grand Hotel in Yokohama and he was shaken out of it. Someone told him that there was a lady caught under a bath tub somewhere up topside and somebody should take a brick and go up and hit her on the head with it to put her out of her misery because the fire was going to get her. Tommy said he wasn't going to stand by and see that, so he went up and broke this lady's leg in getting her out of her entanglement. She didn't have any clothes on and he dragged her down to the waterfront - the Gran Hotel was situated on the waterfront, they call them Bunds out there. Tommy had been quite a strong swimmer at the Naval Academy, he was captain of the water polo team. He dragged this girl into the water with him, towed her, and swam around to a big French liner called the Andre Le Bon, which was in the harbor at the time, put her up. Her husband was so grateful, he was a big contributor to the Republican campaign fund, not to detract maybe, but because it was a very courageous thing, I can tell you that, because not only was it a thing to go back with the ground popping open and the whole business shaken down and fires all around the place, but the oil had spilled on top of the harbor and the harbor itself appeared to be on fire. He swam this girl out. In the first instance, he had gotten her out alive and then swam this distance. I tell you, it took a lot more courage than I would have had, and he richly deserved it. President Coolidge pinned the Congressional Medal of Honor on him. They didn't have anything much less than that in those days. Tommy was a very fine fellow. He's dead now. He was one of my closest friends.

The Wynds came back to Tokyo. They'd lost everything. Then they went down and lived in Kobe for a while. Their mission had housing down there. I didn't go with them because I couldn't. Although I was invited to. I thought it would be an imposition.

Q: What was your actual duty with the Asiatic Fleet?

Adm. M.: Well, I was running more or less as a courier and liaison back and forward between the admiral's staff and the embassy. You see, the embassy moved. The embassy building itself had been burned down. I went to the embassy and found that they were located in the new Imperial which was called the New Imperial Hotel. The thing was built by Frank Lloyd Wright.

Q: Built to withstand...

Adm. M.: It did withstand it. All the people had been laughing before that the first big quake that comes along, this place will fall down. Well, it didn't. It was an engineering marvel when you look back on it. For the next two years or so, the embassy continued to function out of one small suite of rooms, relatively small suite of rooms, in the Imperial Hotel. The ambassador himself, when we had one, lived there, as did his senior foreign service people. The naval attache had managed to keep his office relatively unharmed and the assistant naval attache, who was Hulings - his house did not burn down. The naval attache was Captain Cotten, at that time, and the ambassador was Mr. Cyrus Woods. They had a disagreement and as a result, of course, Captain Cotten came home, so Commander Hulings was the acting naval attache, and by this time Zacharias and Hartwell Davis had both returned to the United States. Their term of three years was up anyway, they having come out in about 1920.

That was the big thing that happened. That winter of 1923, I helped - you wanted to know about my duties with the fleet...

Q: Yes. Where was the admiral's flagship?

Adm. M.: The admiral's flagship was in Yokohama Harbor. It was the Huron. The admiral was Anderson. I forget who his chief of staff was, I think it was Captain Lincoln, and the idea was that they needed somebody to maintain contact - you couldn't communicate with the Embassy. Radios and things we didn't have, so they had to run a kind of a messenger service back and forward, and that was my job. I would go down and contact the flagship, sit on there, and get my instructions from the admiral or the chief of staff or, frequently, the executive officer of the ship, and then I'd take off with that and go up to Tokyo, what do you need, what else can we bring, what should we do, and so on and so forth. At that time, the technique of getting to Tokyo - of course, it was impossible to go along the ground, the roads were all out, the railroads were out - a destroyer would be run from Yokahama Harbor up to the harbor of Tokyo, actually a place called Shinagawa. You'd have to get off there and walk about two or three miles to the hotel. There were no cars. If there were there wasn't any gasoline to run them. It would take about all day to make the round, there and back. That's what I did for two or three weeks, and then finally the admiral decided that he'd done all he could there, and his ships out. The Japanese, you know, are very suspicious. They couldn't understand this business when here comes Admiral Anderson steaming in on the Huron attended by a division of destroyers, their first reaction was to open fire on him. In other words, they felt they were being invaded.

Q: Even in the face of the disaster?

Adm. M.: Yes, that's what I'm talking about. Another job that I had at that time, I didn't do very well. I had to go over - a Japanese rear admiral came in there flying his flag in the light cruiser Tama. Later on he became a very distinguished Japanese admiral and minister of the Navy, Yoshida, or something like that. He was very understanding. He saw the situation entirely and he said to me, "You know, my people are very suspicious of all foreigners, but I understand the situation and I'll see if I can calm them down."

Q: It was hard for them to understand an altruistic...?

Adm. M.: That is correct. Here, Japan had been hit by a disaster and we had come steaming in to take advantage of it. That was their psychological reaction - to take advantage of them in their tribulation. They just couldn't understand how we'd come out there and put out all this stuff - we even put up a field hospital in Yokohama, and in order to get water for it, I helped pick the site out; we put it down just below a reservoir. The main aqueducts from the reservoir, the pipes and all had been knocked out, so that we had to drive in pipes to get water into this tent hospital. The thinking in picking out this site near the reservoir was that we could drive a four-inch iron pipe through to tap the water supply and give us the necessary water to run it. We had the hell of a time convincing the Japanese that we weren't going to tap in something to blow up the town further. You did have that. The first reaction was always one of self-defense. It was just inconceivable to most of them that anything could be done on an altruistic basis. In other words, the Japanese society has been conditioned for centuries - I help you, you help me. It's a reciprocity proposition entirely.

Q: But just outright generosity is not known?

Adm. M.: No, there's none of that.

Q: Is this true of individuals? Do they express generosity voluntarily?

Adm. M.: No. Japanese society - of course, it may be very different now, I'm talking about a good many years ago, and later on when I was assistant naval attache, I found the same thing. You just don't do that. If I do something to you, you've got to consider all the time that you then owe me something in return. Nothing is ever given on either side without a big if or why - they are great people for giving presents. Sure, they give a present. Then you've got to return a present of approximately the same value, and so on, back and forth. You just don't give a guy a neck tie and say, "Go ahead and wear it, Big Shot. That's just because I like you." If you give him a neck tie, he, by damn, comes back and gives you a neck tie of some kind. That's the way their manners are based, and they live within the family as a group, very compact. Well, it's a big family, but I mean they don't have personal friendships as we understand it in this country. Who's he kin to? What's his rank in society? All that stuff comes into it.

Q: Did you, in your student days, get close to Japanese individuals and begin to understand some of these characteristics?

Adm. M.: You just don't do it. I tried. I tried and tried. Some of the fellows tried it. We would try to make friends with the university students and, of course, these fellows were anxious to learn English and so on. We'd take walking trips with them and that kind of thing. You think that you're getting along pretty good and at the end of two or three months, he'd go back to school and that's the last you'd ever see of him. There were some of them that were that way, but there were some rather Americanized or Europeanized Japanese who in 1922 and 1923 gave parties, dancing and that sort of thing, and were trying to Americanize. For instance, in the spring of 1923, I helped teach the current emperor how to dance in our style. Then there's the Okura family, who were very wealthy, but he was not of the nobility at all. He'd made his money by selling fish to the Japanese Army in the Russo-Japanese War, so they said. And he was quite a character, the old man. He was made a baron. In other words, he started out originally as a fish peddler, someone who ran around with a pole on his shoulder - you know, they peddle the fish live in buckets, swimming around, and they peddle it from door to door. That's the way he started, but he built a financial empire of awesome proportions and died a multi-millionaire many times over. He owned the Imperial Theater, he owned the Imperial Hotel, and so on. He was a real acquirer, and one of his daughters, as frequently happens in Japan, had married a man who had adopted her name. The Japanese called this Yoshi. In other words, he was a bright young fellow and Okura needed a man in the family. At the time of the marriage, his boy didn't look like - he had one son who was later on known as the Young Baron - he was going to turn out so good, so this bright young man came and married the oldest of the Okura daughters and took the Okura name. You get that all over in Japan. For instance, Admiral Yamamoto was also that way. He married into a wealthy family. He was adopted. Yamamoto was not his original family name at all. I just use that as an example, but it's not uncommon. I remember sitting here talking to the Japanese naval attache of several years ago, Captain Seki. We got to know them quite well, and came to find out later on that Mrs. Seki was the daughter of Admiral Shima. Admiral Shima had commanded one of the Japanese task forces at the battle for Leyte Gulf and had gotten pasted down there. I didn't know that and Captain Seki remarked to me just very casually, "You know, So-and-So is the family name. My younger brother married one of my wife's sisters. As you know, the Admiral had no sons." In other words, it's important to carry on the family name for religious reasons, and so on. Therefore, here was Captain Seki and he had married one of Shima's daughters. His brother's name now is Shima.

Madame Okura, as we knew her, was very anxious to get a select group of Japanese young people and introduce and mix them with a select group of we people. For instance, I was a youngster and Zacharias was a little bit older, and her daughter was perfectly beautiful, and her daughter-in-law was the daughter of Admiral

Chisaka. In other words, the Okura people were promoting themselves up in society.

Q: They had the money.

Adm. M.: That's right. About once every ten days or so at her home in Tokyo, she would arrange for a party for young people, and we played the phonograph and things like that, and we were learning to dance with the Japanese young ladies, and they were dancing with us. And it was this time that the current emperor, Hirohito - at that time he was Prince Regent - he was a young fellow about in his early twenties, and his current empress was Miss Kuni. She was the daughter, of course, of Prince Kuni, who was an imperial prince. They were meeting from time to time under the wings of Madame Okura, and we were all there. It was a very incognito sort of a thing. There wasn't any fanfare, at least none that appeared to me. A nice thing for a young fellow like me to go to talk Japanese, to meet pretty girls, drink good liquor, and have nice food, and it didn't cost anything.

McCollum #2 - 59

Interview No. 2 with Rear Admiral Arthur H. McCollum, U. S. Navy
(Retired)

Place: His residence in Vinson Hall, McLean, Virginia

Date: 16 December 1970

Subject: Biography

By: John T. Mason, Jr.

Q: Good to see you today, Admiral. I believe the chapter we are to do today begins with an account of your expedition to the Kurile Islands in 1924.

Adm. M.: Yes. In 1924 the U. S. Army Air Force was undertaking the first round-the-world aircraft flight. The route was planned to come through Alaska, down the Aleutian chain, following the Kurile chain of isalnds, down into northern Japan, Tokyo, of course, and then on from there to Shanghai, and around the world. They were using flying boats constructed by the Douglas Aircraft Corporation of Santa Monica, California. As I remember it, the flight took off from the United States and ran into considerable mechanical difficulty. The lead plane with the so-called squadron commander in it cracked up either in Unalaska or the northern Aleutians. So by the time they got to Japanese territory, which was the Kurile Islands, they were reduced to three. All of the people on it were rather junior in ranks, as we understand them now. The leader of the flight at this time was a Captain Smith, who was later killed in an airplane accident - several years later, and the other two pilots were Nelson, who became a big executive later on with the Boeing Aircraft people, and a fellow named Wade, who is around here. He's retired. He was a lieutenant general or something in the Air Force. He got out of the Air Force not too long after that flight and had a very distinguished business career, mostly in South America, and he came back in the Air Force during World War II.

So far as our end of it was concerned, the plan was to station destroyers as station ships and to do a limited amount of resupply, board them, a place to live, and housing and so on, on the route.

Q: And as rescue ships, too, in case of emergency?

Adm. M.: That is right. The Japanese, as usual, were not too happy about anybody poking around in their territory. It's natural with them. But we did get proper approval of the Imperial government, and two of our destroyers, the John D. Ford and the Pope, were told off to go there, and two Japanese destroyers, one for each, accompanied us. I was told off to go to do the Japanese liaison work with it, because of my theoretical language capability. I'd been in Japan then just about two years, so I didn't have too much language, but it was better than what the rest of the boys had. We took off and went up to the Kuriles. The ship that I was on was the John D. Ford and our station was the northernmost of the Kurile Islands, which is Paramushiro. We were stationed actually in Paramushiro Strait, which is a strait between the island of Paramushiro and the island of Shimushu, which is the last one to the north or to the eastward of the Kuriles.

Q: Pretty rugged territory!

Adm. M.: It is rugged. The other destroyer was stationed at – where the Japanese strike force left to strike Pearl Harbor. Hittokappa Bay, it's called sometimes. Other people call it Tankan

Bay, but in those days it was known as Hittokappu, that is Japanization of an Ainu or a Russian word, I don't know which. It doesn't mean anything in Japanese. As I say, we had a Japanese destroyer with each of us. My captain, who was Lieutenant Commander Holloway Frost, was the senior of the two American Captains, so the Japanese division commander, Commander Morita in the Japanese destroyer <u>Tokitsu Kaze</u> was with us. They were destroyers of about the same vintage as ours, which was World War I. Four-pipers we had, and their ships were about the same size and degree of modernity as we were.

We found an amazing lack of information on the Kurile Islands from any modern point of view. The sailing directions were rather vague and the Japanese naval hydrographic office was very cooperative, but we found that they knew almost nothing about it. There was an exchange of hydrographic information between our Navy and their Navy that had been in existence for years and it was working. I don't think there was any pulling of punches, but they just never went up there and they didn't know. The only people who went up there much were fishermen, and they went up usually, as we found out, in fleets of maybe five or six fishing boats, diesel-driven, and they would go up there after the ice went out. They had camps on these islands and they were the only people who knew anything, and they didn't know very much because they were actually using those places as bases to catch fish.

Q: They didn't have any technical knowledge, either, I suppose?

Adm. M.: Not too much. We found our best source of information was a man named Tom Laffin. Captain Laffin was at that time the

President and big guy of Laffin and Sons - and a very wealthy guy - They were ship chandlers and stevedores and so on. Captain Laffin had come out to Japan in command of a sailing ship in the late 1880s or early 1890s and had stayed there and gone into the sea otter poaching business. In those days, the Kurile Islands were Russian territory and the big thing there was to catch this sea otter which had a very valuable fur, and they were fished out and killed in a period of ten years, I think. But most of that was done by poachers operating out of Japanese ports - Hakodate, for instance, in the northern island was a favorite port of fitting out, but they came back usually to Yokohama to pick up supplies. Captain Laffin is said to have spent quite a bit of time as a young man in the Kurile Islands poaching sea otter.

Q: Where were those furs marketed?

Adm. M.: Usually in Canton. The Chinese liked them. As a matter of fact, in our early history the sea otter was prolific along the California coast, and they were fished out and the furs taken from places such as Astoria and so on, and marketed again in South China, mostly in Canton. Hong Kong was just starting up in those days.

Q: Are they extinct now?

Adm. M.: Pretty much. You may find two or three of them in the zoo, But I've never seen a live one anywhere. Nor have I seen the fur, but they're gone. So he had a great deal of knowledge and he was very glad to give it to us. At that time, in addition to his other business interests, he was President and a director of the board of the Grand Hotel in Yokohama, which was the hotel there. But the trouble was that his information would be very useful for a fellow running a poaching schooner. As he said to us, "There's no trouble about going on the rocks. Sure, there are no navigational aids, but that place is just full of sea lions and when you get close to the rocks you can hear the sea lions barking. They bark all the time, so you just sheer off."

Well, of course, with four pipe destroyer with the blowers running, you couldn't hear anything anyway. So that's the kind of information we had, and off we went.

We got up to Paramushiro and established very friendly relations with our Japanese accompanying destroyer. They would come over to our ship to visit for the movies and so on, which they didn't have, and they enjoyed, and we'd go visit their ship and drink their sake, which we didn't have. Our relations were mutually very nice. We also had two Japanese officers on the ship with us. One was an Army captain, named Yamase, and the other one was a Navy lieutenant flyer, named Kobayashi, which is a common Japanese name. By the way, he later committed suicide after leading an abortive revolt against the government, along about 1936. He was at that time considered one of the best of the Japanese Navy flyers. He was really quite a fellow, so was the Army chap along with us, and we all got along very well indeed. In addition to myself, there was an Army captain named Clark on the ship with us, also a language student. But Clark had only been in Japan about six months and he could hardly order a glass of water in the language at this time.

The other destroyer had a fellow named Bratten, who was later head of the MID Far Eastern Section to handle the Japanese part of it, and that ship was commanded by a fellow named John McLaren who didn't have any language, but he'd served for the previous two years as assistant naval attache in Tokyo. The USS Pope, I reckon was the name of that other ship.

Well, we went up there and what with one thing and another, time continued to drag out, and these flyers were having a hard time getting down the Aleutian chain. After two or three weeks up there, we had to go back to Hakodate to replenish our fuel oil supplies. We did, and then on the way back we got in daggonedest storm I've ever been in, but we finally made it, and of course the ice was breaking up and flowing out of this place. Then we finally got up there and went ashore. Now, you understand, these islands up there were all blanketed in snow and there wasn't any place to take any physical exercise ashore, except that we found after a while that when the tide went out there was a strip along the beach. As the tide would come in, of course, it would melt the snow and you could walk along this shingle, but you had to be quick to get back before the tide came in. We did that, and then we stumbled by chance into a Japanese camp of fishermen, only there wasn't anybody there, but we could see that it had been inhabited, and lately. I mean there was a fire in the fireplace, or stove, or what-have-you, and so on. What had happened was that there were two caretakers left up there over the winter to look after this place, and when they'd seen this group of five or six of us coming, they'd gone out and hidden in the snow. They thought the Russians had come to kill them. After a while, when they found out that we weren't dangerous, they all came in and we enjoyed their hospitality a little bit. Later on, when the fishing fleet came up, why, they opened the camp for good. That would be in May. Well, after waiting up there nearly a month, the flyers finally did come in. They took off from Attu, it seems to me, which is the furthest south of the Aleutians. It's about 300 miles across there, and that was about the limit that they tried to take this thing, in 300 or 400-mile bites. That's about all those old flying boats could do, twin-engine flying boats. They came down, of course, as usual, and a minor storm or a squall hit just about the time they landed, so instead of landing fairly closely in a group, they landed in three rather widely separated locations, and we had to rush out and get moorings down for them, because where we planned to have the moorings, we had to pick those up and move them and so on, and after spending about three days there waiting for the weather to moderate, they did take off and they did make it to Japan. Their next stop was Hittokappu Bay where the Pope was. The Pope people had discovered a lake up in the hills that was ice-free, curiously. So instead of trying to land in the harbor, they actually landed on this lake. This lake was not shown on the charts. The Japanese knew nothing about it, and I agree with them, I don't think they did. There might have been one or two who did, but it was totally wild, uninhabited country. They landed up there and they backpacked the gasoline and stuff up there to them, and from that place they went on down to Kasumigaura, which is a Japanese naval air training station in the generally Tokyo area, and the Army flyers went through the usual parties of welcome and that sort of thing.

We came on back, and we stopped at a place called Kushiro on the way back. That is the easternmost city of any size in Japan, and there we were greeted with great fanfare. The city fathers came out to see us. We just went in there to pick up oil, but the city fathers had visions of another arrival of Perry and tried to make Kushiro a second Yokohama, Tokyo - Chamber of Commerce stuff...

Q: So they really weren't suspicious then?

Adm. M.: No, no. Not suspicious. We were welcomed as if we were coming down to - they were not suspicious at all. It was a country town, you know, and the mayor had just been elected. They had won a political victory and there was a new town council, and they all came out there in tugboats that were almost the size of our destroyers. They were very cordial and they put on quite a party for us and we went down and talked before school groups and that sort of thing for two or three days while we were loading up with oil and sea stores.

Q: One would gather, then, that that element of suspicion isn't an innate characteristic of the Japanese as a whole?

Adm. M.: Yes and no. That is, most people, like the Japanese, who have lived under a despotism, as long as they lived under it, very much like what I understand to be the Russian secret police system, are suspicious of anybody. By that I mean the shogunate government for two or three hundred years, each little group in Japan - they were set up in groups of ten, there was a man who was supposed to be responsible for the morals and the condcut of those ten people, and, in turn, there were ten more up the line, so you had them cellularized into a police state system. The result is that in a system such as this, nobody can trust anybody else very much. So you are suspicious And, of course, it's to the interest of the ruling class not to expose those people to outside influences too much. It gives them ideas. So that is one of the reasons for it. The people themselves, when you get down to it, are not suspicious, but they tend to look on foreigners as we do, or used to. There's a little bit of suspicion. Not because we're suspicious to hurt us, but they're funny kind of people. We can't talk to them, so we just look at them a little bit askance, that's all. Their morals may not be the same kind that we have, their food is different, so they're just different, that's all.

So far as this place was concerned, they were having a fine time. We were, too, and so we stayed there one day longer than we should have. The man who was really master-minding the job was a fellow who, I found out later, was a retired major general of the Japanese Army, who had fairly recently retired from being the military attache in London. He spoke beautiful English, of course, was beautifully turned out. The Japanese are great people for wearing proper clothes and so on, and the official, formal clothing in those days was still a frock coat, a Prince Albert coat, as we used to call it. The trousers were supposed to match, but the Japanese didn't pay too much attention to it. Sometimes, you'd see a fellow in a Prince Albert coat with no pants on at all, at least not visible. But this general was perfectly turned out in a out away that looked like it was tailored in London. While he had no official position in the city government, he was looked up to by all of these people and was obviously the man who was saying that they ought to put this show on and how it was done. They looked to him for guidance, in other words. He was quite a fellow.

From there we came back to Japan, and about that time I had to take examinations for promotion to the rank of lieutenant, junior grade. We could not convene an examining board which you were required to do by the Navy regulations, in Japan. We didn't have a sufficient number of officers. There weren't that many in the country. So I kept on going on the Ford until we went into Shanghai, and from Shanghai we went up to Chefoo, and there I was given my physical and professional examinations on board the flagship there. It took about a week to do. Then I was detached from the Ford up there and took passage on another ship, the Pope I think it was, back down to Shanghai.

Well, I'd been away from Tokyo, or Japan, for almost three months, and there was no provision in the Navy regulations for me to get any pay. My money was locked up in my pay accounts which were in Tokyo. So I landed in Shanghai with orders to go back to Tokyo. I got off the ship, and I had very little, or no, money and I first went to the consulate to see if they would loan me enough money or buy me passage on a ship. Oh, no, they couldn't do that, but they did say that there was a fellow in Shanghai called a Naval Purchasing Officer. I'd never heard of that, but they said, why don't you try him. So I went over there and I talked to the people in the outer office and got exactly nowhere. Sure, I've got my orders here, but they didn't have any pay accounts. I got rather upset about this business and I reckon I was talking pretty loudly out there, when a funny-looking little fellow came out from the back office and said, "What's all this going on out here?" I said, so he said, "Now, wait a minute. Come on back here and talk to me." I said, "Who in hell are you?" And he said, "I'm Pay Browning. I run this place." After discussing round a little bit I found that he was Commander Browning of the Supply Corps and he was the Naval Purchasing Officer. After hearing my story, he rang his bell and a warrant officer came in, and he said, "Give Ensign McCollum here $500 and buy him a passage on the President Wilson leaving so-and-so." Then I started to argue. I said, "Hey, you can't do that." He said, "Let me tell you something. I'm Pay Browning. I can do anything." So that was another one of the kindnesses that were handed me. The $500 was a mistake...

Q: He'd learned to be a poo-bah ~~in Japan~~!

Adm. M.: Well, the $500 was a mistake because Shanghai was quite a place to visit in those days, and for a young fellow of about 24 years old who had been away from, you might say, the flesh pots for three or four years, $500, I think, was a mistake. But we had a lot of fun spending it. Later on, Pay Browning came and spent a week with me as my guest in Japan. He was a very fine chap. I've never known what happened to him.

So, I came back from that. I got to Tokyo around the 1st of July, maybe later on thatn that. Maybe about the middle of July, and went immediately up to this place called Nojiri, where I'd spent the previous summer, and had rented a cottage. That is what you did. You rented it for the season, and I hadn't been using it, but a friend of mine had now come to Japan, a fellow named Wells Roberts, to study the language. He was a classmate of mine. Later on he was killed when the Houston went down during World War II. Wells had no place to go, so I told him to go ahead and start using the cottage, which he did. So when I came back, I did have a place to go, and after making my report to the acting naval attache and so on, why, I took a train and went on up to Nojiri and spent a very pleasant time until, say, the middle of September, when we had to come back. That's where I first got to know my wife fairly well. I had known her before. She was one of a group of young ladies who were nice enough to come and spend a house party with us, properly chaperoned, of course, in this cottage up there in the mountains. We saw quite a lot of each other that autumn and fall of 1924.

Q: You mentioned Roberts and you've mentioned others who were there studying. There were a considerable number of Japanese-language students, were there not?

Adm. M.: Yes. There were about five. They came and went, you see. In other words, up until 1923 - just before 1923 - there were three of us, Zacharias, Davis, and myself. And then a fellow named McGoon, who had been a chief pharmacist, a chief warrant officer, at the naval hospital in Yokohama, stayed on there to study the Japanese language, as a student. That was a mistake because McGoon, at that time, was a man of possibly 45, maybe 50, and it was unfortunate because he thought he knew the language and, of course, all he had actually was more or less waterfront Japanese, sort of pidgin, patois, that nearly all of those places speak. And when he found out later on that he had to unlearn all that he had learned, he decided it was just too much for him and he committed suicide. Now, that happened in August. I had seen him at the funeral ceremonies for President Harding - you remember, he died about 1923, and we had a memorial service for him in Tokyo, the embassy and the local Americans and so on. McGoon was at that thing, and I remember talking to him, and it was a week or two weeks later that he committed suicide.

Then there were two other fellows who came out. A Marine named Sullivan - W. B. Sullivan - and a Marine named Hicky, both of them, I think, were Marine captains and both were considered as too old.

They were about 40, both of them. I think that's about as far as Hicky went in the Marine Corps. He was a very nervous fellow. Sullivan stayed the route. He never got too good at it, but he had come, as I mentioned before. Then when Ryan left, right after the earthquake. During the winter of 1923-24, Ryan, Sullivan, and myself operated in the old American Embassy compound, as we called it, a sort of a refugee camp for embassy servants, and at one time we had a population of maybe 100 or so. We had stocks of food and we had a couple of trucks, and a squad of Marines to keep order and service the place, and so on. So, when Ryan left, that left a vacancy there, and Roberts, by this time, had heard of it. He was on destroyers out there and he came and talked to me when they came up to Yokohama, and he put in for it, and got it. So he came along. As one would go someone else would come in and take his place.

Q: This reflected an increasing interest on the part of the American government in...

Adm. M.: Well, I wouldn't glorify it quite that high. The Navy was interested in it, that is, the Navy Department was, but it was mostly the initiative of fairly junior officers. Nearly all of them who were serving on the Asiatic Station were making a request for this duty. At that time there wasn't any close selection of these by any kind of a board or anything in the Navy Department at all Later on, that developed.

Q: It was a random thing?

Adm. M.: At this time it was a random thing. Wells Roberts said,

"I think it would be a fine thing for me to do," so he put in a request for it. And if there was money in the till and the Bureau of Navigation, as it was at that time called, had enough money, why, there it went. It was pretty much on that basis. These guys would land out there, and we "old boys," so to speak, would take them in hand and try to get them indoctrinated, fit them up with tutors, and books, and so on. We were constantly improving. Some of these fellows were very, very good. But, as I say, later on, it was quite a quota and they were selected here and checked off and so on. But in those days, up until about 1928, I would say, there was not too much selection. About that time, things got tightened up.

I went out to Tokyo as assistant naval attache in 1928, and found about six people out there studying the language, and I found that, with one exception, the others had all gone through quite a tight selection process. That is, a weeding-out and so on back here - not a formal board - and unlike in the older days when most of these fellows were up from the ASiatic Fleet, most of these chaps were coming from the States. They'd put in for it here and been screened through a process in ONI and so on before they came. It was an informal screening process. Not too successful, as some cases turned out, but on the other hand...

Q: But it was an improvement?

Adm. M.: The end product was good. There were a couple of mistakes made. Some fellows couldn't make the grade, and others were unfortunate in personality and so on, but, by and large, the percentage of failure was very small and while, of course, you had varying degrees of excellence with these people - some were very, very good and some were just so-so, and others were a little bit below par, but nearly all of them ended up with a useful knowledge of the language, and they were a godsend to us during World War II, I can tell you that.

So we spent a very pleasant winter of 1924-25 there. Tokyo had gone into a typical tailspin, like we do here. As you know, our Congress passed an immigration bill that restricted Japanese immigration to this country, and there were riots in Tokyo and for a while people doing sword dances at the tea dances at the Imperial Hotel and getting very shut down on all contact with foreigners. It was quite dangerous to go out for some of the Japanese, not the foreigners. They were threatened, but it didn't make too much of a difference. But you did have that element of it.

My wife and I became engaged sometime in 1925. You know, we were not allowed to be married out there at that time. We had gone out unmarried. So we couldn't be married out there without going through so much red tape that it wouldn't do, so I came home alone and she followed two or three months later.

Q: Did you ask for orders back here?

Adm. M.: Well, my time was up. My orders were in, and I had requested duty in submarines, which was rather unusual in those days. Most of the people who went in to submarines were already married or were shanghaied into it, at that time. I mean, they were just told off.

Q: Why did you want submarines?

Adm. M.: Well, the two fellows that I had been connected with in Japan, Commander Hulings and his successor Commander Hine, were very kind to me, and I had a great deal of respect for both of them, had served in submarines. Both of them were submarine officers, and good ones, and they urged me to go in to submarines, so I did. That's about the size of it.

So my wife and I were married in Rochester, New York, in September - no, October - of 1925. That about finishes up my Japan business at this time.

Q: Tell me about New London.

Adm. M.: Well, New London is quite a place. First of all, I came back home and went down to visit my mother. I had a nice long leave of two months, which nowadays is unheard of, and then if I wanted more I could get it. I had a lovely time in this little town of Marion that I more or less grew up in. Then I came back up here to Washington, because at that time my youngest sister was one of the dietitians at Walter Reed Army Hospital and I wanted to see her, and when I came to Washington, I thought well, I'll duck into ONI and see what's going on. So I did, and I bumped into my friend John McLaren, who had been an assistant naval attache in Tokyo and also had command of the Pope in the Kuriles. He was sitting on what they then called the Japanese Desk, just the one person, and he said, "Why don't you stay here for a couple of weeks?" And I said, "Well, it's all right by me, but my orders are to go to New London." He said, "Goodness, that school doesn't start till the 1st of July, you know - I mean till the 1st of September, or whatever it was."

Q: Tell me about ONI at that point. How big an operation was it?

Adm. M.: ONI was basically a library-type operation, and that is what later on led to so much confusion. In other words, what you did was you had a few naval attaches, not many, scattered around the world, you had consuls, and so on, and the reports would come in, and it was primarily based on materiel. And these desk officers were the people who corresponded for their areas on matters of interest to the attache and so on, and the report was sent to them, and they took the reports and routed them around to the various bureaus of the Navy Department. As you know, in the Navy Department in those days they were all what nowadays we would call technical bureaus, with the possible exception of the Bureau of Navigation, which was personnel and training. The other one that was not a technical bureau like ships or engineering or ordnance and so on or civil engineers, construction and repair, was possibly the Marine Corps. The Commandant of the Marine Corps was there. So what you'd do, you'd check off all these reports that would come in and you would route them around the circle in the Navy Department, and after a month or two of kicking around the place, they finally came back and you sent them to the archives, the archives of ONI, where they were docketed and filed in a book, so that if you wanted to know anything about Japanese torpedoes, you went to Mr. Lanigan, who was the head archivist, and he pulled out the folder and handed it to you.

Q: Was there any interest at all in economic conditions and political situations?

Adm. M.: Oh, yes. The main trouble was to keep our attaches from writing too much about economics and politics. It was easy to write about economics and politics, it was difficult to find out what was the number and the size of the torpedoes carried by the umpteen so-and-so. But the great stress - and, of course, from the State Department there the reports of their ambassadors would come in due time, their dispatches, they would call them, which, as you know, in State Department parlance is a written document. It's not a telegram or anything of that sort. The reason I'm stressing that, is that there's a good deal of confusion in the mind of some people, writers and so on, because they tend to take the term "dispatch" to mean something sent by telegraphic means of some sort, and it isn't at all. As used in the parlance of those days, it was frequently a rather lengthy written document. You had to allow for lag time, because a State Department dispatch or a report from the naval attache in Tokyo took approximately three weeks in transit. It came by ship across the Pacific and that, depending on the ship and so on, took anywhere from two weeks to ten days. Then it came by train and by the time it got here, three weeks was pretty par for the course. By the time the report had been mailed - the reports from Tokyo, for instance, were taken down by courier and placed aboard ship, in a sealed pouch, aboard an American merchant ship, of which at that time we had quite a number. We did not send those kind of documents on foreign ships. So, again, you had to accommodate the mailing schedule and so on to the schedule of the merchant ships. Those documents were sent in, as I explained, and they were routed around, then placed in the archives, and the archives was a library operation. In other words, if someone in War Plans needed some information on something, he went there just as a researcher would do in a library, and research the archives for it.

Q: Did the functions of ONI at that time - were they considered of real importance to the Navy high command? Did ONI have a real status?

Adm. M.: Yes, I think it did, but I can't judge that. I was not in the Navy high command level. ONI, actually, at that time and always had had, a sort of a dual position. It was the intelligence group to service the chief of naval operations as part of his staff, and was put in for that reason. And it was also, only parenthetically, to service the high command afloat. Each ship was supposed to have an intelligence officer, and usually it was the navigator who, among other duties, intelligence was his job, and that amounted to making reports on harbors and hydrographic type of information. Each ship had one, but it didn't work too well, and so far as the flag commands were concerned, I don't know that, with the exception of the Asiatic Fleet, any of them had a man who was - on their staff - who was full-time intelligence. If there was any, it was just a part-time job. You had to have an intelligence officer, so why not the flag secretary, he's everything else? So, you put it on that basis, and as a result it wasn't particularly effective. In a sense the district intelligence officers, which were fundamentally a security service, were useful, and, depending on the commandants as to how they made use of it, some of them were very good and others were very bad. It was a spotty operation and some guys didn't like it at all, and usually that was a full-time job on the so-called staff of a commandant. Not at that time, but later on, those people corresponded directly with ONI. In other words, while he was on the commandant's staff, that is true, he was a staff officer in a technical specialty, so he had a direct line back and forward to ONI. I mention that because in one case Mrs. Wohlsteder in her very able book on Pearl Harbor, for instance, stresses the point that these people were not in any way a pipeline to and from ONI. Of course, this was much later, but they were members of the commandant's staff and so on. Well, that is true, but like a good many other things in the Navy, that isn't the way she worked! There wasn't any hesitancy on the part of ONI - I'm speaking now in terms of the 1930s - to send what amounted to orders to a district intelligence officer. It didn't come in order terms, you will so-and-so, but "you are requested to do so-and-so." And it was his job to keep the commandant informed of what he was being required or requested to do, and if the commandant objected to it, why, then he came back at us. But, to all intents and purposes, that guy on the commandant's staff was ONI's man.

Q: And, I suppose, when World War II came along he was the counterpart of the B Section, wasn't he?

Adm. M.: That's correct. The B Section ran those fellows, by and large, and they did then. Reverting again to 1925, these desk officers were more or less just correspondents and their other job, the important one, was liaison with the Japanese naval attache at the Japanese Embassy here, in the case of Japan, and China the same way. So they were in a diplomatic situation. I never liked that set-up myself. I thought it was wrong to have intelligence and, you might say, foreign liaison mixed up together, but they were, as you remember. And as a result of that, they did go, and it was very interesting and rewarding, you did hit the diplomatic circus around Washington.

Q: I would think it would be an effective relationship in the case of an allied power, where you were simply exchanging information and doing it in a fairly open fashion. Where you were dealing with attaches from powers who were potential enemies, I would think it would be quite different.

Adm. M.: It was quite different, and the Japanese were, at that time, socially rather difficult. In the first place, they didn't have any of their wives with them, so they were living a rather restricted bachelor type of existence.

Q: Why didn't they bring their wives?

Adm. M.: Mostly because the Japanese ladies spoke very little English and they didn't think their manners were up to circulating around this sort of thing, so they didn't. Now, occasionally, they did, and when they did they were much more successful. I can remember, going back to 1928, Captain Sakano, who was the Japanese naval attache here at that time, had his most delightful wife and children with him. She was very acceptable, but he was relieved by a fellow named Kobayashi, or something of that sort, they came and went, who did not. So you never knew from one moment to the next what you were going to be up against, and the matter of arranging a dinner party or something of that sort, where you've got maybe half a dozen Japanese men only to sit down and have a relaxed dinner party was very difficult, unless you kept it strictly on a stag basis, which was quite different than, say, the people that were dealing with the French or the British, where they were very social. You had a different set-up.

But that's what these fellows did, and again adverting to McLaren, he said, "Why don't you spend about two weeks here in Washington?" I said, well, that was all right by me, if I could get...He said, "We can arrange for that." I said, "What's the catch?" And he said, "I want to take some leave. I want two weeks' leave and I've got to have somebody to sit on this desk while I take two weeks' leave. It would be fine indoctrination for you, Mac." And I said, "In the first place, I'm broke, Commander, and where in hell would I stay?" So he said, "I'm getting out so why don't you take over my apartment and stay with the fellow that I'm rooming with out there, my apartment mate. Won't cost you a penny. Just move in." That was fine with me, so I spent two delightful weeks in Washington, and found that McLaren's apartment mate was a fellow named Frank McCord of the class of 1911, I reckon. Frank was captain of the dirigible Akron when she broke up here, and he was killed. A very fine man indeed.

When Mac came back from his leave, I went on up to New London, cooled my heels until school began up there, then went to school. I was having too much fun to study very much. My intended bride came as far as Rochester, New York. She'd gone to school in Rochester. She finished at the University of Rochester, and then she got mulish and wouldn't come any further. She insisted that if I wanted to marry her, I had to come to Rochester to get her. Well, it was not too easy in submarine school to come by leave, but at that time we would go out periodically on these submarines for indoctrination. Maybe, they'd take a group of 15 or 20 of the officer students and they would go out for a couple or three days in a submarine. I was detailed to go out on the S-51. I was living in Bachelor Officers

McCollum #2 - 81

Quarters there, and a fellow who was married and kept his books and so on in there because they weren't supposed to take them home, came and asked if I would swap with him - let him take my place to go out on this S-51, on account of he had some married business coming up, so I said, why sure, it didn't make a damn bit of difference to me. Well, of course, the S-51 went down and she was sunk. There were only three people taken off of her. Well, with that, my lady got pretty excited up there in Rochester, and I thought I could persuade her to come down, but she said, "Not on your life. You come up here and get me," so I managed to get leave and I went up there and married the girl and brought her down to New London, where we set up housekeeping. They always laugh because immediately we got married, my marks in school improved materially.

Q: You had sowed your wild oats and were ready to settle down!

Adm. M.: Well, when we finished there at New London, I still wasn't high enough standing to get a preferred drawing. Everybody wanted to go to Hawaii, so I ended up going to Panama, where we had a division of, at that time, the oldest active boats in commission. We did have some older ones, but these were the Os, 0-1, 0-2, 0-3, and so on.

Q: At Coco Solo?

Adm. M.: At Coco Solo. It was Submarine Division 8. Up in New London, they had two or three older boats, the N boats, the N-3 and N-4, and so on, which you see were before the O. We lived in Panama there in various ways. It was quite interesting and after about a year on the 0-7 I fleeted up to her command as a lieutenant, junior grade.

Q: What sort of a complement did the O-7 have?

Adm. M.: About 32 men. Supposedly, she carried three officers, three or four officers, and about thirty to thirty-five men. I've forgotten which. Thirty-two is the figure that sticks in my mind. She was an old-fashioned submarine. She had diesel engines, propulsion on the surface, and a storage battery arrangement - the usual set-up. The crews were pretty stable. They were fine people. They weren't too highly educated as far as literature is concerned, but they were manually very capable people. We didn't have so much coming and going. The submarine crews, at least in Panama, were fairly stable. In other words, there wasn't a constant flux of new personnel coming and going, as there was on the surface ships. So after your crew was fairly well trained, you didn't have a lot of the problems that go along with constantly training rookies, you might say, as was the case in the surface ships to a great degree.

We had a very good outfit down there and, incidentally - after I'd been there about six months or so, your friend Bill Heard came down to take command of the division - Submarine Division 8, and we thought we had a very fine submarine division htere, and we did.

Q: What provision did you make during this period for the Japanese language? Did you continue to study?

Adm. M.: No. I was too busy fooling around with a new wife and learning about submarines. A Japanese training squadron did come through and, at Bill Heard's suggestion, I went down and I was made the liaison officer with the Japanese admiral, Rear Admiral Nagano, who was later chief of the Japanese general naval staff at the start of World War II. He had been a former naval attache here in Washington. I had met him in Tokyo when I was a student and he was a student at the Japanese naval war college at the time in Tokyo, and he was a very fine person. Curiously, for a Japanese as a rear admiral he was still a bachelor, which is very unusual. Later on, I understand, when he got to be a vice admiral, he finally did get married, but at that time he was unusual among Japanese officers of any age at all in that he was a single person. He was a very capable chap, in my judgment. He came in, the usual set-up, with three old cruisers, and anchored in Colon Bay and we gave him a series of parties and I was in very much demand, and my wife was too, because we pattered a little of the language. Most of these midshipmen, while they were supposed to study English, their English was just like my Spanish which I studied at the Naval Academy and was not exactly colloquial. That's the only contact that I had with Japanese at that time.

Q: But you fully intended to use the language again?

Adm. M.: Oh, yes. But we went to Panama in 1926, January, as I recollect, and in 1928 I was detached from command of the O-7 and ordered to the S-11 as executive officer. She was a bigger submarine, more modern, and so on. That was mainly for the purpose of paying for my passage north, because I was under orders then to be detached. In other words, my shore duty time, theoretically, was coming up. And a fellow named Bennehoff - his name is very close to that of my wife's maiden surname, spelled slightly differently - was a captain and he'd been in submarine school with me - O. R.

Bennehoff. We came north and we put in to Miami, Florida, to attend the festivities of the Shrine Festival which was going on down there, and this was the first year that Miami said that she was a sea port. Someone had told them that these submarines didn't draw any water. Well, as a matter of fact, all of these submarines were basically deep-draft ships, but not much of them shows above the top of the water. So we were finally dragged into position alongside a dock comfortably resting on the mud bottom there, in the S-11. And I've never seen such swarms of people in my life. We were just mobbed with people coming down to see these things, these boats. It was quite a job. You had to run them down the forward hatch and run them through the boat and up the after hatch, thank goodness nobody broke their necks or their legs on the ship, because you had to climb up and down hatches on ladders and so on.

Q: I'm surprised, knowing Shrine conventions!

Adm. M.: A Shrine convention was all it was, but, you see, at that time Miami was either in its first or second depression. All the banks were closed. You couldn't get any money ashore. Everybody was broke. It was all steam and no relief in sight, as far as Miami was concerned. But the Shrine convention was, as usual, a howling success.

So we came back from that and came up to New London and fooled around there, whereupon my captain immediately said, "Mac, you've been captain of a ship. I'm going to go off for a month." I said, "What are you going to do, Benny?" And he said, "I've got to go and get myself married," so he took off. I was acting captain of that S-11 for a month till I could get Benny back. Then they gave me a month's leave, and my wife and I took a delightful motor trip. We bought an automobile up there in New London. I remember it was a car, it seems to me, was called an Essex, or a Hudson. I've never been much up in that country, and we drove over the old Cherry Valley Turnpike to Rochester. It was just lovely. Time was right, we were young, and staying in these old inns and so on. So we went to Rochester, where her mother had come on vacation from Japan, and spent a month with her, then we came down to Washington. By this time I was told that I was going to go to Japan as assistant naval attache. My wife had not been well and I didn't want to go to Japan. I thought, my goodness, I've just come back from that place three or four years ago. I've been out of the country for three years, I think I ought to have a little time here. I did my best to get out of it, but I didn't carry enough persuasiveness, I suppose. Anyhow I was sent, and another thing that got us both was that we didn't have any proper clothes to go out there and very little money to buy any. My uniform rig was not too bad, but I knew that in Japan I had to have a full-blown civilian rig, which meant dinner jacket, evening dress clothes, and formal attire, morning coat, top hat, and so on. The only way I could figure out to get this was to go to a tailor. In those days, we still had tailors, naval tailors, they were called, who you went to and you ordered your clothes from them and sometimes you paid them and sometimes you didn't. But it was a very nice arrangement, so I went to one who was considered rather high priced at the time, and I got two civilian suits and the rest of the rig and so on, and was in hock there. My wife went down to Jelliffe's and got evening clothes and whatever else women get. We also put that on the cuff, so by the time we sailed for Japan we were really very deeply in debt to tailors of one sort or another.

Q: The Navy had no provision for this side of one's duty?

Adm. M.: That's right, none. Of course, I had a maintenance allowance that they grandly told me was going to be $250 and that's fine, but when does it start? Well, when you get there, which wasn't much good. Besides, it could only be spent to give parties to foreigners. You couldn't spend it on your own people, in theory, anyway.

We finally went to San Francisco, took passage on the President McKinley, and went to Japan. I got a rather disturbing telegram in San Francisco. The then-director of Naval Intelligence was Captain Alfred W. Johnson, later Vice Admiral A. W. Johnson...

Q: Alfie Johnson!

Adm. M.: Alfie Johnson. He and his wife were charming and were very kind and considerate of my wife and myself in Washington, but I did get this telegram from him when we were in San Francisco, "Don't be surprised if and when you arrive in Tokyo, your first duty would be that of shipping the corpse of the naval attache home. The naval Attache, at that time was a fellow named George McCall Courts, and his assistant was a fellow named Jack Creighton, and I was supposed to be relieving Jack Creighton. Well, Jack had persuaded Courts to let him go before I arrived, so that he could take a motorcycle tour - he was a motorcycle enthusiast - of Europe on the way back, and Courts had agreed to that. Apparently, what had happened was that about two or three weeks after Jack left and about that time before I got there - more than that - Courts came down with a bleeding ulcer, duodenal ulcer, of some sort, and he wasn't expected to live and the thing looked pretty bad.

We arrived in Yokohama not knowing quite what to expect. I had never met Courts, I didn't know him, I didn't know what the situation was. Much to my amazement, the fellow who met me, came down to the ship to meet me, was Zacharias, and Zach was very much disturbed. He thought that this illness of Courts' had deranged him mentally and that he ought to be relieved. Well, that's one thing to say and another thing to do. He wanted me as the assistant naval attache, with orders as such, to relieve Courts forthwith and send him home invalided. I said, "Zach, somebody's nuts, either you or me. What I've got to do is to look over the situation, and consult with the doctors." He said, "Well, Mac, there it is. The guy's been operated on, he can't do anything. We've got this coronation of the emperor coming up here, the commander-in-chief of the fleet is coming, and all this. You've got quite a fandango to put up with."

Q: What was Zacharias' relationship...?

Adm. M.: Zacharias had been navigator of the flagship on the Asiatic Fleet, and he had come back to Japan, had promoted what we called a refresher course. In other words, he had finished the language course in 1923. This was five years later, and the Navy Department had authorized him to come to Japan to refresh his memory in Japanese, and that's what he was doing. By this time, he'd married a very nice lady and they had two little children, two little babies mostly.

Well, it became apparent, when I got to Tokyo and started talking around and finding out about this thing, that somehow or another Zach and his family and the Courts and their family were not getting along. There was a certain amount of friction there, for one reason or another, and when I first went up to see Courts, I was supposed to call on him right away, he was lying in bed and I've never seen a fellow look any whiter. He looked white as a sheet. I found later on that that was his normal color.

Q: I suppose he was bleeding internally?

Adm. M.: Yes, most of the time, and he looked at me and he said, "McCollum, why haven't you reported to me first?" And I said, "Well, Commander, I did come up here yesterday to report to you, but I was told by Commander Zacharias, I presumed with your concurrence, that you were not seeing anyone until the next morning, and I'm here at ten o'clock." He said, "Oh, I see, all right. Don't have anything more to do with that fellow. Come to me directly hereafter." Then the next thing I knew, I went down to pay my respects to the American ambassador, who at that time had his office in an office building down in Tokyo. The embassy was not built at that time, or re-built since the earthquake. And the minute I walked in there, I was greeted by Colonel Charles Burnet, who was the military attache, and he'd been military attache there before. This was his second, or maybe third, stint at it. He was a cavalry officer. He said, "Mac, you've got a rather sticky situation between the Courts and the Zacharias," and I said, "Yes, I reckon it is." He said, "What are you going to do about it?" I said, "I don't know. Most of those things simmer down after a while." "Well," he said, "let's go and see the ambassador." He seemd to be acting as factotum. Ed Neville was the counselor and the ambassador was a fellow named McVeagh. He was a New York lawyer, and he had a son who later on distinguished himself in the diplomatic service, ambassador to Greece and so on and so forth.

This was the father, and he didn't spend too much time in Japan, I found out. He preferred to spend his time in Santa Barbara. He would come to Japan for two or three months out of the year, leaving Ed Neville as charge d'affairs, a.i., as they used to call it - <u>ad interim</u>. Ed was a very capable fellow. Then the ambassador would sail off, and in about six or eight months, he'd come back to Tokyo, in time for the fall garden party and so on.

The first thing he said to me, and he talked very pleasantly, was, "Well, I think the time has come when we have to resolve this situation." I said, "That's all right with me." And he said, "I'm going to send a telegram to the State Department and ask them to transmit it to the Navy Department, that now that you have arrived I would suggest that the services of Commander Zacharias are now redundant." So the next thing I knew was that Zach got orders to leave, and that was it.

The big trouble there, you know, was that you have this coronation of the current emperor, Hirohito, coming up. Of course, he had been emperor for about three years, but in those days that was roughly the official mourning period for a deceased emperor. You see, his father, the Emperor Yoshihito, died in the latter part of December of 1926, I reckon - no, it must have been 1925, because the first year of Showa, which is the present time era - these time periods are adopted nowadays by each emperor at the time of his assuming the imperial power and they last through until his death, by order, in other words, it slopped over a little bit, you see. The period before him was known as Taisho, and these are usually the posthumous names of the Japanese emperors. But that's been all regularized. Before that, under the old system, you could have a time period that would run, some of them two years, some three, some four. The astrologists would say this is unlucky and they'd change it, so it didn't fit. The Japanese, when they became Europeanized, so to speak, settled on this thing, and the first of these name periods coincided with the reign of an emperor was the man who assumed the emperorship at the fall of the Tokagawa shogunate. That would be the emperor Mutsuhito, actually better known as Meiji, which was his time period, and that was his posthumous name. His son's posthumous name is Taisho, and his son's posthumous name will be Showa. That coincides with the time period.

So the coronation so-called - they don't have a coronation, there is no crown - but the accession ceremonies were being held in Kyoto, at the old imperial palace down there. The old imperial palace in Kyoto, other than some lovely decorations inside, isn't really such a much. It's a wooden frame rambling building in the Japanese style. It's a Japanese gentleman's residence. It sits in a park with a garden. Not a moated fortress, like that thing in Tokyo. That thing in Tokyo was actually the fortress of the Tokugawa, as you know, and was taken over by the imperial people. Basically, it is a medieval castle, whereas the one in Kyoto is really the residence of a well-to-do Japanese gentleman, built in that style, very open, and parks and so on.

The number of people who could go to that was limited, so each embassy - the ambassador, of course, and the counselor and one or two others - so there was a great deal of competition to get tickets of entry to this thing. And that is what Zach was very much interested in. He said it was only proper that the Navy should be represented. I couldn't see why. I didn't think the Navy needed to be represented at the accession ceremony. Zach laid great store by it, and, of course, he didn't have a ticket and he wanted one. He insisted that I try to get one, and I said, "Zach, I could care less. I know this guy and I don't want to go down there particularly. I'm not prepared for it. My clothes are not in shape. Hell, I've just gotten here." So that was all there was to it.

Anyhow, Zach went home and we were all the best of friends. Things leveled off, and the emperor did successfully ascend the throne without any representative of the American Navy, as far as I know, being there.

Q: The NA couldn't go because of his...

Adm. M.: No. He didn't have a ticket either. They only had about four or five tickets parceled out. I think the ambassador had one, Ed Neville had one, the military attache had one, and I don't know what happened to the others. That was about it, and they were all pretty much the same way. I don't think the British naval attache went, a fellow named Robinson. I'm pretty sure he didn't. Who went, I don't know. I think probably Colonel Piggott, who was the British military attache, did go.

Then, of course, they had a great holiday, a naval review, and up from all over the Asiatic came the foreign representation. There were the British and the French and the Italians. I don't believe the Chinese came. They weren't thinking too much even in those days of the Japanese. And here came Admiral Bristol. He was commander-in-chief of the Asiatic Fleet, a very distinguished person, and he was the senior foreign naval representative and he took his duties rather seriously, of course. He had only one cruiser, the Pittsburgh,

I think it was by this time. The British had three, at that time, very modern heavy cruisers of the Kent class, 10,000-tonners with 8-inch guns, commanded by a World War I hero, Vice Admiral Sir Reginald Tyrwhitt. He had had command of the Dover Patrol during World War I. The Japanese Fleet was in, all decked out. The commander-in-chief of the Japanese Fleet was a fellow named Admiral Kanji Kato. Actually he insisted his given name was Hirohara. Admiral Takarabi was the commander-in-chief of the naval review, which made Admiral Kato very very mad because he said Takarabi was nothing but a damned politician, which he was, but he was one of the senior admirals of the Japanese Navy. He was the son-in-law of Admiral of the Fleet Gombei Yamamoto who had been prime minister of Japan three times or something of that sort. Kato, who claimed that he was a real sea-going officer, resented very much that this what he called a politician was titular Commander in Chief of the Review and he didn't hide it, he was very outspoken about this business to all and sundry that would listen to him. He, of course, was flying his flag in the Nagato, which was the newest of the Japanese battleships, great big 16-inch guns. Takarabi was flying his on an old decrepit cruiser called the Kasuga, which was about the vintage of the Chinese-Japanese war, because that was the only ship that Kato would make available to him. So there was some real fighting there, too.

I was shuttling back and forward all the time. They had quite a severe protocol. When these people like Admiral Bristol for instance, came to Yokohama, instead of just making their calls locally which is usually the case, they were expected to come to Tokyo and pay their official respects to the Minister of the Navy and to the Chief of the Japanese Naval General Staff, and to leave cards at the

Imperial Palace and at the official residences of the imperial princes, of whom at that time there were some seventeen. So, you'd bring Admiral Bristol up to a place like Tokyo and it took two or three days to get through this round of calls. We were all dressed up, of course, in frock coats and cocked hat and so on. And Bristol, I didn't see how he was going to stand it. He was about 63 years old at that time. But that old gentleman, you know, he just bore up perfectly. He had a routine there. He had an old Marmon touring car driven by two Marines, and he wouldn't use the naval attache's car which was much more comfortable. It was a Buick and had a Japanese driver who knew his way around. In other words, he'd made the route before, we had to make this kind of route every New Year's, we had to duplicate this kind of thing, we naval attache people. He insisted that these Marines drive him, so he had two Marines up there in the front seat of this World War I vintage Marmon and our Japanese chauffeur squatting down out of sight to tell the Marines where to go. In the back seat was the Admiral sitting in the middle with his chief of staff on his right, his flag lieutenant on his left, and me squatting on a little jump seat, all those, of course, dressed in full regalia with swords and so on. But the old man had this thing down to a science. We'd leave one call and he'd take that hard hat of his off, set it in his lap, and in just nothing flat he'd be sound asleep. I started to talk once, and Castleman, the chief of staff, shushed me down. And shortly before we'd be driving up to the gate, say, to the Chief of the Naval General Staff's office or residence, or whatever it was, somebody would give him a nudge, the old man would put his hat on, here would be the guard of honor standing out to give him ruffles and flourishes, and he'd come in saluting and move down the line, then we'd go in and usually have a glass of champagne with the chief of general staff, and I would arrange with his aide for the chief of the general staff to send his cards back up to the residence so that calls which were supposed to have been exchanged in person - of course, this was just a card game.

Q: Was this a form of European veneer that they had assumed?

Adm. M.: I don't know. Maybe so. Yes, I understand that it was copied more or less after the courts of England, although I have no way of knowing that. But that's what they did. You never saw these people. You saw the Chief of the General Staff, of course, and you saw the Minister of the Navy, that's for sure...

Q: But the imperial princes you didn't?

Adm. M: The imperial princes you didn't see, and neither did you see the emperor. You merely went to the door and a chamberlain, which is a high class name for a servant of some sort, took your card and then in a little while somebody from that menage would come back around to the naval attache's office and leave the return cards. I remember I was shocked when I first went to Japan back in the 20s. I had some calling cards, sure, but I didn't have them all made out, you know, with attache of the embassy and so on, and I said, "Well, what do you do with these?" They said, "You've got to have some calling cards. Everybody uses calling cards." I said, "How many do I need?" "Oh, as a starter, maybe 500 or 600." That just stunned me and I said, "Good heavens, how in the world am I going to use them?" "I'll show you (this was Zach talking). Get 500 or 600 cards." In the embassy we had a factotum named Ito, at the time, and Ito had a pigeon hole file like an old-fashioned post office, with name labels on it, and he kept your cards, and at the proper time Ito would send your cards to the proper embassy or imperial prince, and at the proper time they would send one back which he would put in your pigeon hole. So, for instance, the British had, say, the Queen's Birthday or the King's Birthday, Ito would send your cards to the British Ambassador and so on. You had nothing to do with it. That's exactly the way this scheme worked. It was a card game.

The parties were incessant, of course, and were very demanding, and Admiral Bristol insisted - I tried to get him to stay in Tokyo, we could have made arrangements at the hotel or at the naval attache's residence - but, no, he had to go back to his flagship. He didn't feel comfortable off the ship at night, he said. Well, my sould, some of these darned parties would run on until one or two o'clock in the morning, and he would get in this old Marmon of his and tool back down to Yokohama, only to come back bright and early the next day to camp out at the naval attache's house. The naval attache was still sick in bed upstairs.

It was quite an occasion, but it lasted, thank goodness, not more than ten days. I was worn out at the end of this time. My wad had been shot, but the old man was still going strong. One day I got up courage to ask him, "Admiral, how do you do this?" And he said, "Well, you know, many years ago I went to sea as a flag secretary for a fellow named Admiral Beardsley. In those days when a rear admiral went to sea, he had two people on his staff, a flag lieutenant and a secretary and that was me. The admiral would wake up in the morning and he'd send for me and give me a lot of jobs to do. I would start doing the jobs and the admiral would then take a nap, and about the time the admiral woke up, he'd send for me and give me a lot more jobs to do. So the only time I got to sleep was when the admiral wasn't quite awake yet. I got the habit of taking naps all during the day. Otherwise, I couldn't have kept going. I've kept it up to this day and it does something for me." It sure did!

I remember this British admiral, a great big, raw-boned Englishman, named Trywhitt, turned to me one night at one of these geisha parties that the Japanese Navy was giving for us, and he said, "How in the world does Admiral Bristol take it?" And I said, "I don't know, Admiral." After a while I said, "I wish you'd start to go home," and he said, "I can't. He's the senior one. He's got to leave first."

One of the most amusing things, I think, at that party was that down in Yokohama the commander-in-chief, not Admiral Takarabi who was the titular commander-in-chief of the review, but the actual commander-in-chief, Admiral Kato, gave a dinner on board his flagship, the Nagato. We were all going and, unfortunately, the weather kicked up pretty bad. It was very rough. The American contingent came first, and we got aboard all right, but as the British contingent was coming a wave came along and washed Admiral Tyrwhitt's pants off of him. So he arrived on board the flagship and started making apologies, and Kato said to him, "Tyrwhitt, think nothing of it. I'll loan you a pair of mine." Well, of course, Admiral Tyrwhitt was about six feet tall and Kato was about five feet, and so the pants were a rather high-water set of gold-striped pants, which everybody laughed about.

Q: What was your specific assignment as assistant naval attache? What sort of reports were you expected to achieve?

Adm. M.: They weren't very clear. We used to get guideline reports from the syllabus of stuff that the Navy Department, ONI, were particularly interested in, and we would try to cover that as well as we could. As you know, we were not in any sense supposed to be a secret service of any sort at all. The function of the naval attache, other than being a naval advisor to the ambassador, was that of - he occupied pretty much the same position to the Japanese Navy Department as the ambassador did to the foreign office. It was that sort of relationship. The Japanese Navy, as you know, was not one department. It was actually two, quite separate. The Ministry of the Navy was primarily an administrative set-up. In other words, supplies and logistics and personnel and so on and so forth. The command functions, operations and that sort of thing, and intelligence, were operated by the chief of the naval general staff. Now, you understand, as a member of the cabinet under a premier, the Navy minister was, in a sense, a subordinate of the prime minister, or the premier, who, in those times, was usually a civilian. However, the Navy minister did have, and so did the war minister, the rather unusual privilege of direct access to the emperor, who was the theoretical center of all power. So that, without going through the prime minister, the minister of the Navy could go, on occasion did go, direct to the emperor.

Now, the chief of the general staff was not a part of the government. In other words, he was the command function. He was the emperor's chief of staff. That's what he was. So that all operations, ship movements, intelligence, what we think of as the war-making aspects were his baby, and he was not subservient to and he didn't report to the prime minister, he was not beholden to him in any way whatsoever. You had a twofold job there which caused some bemusement among our people. It wasn't clear-cut. Theoretically, the minister of the Navy was a subordinate of the prime minister. Actually, he was almost the prime minister's equal. And you had another thing that had grown up in Japan which also caused some concern, and that is that the minister of the Navy had to be, by law, an officer of the active list of the Navy. Didn't say what rank. And the same for the Army. Actually, of course, he was a very senior officer, usually a full admiral, and when the prime minister, in order to form a cabinet, and present it to the emperor, for validation, had to fill under this system every post, some of which he could hold himself. In other words, he could be prime minister and also foreign minister.

Q: He could hold several portfolios?

Adm. M.: He could hold several. Actually, very few did, but he could hold several. But the difficulty there was that the two posts that he could not hold was either that of war minister or Navy minister, because that guy had to be an officer on the active list, not a retired guy, of the Army or the Navy. So what happened is that if the prime minister's actions in his cabinet did not suit either one of these two fellows, after proper consultation with their peers, that is, their brother officers of like rank and so on, they'd resign. And if they resigned, then the prime minister had to hunt for an officer who would take over that job, and, of course, it would be so rigged that he couldn't find one. So when he couldn't find one, his cabinet had to resign. So you had a situation in which the war and the Navy ministers could, upon occasion - they were very careful not to over-exercise it - but they could destroy a political cabinet quite easily.

Q: Back in that time, what was the relationship between the Japanese Army and the Japanese Navy? Was it amicable?

Adm. M.: They were friendly enemies. That stems back to the revolution of 1867 and 1868, when the Tokugawa shogunate was destroyed. That was done by a combination of feudal lords. At that time the Emperor Meiji was about fifteen years old and he had very little to do with it. He was still a cloistered emperor. His father, the Emperor Komei had died of smallpox. He was apparently quite an able person, but he only ruled about five years. He did quite a bit of politicking and he fomented what amounted to a rebellion against the authority of the shogunate by certain of the powerful nobles, the feudal chiefs, and it so happened that most of these fellows were from down in southern Japan in Choshu province - I'm using the old name - which is down there centered around the straits of Shimonoseki and from there north on the main island.

Then the group of Satsuma people - that is a group of the southern clans, Saga, Satsuma, and so on in Kyushu. They were furthest away, of course, from the center of Tokugawa power, which was in Tokyo. These fellows finally cooked up this revolution and they came up and they dragged out an imperial prince and waved the imperial standard around, the first time it had been seen, they say, in battle for 2,000 years or something like that, and they moved against the Tokugawa shogunate in a war. It was actually a civil war. When the business came of parceling out jobs that rightfully belonged to the victors, then you had immediately a competition between two of the most powerful of the feudal lords. One was the Prince of Satsuma, and the other one was the Prince of Choshu.

In the rearrangement that took place at that time the Choshu clan, or the Choshu clansmen, being a little bit closer to Kyoto, the then-residence of the emperor and in a position to menace him and the imperial court more directly than the Kyushu clansmen, headed by the Prince of Satsuma, parceled it out. They had a brief fight among themselves that didn't amount to very much. But they parceled it out so that the Choshu clan took control of the Army, and the Satsuma clan took control of the Navy. For years you couldn't get anywhere much in the Navy unless you were a Satsuma man, and you couldn't get anywhere at all in the Army unless you were a Choshu man. Not only that, the generals and the admirals also doubled, on occasion, as prime minister. For instance, one of the reasons that the current emperor was so late in the Japanese fashion in getting married - he was about 23 or so before he got married - is that Field Marshal Prince Yamagata, who was the actual power in the Choshu clan - he had been premier several times, a field marshal in I don't know what war, maybe he was a political field marshal - anyhow he was a politician as much as he was a soldier, and so was Admiral Gombei Yamamoto whom I have mentioned before. These fellows would alternate. Yamamoto was a Satsuma man, of course, but he was not the Prince of Satsuma. The princes of these feudal clans, by this time, were, under Japanese fashion, pretty much figureheads. The name of the Prince of Satsuma still is Shimadzu, and I've forgotten what the name of the Choshu fellow was. So as long as Prince

Yamagata lived - there was not a princess of suitable age for marriage that belonged to the Choshu people. So Yamagata blocked any imperial marriage under the Japanese imperial concept of that time, by the time the emperor or Crown Prince got to be about 15 or 16 he should have been married.

Q: So he simply had to wait?

Adm. M.: He had to wait until some of these Choshu princesses grew up, or Field Marshal Yamagata died. Yamagata finally died, and so they made a compromise selection in the present empress. She was a Kuni, who vaguely was associated with this Choshu clan, and not the Satsuma clan. Kuni was, of course, one of the colateral branches of the imperial family, and he was a titular field marshal in the Japanese Army. The Japanese Navy and the Japanese Army always had an imperial prince of some sort who was promoted up to a suitable rank and so on. Usually, the one in the Navy was either Fushimi or Higashi Fushimi. Fushimi, like all names, is the name of a locality, and Higashi means East, so you had the two Fushimi families that were usually Navy families. Kannin and Kuni were Army families, and usually the heads of those families were, by the time they got to be about 45 or 46 years old, Fleet Admiral or Field Marshals after they went through the motions of being promoted through the ranks. Every New Year's Day, British fashion, when the honors would be handed out, they would be boosted one peg up the ladder. So you ended up with usually a Fleet Admiral or a Field Marshal of one or two of these imperical princes, and most of the time they did not function.

Q: That explains, then, that traditional rivalry between the two services.

Adm. M.: That is correct. Of course, later on, that started to break down, because that was based on the old so-called Samurai type of Army, a gentry type of Army, knights, and so on, but when the Japanese introduced conscription for both the services, there was a tendency to water it down. In other words, people from other families and other branches came in. For instance, Admiral Yamamoto, who was the commander-in-chief of the fleet at the time of Pearl Harbor, came from northwest Japan. Technically, he was not a Satsuma man at all, and therefore his promotion was rather unusual. On the other hand, his boss, Admiral Nagano, who was chief of the naval general staff at that time, personally was not a member of the Satsuma clan, but he had Satsuma clan connections. But it was being watered down, which is natural as you bring in the citizenry to the Army, and also make entry into the officer corps of the Army subject to quite stiff examinations, which they were, and there was no monkey business about them. You tended to get a broader spectrum of people in there, based on brains and capabilities and so on, rather than mere family connections.

Q: An evolutionary process.

Adm. M.: That's right. But you did still have that rivalry. There was always a sense of contention for control of the government between the Army faction and the Navy faction, and of course the Army had pretty much the better of it because, after all, they do control the police and so on, which is always the case. It's very difficult for a Navy to make a political revolution, but it's fairly simple for an Army to do so. It's like our Army - I don't draw any connection - but part of the Army's function is to maintain civil order, and the Navy does not, theoretically, have that function at all, and when you start maintaining civil order it's not very difficult from that point on to take over the running of the whole civil establishment. That, in my judgment, is why you see, for instance, in South America these fellows are all Army people. You very seldom see a naval officer up there in the top flight of presidents, and those armies just like a lot of the European armies, and the Russian Army, their prime function is to maintain civil order and to maintain the despotism of whatever is in the ascendency. The Navy only can play a pretty fringe part in that. They're not very well placed to pick the fruits of politics.

It's been said, of course, that the Japanese naval officers were very much better educated and much more broad-minded and so on than the Japanese Army officers. That might have been true, although I had known a good many Japanese Army officers who were very well educated and very well indoctrinated, foreign style. For instance, in this country, the Japanese Army maintained as many language students and many officers in this country, as the Japanese Navy did. So they were exposed in equal numbers, at least, to the influence of whatever it is that our type of civilization could hand out. Not that they liked it particularly, but nevertheless that is the case. I don't agree that the Japanese Army officers, per se, were narrow-minded bigots, whereas the naval officers were pleasant, smiling gentlemen. That, in my judgment, simply isn't true. For instance, coming back to a later period, the Japanese Navy in about 1933 and for the next six or seven years went through an outrageous purge of the higher ranks. In one three-year period, practically every high-ranking Japanese naval officer was placed on the retired list, particularly those who had studied in England or this country and so on. They had to be very circumspect about it and only a few of them got by. Admiral Sakano was one, and any number of others. Admiral Baron Oi was another one. You could just pick them out. Every year when the list would come out, well, who's the next.

Q: They wanted to eliminate that cultural influence?

Adm. M.: That's right. Anyone who might be soft on this new type of nationalism that was being preached in Japan, which, incidentally - I don't say it predated, but it certainly was indigenous and had nothing to do with Nazi Germany. The Japanese have been great mystics. They doll this thing up in a form of religion, and they have a religious ritual that goes along with it. You have Kodo - the Imperial Way, Hakko Ichiu means eight directions the world under the Imperial sway, that's Chinese for one unity. In other words, the entire world under Japanese domination. That was the philosophy of it. Basically it is the cult of emperor worship. That was being promoted by the then war minister of Japan. They always put this into metaphysical terms, so to speak. They love it.

Q: In the period when naval officers with U. S. training or English training were being dismissed, did we take cognizance of this and know what it actually meant in terms of direction?

Adm. M.: Well, yes, I think reports were made. How much of an impact that stuff made in the Navy Department and so on, I just frankly don't know. My guess would be very little. I'm sorry to say that in my judgment a great many of our senior officers in the Navy didn't seem to understand the Far East too well, and that's a little bit amazing because most of them had had duty at one time or another, frequently in junior capacities, out there in the Asiatic Fleet. But in the Asiatic Fleet basically you had very little contact with the Japanese.

Q: You were floating...

Adm. M.: You were floating and, maybe, once or twice a year you might send a squadron of destroyers on a so-called courtesy visit to Japan and there would be a week or two of gala parties and that sort of thing. And you'd say well that's dusted that one off and on leave you'd come up there, but you never got any real - social arrangements were rather stiff and formal. Neither side seemed to be willing or could give a great deal. But I don't think that very many of our officers actually in the Navy Department really knew or paid too much attention to what the heck was going on in Japan. They'd read the reports, that was fine, but it was much more fun to read a report of who was sleeping with the wife of the Spanish foreign minister. And, of course, you must remember, as I know you do, the enormous influence of our great eastern universities which orients our minds towards Europe constantly. The Far East, Asia, Japan, and those far-off places relegated to something - we don't want to hear about it.

Q: That's perfectly true, and yet in terms of the Navy, up at the Naval War College, the potential enemy was always the Japanese!

Adm. M.: That's right. But you'd go up to one of these fellows – I remember once I was talking to a member of the General Board of the Navy and he had been a very brilliant, capable officer, but he was verging on being a little senile and he didn't know it and it wasn't too apparent because he was a big fine-looking man. But he said to me one day that he had become convinced that the Japanese were covering up and, to prove his point, he had three fairly consecutive issues of Jane's Fighting Ships, and he pointed out to me, "Now, that ship, what is that?" And I said, "Admiral, that's the Mutsu." He pulled out another volume and in this one he said, "What's that?" I said, "That's the Mutsu." He said, "Have you noticed that it's spelled differently?" I said, "Yes, Sir." He said, "These funny characters, they're different." I said, "Yes, Sir, but it's still the same ship." He said, "The hell it is. It's two different ships. They're just covering up." Of course, what happened is that the Japanese, some time in there, they didn't develop the new form of romanizing – that is writing in Roman letters – before that, most people had used the orthography developed by Dr. Hepburn or Professor Chamberlain or something like that, and they were slightly different.

Q: Because of their contacts with the Western World, they had to.

Adm. M.: M-u-t-s-u is the way it had been spelled, but some time in the '30s the Japanese employed a German philologist to revise this business, and he had come up with something and it was adopted officially. So that instead of spelling it the way everyone had done before, M-u-t-s-u, it was now spelled M-u-t-u. In some places, it got rather ridiculous. Shosha, for instance, is the term for lieutenant commander or major, but by the time this German got through with it that came out Syosya and it didn't make any sense at all. We couldn't even pronounce it. So you had this change in writing Japanese in its romanized form. As you know, the Japanese did not, usually, carry on the stern of their ships their names in romanized form. They usually carried the ship's name in Chinese characters, but they also carried the name in their syllabary which is known as the kana. Well, there are several different versions of the kana, and they're derived basically from the Chinese characters, but they look different. The two commonest of the kana are the ones known as the Hirakana and the Katakana, and sometimes in some years the Japanese would put Katakana on the sterns of their ships, and then later on they thought that was not artistic enough and they'd change to the Hirakana. And that, of course, is what the admiral was talking about. And you couldn't convince him. These sneaky bastards, you know, are hiding something from us.

Q: Something under the vest!

Adm. M.: That's right. So you did have that, and I remember not too long before World War II, we got an urgent message from the admiral commanding the Ninth Naval District, I think, with headquarters in Chicago, did we know that Japan was one of the most highly electrified countries in the world? Well, of course, we did know. And he said, "I have just listened to a lecture by Professor So-and-So (limey, I think) and this astonishes me," and he wanted to know why he hadn't known this. Well, of course, it was because he hadn't read the ONI bulletin, that's the reason. It was as simple as that.

Q: Or, maybe, just a newspaper!

Adm. M.: Yes. The electrification of Japan, of course, used their terrific potential of hydroelectric power, and it was being exploited. A great deal of the exploitation was done in the early 1920s and early 1930s and was financed by American capital, and a lot of the equipment that went into it was manufactured in this country by such people as General Electric. Obviously, we weren't entirely dead to the possibilities, and the result is that we had a plethora of material on the subject.

Another thing, of course, the Navy never did have a proper staff, and I think that's one of the troubles. I must say that I am not too much of a proponent of the Army general staff system. I think that the tendency in that is for the commander that the staff is supposed to be serving to get completely submerged under the staff. That is the difficulty with the so-called general staff system. The Navy never had such a system, and the result is that there was never any thoroughly understood basis for what a staff should consist of - and who did what and their relationship, as there was in the Army where you have a G-1, G-2, G-3, and so on. Of course, there are so-called special staffs, such as engineers, medical, and so on. The Navy never had that and it was always a question. I can remember, every time we had a change in commander-in-chief of the fleet, we went through the same process. You would rewrite staff instructions, that was the first thing. Whether it followed the War College format or not, never mind, if the admiral liked the War College, he did; if he didn't, why, he followed something else. But every one of them was enough different so that there wasn't any clear-cut understanding between the staffs as to what they did. For instance, the staff of Admiral Hepburn that I had the privilege of serving on for two or three years in the middle to late thirties, operations was the key to running that staff. In other words, Operations ran the fleet, the tactics, and arranged the schedules, and also did the planning - that is, from the point of view of operational planning. We did have a plans officer on the staff, but he was the war plans officer and, in our case, he happened to be your friend Admiral Cook. But he was in some very high-flown level. He dealt with the war plans of the Navy Department and their job was to keep these books up current to use. He had very little impact on the day-to-day operational planning of any sort. In other words, it was a war-planning function - the Orange Plan and the Red Plan and the Blue Plan, all that category of colors that he had. It was a bookkeeping proposition. He kept them up and then he corresponded back and forth to polish these things up. Now, for instance, in the Army plans and operations were one, that's G-3. Actually, it was two sections but there was one officer at the head of it. The Navy function, as we developed it later on, plans were separate and operations were separate. They worked closely together, but there was an assistant chief of staff heading each one of them. But the Navy Department never had such a set-up, as you probably realize, and the result is it was all confusion as to who did what to whom, and the guy who got there first and occupied first base was the one who was there.

Q: During the period that you were assistant naval attache, would you say something about the relations between the two countries?

Adm. M.: Between the two countries, it was improving. It was almost a return of the era of good feeling. The prime minister of

Japan was a distinguished Army officer named General Baron Tanaka, and he got some notoriety from having written a thing that was called a Tanaka Memorial, which was a plan for world conquest by Japan, which Tanaka denied, the Japanese denied, the Chinese insisted was true, and so on. It was quite a cause celebre at that time. The minister of the Navy was Admiral Takarabe and this was the time that the London conferences were coming up, in the 1930s, and he was disposed to moderate the influence of the warmongers and he tried to tie this thing down. In other words, he was prepared to make an accommodation and he carried enough political prestige in his person, as well as his prestige as a full admiral in the Japanese Navy, to carry it through.

I remember we got a new naval attache out there, a fellow named J. V. Ogan, who relieved Courts, after Courts went home, and we had very good relations with them. The chief of the naval general staff was Kantaro Suzuki and our relations with him were very good. He was kicked upstairs - he didn't like it - to be Grand Chamberlain to the emperor and Head of the Imperial Household. He was succeeded as chief of the naval general staff by Admiral Kato, and I never will forget that when I suggested to Captain Ogan, when the Admiral had taken over his job of being Grand Chamberlain, that we go up and pay a visit to him in his new job. The old man was so pleased with us, he could hardly speak of it. He said, "You know (he talked German pretty well, but his English was limited), McCollum, you are the only foreign naval attache people who have done the courtesy of calling on me in this god-damned civilian job," or words to that effect in Japanese. From then on, we had it made because he was - you know, he led the Japanese torpedo attack at Port Arthur - by way of being a national hero as well as a distinguished admiral. I first met him when he was commander-in-chief down at Kure. Following the British system, the officers in command of these what we would call naval districts, were termed commanders-in-chief. For example, Commander-in-Chief, Yokosuka, Commander-in-Chief, Kure, and so on. (Parenthetically Admiral Saraki at great risk to his own life took over the premier ship of Japan in 1945 and insisted on capitulation to the United States.)

Q: I suppose, at that point, the foreign embassies looked upon him as a has-been, when he got put upstairs?

Adm. M.: I don't know what the foreign embassies thought but he wasn't put upstairs because the job that he went to, Grand Chamberlain to the emperor, was one of the most potent political jobs in Japan. The way he jerked the strings is the way the emperor bowed. They were trying to get someone to counterbalance, you might say, the Army effect and they picked on this fellow who was more or less a middle-of-the-roader and had all the prestige of being a national hero and so on and so forth. But that didn't mean that he liked the job.

We would go out and make these inspection trips in Japan, and this was always arranged by - through - the Navy Department that if we paid a visit annually - we'd go down and pay a visit, sometimes semi-annually, to Kure. We got to Sasebo less often because it was more remote, a little bit harder to get at. We would go to Yokosuka upon occasion, then pay visits to the important industrial plants, such as...

McCollum #2 - 112

Q: Did you have ready access to naval bases?

Adm. M.: No, no. That was arranged with the Japanese Navy Department. We would come down and make a call and we would give them two times that we would like to go, and there was a negotiation going on. Well, the admiral's too busy, not now, or you'll have to come at another time. There was always a negotiation.

Q: When you got there, did you see anything?

Adm. M.: Not very much. They weren't taking their hair down, you understand. Neither were we. I remember once, as I was going through the Kawasaki shipbuilding yard at Kobe with Commander Hulings - this was some years before - and the Navy Department was riding us to find out what submarines the Japanese were building. Well, we knew that Kobe was full of German submarine construction experts, so that somebody was building submarines. Kawasaki is a big industrial plant, it's a ship yard and a manufacturing establishment, and the Navy inspector of material there met us, a commander, and we were shown through there. We saw the very interesting development of thread-in screws and things of that sort. Nuts with bolts on the end of them and all that kind of thing, how they were made. It was very interesting, of course, but all of a sudden, in one place, I couldn't understand why Hulings stopped, stood for a while, gazed around, and looked at something. When we went back to the hotel, he said, "Mac, they're building submarines all right." I said, "How in hell do you know?" And he said, "Well, you know that when I stopped in the middle of that plant, at that foundry place?" I said, "Yes, I remember that and I wondered why you were dragging that out.

We've seen lots of moldings and foundries and that sort of thing before." He said, "I was standing right on the cylinder head of a submarine diesel engine." He was a submarine officer. It never occurred to me. I was an ensign. I didn't know a submarine diesel engine from nothing.

We went off some place else and came back and I was foolish enough to say that I would go down there and find out whether they were building submarines. At that time, they had tied up at this yard, for repair, an American merchant ship called the Steel Arrow. So I went down to the waterfront in Kobe. I was staying at the Oriental Hotel, and got me a sampan - you know, a water taxi - and told the guy to paddle me out to the Steel Arrow. We paddle out there all right and I went aboard the Steel Arrow, and the chief engineer was the watch keeper - the other officers were ashore - and I had neglected to hold the boat. In other words, I paid him off and he went back. So after chatting with this very fine man, we went up on the bridge and looked down, and, sure enough, you looked down on two large dry docks and there were six submarines under construction. Well, the time for me to go back ashore came and I didn't know how the heck to get ashore. Couldn't hail any boats. There weren't any out there. It started to rain. Finally said, "I'll chance it." The only way you could get ashore - I thought that maybe I could walk across the yard and mix in with the afternoon exodus, when shifts changed. So I did, and it was pouring rain. About the time I was almost at the ferry and thinking, "Thank God, I wiggled through that one all right," all of a sudden this guy looked up at me and he said, "Ano" meaning hello, and it was this commander who'd shown us through the yard.

As soon as I got back, I checked out of that hotel and got the next train for Nara, which was a picturesque tourist joint. I had no idea of having a visit from the Japanese chief of the secret police!

Q: What was the penalty for doing that?

Adm. M.: I don't know. I never found out. If you got out of it alive, you'd be lucky, I should think. Just shows you how young and foolish one can be!

Getting back now to the naval attache business, we would make these trips and wrote reports on them.

Q: Did you do anything about naval aviation?

Adm. M.: Yes, very much so. That was very much in the front. We were very busy on that, and we were following the development of that almost from its start, very closely. The Japanese also were building up at that time a commercial airplane manufactory. The Navy favored one outfit, the Army another. Anyhow, the pie was cut around. The Nakagima factory later built the Zero fighter. We were following that very very closely, and about once a year, a naval aviator would come up from the Asiatic Fleet to Tokyo and I would usually be told off to go around with him to the various air stations and so on, so that he could get a first-hand look at it and I would try to do the talking.

Q: Were the Japanese as careful about their aviation as they were about submarines?

Adm. M.: Oh, yes. But it was a little bit more difficult for them to do. It's very difficult to hide a plane entirely. The naval aviation training station comparable to ours at Pensacola was located on Lake Kasumigaura, which is near Tokyo, as I think I've mentioned before. It was quite an extensive operation, but it was primarily first- and second-stage training for naval aviators. The working air stations, there was one at Yokosuka and one across the bay from Yokosuka, and they were supposedly defensive stations to defend the lower regions of Tokyo Bay. And there were others scattered around. There was one at a naval base in northeastern Japan. The one across the bay from Yokosuka was called Oppama. We would usually go around and make out a list of the number of them and, after, as I say, negotiation with the Japanese Navy Department and with the factories and so on, we would get on the train and go around and make this tour of inspection. We would be met every place by local Navy representatives, other than, of course, we weren't met in such cities as Kobe or Osaka. Those are big cities and we only saw those guys when we went to the factory. They were more or less representatives of the service there in the factory. Most of the time, we found them very decent chaps, but obviously they had their instructions. In other words, they weren't giving anything away for free. Occasionally, they would come and point out something, but usually it would be coming through and they courteously answering questions. You'd have a cup of tea when you arrived and a cup of tea when you left.

There was a naval aircraft factory adjacent to the Kure naval base, the navy yard, you might say, and this was a place to develop experimental types, new things. It's something like the Naval Research Laboratory, was run on a thing of that sort, get it to a certain point and say, well, maybe this is what we want, then turn it over to a manufacturer who would take it from there. That was their function. The Japanese followed the British custom. You know, their officers were highly divided into corps. In other words, you had the line, you had the engineers, which ran the engines of the ships, and you had all kinds of ordnance engineers, aviation engineers, naval constructors, paymasters, and so on. The fellow that headed - this rear admiral - this thing was one of the bright stars in the Japanese Navy you might say, specialty corps. He was very bright, very capable. But he was what we would later on have called an AEDO. He actually started out in life as what they called an ordnance constructor, then he developed an aviation specialty. So they were highly specialized and very good at it.

On one visit we were given a tour of the Japanese naval academy, the line naval academy. The Japanese had three naval academies. They had a line naval academy, they had a paymasters' academy, and they had an engineer academy. When you say Japansese naval academy, you've got to know which one you're talking about. The line naval academy, where the command line was educated, was located on an island in the inland sea, not very far from Kure, called Eta Jima, and we were entertained there by the Superintendent, who at that time was this Admiral Nagano that I mentioned several times before. Captain Ogan and myself were there and he entertained us very nicely. We had dinner that night, not fancy, we sat on the floor and ate sukiyaki, which the admiral personally prepared. The next morning we got up at the crack of dawn to watch the midshipmen, I suppose you'd call them, come out and exercise. They'd start the day with physical exercise before breakfast, about five o'clock in the morning, all armed with rifles and went through rifle drill, bayonet drill, and quite a lot of noise and so on. Admiral Nagano laughed and said, "You know, we make them yell to increase their war-like spirit. They don't have enough of it." But you did every once in a while pick up something. To get to Eta Jima, we were provided with a motor boat and we went across this great bay there that Kure is located on, a part of the inland sea, to the island where we disembarked, and the next morning after the festivities of getting to breakfast and so on, and eating with the midshipmen, and we were given the whole works. Admiral Nagano was very courteous and very understanding and handed us everything, and said, "You people have got to make out a big report on this. If there's anything I can give you to fatten it up, it's fine by me." When we went back, I noticed a funny thing that I hadn't ever noticed there, because, over here, anchored were a number of target rafts, battle rafts, we used to call them, where you would rig a sort of a batten arrangement stuck up there with heavy rafts mostly under water. But one thing that I noticed was that all of them were designed - you could take a look at them and they looked just like a Mississippi class of battleship silhouette, clipper bow and all. In those days, our Navy was the only one that had major ships with what we called clipper bows. And, you recollect that all of our latest battleships, about eight or nine of them, all had this clipper bow cut away in front.

Q: And they were the targets!

Adm. M.: And they were the targets.

Q: Did you query them on that?

Adm. M.: I didn't query them, but I reported it to the Navy Department. They didn't need any querying on it. I reported it to ONI. I don't know what they did with it.

But you know the Japanese were much more realistic than we were about that. They were training their officers, as we found out later. They could recite these ships' names of ours. Now, it is just as difficult for a Japanese to learn to pronounce a thing like "Mississippi" as it is for us to learn to pronounce something called "Hirado." Yet our guys never seemed to even catch onto it. Even way late in World War II, I had an admiral ask me - I was urging that we go out and deliver a torpedo attack on a couple of Japanese battleships, and this admiral looked at me and said, "What kind of guns are they armed with? My Lord! I was the intelligence officer, of course, and I was supposed to know that, but here was a guy who was going to fight them and he didn't know whether the guns had a 12-inch reach or a 16-inch reach, and it makes some difference! I mean those are some of the basics that people should know. They didn't. Our people, you know, were kept so awfully busy training, training, training, and training between the wars, they were so damned busy training that they couldn't figure out what the hell they were training for!

Q: Intelligence, as such, was not terribly important. I mean, our

McCollum #2 - 119

whole intelligence set-up was of lesser quality, I think...

Adm. M.: Of course, the trouble is that...

Q: It wasn't tied up with operations.

Adm. M.: No, it wasn't, because operations - from 1933 to 1938, when I served both on one of our battleships, the West Virginia, and the last two or three years of that, on the staff of the commander-in-chief of the fleet. The big thing was operations, target practice, what score did you make? Did you have an E on your gun turret, and so on? In the meantime, when you yourself were busy with your cut-down turret crews, trying to make a score with these great guns on a perfectly silly type of target practice, which we called short-range battle practice, which should have been abolished at the end of the Spanish War, the rest of the time was being spent out umpiring, observing on other ships. The result is that I spent very little time on board my own ship; and I'm telling you that the work and the reports were terrific. The result is that you didn't have time to think about what it was all about. The minute you got through with one year, you had a bunch of new sailors to train, and that's what it amounted to. So that the main thing was, how was your battle efficiency score? That's what you got promoted for. It didn't make a damn bit of difference whether it was useful or not. You'd get promoted because you had three or four Es on the turret. That's fine. I was fortunate in having four Es on a turret that I commanded. It was nice. I got letters of commandation from the Secretary, no less, on it. My sailors all wore a white E on their jumpers with hash marks under it. Not many of them had that. That was good. But what relation it had to fighting anybody, I don't know.

I came back from Tokyo to the battleship, West Virginia, in 1930, and I found people talking about, well, we've got the world record in this. What the world record meant they didn't know. One day the gunnery officer, who was a close friend of mine, a fellow named Jack Buchanan, I said to him, "Who do we have the world record over? How can we compare, for instance, with the Japanese? Or the British, for that matter?" He said, "Mac, you're too damned intelligence-minded."

Interview #3 with Rear Admiral Arthur H. McCollum, U.S. Navy (Retired)

Place: At his apartment in Vinson Hall, McLean, Virginia

DAte: Wednesday morning, 6 January 1971

Subject: Biography

By: John T. Mason, Jr.

Q: Good to see you again this morning, Admiral. We're coming back to the States and you're going to take up an assignment on the West Virginia.

Adm. M.: Yes, we came back from Japan on the SS President McKinley, and it seems to me that we arrived at San Pedro, California, rather than San Francisco, but I may be mistaken on that. I remember now, we stayed with her because she came down and ended up at Los Angeles Harbor, San Pedro. We disembarked there, and I went out to visit with people on the West Virginia, which was then at anchor in San Pedro Harbor, and everyone wanted to know when I was coming aboard. My orders had been issued the preceding February, which was a very long time. One of my friends on the ship laughingly said they had come to think that I was some sort of a ghost, they didn't seem to expect to see me in the flesh. My wife was quite pregnant at the time and we were anxious to get settled into an apartment and make connections with a proper kind of a baby doctor, obstetrician, I suppose you'd call him, which we did. Then the West Virginia sailed off, as they had a habit of doing, around the 1st of July to go up to Bremerton, or anyhow up in that area, and I was anxiously awaiting the arrival of a child, and my wife, although a mathematics major, seemed to have miscounted because we were unaccountably delayed and I even had to ask for an extension of leave, which made it an unheard-of leave period of about two and a half months. Fortunately, events happened just before my leave was over. I then left my wife and infant son, after I got her back from the hospital, and we had a practical nurse, and I went on and joined the ship in Bremerton. She, the ship, was then in dry dock.

In those days, the battleships and most of the other ships had a dry-docking period about once a year, and on the West Coast there were only two areas where the dry docks were large enough and the water was deep enough to take battleships. One was at Hunter's Point, near San Francisco, which at that time was nothing but a dry dock. It belonged to the Union Iron Works, a subsidiary of Bethlehem Steel, I believe. There was a dry dock at Mare Island, at least one, that was big enough to take a ship of battleship caliber, but the trouble there was that the upper bay where Mare Island is located was progressively silting up, and it was very difficult to work a deep-draft vessel up there. So much had to be unloaded off of it to lighten it and so on, so that, for practical purposes, there were only two areas where you had a dry dock: one, the Union Iron Works at the southern end of the bay, south of San Francisco; and the other one was at the Bremerton Navy Yard. There, of course, you had plenty of deep water - Puget Sound is very deep - but you do have some hair pin curves in there that gave you some problems in working a heavy ship around. Those old battleships were very heavy, they were very clumsy, and they were relatively low-powered. For instance, the West Virginia - she was an electric-drive ship, that's true, very modern, but her total horsepower was somewhere in the neighborhood of 29,000 to 30,000, whereas a four-pipe destroyer had about the same. The West Virginia weighed 36,000 tons, and a four-pipe destroyer weighed about 1,000 or 1,100. And, to show you the distinction, the last - my one big-ship command, the Helena, to come up with the difference, which was a heavy cruiser built at the end of World War II, she carried 180,000 horsepower and handled very, very well. But those big, heavy ships of relatively low power were rather clumsy to handle. Fortunately, with an electric-drive ship, you had almost as much backing power as you had power ahead. Of course, the difference being the slip of the propeller. The propeller is more efficient driving you ahead than astern.

Well, I joined the ship there and everybody greeted me with open arms. They finally said I had materialized and, for a while, they didn't know exactly what to do with me, and I was finally told that I was to be the Torpedo Officer. Well, the West Virginia, along with other battleships, did have torpedoes, one tube along on either side up near the bow, a torpedo tube, down well below the waterline. They were submerged tubes. In other words, they came out with a spoon. The big thing in the Navy in those days was the annual competition, training competition, in gunnery and engineering and communications, and so on. They were all competing for points, one against the other. I looked up the record, and the West Virginia, the battleship that had these underwater torpedo tubes, only worked them out about once every two years.

Q: That was an active job you had taken over!

Adm. M.: Yes. So the word came down that the Executive Officer,

Commander Russell, figured that I was one of these diplomatic dilettantes and he didn't know quite what to do with me and that was a job that he figured I couldn't do much harm at. About two weeks later, the Gunnery Officer, Lieutenant Commander Jack Buchanan came to me and said, "I told the executive officer that you, after all, had been in submarines and had had command of one of them, at least - and in spite of this diplomatic nonsense, why, we shouldn't waste you on a thing like that. How about taking over turret 4?" Those ships, of course, were armed with 16-inch guns and you had four turrets on them, two forward and two aft, and No. 4 was the aftermost one. I said that would be fine, although I was a little disappointed because this turret at that time had one of the highest gunnery scores in the Navy. It had an E with a hash mark, which meant that it had won in two years consecutively prizes for excellence in gunnery. Of course, that put me on the spot. I mean, here we had one coming, what's this new guy going to do with it? Fortunately, when the cycle started again, we were able to do it. But those Es, you know, were given only for short-range battle practice, which in many ways was a very dangerous practice because it was fired with reduced charges which were usually made up of powder on the verge of deterioration and much lighter than the standard bag of powder. One bag of powder for a 16-inch gun of that size - the full charge - weighed about 120 pounds. These reduced charges would come in all sorts of shapes and sizes and so one would weigh, oh, maybe, half that of a full charge. The trouble is that the silk bagging, enclosing the powder was on the verge of rotting and the loading was such that you had to ram it in with a power rammer. The power rammer was no

McCollum #3 - 125

problem with the proper bag and the proper charge, but if you hit one of these rotten bags with a power rammer, you scattered powder all over the gun room which isn't good, not recommended, anyway. And we did just that two years later.

I had a very instructive period on the West Virginia. I served on her for three years. I was what they called a Watch and Division officer. In other words, I commanded the Fourth Division and stood officer-of-the-deck watch and that sort of thing.

Q: And you had the fourth turret?

Adm. M.: And the fourth turret. But, as a result, every year I got a letter of commendation from somebody for excellence in gunnery, usually signed by the Secretary of the Navy, Mr. Swanson, at that time. That didn't do any harm to your records. I also got the opportunity for the first time - for me, at any rate - of meeting and getting to know officers of rank and distinction. For instance, we wore the Vice Admiral's flag. In those days, all the battleships - of the battle force - were commanded by a Vice Admiral and the West Virginia was his flagship. When I reported on board, or shortly after we got back to San Pedro, Vice Admiral R. H. Leigh, later Commander-in-Chief of the Fleet, broke his flag as a Vice Admiral, and, of course, we had his chief of staff and other people. Admiral Denfeld, who was at that time a Commander and was Flag Secretary on Admiral Leigh's staff. And it didn't do any harm for a young officer - theoretically, anyway - to get to know and meet some of these people who were on the way up. Of course, later on, as it worked out, then the vogue went to airplanes and airplane carriers and stuff like that, this business on the gun ships didn't stand you in too good stead, because a revolution came on in the Navy and its gun ships were more or less downgraded. That was, of course, much later.

Q: Admiral, someone said the other day that the annual competition of the fleet for excellence for gunnery and what-have-you and short-range warfare were really not very effective as a preparation for actual warfare.

Adm. M.: Well, the problem, so far as I know, was the same as is the case now. Your root problem is the personnel's system. In other words, you train one crew and you went through with it, and it was a reduced crew. I never had enough men in my division to man the turret. To command that turret from the handling rooms on the lower decks, where the powder and the shell came from, and up to the gun rooms and so on - to carry it through, you should have had about 120 men. I never had more than about 75 to 80, which meant that any time you went into one of these practices, you had to make special preparation and lay in your supplies ahead of time. In other words, the shells were moved up onto the shell deck before. They shouldn't have been. Put on the shell table, and then they were rolled over and you went and got mess boys and extra people from the engineers who weren't on watch and so on, to fill in so that you could pass the powder up, and you had just about enough people to get one train of powder up through the powder hoist. So it was artificial to a degree. And the Es, for instance, that we're talking about were given on the basis of the short-range battle practice. That was a practice fired at a ridiculous range, about 2,000 or 3,000 yards. It was lots of fun because it honed your gun's crew to a fine point and your turret trainers and elevators and so on. These were fixed loading guns.

McCollum #3 - 127

Every time the gun had to be elevated a little bit and fired and then you had to bring her back to her loading position, which was around zero elevation. Those guns were very long. Well, they were 45 caliber guns 16-inch, that's the length of the rifled part of the gun. The gun with the gun chamber and everything elese was pretty close to 80 feet long, and the muzzles were about nine feet apart. The target that you were shooting at out there was only twelve feet wide, so a very little shift on training would throw one or the other of the shells off, and you had to put both bullets into that target every time. So it really trained these people beautifully, but, of course, it was completely artificial because you never expected to fire those guns at that kind of a range, and using manual operation and people looking through lens sights and so on. You fired those guns, and those guns were fired during the war, but by directed fire, of course, where you readied the guns and they were all fired by a central trigger, so to speak. So what your man was doing now, instead of peering through lenses at the target, was following a pointer. In other words, you kept pointers matched on dials and things like that, to match up with whatever signals were cranked to you from your computers in the plotting room. So, to that degree, it was completely artificial. Yet, that was what the prizes were given on, and it didn't make a darned bit of difference -- you could blow the thing up in long-range battle practice, which was fired in ranges of 25,000 to 30,000 yards, which is more like it. But this short range practice was the one that everybody got the prizes on. The crew got prize money and the men wore a little white E on the sleeves of their jumpers, of which they were very proud. And when they lost it, some of these old salts broke out in tears.

I said something to one of them, my bo'son's mate, about it. I said, "Sorry that we busted up on this one" - this was my last year in it - you lost your prize money - I think it was twenty dollars a piece, which was quite a sum in relation to the total pay of the enlisted man at the time, and he said, "Mr. McCollum, to hell with the money, but we've lost our E."

That was the main trouble and, as I say, you'd hardly get through one of these training cycles before you'd start in another one with a crew fed in to you, your other people being paid off, and it was a constant battle and, of course, the ships were always under manned. For instance, a ship like the West Virginia, when she was fighting in the war, would carry a crew of 1,500 to 1,700 men - I don't know. But at that time the total crew on board was around 800. As you know, a warship is manned on the basis of manning its fighting equipment. so from the point of view of merely operating the ship, that is, the engines, the watches, and so on, you have a vast excess of personnel. Even with reduced crews, you have that excess. So what happens now is that, in order to keep these men busy, you went into the spit and polish routine. You do have to keep men busy, young men, anyway. And the next thing you know the shining of the brass and the scrubbing of the decks started taking precedence over things of more import. You did that. In other words, if you had a nice clean deck that shone white and clean, that all helped out. Most of us didn't realize it at the time, but what it amounted to was made work, largely to keep these people busy. Even with reduced crews you had that problem, and you did do those kind of things.

To my mind, this whole competition business was pretty academic. People were talking about having world records and this and that.

Well, they didn't have any comparison with anyone else, to match what they were doing. Because if you're going to make a world record, you obviously have got to have some standard with which to measure your accomplishments. The norm has to be somewhat the same. I don't think the Japanese ever told us what their norms were!

Q: No, I imagine they didn't!

Adm. M.: I just used that as an example. But they were very professional and, of course, the Depression was just starting and we got an increase in the basic intelligence of our enlisted men. The educational level started going up. For instance, the bo'sun's mate of my division, a fellow named Okinowic (phonetic), a first-class bo'sun's mate, had the equivalent of maybe a third-grade education. He'd been in the Navy then about sixteen years, and he was very, very good. My leading petty officers under him - I don't think any of them had more than a third- or a fourth-grade education. My Coxswain, which is the lowest grade of petty officer in that type of position, all had been in the Navy seven, eight, ten years, which is unusual. Promotion was very slow, tight, and a great deal of stress was being placed on book learning, which these guys had trouble mastering. They could frap a boat fall very nicely, but they couldn't do some of these sums that came in the books, and that made a problem. Then, you had a problem with these brighter young men. We even started getting fellows in there who had been to college for a couple of years. As a matter of fact, one disgusted Commander said to me, "It's harder to join the Navy as an enlisted man now than it was for me to get into the Naval Academy." These people were exceedingly good, and they became very professional, and a large part of those people became officers during World War II.

Q: Reserve officers?

Adm. M.: No, most of them were regulars. I don't know how many people from my division, my old division on the West Virginia, came through Australia in 1942 and 1943 and said, "Remember me?" I'd say, "Who are you?" And they'd say, "I'm old Olson" and I'd say, "I remember you." "Guess what, I'm a Chief Gunner now."

I had always felt that the personnel policy was wrong. I don't know how else to express it. The very great stress on what amounted to primary training, you had a training cycle and it started the 1st of July and it ended the following June, and you went through a regular series - I'm speaking largely of gunnery now, and the engineering was the same way, the scores and the speed trials, and so on and so forth. You went through a regular progression of events. Theoretically, each one a step up in complexity and so on. Well, by the time you got through with all this business along about in the following May or June, that was fine, but then when the 1st of July came you'd start it all over again. The same routine - antiaircraft fire, and so on and so forth. You started with the lower type of practice. I'm stressing gunnery because that was the department that I was in, but the same thing applied pretty much to the others, elementary class of stuff and then you step it on up and so on.

We had another thing, that each of the battleships was supposed to furnish what they called a nucleus crew, in case of war, for a destroyer that was in the Reserve Fleet, or nowadays we'd call it mothballs, and, of course, the West Virginia along with other battleships, supplied such a nucleus crew, and we had a so-called battle efficiency inspection by the Admiral. You'd line up these nucleus crews and they'd count heads. They came to about 35 or 40 bodies. Well, who were these characters? You looked around at them and you found that the prospective commanding officer of this destroyer. Who's his executive officer? He's the Spot 1 on the battleship. Now that's the fellow who also tells you - talks about the range - to move the shots up or down or to the side and so on, so you hit the target.

Q: Your most accomplished men!

Adm. M.: Exactly. Then you looked around and found out that they had a bo'sun's mate, and who is he? Happened to be a fellow named Filius. Who was Filius? Filius is the main battery director pointer. He's the guy who looks and pulls the trigger, shoots the guns. So what you did with a situation like that - they were supposed to be, had to be by orders, more or less experienced people, and they were, but if you had a team that has worked together, you completely gutted them to outfit this destroyer, and where did that leave the battleship?

There were a lot of inconsistencies, and I don't know what the answer to it is. In those days, the total strength of the Navy - and we never attained it - was 87,500 enlisted and about 5,000 to 7,000 officers. 5,000 to 5,500 line officers and a couple of thousand staff officers of one sort or another, paymasters and doctors, chaplains, and so on. So you had a rather small, well-knit force. You got to know a great many enlisted men, and most of the enlisted men got to know you. They didn't know who their captain was because he was too far up the pole, but they knew who their lieutenants were. That was the way you had this competition run. I've often envied the amount of time and the effort spent on these things. It was enormous. The labor involved for the officers was terrific. We were always observing somebody else. In other words, umpiring a match, you might say, so that we spent only about a third to a half of our time on board our actual ship. I'd go off on, say, the Arizona to observe long-range battle practice, and be gone for a week. Couldn't get back. Then the guard from the Arizona would come over and observe us and stay with us for about a week because they couldn't get back.

Q: That was in a sense busy work, too, wasn't it? The counterpart of polishing the brass?

Adm. M.: Yes. Well, that was part of it, that was very important because it had to do with the competitions. You were really strapped, and I was also for three years a member of what they called the anti-aircraft board. Antiaircraft batteries were in a state of development, and in those days the battleships were armed with a 5-inch 35 caliber guns, and every year we would recommend strongly to the Bureau of Ordnance that these guns be housed, at least splinter-proofed. One of the reasons for that - I wasn't entirely disinterested, because observing these antiaircraft practices, I was usually what they called a safety officer, as was most everyone else. That means you were stuck out looking through a check sight, they called it, to make sure that your gun isn't shooting at the airplane that's towing the target rather than the target. Well, those check sights didn't have any seats to them and you were stuck out pretty close to the muzzle, so you really took a beating from the blast, not only of your own gun, but of the adjacent gun. A little shielding would have been very welcome. Nevertheless, we always got the standard reply back from the Bureau of Ordnance that they understood and it was in their plans, but as long as it was in an experimental stage of development, they didn't think it appropriate to encase these guns in a splinter shield. Well, of course, the minute the war hit, that's the first thing they did, put splinter shields around them, otherwise you'd get the whole crew killed.

Q: Admiral, I suppose some of these circumstances you describe as peacetime operations in the fleet were almost inevitable. I mean, you were a part of a war machine, but existing in peacetime.

Adm. M.: That's right. It's inherent. The same is true in the Army. I don't care how you figure it out, you cannot keep in peacetime an outfit honed to fighting efficiency. It's just not in the cards to do that. You do all sorts of things. For instance, another big thing in those days was an athletic program. We all had football teams and baseball teams and basketball teams, and they competed with one another in athletics. It got to be quite a big thing out there, at one time. We'd end up with the championship team and we'd go up and play the Army at San Francisco. More or less professional teams, actually, and with all the hoop-la that goes along with college football. We also had bands and cheer leaders and so on.

It's very difficult to take anything of this sort, any kind of a war machine, and keep it honed and keep your eye on the war-making potential, and keep yourself limited to - and it is limited - proper objectives for war, because you've got to do something in the meantime to polish it up. Another thing was like everything else. As you know, Admiral William S. Sims of World War I fame, was the one who insisted that we start using target practice and so on, and he got to be quite famous for it. As a result of that, under various names, within the Office of Naval Operations, it was called the Fleet Training Division. In time of peace it was probably the most important division directly under the Chief of Naval Operations. They ran all the competitions and the target practices, made the rules, and checked on the final results. They were the final arbiter, you might say, and I never will forget that when the war came, the people in Fleet Training didn't know what to do with themselves. They tried to figure out some way to keep busy and couldn't quite do it, so it more or less faded away very quickly, which was too bad because they had some very able officers in it.

Most of the time on the West Virginia was quite routine. We did another thing that, in the light of later events, was quite interesting, also again very primitive. We did these supposedly landings on defended beaches. It was quite a trick to do it. We did that in motor launches from the ship. You'd load a motor launch. These big 50-foot motor launches that would carry about 90 people - and you had a crew to run and handle the motor launch - a crew of maybe a dozen people. These were heavy wooden boats powered with a gasoline engine in the stern. You'd go charging into the beach and when you got to a certain point in the breakers, you'd drop a couple of anchors from the stern and run out the lines and then you'd drive your boat into the sand, that is, on the beach. About that time, you had to have about two people on either side of your bow who had to jump off and wade ashore with lines to keep the boat from yawing off from where she belonged. Then the sailors and Marines would go over the bow...

Q: You weren't anticipating, then, the Japanese pillbox on shore?

Adm. M.: They were supposed to be there but that was the way it was done, and it was a lot of fun, but also I've seen those boats upended completely in the surf off a place like off Haleakala in the Hawaiian islands, just turn completely up-ended, spilling all 90 or 100 people into the water. Some of them would be hurt pretty badly. But it was an exercise in seamanship, all right. There's no question about that. But compared with what we were doing with our LSTs and LCIs and so on in the war where you had anchors all ready and cables on the stern to drop off, and you ran them into the beach. Your ship with a square bow would beach pretty well, with their engines going full ahead. A far cry from that, I can assure you. But we were working on it and we did have a so-called Fleet Marine Force in being, which was supposed to take care of these things, and did after a fashion. Those things, of course, were effective and were used to that degree in more or less the police actions that had been current during the twenties and even in the early thirties in Central America, and the Caribbean islands. For instance, in the case of Sandino up in Nicaragua around in 1926, that was the technique. That was the way the Marines trained and went ashore in the same type of boats. They didn't have special boats at all. The boats were carried by the ships. In this case, they weren't as big as the ones I was talking about because the ships that carried them were smaller. But they did go ashore in Nicaragua, sometimes against light opposition, not too much, but they did go ashore and, of course, the ships were always there to wait on them with counter-battery fire and that sort of thing. Basically, it was jungle warfare there, and they did it very well, I would say. Of course, we always think of Marines, but a good many sailors participated in these landing forces, too. In those days, you had a number of special service squadron ships down there, cruisers built for that kind of job, with copper-sheathed hulls and thins like that. They had a Marine guard on board of maybe 50 men, but when they would throw a landing force on shore, they would throw the 50 Marines and about 200 sailors. That's what it amounted to, 200 or 300 sailors would go ashore as infantry, and sometimes as artillery. That was more or less the way life was in training on the West Coast, at least, at that time.

Q: That's a very vivid picture you've given me of that sort of an operation.

Adm. M.: I'm probably being overly critical. As I say, in my opinion, always the root of the trouble has been our personnel system. As long as we turn over a ship's crew in whole, or in large measure, every year, we're going to have it. In the old days, way back in the wooden sailing ship days, what you did, of course, was that you enlisted a crew on a ship for, say, a period of three years. That crew stayed on that ship for three years, and you trained them for that period. The British still do that kind of thing. And after their three years are up, in the British Navy, the ship is brought back into a Navy yard, as we'd call it, and the entire crew, the captain, the officers, the whole business leave the ship and turn her over to the dockyard. And when the ship is ready to go again, she's fitted out with a crew, just like she's fitted out with new guns and so on. Of course, essentially, that's what we did during the war. For instance, I came in to take command of the Helena, to give an example of that, in 1945. I had what we called a nucleus crew. These were people who followed the last stages of construction of the ship and were also to be the key petty officer and officer leaders of the crew. My executive officer was at Newport with what we called the balance crew, and that was by far the largest number of people. They were the people undergoing primary training. In other words, you had a crew to man a turret, who had trained there in mock-ups and so on. Then, shortly before the commissioning, this crew came down and went aboard the ship. She was then commissioned, and we went down to Guantanamo, in the case of the Atlantic, and went through a series of training exercises but with that crew intact. You didn't change them, and that was the crew you were going to fight with.

I don't know whether it's possible to do it or not with the kind of laws we have, but certainly the old type of constant turning over of personnel is not good. You do have to have a compromise, and one of the things that we had to do then and we'll have to do again, is that these people have to be sent to schools. You take a radioman. He can go so far in the old Navy system of striking, which in effect is a system of apprenticeship. He's observing, following a more experienced or a senior person who is teaching him - we called him a striker. Well, it comes to a point then when he ought to go off to school to get a little more schooling and technical knowledge. That means he's off the ship. And you always had a drain of people at these technical schools, and you were never sure whether you were going to get the same guy back or not. So it does have its problems, and I'm not sure, from what I've heard, that these people nowadays have really solved that problem. I still hear the same sort of talk going on about turnovers and so on, and that, of course, in my day, is what made the submarine service so satisfactory, because you got a crew and you kept it. You didn't change them all the time, or if you did, you did it so slowly that it wasn't a panic. You might send a fellow to school but you knew you'd get him back. But with these big ships, and particularly on destroyers, my goodness, on this east caost here you were lucky if you had the same bodies one year after the next. It offers a problem, I'm sure, but I'm sure that we ought to be capable of solving it, but I'm not at all certain in my own mind that we have solved it. Maybe it's insoluble. I don't know, but certainly the old system was very defective.

Interestingly enough, based on these competitions and so on, the Asiatic Fleet, as they called it, consisted basically - the fighting component of the Fleet - of a squadron of destroyers, and in those days a squadron consisted of nineteen ships, and that outfit on the Asiatic station - Destroyer Squadron 5 - consistently won top honors. The reason was very simple. You sent a sailor out there to the Asiatic Fleet and he was there for three years. When he was sent to a destroyer, he was there for three years, and at three-year intervals you had a shift there. But consistently that Destroyer Squadron 5 won top honors in all types of competition.

Q: So you had the contrasting system.

Adm. M.: That's right.

Q: Well, having spent three years in the West Virginia, you went back to your real profession, didn't you?

Adm. M.: My real profession was that of a naval officer and a ship commander. I went back to ONI in August, 1933, if that's what you mean?

Q: Yes. Tell me about ONI in 1933. How comprehensive was the set-up? What were the objectives? What was the status of ONI vis-a-vis the rest of the Navy, and that sort of thing?

Adm. M.: I think I've mentioned somehwere before that the concept of ONI at that time and for many years past, with the exception of the security intelligence, or domestic intelligence, as we called it, was primarily that of a library operation. Information, largely from public sources, books, periodicals, writings, and so on, were gathered and were sent, in to ONI from various sources abroad. We subscribed to a magazine, for instance, and that was kept in a place we called the Archives. The Archives were basically a library, and if you wished to know anything about a subject, you went to the Archives. You had to have a card to get in, which wasn't difficult to get, and then you got one of the two or three librarian-type people in there, who'd been there a great many years and seemed to be more or less continuous, they would find the data and assemble it for you, sit you down at a desk, and say, all right, go to it. There wasn't too much evaluation done. In the first place, we didn't have the manpower to do it. When I went back to the Far East Section, as Chief of the Section in 1933, I relieved a man named Hartwell C. Davis, who was some years my senior. At that time in the Far East Section, we were responsible for the entire Far East - Japan and China, the Philippines - but we were not responsible, for instance, for the British possessions. The British Desk was responsible for Malaya which was, at that time, a British possession.

Q: The whole empire.

Adm. M.: It was called the British Empire Section. One of the other desks handled the Dutch business. This was what they called a Central European Desk, which was responsible for the Dutch East Indies, for instance. We in the Far East Section were responsible for answering questions about our then island possessions. That was taken away from us later and put into the Central Division, which was just as well because it didn't belong to us, anyway, but at that time Samoa and Guam and so on we were supposed to know about, those things that had nothing to do with intelligence; that had to do with naval government. Both of those islands, as you know, were governed by a naval government at that time. But any questions that arose on policy and so on were always referred down to us and we'd come up with a recommendation and go up the line with it.

My office consisted of myself and one assistant. The one assistant was a Marine first lieutenant. I was a lieutenant. He was a year behind me at the Naval Academy. A fellow named C. C. Brown, and he was a qualified Chinese linguist and probably one of the better ones, as far as I know. I know no Chinese. These were the two of us to cope with the correspondence, the direction of the naval attaches - we had a naval attache in China, of course, and then one in Japan, and those were the only ones we had, so we were luckier than some of the others who had four or five naval attaches that they had to wet-nurse all the time, from the departmental point of view.

Q: Did you maintain monographs?

Adm. M.: Yes, we had a monograph, but the monograph, again, was an encyclopedic work, and it was a tremendous job to keep an encyclopedia up to date and so on - constant revision. You just couldn't cope with the clerical task. For instance, we had one secretary, Miss Sublette. I first met her when I was going out to Japan in 1928. She was very good. She wasn't an expert stenographer. She couldn't take dictation, but she finally taught herself to type. She was all right and she turned out later, during the war, fine. That was it, so about every two weeks, based on the ship-sailing cycle, we would get a bag of mail from our attaches and other places out in the Far East. That would be brought in to our office by messenger, and the only technique possible was to dump it all on the table and sort it out. In other words, with periodicals, newspapers, and stuff like that that they sent us - you didn't have time to read it all. You might pick out one or two to keep, but the rest of it we'd shoot to the Archives right away. We'd send out a list that would go round the Navy Department saying what our acquisitions had been. So, as I say, it was almost entirely a library type of operation, as far as headquarters were concerned. We had neither the personnel nor the facilities to do otherwise. ONI has always been bogged down in this matter of evaluation and, you might say, the publishing aspect of it - getting it out. It takes a lot of people to publish a book, and we never had that. One of the things that we tried to do and did do, was to clear up what the Japanese ships looked like. We had pictures of them and so on, and from these pictures and from other published data, we started the building of a series of models at the Washington Navy Yard. It was supposed to be a highly secret job. We did build these models and they were pretty good, and we published pictures of them in a book along with angles of approach and so on. They used that for recognition throughout the war, and those books were kept up to date. So far as the monograph is concerned, it was almost impossible to keep that thing up to date with the manpower available.

Q: Yes, I would think so. Did you draw on the facilities of the Department of Commerce for things like information on oil refineries?

Adm. M.: Oh, yes. The technique was that there was a complete exchange - I don't know how complete, it's very difficult to say - but reports from the State Department and from the Commerce Department were also sent to us, and if they applied to the Far East at all, we got them. In other words, the ambassadors' dispatches to the State Department, the reports of the commercial attaches, and so on, they all came in, as did the consular reports. If there was anything affecting us in any way, we got it. At least, we were supposed to get it, and that just added to the burden of the tremendous influx of stuff that we had to try to get sorted out and sent around.

I was there only about two years that time, but we did do one or two things there that I think were helpful. I found that there was almost a total lack of material such as dictionaries, gazeteers, etc., that a translator of the Japanese language must have in order to operate on the written word. So we instituted a system in which the Naval Attache in Tokyo every month would send us a selected group of books which we selected, of dictionaries and so on. We called them a translator's kit, and I designed it so that we could hand this to a translator and he could at least cope with some of the problems. Otherwise, we were depending on such books and periodicals that I had.

You see, all of the books relating to the Japanese language in those days were either published in Shanghai, by Kelly-Walsh and Co., in Japan, or in London. There was nothing of that sort published in this country whatsoever, as I recollect. So we were dependent on foreign sources for this material. We built those up so that we kept - I thought at that time that we'd have to have at least ten of these kits. They didn't cost very much so we just kept them coming. I think about $10 or $12 per month or something of that sort was what the Naval Attache normally spent for these complete kits, and he would send it in the pouch, the usual mail bag, so we were building that up. We also started setting up a card index on all Japanese ships and kept that up to date, which was fairly easy to do - ships and aircraft.

Q: Warships?

Adm. M.: Warships, yes, not so much merchant ships. And we instituted a scheme which also wasn't too hard to do and which proved very fruitful during the war, in which we investigated the speed curves of Japanese merchant ships, particularly the larger ones. That was done through the cooperation of the pilots and the engineers who went on board the ships. They had speed curves in their engine rooms and on their bridges. So that we were able before the war started in 1941 to publish pictures and silhouettes, and speed curves of the major Japanese merchant ships. From the point of view of submarine warfare that was very useful, because up until about that time the most useful way of determining the speed of your target ship was from counting the revolutions of the screw. Therefore, if you had the speed curve, you knew how many revolutions it took to make a knot, then you had her speed. That was much better than a seaman's eye basis, with saying it looks like the wave in front is pretty big, maybe she's going ten knots, and so on. It had a very useful purpose, as did some of the other little things that were done.

You have to judge a little bit, I think, about a place like ONI by the caliber of the officers assigned to it. The Far East Section, of course, was never very popular. People didn't particularly like the Japanese at that time, and it wasn't attractive in many ways but...

Q: Also, the language was a handicap for most of us.

Adm. M.: Yes, that's right, but most of the Japanese officers over here, of course, spoke English pretty well. But the other officers that I knew in ONI, for instance, the head of the British Desk at that time was a fellow named Monroe, and Hamilton was the head of the Italian-Middle Eastern Desk. Amsden, I reckon, had the Central European Desk. These were all officers of high professional caliber, anyway. You see, this business of intelligence when you're trying to estimate what an enemy will do, or evaluate what he will do, you're a little bit in the position of a race track tout. All you can do is to say to your Admiral, or whoever it is, well, I think they'll do so and so, and of course, if you guess right and the admiral wins, he puffs his chest out and beats himself on that chest and says, what a great man am I! But, so help me, if he fumbles, regardless of what you've said, you are the culprit. It's one of the professional hazards of the business. You can't get around it. All through World War II the only admiral that I know who ever said his intelligence was superb was Nimitz at the Battle of Midway. The other times they were all saying the intelligence did them dirt. I don't care how you slice it, how much you've told them, or what you said, if they fumble or stumble at all, it was always the fall guys in intelligence.

Q: Nimitz had a right to say it was superb on that occasion.

Adm. M.: That's right.

Q: How frequently did operational people in the Navy Department query ONI in those early days for information which had to be obtained from the attaches?

Adm. M.: We welcomed it, and sometimes they did.

Q: In other words, did they use ONI with great regularity?

Adm. M.: Oh, yes. The only operational part you might say of the Navy Department was the Office of the Chief of Naval Operations. The rest of it, by and large, were Technical Bureaus. But we had that all the time. In other words, the Bureau of Personnel was very much interested in the personnel levels of the Japanese Navy, their systems of promotion, what were the personalities of their leading officers, which we got. The Bureau of Ordnance was particularly anxious to get a line of the latest ordnance developments. Those things backfired because, at that time, ONI was not supposed to evaluate, as far as I know, ever evaluate any technical material. If we got a report on a new Japanese torpedo or a new gun or something like that, that went to the Bureau of Ordnance who did the evaluating, and then it was returned. That was on the theory that a technical bureau on technical matters was better able to come to a valid evaluation than just people like myself, and there's a great deal of merit in that, but it never did work because the technical bureaus either didn't have the men or the people or what-have-you to set up a special section to do that kind of work, and that's what it took. In other words, you couldn't send, as I did, a piece of information up to the Bureau of Ordnance and have it land on the torpedo desk while that guy's busy building torpedoes, and this is just an extra chore for him which he doesn't particularly enjoy. So you don't get actually the measured evaluation that you were supposed to get, and the same is true from the engineering point of view or the hull design business. But you had to keep abreast of those things, and we did, so little by little we in the Far East Section, at least, started evaluating anyway. We sent it to the Bureau. Well, it took about a month to get it worked through one of the technical bureaus. You'd send a piece of paper up there, the guy would be on leave - there was only about one person on each of those desks up there - or else it would land on the desk of the principal technical engineer. He'd pop it off on one of the youngsters around there and you might get something good out of it, but usually and unfortunately, the tendency was to judge technical developments on the basis of our own technology and on the assumption that our technology was superior to any other. So if something was reported that the Japanese did have and we didn't then, obviously, it was wrong. That was the reaction.

Q: What was the origin of this assumption that ours was better than anybody else's?

Adm. M.: That's the American assumption, that's all. In other words, we are the people who invented modern technology. For instance, we got a report of this Japanese 24-inch torpedo, and we had it about two or three years before the Japanese started using it on us, and we had it in detail, we had its speed - 45 knots up at a distance of 10,000 yards, which was phenomenal. It went to the Bureau of Ordnance and we reported it carried roughly a 1,000-kg charge of TNT in the warhead. Well, that's roughly 1,200 pounds of TNT and we got quite a technical dissertation back from them.

Q: Had you put an evaluation on it?

Adm. M.: Yes, yes. We said that the source was impeccable, we thought, and 24 inches. Well, after all, the 24 inches, you understand, was an approximation because the Japanese used the metric system. Curiously, a 533-mm. torpedo is the equivalent of roughly 21 inches, which is the standard big torpedo. 583-mm. is equivalent to about a 24-inch, and that was what this was. Well, the Bureau of Ordnance came back and said that, in the first place, a 1,200-lb. warhead would be so long that its center of gravity, which is the origin of the burst, would be so far back that it would have a not materially different effect from our own torpedo which, at that time, carried 000 pounds of TNT; that the speeds were completely ridiculous, that no torpedo could go that far so fast. Of course, that was based on the fact that our torpedo used, as most torpedoes did use, an alcohol-steam air source of power. In other words, the alcohol burns and creates steam and so on. But the Japanese used pure oxygen instead of the air we used and this gave their torpedo its long range at high speed. Oxygen is much more dangerous to handle, of course.

Q: And very concentrated!

Adm. M.: Very concentrated. The thing is – not only that, but the thing was typical throughout our economy – not only in the Navy, you got it in industry and everywhere else. They couldn't do it because we hadn't done it.

Q: In this case, then, they discounted it almost completely?

Adm. M.: That's right. They only came around to our point of view when the Japanese started blowing the tails off our cruisers down in the Solomon Islands. Our people had forgotten, or did forget, that the Japanese were probably the premier torpedomen in the world, and for many, many years, right up until World War II, the cream of the professional fighting men was directed towards their torpedoes, and that was because the Japanese were among the first people to use torpedoes in an attack in 1905 when they used them against the Russian Fleet at anchor in Port Arthur immediately prior to the declaration of war and without any declaration being made when Admiral Togo launched his torpedo flotilla against the Russian Fleet at anchor and sank a couple of ships with these torpedo boats. From then on, the torpedomen were the top of the gunnery echelon in the Japanese Navy.

Q: That, in itself, was a fact that BuOrdnance should have considered.

Adm. M.: That's right. Well, of course, from the Bureau of Ordnance point of view – and I'm speaking more or less as a proponent of the torpedo – was always on the gun side, and they had a measure of right in that. It depends on what weapon you select. But our torpedo had stood pretty well still. It got bigger. The torpedo I had in the submarine O-7 that was built in World War I was an 18-inch torpedo, but the way she operated and the way it ran was essentially the same as our destroyer and submarine torpedoes in World War II. They were bigger and maybe a little bit better and a little bit less cranky than the others, but not much.

Q: It must have been a little bit discouraging, then, to meet with this type of attitude on the part of the technical bureaus?

Adm. M.: The thing is that the technical bureaus welcomed it and they were very quick. If you sent out a report, for instance, that they didn't agree with or they thought that they were being given a black eye because of this report, the pressure became very strong for you to withdraw it, regardless. In other words, you can't make us look that stupid, you can't make us look that bad. The Japanese Zero fighter had been used in China during the unpleasantness over there. Well, there came a time, eventually, when one or two of these things were knocked down and our people up in the hills around Chungking - this was later on, of course - were on the job and they secured dimensions and so on of this thing with self-sealing tanks and so on and so forth, and with auxiliary tanks put on the side. We pushed this out, and the Bureau of Aeronautics just hit the ceiling. They said, how come you say that a fighter's got a range of 1,500 miles, and I said, well, it's got a range of 1,500 miles because they've got these belly tanks on them and we know that they are escorting bombers from fields in northern French Indochina to bomb the Salween River bridges which are 750 miles away. We know they go there and back. So that means a range of 1,500 miles. And in spite of that, the report was withdrawn. This ship can't have these charactieristics! But we actually had the material. And, again, somewhat earlier. The Japanese back in about 1932-1933 had quite a little war around

Shanghai. Their ships were firing on targets ashore. Some of the bullets went off good and some went off bad, so we had a wonderful opportunity to pick up a lot of Japanese materials, some expended and some not, and our Asiatic Fleet Intelligence officer at the time, a fellow named Smith-Hutton, was very much on the job and, with urging from us, he had parties scavenging stuff and finally got a whole shipload of this junk back here. We made a report to the Bureau of Ordnance about the shape and range of the Japanese 8-inch projectile. This was the time when the 8-inch cruisers were very much in the development stage. And we got a report back from the Bureau of Ordnance saying that this was impossible, that the projectile didn't fit the proper norms, and it wouldn't go the distance.

Q: But you had the visual aid there.

Adm. M.: We didn't have it at that time. I had a friend Charlie Wellborn, from my class, who was on the gun desk at the Bureau of Ordnance, and I went to Charlie and I said, "Look, Charlie, we have got this material. We haven't actually got it yet but we've loaded it on a ship and it's coming here and we're sending it up to Dahlgren, and you people can look at it. What is the reason that you don't want to agree with us?" He said, "Well, my principal engineer tells me that it has a completely outrageous coefficient of form." Now, the coefficient of form of a projectile is the ratio between its diameter and its length. It's a ratio and it's used as a measure. It's got to be so long and so thick. "It's a coefficient of form that will just not fit in anything at all." Well, a week or two later, this shipload of stuff - junk, mostly - got down to Dahlgren and Charlie and I went down and looked at it, and measured it and sure it did measure up and I said, "There's your coefficient of form." Well, of course, what the Japanese had and we didn't have at that time was what was later on called a long-point projectile, an 8-inch projectile, which is longer than normal, so you have a rather odd coefficient of form, that's for sure. But it also gives the shell about 2,000 or 3,000 yards more range for the same amount of propellant that goes behind it. As a result of that, we started changing the Portland class of heavy cruisers - the cruiser was coming out and we changed her shell-handling arrangements so she would fit the long-point projectile.

Q: It seems to me, Admiral, that the basic understanding, concept of Intelligence, was quite wrong, then, on the part of the Navy as a whole.

Adm. M.: No, I don't think so. These people were very anxious to get it, but, you see, one of the difficulties - as it is in any manufacturing outfit - is that we are pretty good, and that goes for General Motors and it goes for the Standard Oil Company and everything else. If we can't do it or haven't done it, it can't be done. It's awfully easy to fall into that sort of mentality, and I'm afraid we had our share of it.

Q: It's a pretty dangerous state to be in.

Adm. M.: Yes, when you're fooling with some things. On the other hand, of course, if you pick up every rumor and start believing it, you can go into a complete tailspin, too. At that time, one of the things that was handed over to me in ONI was a set of drawings on a transparent type of paper, almost a cloth, and these purported to show the Japanese gun emplacements in the mandated islands, and it was supposed to be from an exceedingly valuable, precise and exact, source. I got to looking at this thing one day, and I took out these drawings of shore gun batteries, 16-inch guns here, 8-inch gun there. And this was believed. We had it, the British had it. We were swapping back and forth with the British and the sources were the same.

In studying some of these line drawings - they were not typographical drawings - but we did know the elevation of the island, and those were put in and so on. It all of a sudden occurred to me, in looking at one of these maps, what a tremendous job it was to get a 16-inch gun, judging by the ones that I had had on the West Virginia, about 80 feet long and weighing about 100 tons stripped, up a 1,600-foot jungle-covered mountain without any wharf facilities whatsoever, from a beach. And I just didn't believe it could be done without leaving scars at least where the railroad or cable or whatever had hauled this thing up to the mountain top. We, in those days ran ships back and forward through the mandated islands. We did not stop at the ports because the Japanese didn't like it, but there was no reason that we couldn't sail through there, and it was a fairly simple thing to put this and other islands under observation to see if from visual sightings and so on, using optical instruments, there was any sign of the work that would have to be undertaken to put in such gun emplacements. On those tropical islands, as you know, you just don't put heavy weights ashore like that without equipment of some sort to handle it. And when you have to cut through a jungle to get a thing of that size up there, you're bound to leave a scar that, even with jungle growth, would last several years. Couldn't see a sign of it. Well, a lot of people in the Navy Department didn't like to believe the Japanese weren't arming those islands, and I will say here and now, I never believed they were myself. I didn't think it was possible or practical. They were building airfields, sure, everybody was building airfields, but they had as much of a commercial use then as they do now. In other words, this thing was finally blown up. It was considered one of the most exact and precise bits of information that the Navy had gotten. Actually, as we found out much later on, both the British and we were buying this material from the same source, who was concocting it. Some Hungarian fellow was cooking up this stuff and selling it to both sides.

Q: But not based on fact?

Adm. M.: No, no. He put a gun anywhere he had a notion to put it. He'd never been out there, didn't know anything about it.

Q: Had the Japs begun, in the early 1930s, to do this on the mandated islands?

Adm. M.: No. They did very little, actually, except what we would call field fortifications. In other words, emplace a few antiaircraft batteries around places like Truk and so on, but this was after the war started or immediately before and after they had abrogated the treaty. There wasn't any way to check that, out ahead of time because you can put in light artillery, quite quickly. You notice here that of the Japanese pillboxes on those various islands during World War II very few had heavy guns in them. I mean guns as big as a 5-inch. They might have had a 20-mm. or 40-mm., that kind of thing which does a terrific job against personnel, of course. Very few of the pill boxes found during World War II had a gun of a caliber as much as 5 inches. A 5-inch gun to move around in jungle territory is a pretty heavy piece of equipment, and the Japanese preferred to use tanks. That was better for them. A tank, of course, in those days, carried quite a light gun, an 88-mm. or something of that sort.

I don't know of anything that would indicate the Japanese did other than live up to their Treaty commitments. Now, I'm speaking of the Washington arms treaty. The tendency on the part of a lot of our officers was to doubt it. They were always expecting to catch the Japanese out in a violation. One of the main points at issue that was constantly thrown at us in the Far East Section was when periodically the office of the Chief of Naval Operations said, well, now, let's send a ship in to Saipan, or pick out a number of islands for a visit, and the stock answer by the Japanese was they would be very glad to welcome the ship at any one of their open ports, and the open ports were these. Then the boys up in the Central Division would hit the ceiling, what the hell's the use in all this treaty. As usual, the treaty governing the mandates said that there should be free commerce and so on and made it sound very good. But it made them mad when I pointed out to them that that was fine, but that thing was based on the basic League of Nations agreement that the laws of the mandatory power obtained in the mandated islands. Under our law, of course, all ports are open, except a very few that were closed, Pearl Harbor, for instance, and one or two others. Under Japanese law, all ports are closed except those that are open. So, the Japanese were perfectly correct in turning us down. I mean if our diplomats hadn't sensed that in signing the treaty, that was the time to have made the change, not later on and squawking about it.

(Our State Department was not of much help.)

Q: But that was the source of our suspicion, their sense of secrecy or whatever you term it?

Adm. M.: That's right. And in a measure they were right. They said, well, they didn't have facilities in a lot of these ports to entertain foreign ships. And not only entertain in the sense of amusement, but I mean customs and pratique, and all that sort of business. And they didn't. They could have had, of course, but they just didn't. But they were very liberal, by their lights, in the mandated islands. They offered us this port or that port, three or four of them were open and we could go to any one of them at any time, that is, if we had made the proper approach for a warship to go in, of course. You had to approach the government. You don't just go calling. I must say that I had never felt that the Japanese were other than impeccable in following precisely the terms of the various treaties and pacts, and so on, that they engaged in, until such time as the pacts were abrogated.

For instance, the Japanese didn't even start laying down their super battleships, the Mushasi and the Yamato, until after the London Naval Treaty had been abrogated. The abrogation date on that was 1936. That's why none of those big 18-inch, 60,000-ton monsters - there were only two of them - came into being until the very end of the war. It took about five years to build one, and that's just about the time that had elapsed. There were two other hulls that were converted before they were finished into monster aircraft carriers, both of which were lost at sea. In other words, our submarines got both of them - one on its trial run from Kobe and the other one somewhere else. That shows that they weren't fudging, they went just as far as the law permitted, don't misunderstand me, but they didn't exceed the bounds. A lot of our people felt that they were sneaky, underhanded folks, anyway, and you couldn't believe anything they said. They didn't like to admit that these Japanese people were playing the game strictly according to the rules, which they were!

Q: Did the Japanese Embassy people - the naval attache and others - substantiate this point of view, or were they helpful to you in the 1930s in imparting information when you went to ask for it?

Adm. M.: No. The Japanese naval attache in 1933 when I came here was a fellow named Masashi Kobayashi. His surname is Kobayashi, and his given name is Masashi. You see, the naval attaches were primarily interested in obtaining information, and we would swap information back and forth. In other words, if the naval attache wanted to make a visit somewhere, we'd arrange it for him, and in return, of course, our naval attache in Tokyo would ask to visit something, and so on. So there was a sort of a reciprocal arrangement.

One very amusing reciprocal arrangement we had and probably the oldest one standing was an exchange of hydrographic data between our Hydrographic Office and the Japanese Hydrographic Office. That had to do with sailing directions, of course, and charts and maps, and so on, coastal areas, tide tables, etc. I never will forget that about a month and a half after the war started, in January of 1942, a chap came up to me in great annoyance, saying that he had for twenty years had the job of sending this kind of material to the

McCollum #3 - 157

Japanese Hydrographic Office and this stupid Post Office of ours is now refusing to handle anything and sending it back to him. We had been in a state of war for about two months. I got curious about it and came to find out that the same kind of people were running the Japanese Hydrographic Office because their material was still coming through fine.

Q: Hostilities! But you said that they didn't help to dissuade people who thought the Japanese were secretive and so forth - the representatives here.

Adm. M.: Unfortunately, I had known this naval attache, Kobayashi, when he was assistant naval attache. He followed the usual course. He took their course of English language in this country for two or three years, or whatever it was, then the one of them that did fairly well, the more senior one, was told off to be the assistant naval attache. That was the system, and he had been the assistant. I forget who was the naval attache here at that time, but it probably was Captain Sakano.

It frequently depended on the personality of these fellows. I mentioned Captain Sakano. He was the Naval Attache in 1928 when I went out to Japan as assistant naval attache. He was extremely popular in naval circles in Washington. He had a nice wife, a lovely family, and he played golf in the golf tournaments, and so on - a very personable fellow. But this particular Kobayashi was not the same type of person at all. He was very short, sort of fat, a Buddha-like type, and you just didn't have any meeting ground with him at all. I mention this Kobayashi because later on there was another Kobayashi, Kengo, who was naval attache here in the late

1930s and he, again, was a very personable fellow. I had known him first when he was aide to Admiral Suzuki in Kure back in 1924. He had a charming wife and they were very acceptable socially in Washington, among other things, and he got around quite well and knew a lot of people. Again, it was a matter of personality. His immediate predecessor was Tamon Yamaguchi who went down with his carrier division at the Battle of Midway. Yamaguchi was a very able man, but he overstepped the bounds by using language students around here in the spy business and we had to have him ordered home.

Q: You mean spying on installations?

Adm. M.: Yes. They developed quite a system and, frankly, I tried to develop the same system out in Japan and it didn't do too well. There are places, for instance, in every country - and Japan is no exception - where, because of natural geography and so on, there tends to be a concentration of naval activity, and one of those places, of course, in Japan, is the Inland Sea. We could travel back and forth in the Inland Sea, but there were no open ports, as such, in the Inland Sea. There were open ports on each end, of course. On this end of the Inland Sea, you have Kobe and Osaka, and on the other end, you have Shimonoseki and Moji, Shimonoseki being on the main island and Moji on the southern island. Those are commercial ports, and there was never any stoppage of anyone moving through the Inland Sea. The Japanese didn't consider it a closed sea. As a matter of courtesy, when we had a destroyer or a destroyer squadron come visiting in Japan, we would give the Japanese Navy Department their prospective route, and if there was some objection to it, they would say so. They were usually very frank in saying, well, we're holding maneuvers down there right then and it would be very inconvenient to have you guys steaming through there. In that case, because it was an inland sea it was pretty well closed, and we always honored it. Theoretically, under international law, we didn't have to, but we always did. On the other hand, if the operations were taking place on the high seas, as frequently happened, there was no reason in the world why we couldn't steam through that area any time we wanted to, and sometimes we did.

We had a naval review up at New York and President Roosevelt reviewed the fleet in 1934, and we made quite a big shindig out of it. All the naval attaches then resident in Washington were invited to attend, and they did. I was told off to be the guide, you might say, of these people. We had the British naval attache, at that time Captain Sir John Dewar, who was a very nice personable fellow trying to be very helpful. We had a French naval attache, the Italian, and the Japanese - I don't remember whether the Chinese had one or not but I don't think so at that time. These people were all assembled, we all went to New York, we got train accommodations - it was a package deal, and I went along as their usher, you might say. The Russian naval attache was quite new, Admiral Oras, and his assistant. They all were taken on board the cruiser up there in New York. It seems to me it was the <u>Augusta</u>- a heavy cruiser, and we went out to watch the President steam down the line of ships as they came in, all of them saluting, with the guns going and the bluejackets manning the rails, and so on. Quite an impressive sight.

But this Japanese naval attache Kobayashi came on board the cruiser loaded down with long-range camera gear. Well, it just gave a bad impression. I don't think he could have seen anything, anyway.

McCollum #3 - 160

I asked him if he would mind if I took care of it for him for a while, which I did. He didn't like it particularly.

Q: Did ONI have any voice in the selection of our attaches for the Far East?

Adm. M.: Oh, yes.

Q: In the actual naming of them, or only in the training of them?

Adm. M.: Naming of them. The naming of the naval attaches in the Far East were always referred to ONI. In other words, appointment, or recommendation for appointment, came from ONI, and one of the main jobs that I had there was to scurry around and try to get suitable officers to serve. You see, we were caught, we had no Japanese-language qualified people, with the exception of Captain F. F. Rogers, of the rank of captain, or even, at that time, Commander. It seems to me our highest ranking officer after Rogers was Lieutenant Commander Zacharias. So the problem was to get a man of sufficient rank and prestige to be suitable from the Japanese point of view, and then pair him with an assistant who was qualified in the Japanese language. That's what happened with me in 1928. I was the first one that went out under such a scheme as that. The naval attache, as I remarked before, when I arrived in 1928 was a commander, but quite a senior commander, named George M. Courts. His assistant was a fellow named J. M. Creighton, whom I relieved but Creighton had left before I got there. Neither Courts nor Creighton had Japanese language capabilities, I was the first guy to go out there as Assistant Naval Attache with a Japanese language capability. After Courts went home, he was relieved by quite a senior captain in the Navy, a very fine officer, named J. V. Ogan, who was a bachelor. One of the problems was to get someone who was willing to go to Japan of adequate rank and experience so that it didn't look like we were just pawning off a nobody on the Japanese, which we weren't and didn't intend to, and then try to back him up with a language capability trained officer, which we did do.

Later on, in the early 1930s, Captain Rogers went out there as the naval attache, and he was the first Naval Attache who had any capability in the Japanese language. In the first place, we had to persuade him to go. If you got one senior enough, he felt somewhat that he was shunted off - I mean, speaking from our naval attache's point of view - selection to flag rank was an ever-present problem and most of them were hopeful of making it, but not many did. Ogan was an officer of very great distinction in the submarine service. He spent many years in the submarine service. As a commander, he was the first division commander of the then-considered very modern V boats, later renamed the Bass, Bonita, Barracuda, and so on, he was executive officer of battleships, served on staffs, and had had a distinguished career. He had one advantage. He was not married. He didn't have household problems with a wife and so on. A lot of times the ladies weren't too anxious to come out there to Japan, particularly if they had teen-age children, as most of them did. That can be understood. So, that is what we had to contend with. Now, the job in China was very much sought after. That was because of the social amenities of Peking It was a very pleasant and, at that time, quite a cheap place to live. Japan was not! They had lots of social activities and so on, so that the job as naval attache to China headquartered in the old legation quarters in Peking was very much sought after. Despite the fact that the Chinese government had moved its capital to Nanking, none of these fellows would go down there, neither would the ambassador, for that matter. There was a measure of justification for that. We had treaty rights and so on involved in the extraterritoriality of the legation compound with its guard of Marines, in our case, and soldiers, in the case of the Japanese. All of the foreign powers signatory to the Boxer Protocol, I believe they called it, in 1900, were in there with their own guard forces, and our Marines were kept - that is, one Marine detachment was kept up to strength, and that was also considered a prize job. We always had a very distinguished Marine lieutenant colonel which, in the old days, was a very high rank, commanding what they called the Marine Guard. Of course, the British had the same thing, and the other states. So, you had a very pleasant social life with lots of activities - polo-playing and drinking at the clubs, and so on - that Japan simply didn't offer. In many respects the Peking job was rather avidly sought after, whereas the Tokyo job; the guy usually did it out of a sense of duty, which is a little different thing. But, on the whole, we had, I think, very able men. I mentioned Ogan, for one, and Courts, his predecessor, whom I didn't know too well because, as I told you before, he was quite a sick man when I arrived in Japan, and as soon as he felt fit to travel, why, he traveled. There was a short interval there of about a week or two when I was holding the job down, and Captain Ogan then arrived, and he was followed, I think, by I. C. Johnson.

Q: Admiral, the fleet engaged in war games in the 1930s and the use of orange as the potential enemy - the Naval War College was always working on problems of this sort - the orange was obviously the Japanese, were you drawn upon for information or assistance in the development of such war games?

Adm. M.: No. The war games, as played, and later on when I was assistant and later on acting operations officer of the Fleet under Admiral Hepburn, were not necessarily drawn on - the Japanese. Of course, they were always the potential enemy, but a war game to be really realistic in terms of search and location and bringing in the intelligence of the enemy, can be a very long-drawn-out affair, and the time and the fuel and the cost of all of those things was somewhat limited. So that you have to rig them with some kind of artificiality. And we did have an artificial fleet set-up. In other words, the fleet was organized into so-called task fleets. You had the battleships and you had cruisers and you had destroyers and aircraft and so on, and Admiral Hepburn, my boss, was constantly badgering the Navy Department to get away from this concept. In other words, you had the scouting force with their cruisers and an aircraft carrier or so, they would go out and search and find the enemy. Then the battleships were brought in and sank the enemy. That was the theory, anyway.

Admiral Hepburn, back as early as 1936, when he assumed command, in one of his first letters to the Navy Department said, let's stop this business and organize around either a division of battleships or a carrier with a division of battleships, small striking forces, because you're never going to go out there and fight one of these wars that are more or less traditional with a line of battle and so on. Well, the Navy Department would nearly always come back and tell us, yes, they knew the validity of his argument and he was right; but from the point of view of training there was nothing that would beat a war game that exercised each element of the fleet to its utmost and in coordination with the other elements. So the job on the staff - I'm overstepping myself now, reaching ahead in time - the war game was devised by the operations staff of the commander-in-chief. In my case, when I joined that staff, the operations officer was the then-Captain Ghormley, who was a very brilliant staff officer. He was relieved by Admiral Furlong and between Admiral Ghormley and me being parceled out to do some of the, you might say, dog work of the business, the war game would be devised there, and it would be submitted to the War College and to the Navy Department for their OK before we undertook it. One of the major problems was that you had to bring in all of these forces so that each outfit would be exercised, so it did have some touch of reality. For instance, we actually carried out a daylight attack - a dawn attack - on Pearl Harbor in 1937. Carriers moved in at dawn and delivered a surprise attack on the Army and Navy installations and so on. Of course, sham stuff, but there it was, backed up by the battleships and the cruisers which came steaming in under the cover of aircraft and went through the motions of bombarding places like Diamond Head and Fort DeRussey and so forth. So, it was in our minds all the time. The problem there was to take the training of the War College who, you see, were not bound down in working their war games. They were not circumscribed by fuel budgets, for instance, and there's an enormous difference in the fuel consumption of a destroyer charging around, say, at 30 knots, and one that's going 15 knots. At one time, we were trying to fight these war games with speeds limited to such things as 15 knots, which was perfectly ridiculous. But, what are you going to do...

Q: We were in the Depression.

Adm. M.: Not only the Depression. You had a certain amount of fuel and you couldn't exceed it, I mean, there wasn't any more. When that ran out, the bucket was dry. So you did have to have those more or less practical considerations which did not inhibit in any way a War College operation. For instance, a War College war game could last for a month or two, which was out of the question for the Fleet, we couldn't do it more than two weeks because, as I say, of limitations of time and fuel and food and so on. When you ended up and you always had to pay a courtesy visit. In the case of the Hawaiian Islands, it was all very pleasant, you'd go out and fight the enemy like hell, and then go in to Pearl Harbor and go on the town for a week, you know.

Getting back now to the selection of the attaches, that always was a prerogative of ONI, and it was always taken very seriously, and the effort was, as I said, to get someone who was thoroughly qualified from a technical or, you might say, professional point of view.

Q: The field, for you, in the Far East was pretty limited.

Adm. M.: Well, we had just the two attaches. The one in Peking and we never had any trouble filling that job. But you'd usually have to peddle the Tokyo job around quite a bit.

McCollum #4 - 166

Interview No. 4 with Rear Admiral Arthur H. McCollum, U. S. Navy
(Retired)

Place: His apartment in Vinson Hall, McLean, Virginia

Date: Wednesday morning, 13 January 1971

Subject: Biography

By: John T. Mason, Jr.

Q: Good to see you again this morning, Admiral. Today, I think you resume your story by telling me about your transfer in February 1935 to the hydrographic office in San Pedro.

Adm. M.: The assignment to the branch Hydrographic Office, as it was called, was supposed to be a cover. It wasn't a very good one. My job there actually was as Assistant to the District Intelligence officer with my offices at San Pedro, with a special assignment of liaison with the Commander-in-Chief of the U. S. Fleet, who, at that time, was Admiral J. M. Reeves. It had fortuitously come to the attention of Admiral Reeves that confidential documents mostly relating to gunnery exercises were being stolen from some of the offices of some of his ships and were getting into the hands of the Japanese intelligence.

When I arrived, the job was to try to locate the Intelligence agent who was responsible for employing the people who actually did the stealing. We knew that a man named Thompson, who had been a yeoman, I believe, in the Coast Guard and had also served a time in the Navy, was the person along with a young confederate of his named Turntine, who was doing the actual stealing.

Q: How was it discovered, Sir?

Adm. M.: His companion, Turntine, and Thompson had a falling out, and Turntine, who was about 18 or 19 at the time, maybe less, appeared on the flagship and, you might say, turned Thompson in. They had a quarrel. Some people say it was a lovers' quarrel. I don't know, but it was that sort of a relationship. At that time, the only clue they had was the name Tani that Thompson referred to as the man who employed him, and, of course, the suspicion immediately centered on the Japanese fishing fleet, so called, which was more of a mirage than an actuality and operated out of San Pedro. There was a man of Japanese ancestry who was master of one of the tuna clippers and his name was Tani, but as we looked at the situation it became more and more apparent that Tani was a cover name. As are most Japanese names, it was fairly common. Its one ideographic representation means "valley." It seemed to me unlikely that Tani the master fisherman would be involved in a thing of that sort. He had neither the technical knowledge to designate what was wanted, nor the capacity to treat with people like Thompson.

We had put on active duty a reserve officer named Le Baron who had been a former detective of the Long Beach police and had served in the Navy in World War I as an enlisted man. He was a lieutenant in the Reserve. He had been on active duty and from the police officer point of view was investigating the situation, and without too much success. We had in the Los Angeles area a very fine organization of Reserve Intelligence officers, an organization that had been devised by Captain A. A. Hopkins, who was a Reserve intelligence lieutenant commander. He was the captain of a special force of the office of the Sheriff of Los Angeles County. The Sheriff was Eugene Biscailluz, a very popular - nowadays we would call him a Spanish American or a Mexican American - politician. He was from an old Spanish colonial or Mexican colonial family of distinction in southern California. He very kindly made the facilities of his entire staff available through Hopkins to me in any way that I might require.

Now, in Los Angeles at that time you had two police forces. One was the sheriff's force, who was the Sheriff of Los Angeles County, and there were parts, of course, of what we now call Greater Los Angeles that were not included within the Los Angeles city. The city had its own police force, the metropolitan police force. There again we were very fortunate. The Mayor of Los Angeles at that time was a man named Shaw, recently relected, and his political and private secretary was a retired Navy lieutenant, his brother named Joe Shaw. Through this connection, the facilities of the metropolitan police department were made available, notably through Lieutenant Layne. They were very useful, of course, in such things as checking automobile license tags and, in cases of necessity, making a pick up of someone under suspicion. These things were all new to me. I had never done this sort of work at all.

Q: How did it happen that you were transferred from foreign intelligence to domestic? Simply because of the Japanese aspect?

Adm. M.: Well, they had a Japanese aspect out there and no one seemed to be grappling with it, and Admiral Reeves was in Washington on other matters, and this was one of the things on his mind, and a man who was serving on his staff, who was a very close friend of mine and still is, named Joe Rochefort, had suggested to Reeves that if he could shake me loose from there, I would be able to handle this stuff. I didn't thank Joe for his kindness, particularly. So Admiral Reeves told the then-director of Naval Intelligence, Captain Puleston, that he wanted McCollum. So McCollum went.

There was a great deal of confusion and continued to be confusion over the so-called Japanese menace in southern California. There was a feeling of mistrust of these people, whether they were American citizens or not, some of it justified, most of it, of course, not. The potential was there, I suppose, but it's one thing to have a potential, even a small potential, and another thing to exploit it.

It was quite apparent that something was going on, and that Thompson was the immediate thief. Through Rochefort, who was the Fleet Intelligence Officer, we arranged to have Thompson pick up data that was doctored, because, of course, in this sort of operation one doesn't make arrests, one wishes to develop the situation so you would have an understanding of it, and then control it, so to speak. The last thing it is desirable to do is to make an arrest, because then you have the whole thing to do over again. As long as you are in a position to control what information is fed out, you have attained your objective pretty much.

Q: And in the long end, you're apt to get ahold of all the people involved!

Adm. M.: That's right.

Q: Was Thompson a young man?

Adm. M.: No. He would be a man in his thirties, I would say.

Q: Was he vulnerable because of his sexual proclivities?

Adm. M.: I don't think that entered into it. I think it was a matter of money. You must realize this was the Depression time, and these people didn't have any jobs, and Thompson wasn't the stable type of character who would hold down a job. He was able enough in some ways. He was a stenographer and a typist, but he was a floater and a drifter, and where he could pick up, in those days, two or three hundred dollars a month for taking a pleasant trip out to one of the ships and picking up something and coming back with it, especially after he was given prepared data, at no cost to himself, it made it very attractive to him.

Thompson had arranged with his principal, whom he still referred to as Tani, to deliver data to him. This stuff was run on a very detective-story kind of basis. In other words, a lot of false names and mail drops and so on were used in various places, and we decided that when the delivery was made, it was to be made at a certain street corner in Los Angeles.

Q: By Thompson to the other man?

Adm. M.: Yes, that's right. And we would have observers there to observe the rendezvous. Le Baron was to chaperon Thompson, and Lieutenant Joe Shaw got into the act. He insisted on coming with me, and we pulled into a parking lot, with which he had connections, being the mayor's secretary, which looked out at this pick-up point. Well, the time came for the pick up and Thompson did not show. We sat there for a while. We noticed a Chevrolet automobile came by two or three times. It would pull up to the corner and drive very slowly and almost stop. I was quite a neophyte, but Joe Shaw had the prescience to jot down the license number of the car. Well, after we'd waited for about an hour for Thompson to show up and this suspect car, I might call it, didn't show up any more, I got pretty upset and went back and found that Le Baron had not produced Thompson because Thompson had word, or said he had word, from this Tani that he couldn't make it. Well, I told Le Baron in no uncertain terms that that was no excuse not to have his man there on the spot. It would have been very nice, because we had cameras ready to cover the tryst.

Well, suffice it to say, we did trace the ownership of the car. It was registered in Palo Alto, Stanford University, and in the name of a special student at Stanford, who was a Lieutenant Commander Toshio Miyazaki. That commenced to fill in, in my mind, because I had not been unaware that the Japanese were using their language officers over here as, you might say, spy masters in a sense. I went up to Stanford and talked to, I believe it was the Dean of Men or one of the deans, and asked if I might have a list of the students at Stanford - I told him who I was and what I wanted, of course - and was flatly turned down, as he said he didn't think the university would care to get involved in anything of that sort with the federal government, which is more or less the history of Stanford, pacifistic and non-involvement with government and so on. Of course, the heck of it was that they, along with practially every other university, used to publish a little booklet, a digest of students, and it was published by various people, but you could buy it out in town at almost any stationery store. So I went out and spent 25 cents of the government's money and bought the book. Sure enough, this Toshio Miyazaki was there. So, we started covering him, and the next time we had a successful tryst, in which we took photographs and so on. It was pretty well determined what was going on and who was the principal.

Q: You mean this Japanese student actually turned up at the next tryst?

Adm. M.: Oh, yes.

Q: How did Thompson have free access to these documents? By virtue of his position?

Adm. M.: It was pretty simple in those days. You must realize that the ships in San Pedro Harbor were open to visitors every weekend, and while we had a system on those ships - we used to call it rig ship for visitors - where you had guards posted at various places, but the guards were primarily people to safeguard the visiting public from falling down hatchways and things of that sort. They were really ushers more than guards. They were posted around so that the ladies and the children could come around and look at the parts of the ship that were open, and we were very liberal in what was open.

A fellow like Thompson could come on there and he could sit down and start making friends with the enlisted men, and, of course, he knew enough that one of the places these things were kept was the gunnery office. Well, the gunnery office was just a little bit of a partitioned-off place on the berth deck somewhere and he could go in there and sit down and chat and make friends with the gunnery yeomen, you might say, and talk about things, the old Navy and all that sort of stuff. Then he'd suggest that maybe they needed a couple of drinks - this yeoman would go to the soda fountain and buy a couple of cokes, Thompson would pay for them. Well, while the yeoman was gone to buy the cokes, Thompson would take the material. Simple as that.

As long as you're going to leave those ships open the way they were, and no one was too worried in those days about things being robbed off the ships such as minor thefts of clothing and supplies...

Q: But when gunnery reports began to be missing, then there was suspicion?

Adm. M.: Well, they began to be missing, but, of course, there was a cover-up. Usually, those reports were in the process of being typed up by the yeomen and if the typescript copy was gone - usually they were prepared in long hand originals - the yeoman could always retype them without further ado. There was no definite checking - you got copy No. 1 and you must account for it, and so on - so it was a rather free and easy situation, and the same thing applied to other things. Later on, as I'll tell you, about anchorage charts, most of these things were marked "restricted" or "confidential" and so on, but actually they were not too confidential in my point of view. Nevertheless, there was a stamp on it. They shouldn't have gotten out. There's no question about it.

We played this thing along, through Thompson, feeding Miyazaki with information that we thought would keep him happy and, at the same time, mislead his principals back in Japan, up to a point. You can't mislead them too much, or else they smell a mouse.

Q: The authenticity has gone!

Adm. M.: That's right. The next thing you knew, Thompson got very frightened for some reason. He thought the Japanese were threatening him, and he slipped out of Le Baron's hands and disappeared. We didn't know where he'd gone.

Q: Was he AWOL?

Adm. M.: No, he wasn't AWOL. He was a civilian. He was not in the Navy at all, or the Coast Guard. He was a civilian.

Q: Oh, I see, he was a former...

Adm. M.: Former, that's right. All he did was decide that the thing was getting too tight for him, hot under his collar and neck and so on, and he'd better take a powder. So he did.

Q: How long did it take him to be suspicious?

Adm. M.: Who? Thompson?

Q: Yes.

Adm. M.: The thing is that this fellow Miyazaki apparently impressed on him that in case he turned evidence on him, he would be murdered, and apparently he overdid the act somewhere and Thompson got fearful of his life from the Japanese. That is, not from Miyazaki in person. You see, in that time in Los Angeles, as there was in San Francisco, there was a section of town in which the Japanese lived, and certain of these fellows, just as in any other foreign or ghetto community, if you want to call it such, are involved in somethings less than entirely legal. One of the things that was engaged in, so I was told and later had evidence that there was some truth in it, was the dope traffic. Whether Thompson was a dope addict or not, I don't know. He was obviously, after all, a rather unstable individual. In other words, he became fearful of his life, not from us, but from the other side. So he just simply thought it would be healthy for him if he disappeared, which he did. We hadn't the foggiest idea where he'd gone.

About three months or so later he showed up back in Los Angeles and, curiously enough, he walked into Le Baron's office. Of course, what he wanted to do was reestablish contact with Miyazaki because he was running out of money. We weren't paying him anything and didn't intend to pay him anything. We didn't have it. That was about the status of the Thompson case when I went to sea in 1936 on Admiral Hepburn's staff, who relieved Admiral Reeves. We were able to get definite pictures and identification and so on of Miyazaki, adn we passed the word back to ONI as to how the thing was done. How it was operated. We found the same situation up in the Seattle area, and soon got on the trail of a man up there named Okada, who was again a lieutenant commander in the Japanese Navy. Okada, incidentally, was the son of the former minister of the Japanese Navy and a former Prime Minister who was nearly murdered in 1936. These were high-calibre guys, but they weren't really trained in intelligence or spying but the Japanese Navy was very lavish in equipping them. There was another one up in the San Francisco area. That was three on the West Coast, and there were obviously others in other places. But once you had determined the method, the how, it was fairly easy to pick up the who, and the attitude was to follow that.

Now, later on, it came to a position in which the Navy Department ran out of patience with the whole business. Okada, for instance, up in Seattle, Miyazaki in Palo Alto, among two that I recollect, were, in other words, told to go home.

Q: The game was up!

Adm. M.: Well, we just told them they were persona non grata. These people, you see, didn't have diplomatic passports. In other words, they were, in effect, deported. It was thought better to do that than to try to bring a case before a federal court.

Q: The international implications and...

Adm. M.: Partly international implications, partly publicity was not particularly desired on our part as long as we could spot and follow a replacement. We would let one of these fellows play along for a year or so and then kick him out, then we'd have another one for a break-in period. In other words, you were in on the ring, you knew what was going on. Captain Puleston, who was the Director of Naval Intelligence during most of this period, just got out of patience with the situation and said, let's get rid of these scoundrels, and we did, and that was the way it was done - partly we didn't want to raise the question, we had vulnerable students studying in Japan, too, you know. Later on, about 1937 or so, a case was presented to a federal court. Thompson was indicted, he was convicted, and he was sentenced to McNeal Island I believe, for 13 years. In other words, it wasn't just a dream.

Q: What was the charge in his case?

Adm. M.: Espionage. I don't know whether that was the charge or not but that's what it amounted to. We did have an espionage act, you know, the act of 1917, which was a pretty weak act, but it was on the books and under certain flagrant conditions it could be invoked. That did happen and that must have been about 1938, anyway. From then on we developed a situation in which the commander-in-chief of the fleet and the other officers of the fleet had, you might say, a man Friday on the beach, who, in case of difficulty and so on between the populace and himself, could be a sort of go-between. It was an intelligence officer. At that time, the Young Communist League was making a very strong bid to enlist the sympathy of the enlisted men against the officers. Their technique was to take these youngsters, usually high-school children about the grade of sophomores, send them out to the ships to this open-house business and drop newspapers around and so on. One paper that they had was called The Shipmates Voice.

We, with the cooperation of the Long Beach and the Los Angeles police departments, were able to keep that situation within limits. Most of these youngsters didn't exactly know what they were doing. They were just carried away with the idea that hey were going to have a revolution and so on, somehwat like they're doing here now and in other places, but we did have it and, of course, they had their adult, you might say counselors along, in some cases a lawyer or two who would be as much interested in publicity for himself as for them. There was a good deal of misapprehension on a good many things there. I remember once that I was quite shocked shortly after I arrived when I had gone down to San Diego, which, as you know, is the headquarters of the 11th Naval District. At that time the District Commandant was Admiral Tarrant. He assured me that as far as his district was concerned, he hoped I would assure the commander-in-chief that anything he could do in the way of cooperation and help he was there to do. Now that wasn't always the case because there could always be a certain amount of formality as between the forces afloat and the forces ashore - that sometimes happened. But I never will forget that his intelligence officer said, "I have got a picture of every damned Japanese agent in southern California, and what I want you to do - the names are listed in Japanese - is to translate the sutff for me. I've got $250 from the Navy Department and I bought it. Now these are photostats." A And he handed me a bundle of photostats, possibly 50 or 100 pages. I said I'd have to take them back up to San Pedro where I had my reference books and so on. Well, Sir, you know, the more I got to looking at these pictures, the more suspicious I became about them. They were a series of pictures, maybe a half a dozen to a page, such as you would put in a high-school annual, and all of these guys were dressed in evening clothes, white tie, and some in Prince Albert frock coats. The reasoning of the Intelligence Officer was that they had to be important people. It would be impossible to think of them as farmers and tradesmen and so on around there, because how else would they be dressed this way?

Q: Just a simple matter.

Adm. M.: Well, the more I got to thinking about it, the more suspicious I became. Then it occurred to me that a year or two before that, Prince Takamatsu, who is a younger brother of the Emperor, had been in this country on, not a state visit, but a government-sponsored visit with a full coterie of aides and so on. Zacharias, for instance, was his naval aide.

Q: Was at the White House?

Adm. M.: Yes. He was at the White House, and traveled extensively in the country with a retinue and an entourage, and, in due course, he came to Los Angeles and the Japanese community and the foreign community, but particularly the Japanese community, put on quite a show for him. In Los Angeles, at that time, there was a Japanese newspaper and they were very active - I don't know whether it was subsidized or not, but I rather think not - I mean subsidized by the Japanese government, I rather think not. But I got to thinking about it, and I said, all right, now these fellows here are dressed up in the kind of clothes that would be appropriate, from a Japanese point of view, to meet an imperial person. This is the court dress, either a frock coat or evening dress clothes. And these fellows had had their pictures taken so much a head maybe, and they'd go out and rent a rig to put on.

I didn't dare tell this officer what my suspicions were until I could get them confirmed. So I finally called up on the telephone this Japanese-language newspaper. I suppose you'd call it the Los Angeles Times. It was known locally as the Rafu Shimpo - Ra means La for Los Angeles, fu is city, and Shimpo means newspaper or news or periodical, or something of that sort. I said, "Say, you remember a couple of years ago when Prince Takamatsu was over here?" He said, "Who was Takamatsu?" I told him and he said, "Oh, yes, that guy." I said, "Did you people, by any chance, put out a sort of commemorative album or booklet or something?" "I don't know, but let me talk to the editor and I'll call you back in a little while."

Well, in a little while he called back and he said, "Yes, we put out one. We sold them for about $1.50 a copy among the people around here. It was a sort of memorial issue. Business firms and business guys paid a little something to get into it, and so on." I said, "That's fine. Have you got an extra one of those things kicking around?" He said, "Sure, we've got one." I said, "Well, you know, I take your paper. How about sending me one?" He said, "O.K. I'll put it in the mail." After I got the book which had about twice the stuff that had been given me - there it was.

Q: All the suspects!

Adm. M.: All the suspects. You got into all these kind of things. There wasn't really very much to it. The Americans were afraid of these people. For instance, I was presented with a sketch of a tuna clipper, which is a type of fishing boat, as you know, that has become pretty specialized. It was fitted out with an underwater torpedo tube. Well, heavens to betsy, it had gotten into Admiral Reeves' hands and he was saying, "My Lord, are these things fitted that way?" He yelled for me to come and do something about it. Operating out of San Pedro there were only three of some 25 or 30 tuna clippers, so-called, that were mastered by Japanese. The others were Finns or American or what-have-you. I went to the fellow who was a sort of detective in charge of the harbor police, and I said, "Why don't you go down on one of these ships and take a look and see what they've got," and he said, "I'm scared to. If I go down and start poking around one of these ships, they'll kill me." I said, "Oh, don't be silly."

I finally went down, not having any better sense, to talk to these people and found them very affable and friendly. They talked English and they were very happy to show me thorugh their ships. But, of course, again the potential was there. You see, in those days the tuna were caught sometimes at quite a distance away, as far as the Galapagos Islands, for instance, and they were put on ice. In other words, they were refrigerated, and the refrigerating machinery, by today's standards, was pretty primitive. It was basically a very powerful air compressor, and started out initially in ice and you kept the whole business frozen by what amounted to a month or so. These were the days before freon. So they had to have these very heavy air compressors in each ship to preserve the catch. Of course, a compressor like that is required in order to charge the air flask of a torpedo. So you can take it step by step up the line here, and then, all right, all you've got to do is to dream up where to put the torpedo tubes.

I went down and went through them. They were very interesting ships, as a matter of fact, and the masters were very proud to show them off. I got to be right good friends with them, but there wasn't anything to it. It was just a lot of hog wash.

Q: The Japanese had been known by us as very courteous and almost gentle in their manners, why did they then in this period loom as ferocious individuals? How did this change take place?

Adm. M.: You say "we," you're talking about we people on the East Coast...

Q: Exactly.

Adm. M.: ...where there weren't any Japanese but you must understand that out on the West Coast, the Japanese were primarily indentured labor, to start with, all of them. For instance, as most of us know, the railroads pushing east from California, the dirty track work and the laying of the rails and so on was done by Chinese coolie labor. Well, we passed a law in 1885 or 1890 or something like that, which prohibited further importation of Chinese labor. The people who were then building the western parts of such things as the Great Northern and the Northern Pacific Railroads were looking around for labor, and the other labor source they could find was Japan, so we had a lot of Japanese labor indentured, is what it amounted to, recruited by labor contractors in Japan and shipped into the United States. They worked on the railroads. When I was a boy about 12 years old living in Seattle, all of the people who did track maintenance and worked around, say, the King Street station in Seattle, were Japanese. They were the descendants and in most cases the ones themselves who had come over in these labor ships from Japan, and they were called out there Scabies. It sounds kind of bad, scabies, but that is an anglicaization of a Japanese name called "Sukebei," which was a very common given name for peasantry type of people in Japan.

The Japanese in southern California, nearly all of them - they had a sprinkling of professional people, of course, a doctor or two and a lawyer, not many of those - most of them were farmer types of people and they were a cut above, in Japan, the bums, you might say, who were shipped over as day laborers, coolies. These people were sons or second sons of small farmers, and a great part of the trucking, farming, and so on in southern California at the time I speak of, along the coast was done by Japanese, and they had small produce markets and so on. Curiously, they themselves didn't go out for fishing very much. Fishing, particularly this tuna fishing, is a very lucrative business for the people involved in it, but these people were basically farmers and not fishermen and they wanted no part of fishing, or didn't take it up, anyway.

Q: Just to complete that idea, therefore they weren't viewed by West Coast people in the light that we saw them here?

Adm. M.: No. There was a strong element of West Coast people that were suspicious of their loyalty to this country, whether they be nisei, issei, or what-have-you. Part of that was economic, part of it was just a dislike of these funny people that they couldn't talk to anyway. You remember we had such cartoons as Hashimura Togo the schoolboy, and so on, and we had a paper called the Sacramento Bee that was shreiking about the yellow peril all over the country? The West Coast, by and large, viewed people of Japanese ancestry with a certain amount of suspicion and distrust, and it didn't make much difference how you talked about it, it was still there, and you had the same feeling among the officers and men of the fleet.

Q: So it was easy enough to conjure up...

Adm. M.: Yes, that's right. Anything that was bad, tack it on these people.

Another matter of some concern was that we started picking up funny coded messages that were obviously being exchanged between these tuna ships, or as some people said between spy ships and a place on the shore. These things, one by one, we had to look into. Well, it's true that under our laws at the time, the Master of one of these ships did not have to be an American citizen. Although he might have been domiciled in the United States for a long time the Japanese, unless he was born in this country, was not eligible for citizenship. So that, for instance, a Japanese could have lived in this country for 30, 40, 50 years and still not be a citizen, provided he had been an original immigrant from Japan. Some of these fellows, for instance this Master of one of the tuna vessels was such a person. He had lived in the United States for about 20, 25 years and expected to die here. So immediately there were suspicions. But you see we had a catch in the communication laws. The fact was that a guy who ran a radio set for one of these ships had to be an American citizen, and what the Masters would do, of course, was to hire someone to be radio operator, but the requirement in addition to a technical capability was that he be a citizen. Some few were of Japanese ancestry; most were not.

So, after hunting around a little bit, I found a fellow who had been a third class Radioman in the Navy and had gotten out and seemed to be doing very well for himself. I asked him what he was doing when he came in to see me, and we had a very nice chat. He was a very nice young fellow, a man in his late twenties I would say, a family man. He said, "Oh, I find radio operators for these tuna ships, and put them on there. I get a fee for that." I said, "So then, what?" He said, "Well, I put them on there, they get their money, and I get a fee for it and I get a cut off the catch. It's turning out pretty good." I said, "What else do you do?" He said, "These fellows usually go out and they like to hunt in groups of three to four ships to catch fish, and I make up simple codes to give them for their buddies so that they can talk around with each other as to where the fish are. Do you want them?" So I made an arrangement with him, and all this chatter had been going back and forth and it was all to do with fishing.

Q: It wasn't confined to the Japanese ships?

Adm. M.: Oh, no, all of them. I then found out that the Masters of these ships liked to have in their crew people of varying nationality, Japanese, Finnish, German, Spanish, and so on, so that there was always someone who could chatter back and forth and exchange you might say the fish intelligence when they went alongside. It was a method of operation, that was all. These things were constantly coming up; and once you brought a little thought to bear on the subject, they disappeared. I don't mean to say that it wasn't there. The potential was there.

There was, for instance, a Japanese-owned and operated hotel in Los Angeles called the Olympic Hotel. There wasn't any question that a fellow like Miyazaki, the Japanese spy master there, could come in and out of that hotel in any way he wanted to. In other words, it was a handy place that he could move in and out of, had he cared to. The same was true with some of these other fellows around there. There was a doctor in Los Angeles who was only too happy to assist in this work. His name was Furusawa, and he had lived in the

United States quite a long time. He was a doctor in the Japanese community there. He was a prominent attendant at the functions of the Japanese Consulate. I don't know that the Japanese Consul was directly involved, but again I repeat that these were depression days, you know, and the Consulate at this time made a very definite effort to infiltrate and get ahold of the Japanese-American Citizens League which was just starting up. These were American Citizens of Japanese ancestry, the second-generation boys, and if they could have been controlled, you might say, by a thing like the Consulate or something like that, it was fine. How do you do that? You take one of the leaders of the Japanese-American Citizens League, we'll say, he's just out of college, hasn't got a job, he's a yellow man, he can't get a job too easily, he may be running an elevator although he's got a college degree, that wouldn't make any difference. So, what did the Consul do? He'd get him a job as a secretary at a rather nice salary. That worked up and down the line, so later on we had to go into that situation and you might say nominate a slate of officers from the floor, which we did do, in order to wrest control of the organization from hand picked officers subsidized by the Japanese Government.

That about ends that phase of my duty there. I think one of the most stimulating things I had was the selfless devotion of these Reserve Intelligence Officers. Captain Hopkins had organized them into units. In other words, you had a unit up at Santa Monica with a Lieutenant Commander in command of it. He commanded the Los Angeles unit. The usual unit consisted of maybe half a dozen of these fellows, and they would drop whatever they were doing and come running when the call went out. The trouble, of course, was that they were all people who had to make a living. They weren't paid anything by the Navy. It was all volunteer. One fellow, I knew, used to come from Anaheim or some such place. Anyway, he rode 40 or 50 miles each way on a motorcycle. I mean they were a dedicated bunch of people, but they had the faults of all amateurs. They were overly enthusiastic, sometimes. Enthusiasm is a fine thing, but one needs to channel that enthusiasm and direct it and, above all, keep it within reasonable bounds. It was very interesting duty and the only type of duty like that that I've ever had.

Q: Were you in that time as unflappable as you are now about such things?

Adm. M.: I don't know what you mean. My wife says that I'm very flappable.

Q: I mean looking at a situation and reasoning it through rather than getting excited and suspecting espionage. I mean you went at it in a very cautious, careful way.

Adm. M.: I think one had to do that. The thing is that a lot of these fellows that were bringing in this information were highly excitable fellows themselves. There was one place down there called Scammons Lagoon, which is in Lower California, which is Mexican territory. At one time in the sailing-ship days, way back when the whalers were running down there there was a salt works in the place to cure fish and stuff like that. Scammons Lagoon, sure, it's a lagoon, but we had one fellow in Los Angeles who just insisted that he had pictures and he could produce them of major ships of the Japanese Navy anchored in Scammons Lagoon. Now, Scammons Lagoon has, in certain parts of it (I suppose you could anchor) but there's a bar across there that has only nine feet of water over it. Well, you can't get a 27-foot-draft ship over a nine-foot bar in any way that I know of. But in order to lay this ghost, we had to go down there and poke around and go into that place and assure ourselves that the Japanese had not dredged the bar out, that it was in fact still nine feet deep, and then come back with the dope. Of course, people that dream up a sort of a fairy tale like this don't always enjoy having it destroyed.

I think the trouble is that they started off on the assumption that these Japanese people are treacherous, underhanded people, and so on. You say the Japanese are such gentle people. They are in a sense. But, on the other hand, they are a pretty rough, rugged kind of people. I mean among their own people they don't hesitate to use force and use it in a big way. The Japanese police are famous for what we call police brutality - I believe that's a term we use over here, and it wasn't the type that we have over here, it was pretty hard-hitting. So the funny thing about these Japanese is that they can be very polite and pleasant and that's one of the things that's a matter of suspicion, but that's part of their manners. They can be awfully, awfully rough when the coin is on the other side, I can assure you, and they were. As I say, another thing is that California at that time had a population of about 12 million, I reckon, something of that sort, and the Japanese were filling in, they were displacing what had been wheat farmers with truck farming and so on. YOu have an economic factor coming in. And another thing, just like in other new-comers, these bright Japanese kids would go to school, to the University, get high marks, and then they'd come out into what? Go to work selling vegetables at papa's vegetable stand. They didn't like it, understandably.

The Army intelligence at that time, which was headquartered in San Francisco, I believe it's the XII Corps area, were very much concerned with the so-called Communist angle, but not so much with the Japanese, so they left it more or less to the Navy to develop and keep tabs on the situation among the resident people of Japanese ancestry, which we did. Later on, we actually - I say we, but I didn't have anything to do with it, but the ground work had been laid and later on carried on, with the help of the Japanese-American Citizens League, which got to be very much on our side, these were these misei people and so on, we were able to pinpoint practically every agent of the Japanese government that had any potential for mischief at all.

Q: Before we leave this phase of your career, Admiral, I wonder if you'd tell me a little bit about Admiral Joseph Mason Reeves. You know, he is a naval officer of exceptional ability who somehow or other seems to have been lost in the historical record, and I'd like to have more of a picture of him, as you observed him at close hand.

Adm. M.: I had not know Admiral Reeves until I reported aboard his flagship, the Pennsylvania, in San Pedro Harbor, what it amounted to was to make my manners. Theoretically, I had no reason to report to him because my boss was the Commandant, through the District Intelligence officer, of the Naval District. However, it was made quite clear to me before I left Washington that the man I should look to for guidance was Admiral Reeves or his staff.

He was a very forthright person. He had a flair for impressing his personality throughout the fleet that I have never seen equaled by any other commander-in-chief with whom I've had the privilege to be associated. I don't think there was a sailor in the fleet who didn't feel that he had "the old man with a beard," (as they called him - he had a full beard) on his side.

Q: A handsome man he was.

Adm. M.: He was about six feet two or three, spare, and very straight, and I found him a very kindly person. Others did not. He was very much a strict disciplinarian, but I have never seen a man who so impressed the enlisted men, I think partly because of his beard. Some kid would get in trouble, and someone would say, "Never mind, the old man with the beard is going to look after you." He was a great believer in direct action. He didn't necessarily want to go through channels for this, and other times he didn't expect to go through channels. At this time, he was a widower and he remained so. He had one son that I know of who was an artist and quite a good one.

He also was a man who had very strong prejudices. He had made up his mind, for some reason, that a rather prominent marine artist who was a naval reserve officer was a British spy and he didn't want him around. This fellow was very active in the naval reserve, very good, and so on. Other people, notably Admiral Leahy who was later chief of naval operations, was a great protagonist of this young man - young man, heavens, he was as old as I was, if not older. So we had quite a time, but we found the fellow had actually been born in England. He was an American citizen but when he joined the naval reserve nobody asked him specifically anything like that, and when he was asked where he was born he said Norfolk. Well, he was born in Norfolk, but it was Norfolk, England, not Norfolk, Virginia. That, of course, just confirmed Admiral Reeves' suspicion. Some of us were trying our desperate best to protect this fellow against this vendetta. I don't think we were wholly successful but we were up to a point.

You know, it had been customary for a long time in the fleet that I served in that on Monday morning a ship would get under way to go out to sea for exercises, at eight o'clock. That's all right, but you know on board ship at eight o'clock practically everything happens. They have colors and the band plays the Star-Spangled Banner, the watch changes, they dry down the decks, hang up the mess tables, and so on. Well, the first order that Admiral Reeves issued was that this Fleet will not get under way before nine o'clock in the morning, and that of course made a big hit with the officers and enlisted men, some of whom had to scramble to get back aboard if they had missed the last ship's boat from the dock, which some of them did. He was a man who was very forthright.

I remember once he told an officer on his staff, "I want you to go up to Los Angeles" - I've forgotten just what it was, we were negotiating with the city, probably to build a naval air facility on Terminal Island and we didn't have any money, but we had a new thing that had come through and it was WPA money, apparently, available in some form or another to do these civic improvements. What we wanted was to get a seaplane facility there to service the seaplanes - float planes, the British would call them - which at that time were carried by every battleship and most of the cruisers.

You know, canvas and plywood jobs, more or less.

Q: They were reconnaissance planes, weren't they?

Adm. M.: They were called reconnaissance planes, they were actually for spotting gunfire. Of course, to control gunfire at long ranges the man in the foretop, which was the highest place on your ship, sometimes didn't have the direct vision of the target but if you could get an airplane up overhead he had a very much better perspective and he could get the word back. His reports on the gunfire, the fall of shot, and so on were usually more accurate than what came from the foretop. That's what they were primarily for. They called them observation planes, OU-2 or something like that.

These planes periodically required to be gotten off the ship to have an engine overhauled, which we couldn't do very well on the ship. We didn't have the facilities on the ships. So the technique had been to load them and their gear on a barge and tow them down to San Diego where they had a naval air station and that did the work, which meant that you had quite a job getting these people off and getting them back. If we could have there in San Pedro a seaplane facility with a ramp and a limited machine shop, it would have been very helpful, so we were negotiating that, and the Admiral was sending Joe Rochefort up to negotiate with the City Fathers on this subject to see what could be worked out. He said to Joe, "I told them that I'm sending Commander Rochefort up." Joe looked at him for a minute and said, "Admiral, I'm a Lieutenant." He said, "I don't care what the hell you are. Put on a Commander's uniform and go on up there. You're the Commander." I won't say that was typical, but he said we need a little rank and you ought to be a

Commander anyway, go on up there. So, he was ready to operate quite directly.

Q: He was senior enough that he could do that.

Adm. M.: Oh, yes. There wasn't anybody more senior than he out there and he didn't let anybody forget it. He also was a very entertaining dinner speaker, which is unusual among naval officers. They had a club there of people in Los Angeles called the Jonathan Club. It may still exist, I don't know. It's a luncheon club, not like the Lions or anything, but very prominent professional and business people belonged to this club. I watched the old man get up there and he didn't say anything but he talked for about thirty-five to forty minutes and he had this outfit completely spellbound. One funny or odd story after another. He was really the center of the picture. That is my impression of Admiral Reeves. He said he was a naval aviator. Well, he wasn',t but he had, along with other senior officers, gone down to Pensacola and had taken the aviation course down there. At that time they had a grade below Pilot called Aviation Observer, and some young officers who couldn't quite make the grade as pilot, maybe because of color blindness of an eye defect, or something of that sort, but were still pretty good were rated as Aviation Observers. A good many of the more senior officers, of whom Reeves was one when he was a full Captain and a fairly senior one, as I understand, when he took the course. They were trying to upgrade the rank structure in aviation and that was one way of doing it. They did the same thing in submarines later on. Admiral King was such a person.

Q: Yes, he was not an actual pilot either.

Adm. M.: No. He had pilot wings, he was rated a pilot. But Reeves was an Aviation Observer and wore silver wings instead of gold, or something of that sort. There was a slight difference in the insignia, but it wasn't apparent to one who looked at it casually. He was very proud of that fact and, as a result, he was rather rough on the aviators because he said he knew all about aviators, they were a bunch of lazy scoundrels and he wanted to get them to work.

Q: Was he unduly concerned about espionage in your dealings with him?

Adm. M.: No. He felt that it was a problem. He was concerned because people kept coming to him with these stories of one sort or another, and he didn't have any way or technique of getting to the bottom of the thing. All he wanted to do was get the facts, and having the facts, he'd take it from there. But he couldn't - and I think rightly so - go off on these various tangents without some real basis to go on. Sure, if we've got people stealing things off the ships, we'll take steps to stop it if we know what the problem is. But we've got to know what the problem is. And as soon as you had that, from my point of view, he was not only cooperative, he was pushing from behind, you might say. He did want results, and I think we gave them to him. Later on, we organized each Naval District into what we called the Zone Intelligence Areas, which I again repeat, was devised by Captain A. A. Hopkins of the sheriff's office. That same system was established around San Francisco and up in Seattle. Those were the three West Coast districts. I don't know what they did over here and the Mid West. At that time there were only two naval districts in the middle of the country. One was headquartered in Chicago and the other in New Orleans. There was nothing in Florida. Pensacola, the old naval base, was not operating as such. Key West was in doldrums, it was laid up. I don't know about those, but the three West Coast districts, the 11th, 12th, and 13th, the intelligence set-ups there were organized on this zone basis, so you would take a town or a center of population and you would pick out and talk to a fellow who was willing to do this on part time. For instance, In Santa Barbara we had a zone. The zone there was headed by the editor of one of the local papers, and that sort of thing. You felt free to call these people up on the telephone and say, all right, we've got a report of so-and-so, look into it. And they would look into it, and they'd come back and say there's nothing to it, or there is something to it and we're doing something about it.

Q: Since you were involved with these reserve officers, did you dip down into the ROTC units at the universities?

Adm. M.: No. As a matter of fact, at that time, there were only two ROTC units on the West Coast, one at Berkeley and one at the University of Washington in Seattle. In the whole country, as I recollect it, there were only six, at that time. I think there was one at Georgia Tech, one at Yale, one at Harvard, one at North Western. Anyhow, there were only a total of six, of which two were on the West Coast and they were pretty hard to get into, and they turned out a very fine body of men. I had a couple of them serve with me during the war and they were an impressive group, they were very eager, highly motivated, and thoroughly qualified. Give them a little time and a little help and they got on all right. I had one fellow named Blake who worked with me on ONI, he'd been in China for an insurance firm, with the Star group over there, and when he came back he just wanted to do something. I asked him "What do you know about intelligence?" He said, "Nothing." Anyhow, he was a nice, intelligent, active fellow. Then when the war came on he wanted to go to sea, he wanted to fight, so we finally let him go to sea and he ended up in command of a patrol boat and did an excellent job of it.

I don't know that I have much more to add to this shore duty phase on the West Coast.

Q: Your whole attention was dedicated in that direction, was it? I mean when you were out there as assistant operations officer.

Adm. M.: No, what happened is that when Admiral Reeves quit being commander-in-chief he was relieved by Admiral Hepburn, and he'd made a deal with Hepburn. Rochefort came over and relieved me, and, at Admiral Reeves' suggestion, I took over from Rochefort. Rochefort was Assistant Operations Officer on the Fleet Staff, as well as Fleet Intelligence Officer. I relieved Rochefort so that I became Assistant Operations Officer and also as an additional job, as frequently happened in those days, you'd have two hats, I was the Fleet Intelligence Officer.

Of course, as Fleet Intelligence Officer with the fleet operating the way it was and the time it was, our primary concern was security. There wasn't any way of getting information about, we'll say the Japanese, as far as we were concerned. If we picked up something, all right, but the main thing to do was try to make sure that the matters that should have been confidential or should have been secret were confidential and secret. I was very fortunate. Admiral Hepburn was quite a different personality from Admiral Reeves. I had never known him before, but Admiral Hepburn had had a very distinguished career, also he was a former Director of Naval Intelligence. He had served on the staff of Admiral Bristol when Bristol was the High Commissioner in Turkey, right after World War I.

Q: That was some staff! There were so many people served there of later prominence.

Adm. M.: Yes, and from the intelligence point of view, I had a friend and a helper right at the top. The Chief of Staff, at that time Captain Pickens, was very dubious about some of this Intelligence stuff. He was a Bureau of Ordnance man and a very, very capable person. Later on he got to be one of my warmest friends. He lived over here in Alexandria. My immediate boss was the then Captain Ghormley, whom you will remember from London days. My main job on that staff was to be the Assistant Operations Officer. In other words, Ghormley was the idea man and I was the fellow who did you might say the research. That was the way the job usually fell in together, and, as I have pointed out to you before, as staffs were then organized, the planning, the day-to-day operations, the fleet problems, and that sort of thing, tactical planning, all that was done by this operations staff. Also one of the jobs was to answer letters. Why it came to the operations staff, I don't know, but we at that time would get letters from all over the West Coast, wanting to have naval participation in Rose Bowl Day, or naval participation in Grapefruit Harbor, and so on. Some of these things got to be pretty ridiculous. These chamber of commerce promotions and so on. I remember one that was very amusing, the place was the southern end of San Francisco Bay, believe it or not, my recollection is that it's name was Red Dog, and we got a very, very effusive invitation to come and participate with the dedication of Red Dog as a deep-water port. They wanted battleships and aircraft carriers. Well, of course, if a battleship in San Francisco Bay wants to get beyond Hunter's Point the water shoals pretty much. They would send letters, the letters would come in backed by endorsement by the Congressmen and the Senators and so on, and you had to write a letter to each one. It took an enormous amount of time, actually, and they wanted the letters all different so we couldn't send out mimeographed replies. So when I wrote to this Red Dog outfit to tell them that we'd studied the chart there and we couldn't get a destroyer up there even, I got a very indignant reply back, that the Army Engineers, by gravy, had just cut a deep-water channel down there and they wanted me to know it was nine feet deep! Well, of course, minimum depth to the tips of the propeller blades of a destroyer of that day was about 13 feet. So, you had some amusing things like that.

I remember once the city of Sacramento wanted us to send aircraft carriers up there. Of course, you could go up the Sacramento River, which is deep enough, but you can't get these carriers, which are pretty close to 800 to 900 feet long - that is, the Saratoga and the Lexington and the river there is pretty bendy. You come to

McCollum #4 - 199

a point when you can't bend them around the curve. They couldn't quite see that.

I then went to sea in July of 1936 on the staff of Admiral Hepburn in the capacity of Assistant Operations Officer and Fleet Intelligence Officer, and with Admiral Hepburn's approbation, we organized within the fleet a more or less, you might call it, a security intelligence outfit, so that in every major division we had an Intelligence Officer reporting to me. For instance usually in those days a battleship division consisted of three battleships, and there was a Rear Admiral in command. You picked out a guy on his staff and said, all right, you're the Intelligence Officer, and his Admiral would authorize him to communicate directly with me on Intelligence, with the proviso, of course, that he keep his boss informed of what goes on. It worked out pretty good. Not having to go through a chain of command to have a look round, you were able to have one guy in each one of these big divisions do it for you. And if there was something going wrong on one of the ships, you could call this fellow up or ask him to come over or go over and see him and say, look, we've got this report, I don't know if there's anything to it or not but it may be something you want to look into. Pretty amateurish, it's true, but the security of documents...

Q: You installed a system of classified documents?

Adm. M.: Well, we had the system already. It was a question of making sure the darned things were locked up when they were supposed to be locked up, within reasonable limits...

Q: And checked on periodically to see that...?

Adm. M.: They were checked on. Of course, the big security business always was with the codes and ciphers system, what they called the Communications Periodicals and other periodicals, like the Tactical Instructions, and so on. Every quarter you had to go down the list of the Registered Publications, in your custody and account for them. All of these things had a number on them, and you had to account for each one of them and report. And, my lord, if you missed one they wanted to hang you to the nearest yardarm if they had one.

Q: Maybe they did!

Adm. M.: Even a paper that was subsequently declassified. I remember I lost a torpedo pamphlet on an obsolete 18-inch torpedo when I was a student at the Submarine School in New London. My soul, you would have thought that I had violated the Constitution of the United States, and maybe I had. By the time they got around to giving me Hail Columbia about it, they had declassified the pamphlet! It didn't make any difference. I lost it while it was classified, so I was at fault. And there's some merit of right in that, of course. I will say that I was busy getting myself married at the time and I might have been a little bit distracted!

Q: Had Admiral Hepburn at that point made his survey of the bases in the Pacific?

Adm. M.: I don't know. You will have to figure that one out. I simply don't know. I rather think not. He became Commander-in-

Chief of the Fleet in 1936, about the 1st of July, and he hauled down his flag in February of 1938, having been in the job about a year and a half. Usually Commander-in-Chief job was a year or a year and a half, two years sometimes. They played musical chairs with those jobs. As you remember, all of those top jobs carried extra stars. They were all temporary. So when Hepburn quit being Commander-in-Chief, he reverted to his permanent rank of Rear Admiral, and that was what all of them did. Then, at his request, he became commandant of the 12th Naval District with headquarters in San Francisco, which he liked. He liked San Francisco, as a good many people do. He was a widower. He was a rather reclusive, scholarly, quiet person, but a very sharp tactician, and a very direct and quick thinker. Later on, at the time of the Panay incident, which was in about 1937, he got a private, courier-carried message from Admiral Leahy, who was Chief of Naval Operations. I never knew what was in it, but at that time I was the Acting Operations Officer of the Fleet. There wasn't any operations officer. I was it. The Admiral sent for me and he said, "I want you to put this fleet in a state of readiness for immediate action. I want destroyer patrols established off here, (meaning San Pedro), and I want seaplane patrols sent out to sea. I want San Diego to have tight port security right away, antiaircraft coverage there, antiaircraft conditions here. Now, hop to it. I want to get King, Horne - Admiral Horne was commanding the aircraft carriers that were in San Diego, Admiral King was commanding the seaplanes. He was in San Diego. "I want to get Woodward, the Destroyer Commander. I want them up here right away."

I said, "Well, Admiral, it's getting along towards Christmas.

These people are off." And he said, "I don't give a damn whether it's Christmas or not. Get them up here, and get all these people back on board ship and get going." It was about ten days before Christmas. So we did, and we always called it the Christmas War, and we went to the Christmas War.

Of course, you can keep up that type of readiness and control only so long, and then it starts to peter out. Your men wear out, your enthusiasm wears out...

Q: It becomes commonplace, then, doesn't it?

Adm. M.: Well, not only that, but some of these guys, you know, took it very seriously. I never will forget sometime later on the Chichibu Maru, which is a big Japanese passenger liner, came in to San Pedro Harbor. We got a message in from our offshore patrol destroyer, "I picked up the Chichibu Maru," she'd been picked up by the seaplanes before that, "I'm convoying her into harbor." Well, my lord, I went up on the bridge to watch this operation. And what did I see? I saw a destroyer on this side and one on that side, guns trained on the Chichibu Maru, the passengers gazing down from the decks on this outfit, the men at battle stations, ammunition all laid up, and so on! I went down to the Admiral and I said, "Look, this thing is getting too thick, don't you think so? Don't you think we ought to tell them to cool it a little bit," he said, "No, let them go ahead." I said, "Do you realize that these guys have got loaded guns pointed at this passenger ship?" He said, "So what! We mean business. Let 'em know it."

After two or three weeks, we had to cool it. The ships and the men, both, commenced to wear out.

Q: That's only an intermediate step, isn't it, it had to go on to a conflict, or else recede?

Adm. M.: That's right.

It is of interest to note that one of the things that Admiral Reeves had stressed was the necessity of building up a capability of ship maintenance and repair and supply facilities at Pearl Harbor. Therefore, he had scheduled a cruise of the major elements of the fleet from the West Coast to the Hawaiian Islands for the summer of 1936. That of course meant - we only had two major aircraft carriers. The Langley was too slow and too small. We only had the Saratoga and the Lexington, and we had about a dozen battleships, which were considered the backbone of the fleet. And in the Pacific, at that time, we had a couple of divisions of light cruisers, glorified destroyers of the Omaha class. The heavy cruisers were just coming out. We didn't have too many of them, but they were coming in, so that with a great part of this force we went out to Pearl Harbor, moved in, and moored to the moorings within the harbor, bringing the ships in and taking them out. It took an enormous amount of time to get them in. The first time that we went in, it took us nearly six hours to bring the ships in. Of course, all of them had to come in in single file through what we call a dog leg channel, in other words, the channel made an angle. We went into it and had to make a turn in the channel. The channel itself was fairly shallow, about 40 feet, it had to be constantly dredged.

You must realize, and I'm sure you do, that the battleship of that era as commonly loaded drew about 36 feet, so they had only about four feet of water under their bottoms. The people at Pearl

Harbor had not done this for a long time. They had plans for it, but it hadn't been actually done, so we got delay after delay after delay in getting the ships in. Captain Ghormley and I had estimated, rather optimistically, that we ought to be able to get the job done in about four hours. It took us six and on into the night. Apparently, Ghormley got disgusted and stomped off to his cabin, for which I don't blame him.

But we did get them in. So with that debacle, we had a big conference and decided that we'd try it a couple more times - take them in and out, just as an exercise, tugs and all that sort of stuff. Well, we learned a number of things. We finally got the time element down to about three hours for the number of ships that were there. And that was about optimum because we tried to shave it going out. The original orders had been that the heavy ships, like battleships, would move up that channel at a speed of six knots, or something like that. Well, that seemed a little ridiculous, so we decided to move them in and out at 15 knots. Well, we found a funny thing. We were doing fine. We got about three battleships out at 15 knots, and all of a sudden, all hell broke loose. The Mississippi went aground. She went aground because she was was moving out at 15 knots and with her tremendous bulk in this channel so close to the bottom she pushed the water out of it and her rudder wouldn't function. In other words, we'd run out of water. You did that. So when that happened, she spun just like an airplane. She dropped both anchors and was brought up completely athwart the chennel. Well, there were two other behemoths coming down behind her so we had a regular traffic jam in there for a while.

Q: Her skipper wasn't held accountable for that, was he?

Adm. M.: Oh, no. I think everybody was worried in those days, but Loomis, as I remember, was her captain. I think his son is...

Q: His son is Kent Loomis.

Adm. M.: I think so. This was Sam P. Loomis, as I remember. I didn't know him at all. So we learned that you could push certain things so far, and then you had to wait for nature to take its course. But the thing is that they were working on Pearl Harbor with the idea of bringing it up to snuff as really a first-class place. You know, Pearl Harbor had been a sort of a sleepy place, a very pleasant place. I mean, there was a division of minesweeper type destroyers, one division, and there was a squadron of submarines out there, a minelayer or two, and that was more or less the force, except for assorted tugs and that sort of thing.

Q: The Atlantic was the point of emphasis?

Adm. M.: No, the Pacific was the point of emphasis, but the big supply points in the Pacific were Bremerton, particularly, and then the Navy yard at Mare Island, which, as I pointed out before, for really heavy ships was of only limited use. But you did have a very good yard up there at Hunter's Point. Then, for the destroyers and submarines and light cruisers and so on, they used the facilities - there was no Navy yard there - at San Diego, some of them shore-based, some of them tender-based, and so on. A lot of the interim work, the maintenance of ships and so on was done by tender. That was expensive, but it was considered to be good training. Periodically you'd bring one of the tenders along and they were very capable ships. The Medusa, for instance, and so on, that would come in and do all your repairs. They could do all sorts of things. But the idea was to try to build up the capabilities of the Pearl Harbor Navy yard and of the Naval District to handle the Fleet.

We had a funny occurrence there after we got all snadwiched into Pearl Harbor. An oriental-looking photographer came down to the ship, and it appeared that he was a Chinese man who had served in the Navy for a good many years and then had served as Admiral Hepburn's mess boy, so he said, some time back. He came down and very grandly presented the Admiral with a color photograph, a great big thing, showing the layout of the entire fleet nested at Pearl Harbor. Well, of course, how did he get the picture? It was all supposed to be very secret, Pearl Harbor was a closed port and so on. Well, he just stood up on the hill back of it and took these pictures. Again, you're talking about security. It was supposed to be very secure and here this fellow had them, and in all innocence he was here to make this presentation, which the Admiral very graciously accepted, then he turned to me and said, "Get your people out there to get ahold of all those prints and get rid of them."

The following year, we went back out to Pearl Harbor and that time it got to be pretty much old hat, that was in 1937, and there we did deliver a so-called surprise attack on Pearl Harbor, with the aircraft carriers coming in and delivering the punch and so on, a pre-dawn attack, or an attack at about dawn, the battleships coming in and simulating a bomabardment and so on and so forth.

Q: Were the attackers successful?

Adm. M.: Yes. Nobody was awake that early in the morning in the Hawaiian Islands! Besides, it was all a sham battle, anyway. I reckon that theoretically - they always had a big critique after one of these things, you know. Everybody admitted that the attack was highly successful and that the people ashore should take steps to make sure that they didn't get surprised that way again, but there you have it.

Q: Did you have war games off Panama also while you were with the Fleet?

Adm. M.: Not at that time. We did not go to Panama. When I was serving in the West Virginia in 1933 we did go to Panama, but the emphasis now, following the Reeves trend, was to try to build up the capabilities of the Hawaiian Islands.

Q: I know that Reeves at one point was in charge of an operation when there was an attack on Panama, when he was with the fleet.

Adm. M.: That was the usual mock up. In other words, when you came into town you planned an attack on the place to exercise the people, both going and coming. Then you had games off of Panama, in which you exercised at destroyer attacks against a battle line, and that sort of thing. Some of them were rather dramatic. They used to have an attack called the anvil attack. Tactically, it was a very pretty thing to see. You'd have a line of battleships supposed to be coming down and two squadrons of destroyers, which at that time each consisted of 19 ships each, would come charging across, crisscrossing the bows, and why the heck they didn't run into each other, I don't know, and launched torpedoes and that sort of thing. Very spectacular. The timing had to be to a gnat's eyebrow or you'd clip somebody's tail off. So you did have those kind of things.

When Admiral Hepburn hauled his flag down, which would be in February of 1938, I had tried to get command of a destroyer. I wanted it in the Pacific, largely because we were there. I had a wife and a small child. Nevertheless, I was ordered to the Navy Department in Washington. Somebody had made a slip-up. I had no order with which I could move my family, so I had to leave them behind and come to Washington. When I got here, nobody in ONI, nobody knew where I was supposed to go to work. It was temporary duty with a catch in it. I was ordered to Washington for temporary duty.

Q: Who was at your former desk at that point?

Adm. M.: I think it was Creighton. It was either Zacharias or Creighton. I rather think it was Creighton, but if not, it was a change-over period.

I finally found out that I was supposed to go and work in what was called the Ship Movements Division, that was part of Operations. In other words, they knew where the ships were and planned these things. I went in there and my job there was to put into effect the new Ship Movements Report System. Up until that time, every time a ship in the Navy moved anywhere, by radio - you had a set of offices all over the country called ship movement offices, SMO. You would send a dispatch. In other words, If I sailed from Norfolk at such and such a time and expect to arrive ETA New York such and such a time, and that would be reported to these SMOs.

Jack Redman had dreamed up the idea that running fleets on pretty cut and dried schedules - the schedules were prepared and were approved on a quarterly basis by the Chief of Naval Operations, and it had gotten to be so that they made quite a fetish out of this business. In other words, if a ship was scheduled to move at such and such a time, by gravy, she moved. When she came back in, she was right on schedule. Schedule was the big thing. Of course, Jack got the idea...

Q: Where was Jack then?

Adm. M.: He had been Admiral Hpeburn's communications officer, and he had suggested this to Admiral Hepburn, and Hepburn turned it down. He came to me and I had turned it down. I was Acting Operations Officer at the time, and I said, "Well, that's all very well." Jack's scheme was that you got a schedule and everybody has a schedule, and as long as the ship is operating on a schedule and there isn't any change from that schedule, why send out all these radio reports, we can cut down on all these radio stations at a tremendous saving in cost. You got the schedule, just assume that the ship was going there on schedule, and if it was not on schedule, then the ship will come up and tell you. And it made a very nice thing as long as you could count on a schedule. My argument was that that was all right and good for peacetime operations, certainly very economical and so on, but we were supposed to be training for war, and one of the things you could count on come a war, was that you weren't going to have all these set schedules. People were going to be leaving here, there, and yonder, all over the lot. So what do you do?

McCollum #4 - 210

Nevertheless, Jack came back here to Washington and lobbied it through naval communications and the CNO. There was a big saving there in peacetime.

Q: Was his brother in charge?

Adm. M.: No, no, his brother wasn't in charge. A fellow named Hooper was in charge. It seems to me it was Hooper.

So, I being opposed to it was brought in here to Ship Movements to put into effect this new system, and I did, I put it into effect, because I was ordered to.

Q: Were you converted?

Adm. M.: No, I wasn't converted, never was. Nevertheless, that is presumably what the Chief of Naval Operations, Admiral Taffender, then a Captain and head of Ships Movements wanted. He didn't think much of it, but that was the order from above to put it into effect. We'll try it this way. We'll put it to test every six months and then if it doesn't work and so on. Of course, you had to do a lot of missionary work. Paymasters were screaming all over - how did they know where they were going to get their supplies down to a ship if they didn't have the ship movements in detail, how were they going to do this? Well, after a while, it ironed out. It worked fine and certainly cut down the radio traffic and so on. But the point is that the minute the war came on in 1941, the whole system collapsed.

Q: Just as you envisioned!

Adm. M.: I had been originally ordered to command the <u>Leary</u> and while I was in this ship movements division, I got wind of the fact that the Jacob Jones was going to go to Europe. Well, I had never been to Europe and I had wanted to go, so I managed to maneuver it around so that my orders were changed and I was ordered to command the Jacob Jones. She was in the Navy yard at Norfolk then, and I went down there, I think it was in April, and took command of her. At that time, she was a reserve destroyer and we had a constantly changing crew of about 50 on the ship. That's adequate, of course, to run the ship, engines and watches and things of that sort, but we had a queer assortment of people on there. The ship was being used, as were all the ships in our destroyer squadron 10 operating here in the Atlantic, at the time, as the final duty station of people awaiting retirement. The ships were scattered around, one was at New Orlean, I was at Norfolk, somebody else was at Philadelphia, and so on, scattered all around at various places. We had to train reserves and that sort of thing, and these people shifted around. You had a completely lopsided crew. At one time I had nine chief Commissary Stewards on the ship. These fellows were back here ready to pay off on 20 years' service, and for the last two or three months they had to put them somewhere so they'd stick them on one of these ships. They didn't pay any attention to whether they fitted in or not. Well, it is pretty hard to take a man who's been in the Navy 20 years and gotten to the position of a Chief Petty Officer and ask him to get down here and start scrubbing decks. Well, of course, you don't scrub decks on destroyers, but I mean there is a certain amount of respect to be given to rank and distinction, which we tried to do.

So I worked out in Norfolk there, ran targets for airplanes and that sort of thing. Then in the summer of 1938, I was ordered to operate directly under the Office of the Chief of Naval Operations. I quickly found out, then, that I was supposed to do what we used to call Strawberry Festival cruises. I was ordered up to the New England coast to make courtesy calls to various small ports in New England. My first port of call was Swampscott, and from Swampscott I went to Rockport, then we went to Gloucester, then we went to Narragansett Pier. I don't know what the order of it was, but we'd go into one of these places for two or three days and be entertained by the city fathers, open the ship to visitors, a sort of a gala occasion all around. Very pleasant. The weather, as you know, in New England is to a West Coast sailor pretty foggy. In those days we didn't have any radar. You'd get caught in these little ports, fog would settle in, and you couldn't very well get out. I remember from Swampscott, I made a run for Rockport. It's only about 25 or 30 miles, maybe less, and I was waiting for the fog to lift a bit so I could get out of the port and around through the breakwater there - there was a breakwater near Swampscott. Before I could get up to Rockport the fog had closed in so thick you couldn't see the forward gun from the destroyer's bridge, there were fishermen blowing horns at you all around. We had a radio compass, of course. When I figured out that we were far enough probably north of Cape Ann, we had to do something. We couldn't just float around in the fog for ever, so I turned toward the beach and put out about 8 or 10 fathoms on the anchor, and when the anchor hit bottom, there I was. I anchored.

We had a fine time up there. The men liked it...

Q: Was it largely in the interests of public relations?

Adm. M.: Yes, that's right.

Q: With some idea of recruitment?

Adm. M.: No, no, not recruitment. What would happen in those days was that the Navy Department would have requests from Congressmen or dignitaries to have a ship visit their city or their town at such and such a time, and they would rig up these visits. It was just to go up there and let people see you and be seen and so on. You didn't recruit anybody. The recruiting service did that. Never recruited anybody on board of a ship. Theoretically, you could, but I don't know of anyone that actually recruited anybody, that is, right on board ship. I hadn't seen it done. I had heard of it.

Q: I was thinking in terms of general recruitment for the Navy in the light of the fact that the fleet was building up and the need for personnel was increasing and funds were becoming available at this period.

Adm. M.: Well, the idea seemed to be just going around to spread joy and happiness. I had never been in that part of the country before. I'm a southerner. I went to Narragansett Pier and I brought this one destroyer in there. At that time, they had a big old-fashioned bandstand kind of a thing on the end of the pier there, and obviously it had been at one time a Victorian type summer resort. There was still a summer colony at that time, and they were very kind and generous. We were entertained, we were taken around all the town by the President of the Board of Selectmen, the head guy. He was a dairy farmer out in town, an awfully fine chap, and so on. I never will forget, I got a kick out of him. He said, "Well,

Captain," - I was a fairly junior lieutenant commander - "You don't know what a thing like this means to Narragansett Pier. You know, this is the first time that the fleet has been brought in here since Admiral Dewey visited us." I looked at him to see whether he was pulling my leg, but I don't think he was. He was sincere and meant it as a compliment. He was delighted with it, and so was I.

On the way back from there, we ran as targets for submarines operating out of New London. Submarines, you know, had to have something to fire torpedoes at, and we had one modern destroyer, a new one, the Warrenton, was the target, and I was the other one, the screen. We had to be out on the bow as a screen against this thing and I almost hit a submarine, or the submarine almost hit me. They had quite a todo, a furor, about it afterwards. It ended up that I got a letter of commendation from the Commander-in-Chief of the Fleet, so it wasn't too bad.

Then I was in a fix because I had to come down from there and was ordered in to the Washington Navy Yard to be present at the President's Cup Regatta and, of course, with this run-in with this target business we didn't have any time to paint and clean up the ship. We were out there running up and down madly all day long, then creeping in to the roads there at the Thames River at night to anchor. Then up again early in the morning. The thing that bothered me was that I knew my ship was going to go to Europe and that we were going to be put in the Navy Yard at Norfolk, so it was desirable to go into the Navy Yard with not too much fuel oil on board, the less fuel oil the better. That is, from the Navy Yard point of view, because before your ship went in the dry dock in those days the fuel oil on board had to be unloaded in barges and towed off somewhere else. Theoretically, what you should have done was flood your fuel oil tanks with salt water, but nobody liked to do that because you could never get the salt water entirely out. When you had salt water in your fuel it was just like getting water in your automobile fuel system. It doesn't burn too good. So we were coming down the coast and this darned hurricane was coming up the coast. That was the hurricane of 1938, the one that did raise hell up in New England, at all the places we'd been. I kept watching this thing to make sure that we could get through the Virginia capes. I thought we were going to meet there and I didn't want to meet there. Fortunately, we just beat it in, came up and got into the Washington Navy Yard, tied up at the dock, opened ship to visitors and that sort of thing, for about a week, I reckon.

Then I went on down to Norfolk and got the ship ready to go to Europe, along with her companion, a ship named the Badger. We left Norfolk, and Admiral Johnson very kindly came down in person and saw us off. We were loaded down and I wasn't sure the ship would float. We were going to war, you know, the Spanish Civil War was going on. We'd got 50-caliber machine guns, which I'd never seen before. We got two of them. Beat them out of the Navy Department, extra boats and, above all, we got a full crew. Unusual. We got the whole ship manned. It was a war crew. In other words, we got a complement, not just an allowance. 132 men on board. 132 men and seven officers.

Q: What kind of a role did they anticipate for the U. S. Navy in connection with the civil war in Spain?

Adm. M.: We were down there - well, to give an example of what we did do, we went down there and we had to run mail into the consulates.

You see they weren't letting that through. Consular and Diplomatic business, mostly. You'd go into these places and bring in supplies to a consular post, bring in their mail and take their mail. It was sort of a service business there. We did the same thing out in China, you know.

Q: Yes, I know. What Spanish ports would you go into? Cadiz, and places like that?

Adm. M.: Oh, no, we didn't go into Cadiz. That was already in Franco's hands. There wasn't any great necessity to go to a place like that. Barcelona, for instance, and Malaga. Mostly on the Mediterranean coast. I actually didn't visit many ports in Spain, but we were over there to more or less show the flag and re-assure people of our presence. The squadron, at that time, was called 40-T, the T standing for temporary. I don't know where they got the number. It consisted of one light cruiser, when I arrived out there, the Omaha, that was the flagship, and two destroyers. That was it. The Omaha wore the flag of Rear Admiral H. E. Lackey. When I got out there, he was the Commander of Squadron 40-T. We had known that the two destroyers - we were relieving had sailed - they relieved them about every year. In other words, we had two over there, and the next year two others, and the crews would rotate, too. The Omaha was relieved while I was there by the Trenton, same type.

We had known that the other two destroyers had been very roughly handled by the weather. They tried to hit the great circle course from a place like New York. The same thing would have applied to Norfolk. They got caught in this weather and both of them were nearly sunk. They had to limp back into Boston, and it took another two or three months to patch them up so they could get over there. My executive officer was a very, very fine navigator, and he and I got together and decided that the one thing we didn't want was the great-circle course and the heavy winds in there. He thought that if we would take departure from the Chesapeake Bay lightship and set a compass course due east, that the prevailing wind would push us sufficiently far north for us to make the Azores without laying a course specifically for the Azores. In other words, just head east and the wind will take care of you, and it did. We hit Ponta Del Gada right on the nose, still heading east. The reason we had to go there is that destroyers, like the Jacob Jones, were what they called short-leggers. They were under 1,100 tons, 1,070 or 1,080, or something like that, 1,090 maybe, displacement, but their fuel capacity was more limited than that of some of the others. We couldn't make it all the way across in one jump. We had to have fuel en route, so we pulled in to Ponta Del Gada in the Azores for fuel, at least some fuel, enough to get us to Gibraltar.

McCollum #5 - 218

Interview No. 5 with Rear Admiral Arthur H. McCollum, U. S. Navy
(Retired)

Place: His residence in McLean, Virginia

Date: 20 January 1971

Subject: Biography

By: John T. Mason, Jr.

Q: Admiral, last time when you concluded your remarks you were on the destroyer the Jacob Jones and you had been cruising around the East Coast. You had come to Washington and I think that's where you want to continue your story.

Adm. M.: The Jacob Jones along with the Badger were under orders to go to Europe to join Squadron 40-T, as they called it at that time, which consisted of a light cruiser and two destroyers. We were to go to relieve the two destroyers that were there. We had quite a time outfitting the ships and we did get them equipped with the then-new 50-caliber antiaircraft machine guns. As you know, the only type of antiaircraft weapon available on that type of destroyer was a short, 3-inch gun mounted on the fantail, having a ceiling of about 4,000 to 5,000 feet and very primitive control equipment and largely ineffective, except maybe to scare somebody.

Q: Were the new mountings Swedish guns or were they our own?

Adm. M.: No, they were our own. They were not the Oerlikon. They were 50-caliber machine guns developed in this country, with water cooled barrels and so on, and they were much more effective, actually, than the 3-inch pop gun. About a year before we went over there, a little bit more than that perhaps, one of our destroyers serving in that duty had had bombs dropped on it and had been strafed by either one or the other of the contending factions in Spain, I forget which side it was - I don't think it was ever determined, but she was fired at and she fired back with this 3-inch gun. So we were quite anxious to get these ships re-equipped and we investigated all sorts of things. These destroyers at that time were all supposed to have one ready locker placed at a Naval Operating Base where certain so-called war equipment was supposed to be store. Nobody had looked into those things for years and when we looked into them there wasn't much there, which is quite understandable. In other words, there'd just been no checking done. I don't think it was stolen. It just gradually drifted away. It wasn't much good anyway. They talked about splinter mats. Those are things that you hang around the bridge area, presumably to absorb splinters from shrapnel and stuff of that sort. They just were non-existent.

We did get the two ships equipped. We had to get hand weapons on board these ships adequate to serve part of the crew. In other words, rifles and so on, which we only carried in those days in very limited numbers on destroyers, and steel helmets and that sort of thing that could be issued to the crew so that we, at least, wouldn't be quite as naked as we would have been otherwise.

We sailed from Norfolk in early October or late September and Admiral Alfred Johnson, who was Commanding the Squadron operating in the Atlantic, was kind enough to come down and see us off. We did sail and we moved directly from Norfolk but we had to go to Ponta Del Gada. I debated with my executive officer as to whether we should try the great-circle course, but the two ships that we were relieving had tried it when they went out the year before and they were so badly handled by the weather that they had to put back in to Boston in a virtually sinking condition. So we decided that we would set a compass course due east and hope that the wind would push us up without more ado, which it did, and we made Ponta Del Gada rather precisely, which was very pleasing to both of us. We had to go there because the destroyers of that class didn't have the fuel capacity to go all the way across the Atlantic without refueling en route. So we made Ponta Del Gada and we picked up a limited amount of fuel because in those days all the fuel there had to be imported and it was somewhat more costly than it was in other places where larger quantities were used.

Q: They certainly had very limited facilities there in that harbor, didn't they?

Adm. M.: Yes, fairly limited, but adequate for the types of ships these were. They were relatively small ships.

From there, we went to Gibraltar where we expected to get a full equipment of fuel and other stores. We planned to get all the stores there that we needed. There was a U. S. Navy contractor that came to Gibraltar to see that we got sea stores and things of that sort. Although the British were very kind in making available what they had, we didn't draw off them but we did get our kind of stores and so on through this contractor who gloried under the name of Goldberg Freres. His firm was quite well known and very adept. They had connections around that made them very helpful. We had planned to stay in Gibraltar about two days, but our British friends there went all-out, unnecessarily so, to entertain us all from the two ships. They were always apologetic that Lord Ironsides, the Governor-General of Gibraltar wasn't there to greet us, and so on and so forth. We were just overwhelmed with social engagements and other things. We did have to stay an extra day because we couldn't get some of the supplies we wanted, which I did.

In the harbor of Gibraltar there was a modern Spanish destroyer with a rather large hole in her starboard bow, which she had gotten in an engagement with some of Franco's Navy, the Navy that sided with Franco. This ship, apparently, stayed with the Republican government. Admiral Evans, the Rear Admiral at Gibraltar, was most kind and he told me, on my call to him, that the rumor was already circulating that this destroyer was going to try to mix herself in with us when we put to sea, so she could avoid the blockade of the Franco forces. So, when I went up to tell him good-bye shortly before we sailed, he took me out on his glassed-in verandah and pointed out to the bay and there were two very modern 8-inch-gun cruisers steaming up and down, and he said, "You know what they're out there for, don't you?" I said, "No, Sir," and he said, "They're just waiting to catch you and this outfit coming out together and they're going to blow you out of the water. Are you going to sail?" I said, "I have no option." So we did sail, and I cautioned all hands and talked to the captain on the <u>Badger</u> - we wanted to make sure that our guns and so on were ready, our torpedoes and so on, in case of necessity - but I wanted to make sure to make no sign that the crew was at anything approximating battle stations. In other words, we were on a peaceful mission and we'd just go along that way.

Q: Well, you were identifiable, weren't you?

Adm. M.: Yes, but nevertheless, you never know what trigger-happy people will do. So we did go out and we went right on by these two ships. One was the Canarias, and I forget the name of the other one. They were sister ships, both of them quite new, 8-inch-gun cruisers and were very capable ships.

Q: Were they built in British yards?

Adm. M.: No, no. They were built in Spanish yards, as far as I know. Jane's Fighting Ships of that era will have it. The Spaniards are quite good shipbuilders.

From there we went to Naples where the flagship was. At that time, the squadron was under the command of Rear Admiral H. E. Lackey. He was very cordial, he greeted us, and he said that after another two or three days there in Naples he was going on a cruise with the flagship which, at that time, was the Omaha, down on a flag-showing cruise along the North African coast, ending up in the French port of Sfax in Algiers, and then coming back to Villefranche. He wanted us to sail about the same time that he did but we were to go up to Villefranche and await the return of the cruiser there, which we did. He cautioned me that our principal function was that of showing the flag, creating good will, and so on, and we should be careful to avoid any indication of taking sides, one way or the other. He said that there was quite a tight political situation within France, as between, you might say, the more liberal elements and the more conservative, and so on, and there was always a tendency to get embroiled in some way, and we should be very careful to avoid joining in any of the local riots which weren't very dangerous but took place from time to time. And you know sailors love a riot. They just enjoy it, and it doesn't make much difference which side...

Q: Sometimes they start them!

Adm. M.: Yes. Well, we went up to Villefranche. Our course, of course, lay between Italy and the islands in the Mediterranean, that is, Corsica and Sardinia. We had hoped, as we went along the coast of Italy up towards France to sight navigation lights ashore. It was very overcast so we got no sun, moon, or star sights and we were just far enough out of sight of land that we couldn't pick up any headlands. It was misty, so you couldn't see very far but we rather counted on picking up the light at Bastia, which is the port of Corsica. By the time it was apparent that we had passed Bastia, assuming that our dead reckoning was anywhere near correct, there was no light visible. I heard later that that was not unusual. Sometimes the Italian lighthouses, and the French lighthouses, too, - Bastia, of course, was in Corsica and that would be French - sometimes they worked and sometimes they didn't.

When the time came to head in for the coast, we turned on dead reckoning and headed in. When dawn came up, I was a little bit overwhelmed because it looked like the Alps were falling right down on top of me. We kept merrily along. I'd never been on that coast before nor had anyone else in the ship, except one or two people who we had carried back as passengers from the flagship for what nowadays we would call compassionate reasons - a signalman from the flagship whose wife was having a baby or something of that sort. As we neared the beach these lighthouses - small lighthouses, really beacons - started popping up around. The executive officer who was the navigator also and I were madly looking at our sailing directions and books to see if we could identify them. For goodness sake, they all looked alike to me and to him, too. There was no visible gap. Of course, we were actually farther out than it looked. I mean the height of the mountains made it look like we were right close in, gave you that feeling, but we weren't, but having no identifigable landmarks from which we could take a fix - it then occurred to me that this signalman from the Omaha, the flagship, might be well enough acquainted with the shore to tell us whether we were right or wrong. So I sent for him and asked him if he could identify any of these things, or which one of these things was the leading mark for Villefranche. In those days, a signalman was pretty much like a quartermaster. The rates were virtually interchangeable. He said he couldn't tell from the bridge but if he could get up in the crow's nest he might be of some help. So I ordered the lookout down and him up. There was only one way to get up or down. He got up and in a little while he called down through the voice tube, which was the only method of communication, "You're all right, Captain. You're heading right for it." That sounded like good news, so I stayed on little while longer till we got another confirmation from him, and sure enough, as we got in close enough the hole opened up. The harbor at Villefranche is almost a perfect U to go into. There is a bar or part of a bar across the front, but the shape of it is almost as if it was cut out specifically like the letter U with the open end, of course, in the Mediterranean. It's deep inside and deep outside. I asked him, "How could you be so sure that that was Villefranche?" He said, "That's simple, Sir. I just saw the sign on the top of the Welcome bar." So that's the way we navigated in to Villefranche.

The duty there was very pleasant. As a matter of fact, one of the difficulties we had was trying to exercise the ship battle stations. As you know, Navy Regulations at that time required that once a week you were supposed to exercise the crew at battle stations. Of course, we thought we were in a war zone over there or likely to get in one, so we were very anxious to have the crew properly exercised at their battle stations, which we did. About twice a week or sometimes oftener I'd send the crew to general quarters and we would exercise the guns, wave them around, as they usually do, fire blank 30-caliber cartridges off of them to make a pop to indicate that the guns had gone off.

Well, when the Admiral got back, he sent for me and he said, "What in the world have you been doing? You've scared all the old ladies on Cap Ferrat completely tizzy. They tell me that you've been pointing guns at them, firing at them." I explained to him and he laughed and said, "Well, that's about what I thought but don't let's do it any more. You can go out here where you're out of sight of these people to do these things. These people are all very nervous, and most of them are rather elderly folks here, some of them are widows and they live over at Cap Ferrat, being one arm, one side, of the bay of Villefranche, the other being where they have the city. As you face out to the Mediterranean, on the port side, there's Cap Ferrat and on the other Cap Something else. Anyhow they all called it the Citadel, that was the old fort of the Counts of Villefranche and it's now a caserne for a battalion of the Chasseurs Alpines. So we quit exercising. We didn't frighten the old ladies any more. About once a month one or the other destroyer would take a run down to Marseille to pick up light freight, as we called it - mail for the squadron, and come back and that was about it. Most of the time we were kind of hard put to it to keep our people occupied, so we did a lot of spit and polish, and the ship really shined. We had 132 people on there to do nothing but shine the bright work. The main thing was to keep them from making too much bright work. We also went in rather heavily for athletics and we engaged in rifle matches with the local garrison and that sort of thing. We had their officers out and we visited them. It was all very pleasant as far as that is concerned.

Q: Did you also make intelligence reports on the political situation and that type of thing?

Adm. M.: We didn't, but the flagship did. We didn't know anything about the political situation. If we had anything to report it went into the flagship and they picked it up from there.

Somewhere in the course of our stay there, Franco's forces in Spain had taken Madrid and were gradually overrunning the rest of the country, where some of our Consulates were. In places like Malaga, for instance, they were well behind Franco's lines. By this time, one of the last places to hold out against him was Barcelona. As Franco forces were closing in on Barcelona there was apparently a great deal of rioting, burning, and looting going on by the so-called defensive forces of one sort or another. So the Admiral took off in the flagship with the other destroyer, the Badger and, much to my disgust, left me sitting in Villefranche in the Jacob Jones because he needed a radio link with me and from me to the land wire up to the Embassy in Paris. The Assistant Naval Attache in Paris, Hillenkoetter, came down. He spoke both Spanish and French rather fluently, at least, he spoke French very fluently, and Spanish, I think, just about as well. He came to assist in pulling the consular people and the few remaining Americans out of Barcelona, which they did under some sporadic fire from either one side or the other - no one knew just who was shooting at whom. After about a week or ten days the Admiral and the other ship came on back.

Later on that spring we went to Algiers, the city of Algiers, on a cruise, just the two destroyers. We were rather roughly handled by a storm in the Mediterranean but managed to get through it all right. We found that we were pretty lucky in that regard. On the way back we stopped in at Ajaccio in Corsica. I had always wanted to see the birthplace of Napoleon. We put in there and spent a very pleasant three or four days. We toured the island - a lovely place to look at and quiet. The people were very hospitable. They are not amusing people at all but we all got thoroughly educated on where the Bonaparte family was raised. That was their home base there, and they made quite a thing of it. From the Intelligence point of view, we discovered that one of the most important fellows on the island was the British honorary vice consul. And we found this situation in a great many places in the Mediterranean. In relatively small places there would be an honorary British vice consul...

Q: A native?

Adm. M.: No, he wasn't a native. Honorary meant that theoretically he didn't get paid for it, but he in practically every case was a retired naval officer, as was this fellow, and it became apparent that his primary function was to be there as an observer. Later on, we would have called them naval observers or that sort of thing. But he was very well thought of in the community. The mayor, for instance, and the local Prefect all - he was very much persona grata with them, and he lived rather well, not flamboyantly at all. He was a very nice chap and he had a charming wife, who was an English-woman, of course. I say that because we found out - or I found out rather surprisingly that most of our Consular people in the Mediterranean were married to non-American wives. At that time the Consulate in Marseille was very heavily staffed with the Consul General, Consul and vice Consuls because they were the closest place convenient to the war situation in Spain. And every time we went to make one of these monthly visits there, we were royally entertained by the consular staff people. They must have had eight or nine officer type people at this consulate, and only one of them had an American wife. The Consul General himself, I believe his wife was either French or Italian. We had a Consul in Nice and his wife was American, but he was relieved by a fellow in the due course of time whose wife was, I think Egyptian.

Q: That's because they were career officers and they started out early and...

Adm. M.: It's perfectly natural. They were career officers and they were sent over there and when they got to a marriageable age they looked around for someone to marry up with, and this was about all that was available. And they were charming people. There was a fellow named Abbott that I remember very well who was the Number Two in the Consulate. His wife was a Norwegian girl and she was charming. This is no throwing off, but the fact is that they were not native American. Most of them had never been in this country. I'm speaking of the ladies, now.

Q: In a sense that might give the man a dual point of view, European and American!

Adm. M.: That's right. I just mention that, and it is a problem in an outfit like the Foreign Service where in those days they got these men rather young because they had to, right out of college, then they sent them off to these foreign posts where before they got back here they were due to spend five or six years. You had that situation. Later on, back in 1946 when I was operating along the English coast I ran into exactly the same thing. The Consul at Plymouth, the Consul at Hull, the Consul at Edinburgh, they were all married to foreign ladies. The fellow at Edinburgh was an awfully nice chap and his wife was a Belgian. You did have that situation. It wasn't so marked in London, as I remember, but I do remember that these chaps would come out and they were all nice fellows, but very few of them had been back lately to this country. There was no provision under the way the Foreign Service then ran, as far as I could find out, for periodic tours of duty, you might say, in this country.

Q: In the aggregate, do you think that that was a detriment to the service or that it was an asset?

Adm. M.: I couldn't say that it was an asset. My view would be that they tended to get too parochially involved with the views of the country in which they served, and tended to overlook - in other words, they were out of touch with feeling and so on in the United States, and I do think that that is a definite detriment. I found the same thing in Japan. Fellows that had spent years and years out there with only very brief visits back to this country. They tended to acquire the point of view of the country in which they were serving. Sometimes that's good but sometimes it isn't. I think a man should continue to keep before himself that his primary job is that of a representative of the United States and to be jealous of the privileges and the requirements of the United States.

Q: And automatically you're comparing it with the Navy's system of rotation.

Adm. M.: Well, I suppose you could say that. You see, the way the Foreign Service was set up at that time you had a State Department Service and these fellows never left the State Department. For instance - this is going ahead of the story a little bit - take the Far Eastern Division of the Department of State. For many, many years that Division was headed by Dr. Stanley Hornbeck and for almost as many years his assistant had been a fellow named Max Hamilton, and there was one other, who they called State Department officials, more or less permanent. Because that division dealt with such exotic countries as Japan and China. Usually there were one or two Foreign Service officers temporarily on duty with the State Department in it.

Of course, those fellows had been in the Far East. At the time that I knew it best, the fellow that I ran into was an old friend of mine, Gene Dooman. He had been the Japanese Secretary at the American Embassy, he was the Second Secretary, or had been, and he was thoroughly versed in Japanese, but that was an unusual situation and the same situation did not obtain, so far as I know, in say, the French Desk, or the European Desk, or whatever they called it. But these fellows were pretty well down the pole.

Dr. Hornbeck had first been an adviser to the Chinese government. He went with them to the Versailles peace conference and then gravitated into the Department of State. Since that time he had never visited China or the Far East. Hamilton, his assistant, had started out in life as a vice consul in Hong Kong and he was a Chinese language student-interpreter. But at the time of which I'm speaking in 1941 or so he hadn't been in the Far East or in Asia in twenty years. There seemed to be no scheme for swapping back and forth, which I understand is quite different now, and I think probably to the good. I just mention that in passing.

Now, when we went to Algiers, for instance, we had an American vice consul there, a very nice chap, and he was trying to put on the honors and that sort of thing. The French were being very, very kind and hospitable to us. Admiral Robert commanding the French Navy based on Algiers, he and Madame Robert gave us receptions and that sorth of thing, which, of course, the Vice Consul was trying to return. Well, again, his wife was a very charming girl, but she was Swiss and she didn't feel quite at home on these little ships with the American group and so on, but she was a very nice person. So, we'll pick it up from Ajaccio.

From there we came back to Villefranche and after a time I persuaded the Admiral to let us go to Italy. He was a little bit dubious about going to Italy. At that time it was in the heyday of Mussolini, of course, and he didn't like Americans too well, apparently, but we did go to Italy. He let the two destroyers go down there. We went in to the Gulf of Rapallo and we had a delightful time there, gave everyone a chance to go and see the sights. It was sort of a glorified tourist cruise when you come right down to it. The men had a wonderful time. No disciplinary problems at all. I was very proud of them. They got into no fights with nobody, as a sailor would say. They all came back clean and sober, or reasonably so. After spending about a week at Rapallo and after seeing the sights - it's a beautiful place - and it's got such places as Santa Margherita and so on, lovely little resort communities. Just lovely, to look at. The country itself is not, agriculturally, very productive, I would say, but scenically it's glorious. We then came back to Villefranche and in the summer of 1939 the entire squadron left Villefranche and went out into the Atlantic. There, after a stop of about three days at Gibraltar, we went up to Le Havre and stayed there about a week or ten days, giving everyone an opportunity to go to Paris. From Le Havre we went to Rotterdam and moored along the sea wall in the park in what seemed to be the center of town, very nice. The Dutch people went all-out to be nice to us. One fellow was very disgusted, he set up a beer stall. He understood that we didn't have beer on the ship so he set up a beer stall with this fine Dutch beer, and some guy had set up a milk bar, and this fellow was disgusted because our sailors all preferred milk to beer. We were entertained very royally there and had an opportunity to get around Holland quite a bit. It's not a very big country. We went to Delft, for instance, and to another place on the Zuider Zee. I think the most fancy dinner I ever attended was given by the Royal Dutch Marines; of course, it was subsidized by the government, at the old Weimar Hotel, which I suppose has been bombed out of existence. We drank cocktails and ate hors d'oeuvres for about three hours. I was completely replete. I tried not to eat, but finally we were ushered in to dinner and sitting across from me was a rather heavy-set, completely bald Dutch colonel in full uniform. Surprisingly enough, he was one of the few Dutchmen who didn't seem to speak much English. I remember once he looked over at me as the waiter started bringing the dinner in and I was already so full I couldn't eat anything, rubbed his hands together, smiled broadly, and said, "Ah, the dinnah. She now commance."

This was supposed to be a lunch and we got up from the table at 5:30 in the afternoon, and staggered out of that place, and then staggered in to evening dress uniform and drove 20 miles to The Hague for a dinner at the American Legation. The American Minister's wife couldn't understand why no one would eat any of the delicious food. She was really distressed about it, but it was explained to her later on that we were stuffed to the nines.

Q: This part of your tour on the Jacob Jones was done in the face of what Churchill would term "the gathering storm," wasn't it?

Adm. M.: That's right.

Q: Were there definite signs of apprehension on the part of the Europeans?

Adm. M.: I'll come to that in a minute. The Dutch, as far as I could judge, were supremely confident that they were going to be left alone. I talked to a fellow who was a very prominent businessman in Rotterdam. His name was van Roosevelt. He calimed that his family was distantly related to the Roosevelts in this country, and they probably were. He was rather optimistic. He said that he could see no reason for Hitler overrunning them, and he didn't think the British would, and he thought that it would be too useful to Hitler if he could maintain the Dutch more or less as an outlook on the rest of the world, if they went to war and so on, which he rather thought they would. But he felt that Holland was not so much in danger as Belgium. He was dubious about Belgium - but he thought Holland would probably get by because they would be more useful theoretically neutral to Hitler than they would be had he overrun them. That was his viewpoint. And that seemed to be the viewpoint of the few Dutch people that seemed to be knowledgeable at all and were willing to express a view.

After about ten days or so in Rotterdam, we sailed and went down the coast to St. Nazaire in France, and after a couple of days in St. Nazaire, I was sent up the Loire River to Nantes which, as you know, is a port from which a great many of our early Huguenot colonists in this country sailed. I was sent up there to represent the Flotilla at some sort of local celebration. We were received in the city chambers by the Prefet and we joined in the parade to the local tomb of the "Unknown Soldier," laid wreaths and that sort of thing, and after two or three days there I went back to St. Nazaire. It was while here I got really concerned about the situation so I sent my wife and son home. They made it on the SS President Harding.

St. Nazaire is a very important shipbuilding port. The French Navy, in particular, had a very large shipbuilding program going on there. It was hard to tell whether it was Navy or whether it was civilian, and we got to know the man who in our Navy we would call the Superivising Inspector of Machinery. He was an engineer captain in the French Navy, a fellow named Bronkhorst, and he was quite outspoken when we had him to lunch on our destroyer. He said that they didn't trust the workmen, most of whom were Communists. Of course, he was expressing a point of view, and he was very frank to say he didn't know whether it wouldn't be a very good thing if Hitler would come in there and knock some sense in them. Not that he was pro-Hitler. He was very much pro-French, but he felt there was unrest among the French and there was going to be a blow-up inside if some outside force didn't take over.

Also at that time we became aware that preparations for war were going on apace. There were quite a number of British Army officers in town. They were over there conferring with their French counterparts on the French staff, making preparations to land British troops in that area, and so on, and seeing what small boats could be armed for patrol and so on. In other words, there was a very definite feeling that they expected war at almost any time.

Q: Did the French Navy have in being at that time what later came to be known as the submarine pens used by the Nazis?

Adm. M.: Was that at St. Nazaire?

Q: Yes.

Adm. M.: No, they did not. They were building either one or two very large battleships. I think one of them was the Brittany. She was pretty far along. I think she was fired on by somebody down at Dakar, wasn't she? I think that was the ship. These engineer officers that we got to know quite well. My officers who were even younger than I was got to be very sociable with them. One of my officers spoke rather fluent French, a fellow named Porter, whose father had been military attache in France and he had been raised there partially. He was quite facile with the language, and he got to know them quite well, and they were quite outspoken to us that they expected war to pop at any minute. But there was this feeling that they didn't trust their own common people. That was endemic almost. They just didn't have the confidence in their, you might say, working classes and so on.

Q: The French labor movement at that point had been shot through with the Communist philosophy, hadn't it?

Adm. M.: That's right, and I think that's what these people were fearful of, and most of them didn't have any confidence in the French government, particularly a government such as that headed by Leon Blum, who, I believe, was a socialist or something of the sort. These people were rather outspoken and said flatly the government was Communist.

For instance, going back a way now, while I was left at Villefranche while the admiral and the destroyer Badger went to Barcelona, I was invited to come to a reception at the home of the local military commandant. In other words, the lieutenant colonel commanding the battalion of Chassuers Alpines garrisoned at Villefranche. I went there and I found, much to my surprise, that while I spoke very halting French and could understand very little, that there were a number of rather important officers of the French Army there. These fellows were all in uniform, including Lieutenant General Girodius who commanded the French forces in that region, the regional commander, you might say. There were several General Staff officers with the rank of roughly major general down from Paris and the only person that I could talk to very well was a perfectly delightful rather elderly lady, British lady, who had been married to an Italian nobleman for many years, the Contesse Gauthier Vignaul. She was quite the grande dame of the Riviera. She used to give parties for us.

Then I noticed that champagne was flowing pretty freely. Of course, champagne was quite cheap there compared with our prices - about 20 cents a bottle, and I found that word had come through while the party was going on that Barcelona had fallen to Franco. Now the French government of the day, you understand, was supposed to be opposed to Franco. In other words, they still recognized the so-called Republican regime down there. But to my amazement these officers in full uniform were toasting with glee the fall of Barcelona, and I remarked to the Countess, "Do I understand what's going on here correctly, that these people in full uniform here are toasting the fall of Barcelona to the Franco forces?" She said, "Yes, that's right." That rather shocked me. I don't think any American officer in full uniform would have toasted the success of an outfit that was opposed by his government more or less publicly. She bristled and said, "What do you mean? If we don't stand up for ourselves, they're going to murder us in our beds," meaning the lower classes, again.

So we did have very definitely that feeling of uneasiness there all through the Britanny coast. You know, up the caost from St. Nazaire there are a number of seaside resorts. None of these places are very far away and one can take a bus and go up and come back quite easily and quickly. We did a certain amount of sightseeing, and everywhere we went we found people saying, well, this will be the <u>last</u> season. And certain of the hotels there had floors commandeered for the use of British officers who were already being billeted in them. Of course, this was the tail end of the season and they were probably glad to get the business because I understand a lot of those hotels were not year-round places; they ran seasonally.

We went back down to Gibraltar, pasued there briefly for fuel and so on, and hastened right on back to Villefranche. In the meantime, we'd had a shift of Admirals. Admiral Courtney was now commanding, and we'd hardly been in Villefranche a few days when war occurred. The towns were blacked out after a fashion. When we got back we discovered that our friendly Villefranche garrison had disappeared, and someone said, well, they were just out on their annual maneuvers. Well, it had been customary, I understood, for this outfit to go on what they called maneuvers at what the French called their attack positions. You must never defend, you know, always attack. So they were moving to their attack positions in the Alps. Of course, as Major Andre, the garrison executive officer, pointed out to us repeatedly, that part of France had never been successfully invaded from Italy - ever. The Romans when they finally got around to taking it, came around and landed at Marseille and took it from the other direction. In other words, the way the valleys ran from the mountains, the terrain was such as to make it exceedingly difficult to attack up these valleys that narrowed as they came up into the mountains while the valleys fanned out into Italy. And it's true, perfectly true. I hadn't realized that, but you know there are three roads along there, the Littorale, they call it, the Moyenne, or the Middle, Corniche, and then the Grande Corniche, which runs along the crest of the mountains. Roman monuments are there, all along in that area, and, of course, the top road is the Roman military road. The middle one was cut out later on, and the lower one later yet and clings to the cliffs between Monte Carlo and Nice.

The point is when it was time for the troops to come back from these maneuvers, they didn't come back. They just left. Some time before that we had periodically these scares of war coming up, and the French had finally brought in a full division of Senegalese troops. I have never seen such black men in my life. The French technique of billeting them was to come around and put a number on any house that they saw that looked likely, bring in a load of hay, and put a squad of troops in there, and the local French were just frightened to death of these Senegalese troops. They spoke very limited French, and the French had never seen very many real black people, and these fellows were real black. You walked along the streets of Villefranche at night and you could see their eyes shining before you saw anything. But they had a reputation for ferocity that they took no pains to play down. Not that they did anything, but as long as they had the fear of the Senegalese in them that was all to the good. They were later on moved a little bit away from Villefranche and put on guard duty down around Toulon, the big French naval port.

We stayed there under that situation until time for my relief arrived. I was already under orders to come back to the United States and finally, about the middle of September I was relieved of command of the Jacob Jones by an officer named Woodyard who had been serving on the staff of the Admiral. I always made it a custom that when I was relieved of command, I'd get off the ship immediately. It was not always easy, but after you've had a turnover period with your successor and so, it can only be an embarrassment to him for you to stick around. At least, I've always felt that way. So I got off the Jacob Jones, but I didn't have anywhere to go so I went up town and stopped at the Ruhl Hotel, which was one of the two premier hotels in town.

I walked into this hotel and I said "Would it be possible for me to squeeze into a room in the place?" They said, "Que voulez vous, Monsieur, you can have any room in the place." Everybody had left, so I had a magnificent suite of rooms at a very nominal cost and stayed there two or three days until it became apparent that the train schedules were pretty badly disrupted, and the French naval command and so on were in a state of some confusion. Some time just shortly before I was relieved of command of the Jacob Jones, I was ordered to go to Marseille again for one of the pick-up cruises and also to observe conditions there to see how they were getting along. While Toulon was a naval port, the fellow who actually ran the local naval business along that coast was in Marseille.

Q: Like our naval districts!

Adm. M.: That's right. I went into Marseille and we were reading the French claim that they had sowed mines in the bay and they were very careful to tell us that we couldn't take the usual channel along the Ile d'If to go in but that we had to go round the other way. Going into the port there, I was badly out-maneuvered, much to my chagrin, by one of our very fine merchant ships, the Exochorda. We had read all these things about mines and obviously he didn't want to tangle with mines and we didn't either. I had taken the precaution of calling our Consulate at Marseille to make sure that I had the latest dope from the French naval command there, and I was assured that I did.

Well, anyhow, when I stood in, this Exochorda was ahead of me and the minute he saw me he made a great sweep and came around under my stern and for a minute I thought, how pleasant, what a nice expression of manners! Then it occurred to me that what he wanted me to do was to run mine defense for him, and I tried to out-maneuver him, but he beat me to it. I went up the way we had been told to go and that would be clear of mines, but here was a string of buoys all the way across the bay up there supposedly indicating the location of the minefield. So we went back down and went right up the usual channel which we were told was going to be mined but it was wide open. In other words, that was indicative of some of the confusion.

French trains are normally pretty good. They're right on time and well managed, according to my limited experience with them. But now they were running very sporadically, troop movements were taking precedence, and so on, so it became apparent that it was not going to be easy to get a train from Villefranche to Marseille. Most of the trains in France that I've been able to observe run to Paris, anyway. They don't run east and west. You have to go to Paris before you can go anywhere else, which isn't entirely true. There were a couple of trains that went along the coast. I engaged what amount to a taxicab and loaded my footlocker in it, and we drove to Marseille. That gave me an opportunity also to observe the countryside, and I was very much struck by the fact that I saw no troops, other than rather elderly fellows in rather ill-fitting uniforms that had obviously been hurriedly called up supposedly to be guarding important things. You got the impression that these fellows didn't know what they were doing, that they'd been bar-keepers or businessmen or workmen or something...

Q: World War I!

Adm. M.: Yes, that's right. That type of fellow. They didn't make a reassuring appearance. Another thing that I noticed was that there was no elan for war at all. The people were completely depressed by the fact that there was a war. The English-speaking barmaids - we had two very famous ones, Maude and Kitty - and one who was learning English, Pauline, she was taking a course in pass defense pretty well, and the others didn't need it. They were very frank in saying that they didn't view this thing at all happily, that they just thoug thought it was a calamity. You just got the impression that the people in that area in that walk of life looked on it as a calamity of the most dire kind. You just didn't get any feeling of the French elan that I'd always read about.

Anyhow, I got to Marseille and spent one night in a hotel there, then went down the next day and boarded an American Export liner, a ship called the Excalibur. I'd originally thought of picking it up at Genoa which would probably have been closer than Marseille and quite a bit easier to get to, but the outbreak of war made it doubtful that I could get to Genoa at all, although I had taken the precaution to have a passport. She did come in to Marseille and I did pick her up there, and found that the ship was loaded with refugees, that is, refugee Americans. Most of these people had spent most of their lives in Europe and I gathered that most of them had not been engaged in any business to speak of. They were just living over there. Nearly all of them were married to European women. A large number of people on there had Austrian, very few with Italian wives. These people seemed to be running away from Austria and some few from France. Those ships were supposed to carry about 120 passengers, but we must have had 300. Very few children because most of the people were middle-aged or older, and they were frightened to death to come back to the United States. They had been so long away that most of them had forgotten about life over here. Their ladies knew nothing about the country and they just feared the worst. They were going to be murdered on every street corner by the gangs, and everybody toted six guns around, and so on and so forth. It was rather pitiful.

I did run into a curious thing there. I ran into a fellow named Linton Wells whom I'd known out in the Orient. He was a newspaperman and he was married by this time to a rather famous lady, also a reporter, Faith Baldwin. She was famous because she got to be quite an expert on Soviet Russia. They had been down in Africa on some project. Linton Wells I'd known in Tokyo back in 1924. He was a sort of a free-lance newspaper fellow. He was still doing the same thing. Later on he went on the radio, I understand. He felt the same way about it that I did. He said, "Look at these people. They're pretty sorry Americans aren't they?"

The ship made port in Boston without any trouble at all and other than being very much overcrowded, the ship people did very well by the situation. We didn't have anything like stewards serving beef tea at eleven o'clock and that sort of thing. The ship stayed in Boston a day or two, then came on down to New York. I then took the train and came on down here and my wife met me at the depot and took me home to Alexandria. That would be in October of 1939.

Q: Then you were ready for another tour of duty in ONI?

Adm. M.: Yes, my orders were to report to the Office of the Chief of Naval Operations, but I had been told that when I came back I would be going to ONI.

McCollum #6 - 245

Interview No. 6 with Rear Admiral Arthur H. McCollum, U. S. Navy
(Retired)

Place: His residence, Vinson Hall, McLean, Virginia

Date: 2 February 1971

Subject: Biography

By: John T. Mason, Jr.

Q: Good to see you this morning, Admiral. This was a most important assignment that you had with ONI at this moment in time. Would you tell me about it, Sir?

Adm. M.: After I returned to Washington, or, rather, to my home in Alexandria, I had three or four weeks' leave and helped my family get settled in. They were already pretty well settled. My wife had done a splendid job, so I had just to slide in and start mowing the lawn and raking the leaves. But it was a very enjoyable interlude.

I reported for duty in the office of the Chief of Naval Operations and was detailed to ONI and again detailed as head of the Far East Section of ONI in early November, I think it was, of 1939.

Q: What was the state of the Far East Desk at that point?

Adm. M.: My predecessor who had been head of that section, Commander Creighton, had already gone and in temporary charge, that is, during his basence, was Lieutenant Commander Kramer. The basic organization of the section was pretty much as I had left it back in 1935. Basically, there were three sections within the Far East Section, the Japan desk, the China and Philippine desks. We didn't do much about this latter because the Philippines at that time were still possessions of the United States, although independence was coming on. Also, the China Desk was supposed to look after such odd places as Indochina. But ONI on the whole was organized on the basis of looking after these various places through their mother countries. For instance, French Indochina at that time was the responsibility of the French Desk, and the same was true of the Dutch East Indies, for instance. So that, theoretically, those things did not come under the Far East Section. The Dutch East Indies, of course, as they were called then, were run by the desk we used to call the Central European Desk. It had Germany, Norway, Sweden, Holland, and so on.

Q: And all the component parts of the British Empire were under the British Desk?

Adm. M.: That is correct, and the same was true, for instance there were two little Portuguese enclaves over there, Macao and Timor. The island of Timor is divided in half, roughly, and one half was Portuguese or under Portuguese control, and the other was Dutch. But both of the other desks that had cognizance were constantly cross checking with the Far East Section, and somewhat later on ONI organized themselves so that a desk was given what they called "strategic cognizance" of these areas and that devolved - that was about a year or a year and a half later - on the Far East Section where we had coordination and cognizance over the Dutch East Indies, India and Ceylon and places that we'd never thought of before, and also British possessions - British and French possessions - in the Pacific.

Q: It certainly made sense, though, didn't it?

Adm. M.: It did make sense. We did not have, you might say, the responsibility for collecting information, but to coordinate information. Of course, the British had numerous island possessions and, of course, Australia and so on, and New Zealand, in the Pacific. But I thought it made quite a lot of sense and it worked quite well. But, again, the Far East Desk did not have responsibility for directing any active intelligence-gathering operations in those areas. That was done through the British Desk in the case of Australia, for instance. But we felt no qualms about going to them and saying, look, we need this or we need that, and they would try to get it.

As I have said before, ONI, with the exception of the Far East Desk, continued primarily a library-type operation which collected papers of various sorts and filed them away in their archives, and very little of this could be disseminated because the machinery for writing it up and getting it out was lacking. There were just not enough bodies or enough money to run it. Now there was, as I have said before, a monthly bulletin, but that was largely filled with technical information, ship design, for instance, and that sort of thing. But starting under the direction of Captain Puleston, who was director of intelligence, in 1934, I think, the Far Eastern Desk had been cranked up to be a comprehensive intelligence-gathering, and evaluation organization. We were charged with the job of issuing estimates of enemy intent - we didn't use the word "enemy" but oviously in the Far East we had to keep track of what the Japanese and Chinese might do. Revolution was going on in China constantly in some part or other. Also, back in 1935 we had set up under the direction of Captain Puleston, what was later on called a "coast watcher" service.

We didn't call it that then, but an observation network along the China coast. The heart, the direction, of that was under the Assistant Naval Attache at Shanghai, under, of course, the general supervision of the Naval Attache in China who was located in PekinG We considered, and I think rightly so, that our best source of observing certain things about the Japanese and also the Chinese was in China. We enjoyed latitude of movement there that we didn't enjoy in Japan and these things could be done and were done. The trouble was that they had a tendency to drop off if they were not closely supervised, and it happened. For instance, the Assistant Naval Attache at Shanghai got very ill and, while we didn't know it, the network tended to sort of disappear.

When I got there in November I found that the situation which Captain Puleston had set up with our help, a worldwide scheme of surveillance of Japanese merchant-ship movements, with the thought that if Japan was preparing to go to war with us, she would like to withdraw her more important merchant shipping so that they would be less liable to seizure by us in our ports and South American ports, and so on. I'll talk about that a little later. So these things were functioning, but to avert for a moment to the merchant-ship observation deal, we had tried to get, back when I was head of that section in 1934, the State Department through their consular officers to send us either by mail or by cable reports of the routine movements of Japanese ships in and out of foreign ports that usually were carried in a certain section of the local daily press. Well, the consular people were enthusiastic, but the State Department was less than enthusiastic. They said they didn't have the money or the means and they suggested in a letter that I have, signed by Mr. Hull, not that he knew precisely, but he signed a letter saying, in effect, that they couldn't do it because they just didn't have the means, that meant the money. In other words, it cost money to send a cable, and they weren't geared for that kind of money. That's what it amounted to.

Q: Do you think they fully appreciated the value of such reports?

Adm. M.: Well, they were told. That's all I can say. I don't know that Mr. Hull did. I'm sure that if it had been presented to him in person, but I don't know. Anyway, we couldn't get it through the Far Eastern Section of the Department of State. They just said that they didn't have the money to do it. They appreciated what it was, but the answer was that it would take them two or three years to get the money and they didn't know whether they had the means to go to Congress to get it or not. That's about what it came down to. Of course, they fell back and said, why not have the naval attaches do it. Well, you take the situation in the Far East. You had the Naval Attache in Tokyo, one, and an assistant, and that's it. Of course, he was fairly close to the port of Yokohama and could pick up things from Kobe. We had a Naval Attache in Peiping (inland) China with a branch in Shanghai, and later on a branch in Chungking (also inland), and that was it. Whereas you take the Consular people, they had a network of Consular posts throughout the Far East. At that time, there was a consulate general at Yokohama, a consulate at Kobe, a consulate at Nagasaki, a vice consulate at Moji on the Strait of Shimonoseki. I just use this as an example. There was a consul at

Chefoo and a consul at Tsingtao, at Tientsin, and at Chingwantao, which is the port of Tientsin, a Consulate General in Shanghai, a Consul at Amoy, Hong Kong, and so on down, also in French Indochina they had Consular representatives down at Hanoi, for instance.

Q: So it was logical to use them.

Adm. M.: Well, we had this network of observation stations, and one of the functions of the Consular Service, a primary function, was to keep track of our own and foreign shipping, a very important thing, and they were required to make these reports anyway under standing instructions from the Department of State. They had a chap in Kobe who was exceedingly helpful. He was one of the vice consuls on the Kobe consular staff and he took it upon himself to give us a monthly survey of Japanese merchant shipbuilding in the Kobe area, which was very important because Kobe was a very important - Kobe and the inland sea port of Yokkaichi and Osaka were very important merchant shipbuilding centers. The Mitsubishi and the Kawasaki yards at Kobe were large ship yards and repair yards, were very active and darned good too. He took it upon himself to cover that area and he wanted to extend himself to Nagasaki but he was likely to tread on the toes of the consul down there. It was very useful. I just use that as an example of how these things keyed in.

Well, getting back again to the organization of the Far Eastern Section itself, as I said, there were basically two sections, the Japan Desk and the China Desk, and the head of the Japan Desk was Lieutenant Commander Kramer. The China Desk was headed by a Marine. That was traditional. Usually the Marines had studied Chinese, so we had a Chinese linguist, a Marine who was heading the China Desk, and that covered pretty much everything other than Japan, and they did collate the best way they could the information that came in. Then we started issuing about every week or two a sort of an appreciation of the situation in the Far East, and that was a thing that we mailed out. It was supposed to go to important commands afloat as well as the Navy Department.

Going back again, the Office of Naval Intelligence was organized primarily to serve the Navy Department, and this idea of being an outfit to serve the fleet in outlying areas was a thing that was elaborated and established by Captain Puleston, and primarily confined to the Far East. He thought that that was the important area for us and so did we. Now, for instance, the British Desk so far as I know didn't send out any appreciations of the movements and locations of the British fleet.

Q: Only after the conflict began.

Adm. M.: That's right. The movements of the British Far East fleet were covered pretty much by our desk because we had the people who could do it and were in touch with the situation. The British had a patrol in the Yangtze River, as we did. They also had a fleet of usually three or four very modern cruisers and half a dozen destroyers based usually in the Hong Kong area. The British Far East Fleet and our Asiatic Fleet worked in rather close collaboration upon occasion. It was quite a job to try to get this stuff out and I found when I came there that certain of the things that had been set up and functioning had fallen somewhat into abeyance, principally, again, due to lack of personnel and funds. The world-wide system of reporting on Japanese merchant ships which we had undertaken to supply funds to the State Department if they couldn't afford these things had fallen by the wayside because we couldn't get the funds either - that is, ONI, I'm speaking of now. At least, that is what I was told. So the job of making these reports had been put into the hands of a commercial reporting fellow who undertook I think it was for $25,000 a year, or something of that sort, to provide these reports, which was fine, but of course as long as we could have the consuls doing it or our own attaches, they could still get through their cabled dispatches with very little or no censorship or interruption. The commercial fellow could not.

The minute the war in Europe broke out, even the countries in South America clamped a pretty tight communications censorship on commercial radio and cable so the system folded up instantly. So that had to be revivified. The recognition manuals of the Japanese naval ships which had been produced in the early 1930s had to be brought up to date. They were getting out of date now, at least, they had to be reviewed. First of all we had to find the models from which the pictures were originally taken, and it was such a secret project that they were hidden in the Navy Yard in Washington and nobody knew where they were. Well, after about six months of effort we ran them down. The model-maker who had made the models had unfortunately died and no one quite knew where they were, but we did unearth them and we rebuilt them and touched them up, and we reissued recognition manuals which were got out in the late 1930s, so they were brought up to date. The same was true of the characteristics of Japanese merchant ships, and as I've mentioned before, their speed curve particularly, and the side views. You see, just like in any other maritime country, the Japanese had built a certain number of passenger liners for easy conversion to aircraft carriers or cruises. We were doing the same thing. That was the basis of our subsidizing certain of our ships for ready conversion for naval purposes. That had to be brought up to date, and was built up.

I found again that we were almost totally lacking in the books necessary for the translating of Japanese to work with. I mean dictionaries and gazetteers, geography and stuff of that kind. So we got the naval attache in Tokyo instructed to start collecting this kit. In other words, the papers were reviewed to see what we needed and bring it up to date, because, as I've mentioned before, that type of publication was not published in the United States. Most of it was done in Shanghai, China, by Kelly and Walsh, which was an old-time publishing firm, and London seemed to be the base for a good deal of the rest of it, a place called the Asiatic Society was a great source of periodicals, early people who wrote in the Japanese language. Curiously nearly all of them were British. Professor Chamberlain was a standby, Ashton, Satow. They were all British. I'm speaking now of the 1880s through to about 1910. There were, of course, others that wrote. The French, for instance. One of the best dictionaries on Japanese characters in the early days was one by Bourgois. Later on, another English scholar named Rose Innis produced the ideographic dictionaries for use by foreign students. In Japan there were several very excellent dictionaries, English-Japanese and Japanese-English. They were designed for the use of the Japanese student but it was very difficult without a knowledge of the ideographs, or the foreign student, to read it. But we did have to get this collection.

Back in the early to middle thirties, we had established and tightened up the system for teaching our students Japanese in Japan, and we were very fortunate in engaging a very excellent instructor, a man named Naganuma, who was in effect the principal of our language school in Japan. And, of course, there again, as I pointed out before, our early students out there had been constrained to study textbooks and readers and things of that sort as used in the Japanese primary schools. Well, he revised that whole business and wrote a set of readers, comprehensive readers, so that you could learn the ideographs along with learning to read. He had produced under our subsidy in Japan a very excellent course of instruction in the Japanese language. So excellent, in fact, that it was used by the Department of State for their students out there and by the Army and so on, and we had a constant battle to retain the services of this very excellent man.

Q: The Japanese government never offered any objection to your setting up a school like this?

Adm. M.: It wasn't set up as a school. It was still done on the basis of instructors going to the individual homes of the students. But in running the course and giving the examinations and keeping track of who was doing it and so on, and also to the point of even training the instructors that went to the various houses, this Naganuma was a king pin, key man, and he produced these books. They were called the Naval Tokuhon. "Tokuhon" means "reader" in Japanese, and we called them the Naval Tokuhon.

So we instructed the Naval Attache in Tokyo to send us a full syllabus of that language course out there and along with the teaching material, with the idea that if trouble came we would at least have a way to teach Japanese in this country. We had and had had for many years lists of people who had experience in Japan or who allegedly talked Japanese, knew Japanese and so on, and we had to review those lists. They hadn't been reviewed for some five or six years. Well, people get old, and some die, so the lists had to be brought up to date, which they were. We had no way of checking on all people. Specifically, I mentioned that our main source of people that had had experience in Japan were mostly missionaries, retired, or the children of missionaries. The business community, by and large, did not talk Japanese or make any effort to, whereas the missionaries made an effort. But amazingly enough very few of the missionaries could read Japanese. They could all talk some and most of their children were the same way. They could talk but they couldn't read. They couldn't even read an ordinary newspaper. There were possibly 300 or 400 of these people, at the outside, that were still young enough or that might be trained sufficiently to be of some use in learning Japanese. A good many of the people who had grown up in Japan could talk quite well, but very few of them could handle the written language at all, even in the printed form.

Q: What use did you contemplate for such people?

Adm. M.: Well, for one thing, we needed to get some recruits to beef up our reading of Japanese codes and cyphers. Another thing, it was quite evident that if we got into a war with Japan we were going to have to have someone who could talk to any prisoners that we might take, just as an example, or if we picked up a document find out what it was because up until that time if anyone picked up a document with these funny little wiggles on it they sent it in to us, they didn't know what the heck to do with it. They couldn't cope with it on the spot. Sometimes you can pick up something and say, well, this thing means that bombs are planted here or something. We had that experience later, during the war, in New Guinea. We started receiving in our documents section papers sent in by the troops asking what in the heck does this mean? Well, they were signs stuck on sticks posted round a minefield. But they didn't have anybody who could read them, not a soldier, and a couple of them got blown up before they found out what it was. I'm speaking of that kind of thing that we had in mind. We didn't have anything specific in mind, but we thought it would be useful to have some people who could handle the language. That's what we were trying to do.

Q: Well, not only did you compile a list that was up to date, but did you make any overtures to any of these people?

Adm. M.: Yes, and that was the source of getting people. For instance, in my section that did the translations, decrypting, Japanese codes, there were six or seven, and they were constantly improving their skills and they got to be very, very good. There were Cate, and Woodrough, and Dr. Hoffman, and so on. Woodrough was the son of an American who taught in Japan a long time. Cate was the son of a missionary and his brother, whom we had acquired when we didn't have money enough to pay him went over to the Army crypt analytical section. There was a fellow named Aurell whom I'd known. He was the son of a missionary in Japan. He was a Stanford University graduate. He went into business in Japan and he was about the same age that I was. I'd known him when I was studying out there, and he made himself quite an expert. He was employed in the Army Signal Intelligence Section and during the war got to be a colonel, I think, in the Signal Corps.

In other words, we tried to skim the cream and we were in collaboration with the Far East Section of M.I.D. of the War Department to try to build up a corps of qualified linguists. Going back some years before that, when I went first to ONI, there was only one translator of Japanese in the Navy Department, Dr. Haworth, who at that time was nearly eighty. He was a very fine gentleman, and he and Mrs. Haworth who acted as his secretary, were the sole authorities of anything, including the decrypting and handling of all the things Japanese. This would be in 1933, let's say. So we had to build that up. The first move had been made before I came in there. Zacharias was the prime mover in it to get established a professional civil service rating that could offer a salary sufficient to induce the kind of people we wanted, and, surprisingly enough, the salary authorized for the position, and they were called P-2 positions, professional, 1, 2, 3, Civil Service type of thing, was $2,600 a year, which wasn't a bad salary for the time. But when they asked me in 1933 or 1934 what I thought they'd have to pay the kind of guy I wanted, I said they'd have to pay him $4,000 a year. Well, of course, the Depression came in about that time and you could pick up these fellows. For instance, Cate was a curator of a small museum up in Philadelphia. They came in and they came in willingly and they developed very well.

I had a very fine one in the Far East Section, John Clark. Now John Clark had taught English in Japanese schools for about seven years. He was a Phi Beta Kappa graduate from the University of Pennsylvania, had a doctorate or something or another. He was a very fine man, and he was what we called an analyst in the Japan Section. We had such a person as that in a person named Emmanual Larson in the China Section. Larson had been raised in China. He'd worked a number of years for the Chinese postal service. He was of Danish extraction, an American citizen, and a very competent, able man. Later on, some time in the war, he got tangled up with this *Asia* magazine and people thought he went sour and so on. I didn't think that. My own opinion is that Larson was a very intense fellow, though he didn't appear so, and he just felt that we weren't doing enough and that maybe he ought to get out and do it. Anyhow, he was a very able analyst. He had traveled all over China and sometimes in Japan and in the Far East. He was raised in China, he spoke Chinese, he spoke Mandarin which is, as you know, more or less the official language, although there are other so-called dialects of Chinese which are, in effect, languages. They call them dialects but except that they are rooted in the same basic language group, they are very different. As you know, the Chinese have a tonal language, and one of the dialects has 16 tones, I understand. Another one would have only eight or ten. So in effect they are different languages. They are akin to, but some of them are as much different as French and German, although they are the same Asiatic type of language.

We then had our one clerk who was Miss Sublette who'd been there for quite a number of years. I first met the lady in 1925. She was supposed to look after all the filing, typing, and so on. She was not a stenographer. She couldn't take shorthand, but she was a very nice lady. So the next thing that I thought we needed was to increase the clerical staff, and we did. We increased it with the backing of our then Director Rear Admiral Anderson. We acquired four or five very capable young ladies, most of them were recent high-school graduates who had taken the Civil Service examination and, after screening and so on, came in. And we got at least one man who was skilled in organizing written material and so on, to help us out. We then acquired a Mr. Wild to come along to back us up on the China Desk, with particular emphasis on the southern part of China, that is, French Indochina and so on. He was a very capable person. He talked some of the languages.

About that time, this would be now in 1940, we were very fortunate in acquiring the services of Dr. Hindmarsh, who walked into my office and said, "I'm a Naval Reserve officer and I want to go to work." He was at that time an Associate Professor of International Law with Dr. Wilson at Harvard. I said we didn't have any job that would challenge a fellow of his intellectual attainments, and he said, "Oh, never mind all that. I can type, I can take shorthand. I'll do anything." I said, "What do you want to come here for?" and he said, "Well, I talk Japanese, you know." And I said that was fine and asked him what he based that on. He said, "Well, I was an

Associate Professor of International Law for a year at the Imperial University of Tokyo." That was his field, International Law. He was then a Lieutenant in the Naval Reserve, so I said, "Well, Dr. Hindmarsh, we really haven't..." He said, "But, look, I'll come ahead." So I said, "If you want to come on, we can always get you put on active duty. We've got enough active duty billets left here to upll you in." And, you know, that fellow turned out to be a whiz bang. He could run the office, he could do anything, and he would. It was amazing to us. He didn't like the Washington climate, but he came down here with a wife and three small children, and he was a tower of strength, but he quickly learned that he didn't know much Japanese for the kind of thing we required, but he had a feel for it. A very able person. I have never been more grateful.

We were constantly on the look-out for someone to beef up the professional quality and competence of our staff. One chap that we acquired was just priceless. A fellow named Glen Shaw. I had known Glen out in Japan. He had been a teacher for many years in the Japanese schools, teaching English at the primary level and what the Japanese call their middle school level. I had met him at a place called Nogiri in the summer of 1923 for the first time. I was going over to the Interior Department cafeteria, which some of us favored over the Navy Department's, one day and as I was walking up the steps here came Glen Shaw walking down the steps. We greeted each other and I said, "Glen, what are you doing?" He said, "I'm looking for a job," so I said, "Come on over and I'll give you one." He said, "You must be fooling," and I said, "Where are you looking for a job?" He said, "I've been to the State Department and they say they have no use for me." So I said, "Maybe those fellows don't, but you come on over and we'll see if we can find a slot for you.". He did, and we made him one of these P things, you know, and he was a bird, that fellow. He talked Japanese and read Japanese. He was a real scholar in the language, and later on, he was more of less a tower of strength to these Japanese-language schools that we set up. He was full of ideas, very willing, able - a man somewhat older than I was but that didn't seem to bother him at all. Nowadays, it would take you six months to get a fellow like that.

In the meantime, we had started, as I said before, issuing weekly or oftener appreciations of the situation, usually by radio. That was addressed to the several naval commanders. It wasn't an estimate of the situation, that finally got to be rather formalized because the War College taught a thing called Estimates for Plans and Situations or something of that sort. Very excellent. But of course that thing was designed to make you think in an orderly fashion. Well, that's fine. You start out with listing your forces and the enemy forces, then you state the intelligence. Then, from this, you come to your decision, and from the decision you issue the orders. That was the technique and as I see it, an orderly process of reasoning. But the kind of intelligence we were issuing was just the intelligence, not tell people what to do and so on, but this is what we think to the best of our knowledge. If the Commander-in-Chief, Pacific, wanted to do something about it, that's his business. We shouldn't sit down here in Washington and say, all right, we think so and so, you will therefore sail and so on and so forth. Now, the process itself was perfectly sound but, again, it is an orderly business of thinking. And, later on, as we'll see, that mixing the process with actuality somewhat inhibits the situation. But, coming back again, we were constantly doing this and we were trying to bolster up this corps of about half a dozen fellows who were there de-coding Japanese messages. At that time the head of that de-coding section was a Lieutenant Carlson who had been a Japanese-language student, and they had to have someone of his capabilities out in the Communications Intelligence unit in Corregidor in the Philippines. So Carlson was very reluctantly sent over there. Kramer was very adept at this coding and de-coding and so on was head of the Japanese desk, but he doubled as head of the de-crypting section. The problem here was that while these fellows like Woodrough and Cate, Dr. Hoffman, and several others were very competent in language, sometimes it was difficult for them to convert to naval technical terminology. For instance, you take the Japanese character for a firing pin, that is, the group of characters for a firing pin in a gun, the same thing can be used for a water hydrant and it's a question of fitting it in, and a man with a naval background or some naval background, anyway, was very useful in that respect.

I remember back when Dr. Haworth came to me and said, "You know, I've been studying over these things for nearly three weeks, and I can't figure out what this thing is." He loved to go through dictionaries and so on, but I took one look at it and said, "That's a firing pin," and he said, "What's a firing pin?" As far as his knowledge of Japanese was concerned, it was fine, but you have to have that facility to bring it over. We were then constantly issuing, from time to time, reports on specific subjects, like a

Japanese torpedo, for instance, or a Japanese plane, or a new Japanese cruiser. Those reprots were given rather wide dissemination, but, again, it was a mail thing and it took time for that to get out, but they did go to the forces afloat in addition to the Navy Department. In 1940 we issued the first — not the Far Eastern Section, but ONI — of what was later known as a Fortnightly Summary of the Current International Situations or something of that sort. The first publication went out before the order authorizing it came out. That was around the 1st of December 1940.

The constant effort here was to improve and increase, I just had to get out and get this China observation network set up, and working again. We were very fortunate to acquire the services of a Colonel Williams who was at that time Major Williams. He didn't know any Chinese, he hadn't had any experience in China, but he'd had extensive intelligence experience in Latin America, notably in the Dominican Republic. He was a very smart fellow, and he did go down and he did get the staff reorganized. The job didn't require any particular knowledge of Chinese.

Q: He had to go to China?

Adm. M.: Oh, yes. We sent him out as the Assistant Naval Attache stationed at Shanghai. That's where the action was, to use a modern term. You see, the network in the then state of radio communications, you had observers located at certain posts along the coast where ships were likely to pass, and you equipped them with binoculars and so on and you paid them. Then, when they would see something, they had a little local radio that would come back to a local station, and then that station would retransmit the information to the station in the Philippines. That was your observation network. Tokyo never was cut in on it. We didn't need to compromise then. In other words, the message actually went from this string of stations to the Commander-in-Chief, Asiatic Fleet. I said the Philippines, but he had his radio and they'd relay anything to him. The Asiatic Fleet Intelligence Officer was asked to make demands on this network from time to time to increase their efficiency, which he did. The Fleet Intelligence Officer at that time was Lieutenant Commander Redfield Mason.

Q: He was a very good one, too, wasn't he?

Adm. M.: Yes, a very good one. The problem that was constantly facing ONI was the lack of knowledge on the part of our own people on the Japanese and the terrific propaganda against the Japanese, fomented to a great extent by the Chinese and the missionaries to China who could see nothing good in Japan. The propaganda was exceedingly strong. Our own press took a jaundiced view of anything Japanese, they're funny little people, they can't march, and they can't work, and so on. Actually, at this time that we're talking about now, in the 1940s, Japanese armies had overrun any part of China they wanted to overrun. They could go anywhere they wanted to go, and most of the big Chinese victories, with one exception that I recollect, were more or less propaganda. I remember that twice a year - no, about once a year, a big rice-collecting town, the big city of Changsha in China, would be captured by the Japanese. Then a little while later, the Chinese would announce very grandiloquently that they had driven the Japanese enemy out of Changsha. It was actually a tax-collecting operation. The country parts of China were run on the basis of collecting the tax in rice, that's still the old-fashioned commodity. So when the rice harvest was in and was stored, why, the Japanese set up an expedition and went down and captured Changsha and the rice. Then when they'd got the rice or as much of it as they could carry on one trip - they always left some - it was sort of a gentleman's agreement among thieves - the would withdraw, whereupon the Chinese would come back in and announce that they'd driven the Japanese out. It was as simple as that. There was no fighting on either side. A good many of those things that were happening on the mainland of China were of that kind, but for a whole year the American press was blowing it up as a defeat of the Japanese.

You had the same idea - these Japanese guys can't fly because the pilots are no good. Why aren't they any good? Because as children they're carried on the backs of their mothers or their older sisters, and their older sisters play hop-scotch, and when they play hop-scotch the child's head bounces around and it destroy the balance in the inner ear. It didn't do any good to point out that you've got a thing called Japan Airlines operating on dirt strips, which wasn't unusual in the 1930s, of course, anywhere, and over terrific terrain and using single-engined biplanes mostly. They were running a regular route between Tokyo and Osaka and down to Nagasaki and back on quite a good schedule for the time, and with remarkably few passenger casualties. It didn't do any good to bring that up. Oh, no, they were no good. You'd talk to these fellows, some of those newspaper fellows, and ask them if they'd ever flown in one of those planes, and they'd say, "Me fly in that thing!" So I'd say that the Naval Attache and I flew to Osaka and they'd answer, "Well, you're just a dmaned fool. Get in with a Jap pilot and fly that thing! Not me." Then they'd write these pieces, you know, about how unadept the Japanese aviators were. The Japanese aviators were good, and any time that we would send out something that said how good they were, we would get a storm of, I wouldn't say abuse, but "you can't say this, the papers don't say it."

Q: This sort of thing must have pleased the Japanese intelligence?

Adm. M.: Well, I don't know that they were up on that, particularly, but in late 1940 we had a shift of people in our naval attache forces in Japan, and a young fellow named Steve Juricka had been the Assistant Naval Attache for air in Tokyo. He was at that time a Lieutenant (j.g.), I think. He came back and he had made a very comprehensive study of Japanese naval aviation, and he impressed me terrifically, so I started him on a round of what you might call propaganda talks. I had him appear before the General Board in the Navy Department to tell these people that the Japanese aviators were darned good. They would only half believe. I sent him around not only in the Navy Department, but sent him out in the country to carry the message, but it just didn't percolate. It's awfully difficult for a thing like Naval Intelligence to counter the constant daily drumfire from our press. I'm not derogating the press at all, but you see, speaking now of our press corps in Japan, none of those fellows could talk Japanese. None of them. Wilfred Fleischer was the publisher, I think, of the Japan Advertiser. His father (Mr. B. M. Fleischer) had established this English language newspaper out there. He had been raised more or less in Japan and he was in Tokyo. He could talk a little Japanese, enough to order a glass of beer in a saloon, I suppose. But the rest of them, and I knew nearly all of them, they couldn't talk Japanese although they picked up a little smattering. When they went to interview, for instance, an important person in the Japanese government, the fellow that went with them was an assistant who was bilingual, but he was in every case a Japanese. In other words, he was a Japanese who had been trained by these guys to be their ears, he was also usually a reporter for a Japanese newspaper. So, at best, you were getting your information through a screen and they didn't seem to realize it. I don't think there was any deliberate intent on the part of the Japanese government or the Japanese Navy to carry these people astray, but the people just more or less strayed on their own. You got that all the time. You couldn't convince them, and these boys were pretty good.

There are many fine Chinese missionaries that I've known and very fine Japanese missionaries. As you know, I'm the son of a Baptist missionary myself. These missionary people from China just couldn't see anything good in Japan. I don't care what it was. It's not a question of whether you see anything good, it's a question of trying to come to a balance to pool all the facts that develop them without being twisted to one side or the other. It was one of the things that impressed me very much. The Japanese Kwantung Army was all through this period constantly probing the Russian position along the Ussuri River, and every once in a while they would have a little border skirmish up there, and people were always saying that the Russian armies were no good. Well, the Japanese tested it out. They tested it out once with a full division of troops. They put on a combined operation up there at a place called Nomonhan sometime in late 1939 or early 1940, and the Russian Far East Army under the redoubtable General Blucher pinned back their ears, and no fooling. They wiped the whole division out, and not with a preponderance of force, either. Blucher himself, you know, was quite a character. Like most Soviet Russians, we never knew what his real name was. When he was Field Marshal and Commander-in-Chief in the Far East, which he'd been for fifteen years, this guy called himself Blucher because he admired the old German Field Marshal Blucher. When I first knew about him he was known as Galitzin and he was then training Chiang Kai-shek's armies which at that time were supposed to be Communist. He organized that military school down in Canton that Chiang Kai-shek later headed and made his corps of officers out of. His name at that time was Galitzin. Then he had another name or two.

It impressed me very much, in other words. The Japanese were scared of the Russians and still are. But they tested it out and found the Russians were ready. So later on, when people kept talking to me about the easy invasion, the Japanese were going to have in invading Siberia, I tended to doubt it, because the Japanese had had it impressed on them that such an invasion would be a very costly and difficult project. They had established it empirically, you might say. There were other places where it would seem to be less difficult to cope with.

That was about the way the office was running...

Q: Did Admiral Anderson appreciate the efforts of the Far East Desk? Did he back you up all the way?

Adm. M.: Oh, yes. I had a very close personal relationship with Admiral Anderson. He had been Captain of the West Virginia and I had served on that ship during the period of his command. He got to have, apparently, a very high regard for me. When I came in he welcomed me and anything that I did - in other words, to use the naval parlance, I was Admiral Anderson's fair-haired boy. Anything that I wanted within reason, I got. There wasn't any question about it. Captain Bode who at that time was head of foreign intelligence...

Q: How did you rate with him?

Adm. M.: I rated with him because I rated with Anderson! No, he was really very good, but he, Ping Bode, you know was very much of a martinet type of person who stood on ceremony quite a lot. As far as I was concerned we got along fine and he was helpful. I've seen him treat other people somewhat less well, but I got on all right.

Later on, when we got another fellow in ONI, Ethelbert Watts, a Japanese-language man, he took over and that enabled Kramer to devote full time to the code breaking business. Watts took over the Japanese Desk. Then we got a fellow named Sinclair who came in as an Ensign to pep up the Philippine Desk. He was the son of a missionary to the Philippines. Quite a young man but quite good. And we had here in town an extraordinary fellow, an old friend of mine, named Sebald. Sebald was a graduate of the Naval Academy, class of

1922. He and I had been in the same company. As a matter of fact, we were in the same squad at the Naval Academy. Bill Sebald had been sent to Japan as a naval language student. He studied the Japanese language and got quite good at it. He got Navy Department permission and married a lovely lady named Edith de Becker. Her mother was a Japanese lady of rather high nobility and her father was a distinguished international lawyer, an Englishman, who had been adviser to the Japanese delegation at the Washington Arms Conference on international law. He was an adviser to the Japanese Foreign Office and so on. He had made a lot of money in the legal business out in Japan. In other words, the de Becker family were financially very well to do. They lost a lot in the earthquake of 1923 because a lot of their wealth was in land, buildings, in the Tokyo-Yokahama area.

Bill continued to serve in the Navy until some time around 1931 or so, he then resigned, went to Johns Hopkins and made himself a lawyer - took a law degree there. About the time he got his law degree at Johns Hopkins Dr. de Becker died and his older daughter, Marie, was at that time married to a German or maybe an Englishman. Anyhow, Marie was a very beautiful young girl, I thought prettier than Edith. Well, Bill had gone back to Japan because the de Becker fortune was being dissipated. Primarily, he went out there to see whether he could pull it together, which he did, and in about two years or so he established a law firm there in Kobe headed by himself with a Japanese partner to do the pleading before Japanese courts and so on, which was the usual set-up. It was very lucrative, its headquarters were at Kobe, and it was doing fine, and Bill used to send us reports. He had gone into the Naval Reserve and he was in Reserve intelligence. We tried to tell the Bureau of Navigation to quit sending this fellow routine forms that they sent out to all the reserve people headed "Lieutenant Sebald, Kobe." That just set the Japanese police on their ears, but we never could get it stopped. Finally Bill in disgust said, "I'm going to resign. That's all I can do, I cannot have my business pried into by the police every once in a while on account of being a Lieutenant in the Navy." He did continue to function but a little bit before I came back to the Navy Department, as a matter of fact, in the spring of 1939, he apparently was prescient enough to see the handwriting on the wall, so he liquidated as much as he could of the family fortune and got to hell out of the country before they pulled back his ears entirely. He and Edith came back to this country. They salvaged enough of their wealth for Bill not to have to work too much, but he came into the Navy Department and he walked in to Admiral Anderson's office and said, "Well, here I am. What do you want me to do?" Anderson had never heard of him, so he just looked at him and threw him out. So Bill and Edith went up somewhere in New England and when they heard that I was down here Bill came in to see me, so I talked to him and talked to the Admiral. He asked where we could use him and I said, "Bill, you can come over here and go to work in ONI." He said, "Couldn't you find something more useful for me to do around here? Here I am. I've studied the Japanese language, I can talk it." I talked with Domestic Intelligence then and I said, "Why don't we use this fellow and have him set himself up as a lawyer here in Washington, and maybe, being a lawyer and with his Japanese connections, his family, Dr. de Becker's family, and Edith are well known in Japan among the officialdom. Maybe he could work himself into the position of being a legal adviser to the Japanese Embassy?" Which he did.

Q: This was in what year?

Adm. M.: This would be in 1939. By 1940 he was established as legal counsel for the Japanese in their trade negotiations and stuff of that sort. Of course, the answer was, it was not anything unethical but we were au courant as to their thinking and what they...

Q: It really was helpful!

Adm. M.: It was a helpful connection. Later on, when the war started, Bill came down and said, "I've got to get into uniform or the Army will grab me." So I said, "Well, come on. We'll put you in uniform." By this time the security people were getting real security-conscious and they turned Bill down.

Q: Because he had Japanese connections?

Adm. M.: Sure! Why, I think we've seen this fellow consulting with the Japanese ambassador! Well, dammit, that was what he was supposed to do. I had a hell of a time getting him put on active duty as a Lieutenant Commander in the Naval Reserves. He stayed on and you probably remember him.

Q: I do.

Adm. M.: Later on he went into the diplomatic service and he's been Ambassador to a couple of countries, Australia and Burma, head of the diplomatic section for MacArthur in Japan. He had a brilliant diplomatic career. He's a very capable fellow. Now he's retired and living in Naples, Florida.

That's just some of the side lights. The constant effort was to try to get more and better people in ONI, and to revive some of the things that had been thought of by people such as Captain Puleston and get them functioning them again, which we did because money now was commencing to be a little bit more plentiful. Around the 1934 and 1935 period, money for the Navy was fairly plentiful in one form or another under the New Deal effort to revive the economy and so on. After about 1935 there was a drought period as far as money was concerned for ONI, anyway, and things had to be cut down a bit, and they were. Therefore, one item or the other that were considered less important by the then people there were dropped or allowed to atrophy, and my effort was a rebuilding job there. We did rebuild quite well, I thought.

Again, I stress that the situation of handling the codes and cyphers was such that the translation section was actually part of my section, headed, at this time, by Kramer. The Analysts, as we called them, who worked there, some five or six of them, were all paid for out of ONI funds, and the information that came from that source was supposed to be sent into ONI into my Section. Then we, theoretically, disseminated it.

Q: How did this tie in, then, with naval communications?

Adm. M.: Well, Naval Communications did the actual technical intercept work. In other words, you had intercept stations in Bainbridge Island, in Hawaii, in the Philippines, etc.

Q: There was one in Australia too, wasn't there?

Adm. M.: That came later on. The one in Australia was set up by refugees from the Philippines. The theory was that the communications handled all the radio traffic and the actual interceptions, and that went into three centers, the one here in Washington, the one in the Hawaiian Islands, originally at Ewa, and then the one at Cavite. Originally, that Cavite station - it had a long history. It had been set up first in Shanghai, the first I knew about it back in 1924. From Shanghai it had been moved because it was set up on the top floor of the consulate general building, and the Consul General felt that they were not sufficiently secure there, so they moved to Peking, to the legation compound up there. That lasted a while, but they couldn't get properly set up, and eventually they were pulled out and sent to the Philippines, keeping minor pick up and reporting stations at both Peking and Shanghai.

But the furnishing of the translation group and, theoretically, the distribution of any Intelligence was a function of my Section of ONI. We had a rather constant difference of opinion. The director of Naval Communications, at that time Admiral Noyes, and his predecessor took a personal interest in this business, but they were also, and understandably, anxious that their division get credit for it. By credit I mean by the Chief of Naval Operations. After all, they worked for the Chief of Naval Operations, and this was a wonderful thing to make their mark. Therefore, they were rather insistent that these messages, these cryptic messages, receive special treatment so they could be definitely identified as radio intelligence. To my mind, that was very insecure and very wrong, so you developed a system of the books being carried around where these so-called intercepts which now have gotten right famous from these various investigations. But in order to try to give some background appreciation of what these things were, I insisted that Kramer, who was well versed in the Japanese aspect of it, personally carry these books around and talk to the recipients, such as Admiral Stark, later on the Secretary of the Navy, and others, so that they didn't lose sight of the perspective that these things should be put in. But, even then, it was difficult. After all, Admiral Anderson coined the word Magic for this thing. "Well," I said, "It's not magic. This is just the blathering of some Japanese diplomats that we are getting." He said, "Oh, no. We're reading the mail." "But," I said, "how authentic is the mail? How much does it represent of what these little people are going to do?" And he said, "Oh, Mac, we're reading the mail." Well, what can you do? This had an aura of authenticity that in many cases it didn't deserve. Under the Japanese system, any one of their diplomatic or consular officials could send in a dispatch of their viewpoint to the Japanese foreign office, and of course we picked up a number of them.

Q: That wasn't necessarily the official...

Adm. M.: That wasn't necessarily the official point of view or the one that was going to be carried out at all, but one of these whiz bangs would come through and it would be very interesting, so they would translate it and, my goodness, the whole business would shape up on this thing, and you had an awful time trying to say, "Wait a minute, who is this guy?"

I remember one case when a series of very belligerent messages came out of Mukden. Now Mukden in Manchuria was a Consulate General, but the Consul General at Mukden exercised many of the prerogatives of a viceroy. He was actually a man of ambassadorial rank in the Japanese foreign service, and a very high ranking one, and usually a very capable one, but he was Consul General at Mukden. Mukden, of course, was also the headquarters of the Kwantung Army and of the South Manchurian Railway Company. These things were all subsidiaries of the Japanese government in one form or another, so all of a sudden we got this very belligerent dispatch from Mukden, intercepted it, and it went to the point of saying, well, we ought to take this, we ought to sequester all foreign property, seize all Americans, put them in jail. In other words, a war type thing, and it got pretty tight there for a while, until we finally sent a message out to Smith-Hutton in Tokyo and said, "Where is the Consul General at Mukden?" We got a message back, "I had dinner with him last night." In other words, one of the office staff in the absence of His Nibs himself had cooked this thing up. I was very much amused because about a week later when the consul general got back to Mukden we intercepted a dispatch from there saying, "Disregard my so and so." This was this thing sent out by his subordinate.

But those kind of things do happen.

Q: Didn't that serve to underscore your point of view with Admiral Anderson and others?

Adm. M.: Up to a point, but you know, this got to look awfully good. It looked like real gravy, and it was, as far as the diplomatic stuff was concerned, there isn't any question about it. But what we overlooked was that what we were reading here was diplomatic. Now, the Japanese foreign office was sending these things back and forth, but that did not necessarily reflect the opinion of the Army General Staff, which was very powerful, or of the Navy General Staff, and at that time we were reading almost no Navy codes at all. There was one fairly minor administrative code that was the Navy's and it was interesting but it didn't carry anything in the nature of orders, operation orders, or anything of that sort at all. I kept stressing that instead of trying to decode and translate all this mass of diplomatic stuff, we ought to be spending more time seeing if we couldn't somehow or other de-code Japanese Navy traffic. The Japanese Navy in about 1936, I think it was, had revised entirely their code and cypher system and had gone to a machine-type of system like the so-called ECM machine for their more important messages, and we just simply had been unable to break it. Now, we were able to get the diplomatic machine, but the Navy's stuff was virtually a closed book for us. I think that that is one of the troubles, that everyone was looking so much at this diplomatic thing that we continued to look at that and didn't think too much of the other, me included.

Well, with the situation coming up this way - you see, in addition, as you know, the codes - the breaking and actual reading of the codes, there were a couple of other ways of getting information out of the radio emissions. One is by traffic analysis, the other one is by direction finding. There are a number of other things. Traffic analysis...

Q: That's a very important one.

Adm. M.: Yes. The Japanese were very good at traffic analysis. I think they were better than we were. I am speaking now of later in the war. We didn't know it at the time.

Q: What were your relations with Safford?

Adm. M.: Very good. Safford, of course, was the head of the code and signals section. Only one of his responsibilities was this decoding. Safford himself was a very adept, clever cryptanalyst, I think they called them, but he also had the function of devising our own codes and cyphers, and supervising in a general way their distribution and security. There was a Registered Publications Section which actually distributed them and kept track of them, that is, the codes and the coding machines and so on. Now, that was not only the Communication Publications, but also the Registered Publications Section distributed the ONI publications. They distributed the war plans. In other words, it was a mail distribution business of all secret, confidential books and periodicals and whatever nature, but it was physically located and supervised by the Communications Division of the office of the chief of naval operations.

Q: Periodic days of retribution or something!

Adm. M.: Yes. I had thought and I think mostly that our efforts in the Far East Section were improving. We got to the point where we actually had established a plot within my office there in ONI of where we thought the Japanese fleet was, you know, various units, on charts and so on.

Q: Was this for the benefit of...

Adm. M.: For the benefit mostly of me and my staff so that when they said a Japanese ship was so and so, we had it. We got most of our information at this late date from the code and signals section of the Navy Department - traffic analysis mostly, direction finders some, but direction finding at that time that short wave radio coming in and was a very chancy and a very difficult thing. Direction finding had its place in the sun during World War I when everybody was still using long-wave and continuous-wave transmitters and you could actually beam in on them. They were all fairly short range. But no one quite knew at this time what happened to a short-wave emission. This thing went up to the ionosphere or some place and bounced back in various places in the world. You could take a bearing on it, but whether that was where the actual transmitting station was you didn't know because you might be getting secondary waves.

After the war started we got a very interesting example of this. We got persistent reports in the Navy Department that there was a Japanese ship operating 700 or 800 miles off of the coast of the State of Washington, and we repeatedly sent search planes out to this spot but could find nothing. Yet the radio emissions were very strong. But we were finally able to intercept a couple of the emissions for study. Actually we identified the call signs and they were those of a Japanese submarine division that we knew from visual sighting was operating in the Dutch East Indies. What had happened, as we trailed the thing back, was that the messages had been sent off and after two or three bounces they hit this one spot off the Washington coast. It's one of the things that you have to consider. The long-range direction finding of short-wave radio at that time was not very effective, that's the point that I'm trying to make. It was always open to a little suspicion. But on the whole I thought our people did pretty well.

In the summer of 1941, at the suggestion of Hindmarsh who had talked to people at Harvard, we went up to a symposium there at Cornell which the professors of Japanese of the major colleges in the United States were to attend with some of their pupils. Dr. Elliessief, who was the head of the Oriental Studies Division at Harvard at that time, was a White Russian. His assistant at that time was Reischauer.

Q: Later ambassador?

Adm. M.: Yes. He's back up there now. I knew his older brother better than this boy. That was John who was killed in a bomb explosion in Shanghai when the Japanese were attacking back in about 1932.

They came and I think it was Dr. Kennedy from Yale who came, and we had Miss Florence Walne, she was a Doctor at the University of California. We had a fellow named Yamazaki, I believe it was, from the University of Washington at Seattle. And curiously a chap from North Western University who was a Japanese national.

Q: What was the purpose of the symposium?

Adm. M.: Hindmarsh thought that what we should do was to survey the situation, see the competence and the ability of the various colleges to produce anything in the nature of linguists useful to us. They were going to have this meeting anyway, so we got ourselves invited to attend. So Hindmarsh and I drove up together with our respective wives -- a nice junket you know, up there in the summer time, the beer is good - and we went up there along with a fellow named Charley Moore, a Major in the War Department. Charley Moore was the son of a Japanese missionary and talked Japanese and, curiously, could read it quite well.

We spent three days in conferences and talking with these people and had a wonderful time. It became apparent very, very soon that none of them had anything that we would find useful and understandably so because these schools of "orientalia" or whatever you want to call it, at our big eastern universities - as far as I can remember, Princeton didn't have such a thing - and the schools that had them, Harvard was one, as I mentioned, and the other one was Yale, and their approach was that the actual teaching of the language was more or less incidental. They did teach the language but the language was a tool to get an insight into history, dramatics, art, and so on.

Q: Culture.

Adm. M.: Culture, that was it and, frankly, even from that point of view they were pretty sorry courses, in my judgment. Major Moore got up on the third day and said so very flatly, Army fashion - also he was a Ph. D., you know, and strangely for me I kept my mouth shut, but Moore got up and said, "Well, gentlemen, you haven't got a thing that's any damned use to the government at all." I don't think it was taken in too good part.

Anyway it was decided when Hindmarsh and I came back that what we should do - we had got a tentative agreement from Dr. Eliessief and from Miss Walne out at Berkeley - was to set up a course for maybe fifty students at Harvard and fifty out at Berkeley, which the Navy would somehow get enlisted and would pay. We would also give a fee to each one of these schools for teaching a course that we would provide. This was the Naganuma course that we had with certain modifications that Shaw started working on and trimming down to fit the case. Then we went out and with this list of possibles, all of them youngish men, we started recruiting students for these two courses. In order to keep them out of the tentacles of the draft which was then commencing to operate in this country, we had to put them in uniform in some way, then we had to devise a system of paying for them. So with the connivance of the Bureau of Navigation, later the Bureau of Personnel, we arrived at a system of enlisting these guys, which we could do, as yeomen, second class, in the naval reserve and putting them on active duty. Well, that enabled us to pay these people as yeomen, second class. They would get about $50 a month on the pay scale that ran then, and that was enough for them to get eating money and so on. Then we pushed them into these two schools and put them under the administration of the local Professor of Naval Science and Tactics. There was one at Harvard and one at Berkeley.

Q: Connected with the ROTC?

Adm. M.: ROTC. In other words, they'd pay them and keep their records and all the naval folderol that goes on and has to be done. So that could be taken off the necks of the people who were actually running the courses, Dr. Eliessief and Miss Walne. In other words, these people were paid, their subsistence was done, and any disciplinary matters that came up, they would be rapped on the knuckles, and that was the guy who did it.

Of course we had to persuade these fellows because it was unheard of that these people who had no naval training, no nothing, would come in as second class petty officers in the Navy.

Q: How did you recruit them in the first place?

Adm. M.: Well, we went round and saw these guys.

Q: From what kind of a list?

Adm. M.: The list that we had in ONI. The first question was, how much exposure have you had to Japanese, how good is he and how much does he have. And the courses were set up on the basis, now here's a fellow who at one time was very good and all he needs is polishing up. The courses were set up on the basis of six months, but maybe he could be useful in three months. Later on we had to go to another scheme, but the first ones with this outfit were of rather varying competence. The more competent we didn't need to teach much, but we could turn out people and they could be useful, which they were.

It soon developed that we were having trouble with Harvard. We couldn't get through to Dr. Eliessief who was rather insistent that he was going to teach the language his way. Well, his way demonstrably couldn't produce in the time allotted people that could handle the language.

Q: It would take four years!

Adm. M.: Well, he wanted to teach it in the traditional way, and another thing that complicated it, he and Reischauer had just written a book on how to teach it and they didn't like to use our book when they had a perfectly good book of their own. Well, it became very apparent after constant pressure that we couldn't persuade Eliessief because he would start his outfit and run for a while our way, and the next thing you knew he was back to his old ways again, and because Hindmarsh had been an Associate Professor at Harvard and still had tenure there after a fashion he could go back and forward. In other words, he had the kudos, academic kudos, necessary because he was a Ph. D. in two or three ways. Finally he came back and threw his hands up and said, "We just can't do it up there. I've gone to see the President..."

Q: That was Conant, probably.

Adm. M.: It came as a surprise to me that Presidents of Universities could exercise only mild moral suasion on a full professor. A full professor runs his own department damned well as he pleases and in a great many cases they don't take too kindly to direction from the President.

Out in California you had a different thing. Florence Walne was very much interested, very pliable, and they had had for a number of years a sort of Japanese course out there. It hadn't amounted to very much and Florence was trying to put it back on its feet and she had very little to start with, so she welcomed our material and was enthusiastic about it. She also had the enthusiastic support of the chancellor out there who I believe was Dr. Reineish, was it? A very fine man. And of course California had their axe to grind, which was all right by us. They saw themselves developing a real Department of Oriental Studies there. That was good for us and good for them. The result was that their product very soon was superior to what was being put out by Harvard.

We did have a contract with Harvard that ran, I think, for six months, or maybe a year. These were done with the universities on a contract basis. You contract to teach it and you get paid so much and we'll take care of the paying of the students and the disciplinary administration and so on. So we just phased the Harvard thing out and put all of our marbles, so to speak, at California, and that turned out very well. The first two or three classes were completed, then we started running out of fellows who had any competence of exposure to the Japanese. Later on, we developed a thing of going to get smart boys out of the universities and putting them in and just soaking them with Japanese more or less the way it's done in a Berlitz School for six months. They were taught, ate, drank, lived, slept Japanese, and they did all right.

Q: What relationship did that effort have to the one out in Colorado?

Adm. M.: That came at a later date. You see, after the war started with Japan, we still maintained the school at California. A number of our instructors or professors at the school were Japanese nationals who had been in this country a long time, and others were of Nisei type people, all of them from the academic community. The University of Washington's professors and instructors - they only had about three - came down and joined Miss Walne at California.

What happened there is that in the spring of 1942 I came back from Pearl Harbor - I'd been out there to suggest to Admiral Nimitz that he establish an Intelligence Center out there to serve his command, and showed him the plans that we had prepared in ONI for him, and got his approval. Well, when I got back to San Francisco I had this message from the director of Naval Intelligence saying to see if I couldn't do something to save our language school at Berkeley. I left Washington in early April or late March 1942 to go to Pearl Harbor and it took me a while to get out there because the transportation business was all knocked out of kilter. We had to go out by train to California and finally took a ship from San Francisco out to Pearl. We came back by plane all right, but it was difficult going.

In the meantime, I had heard rumors here in Washington that the Army might sequester people of Japanese ancestry and others in concentration camps. Personally, I was very much opposed to it because we, Naval Intelligence, on the security side, had for a number of years cultivated the Nisei element in the population in California, for instance, and in other places and we felt that we knew what was going on. We had a list of possible enemy agents, where they were, and how they operated, and just merely handed it over to the FBI. At that time, the FBI was under such orders from either the Attorney General or Mr. Hoover in espionage matters or any matters they wouldn't act unless they thought they could bring a case to a presentation, to a jury and so on, within six months, say. They had to do that. So that as for any long-term surveillance business, they were very generous with their advice as to how to go about this thing, but they themselves couldn't take much of a part in it. They had other things to think about. I had heard these rumors but I was assured by the people in the War Department that no such action would be taken, so I felt pretty secure. But I then came to find out that we were in this fix and that General De Witt, who was commanding general of the Corps area out there had issued this order actually putting these people into concentration camps. Of course there was a time lag, about a month or two, and I went up to see Admiral Greenslade who was Commandant of the Twelfth Naval District and talked to him. He said, "Well, my Lord, I don't think that you have a chance to change the General's mind, none." I said, "Why?" and he said, "Well, he's publicly committed." The Navy Department didn't tell me about this. I don't think they knew, and I'd been away about a month and here all this thing had happened.

I did go out to see General De Witt and, as Admiral Greenslade had predicted, I got exactly nowhere. In other words, he was committed, he had made up his mind, he had the approval of the War Department, and he wasn't about to change his mind. That was one of the hardest jobs I ever had to do was to go over there to Berkeley and see Dr. Reineisel, the Chancellor, and tell him that we were going to have to move that school. It was a very difficult job to do. He had been so cooperative, and of course that just slapped down the whole thing, so what we did was we loaded all of the school, the professors, the families, the students, and everything into a group of buses, Fords, and what-have-you, and transported them to Boulder. Initially we didn't know where we were going to take them, but what happened is I got back to Washington and Hindmarsh, in the meantime, was scurrying around the country to see if we could relocate this school somewhere. He was up somewhere around North Western University talking to the people up there. I came back and I went down here to the educational section of the Bureau of Navigation to see if they had any place that we could put this...

Q: You wanted buildings in being!

Adm. M.: Well, we wanted something, we had to get something, and when I went in there I said to one of the heads of the section, a fellow named Will, do you have anything? He said, no, he didn't think he had. Then he said, "By the way, here's a chap that's just in here that might be interested." And I said, "Who is this fellow?" He said, "Well, he's the President of the University of Colorado at Boulder." It seems to me his name was Steinhardt. He was a very nice man and we got talking and he said, "Well, you know, I've got a plant out there," and he started giving me a sales pitch about his plant that he had at Boulder, and he turned the whole thing over, lock, stock, and barrel, to us for doing anything we wanted.

Well, you see, at that time a lot of the Universities were afraid that with the draft coming up their student body was going to be disappearing into the Army. In other words, they were madly looking around for something to keep their organizations going, and in the tempo of the times I can see what it was. I wired Hindmarsh to get out to Boulder and see what the situation was, and wire me back. Well, in two or three days, I got a wire from Hindmarsh saying this place is ideal. So I went over to the Bureau of Navigation and said how about signing us up for this Dr. Steinhardt at Boulder? OK. So we signed up and sent word out to California that we had a place for these people to move to. In other words, we picked up the entire school, instructors, pupils, books, the whole works, just picked them up and bodily transported them to Boulder.

Q: Did Florence come along?

Adm. M.: Yes, she came along. She was the Director of the school. As I said, the whole works. I don't think California had anybody left. And, of course, they were out of the zone then so that...

Q: So that General De Witt couldn't put them...

Adm. M.: Well, not only that, but the rest of them. In California, as I've hinted before, there was always a certain amount of suspicion and prejudice against people with yellow skin, and there was almost none of that in Boulder. As long as they weren't Indian, they were all right! But that's where Boulder originated, and from then on Hindmarsh was more or less the Washington representative of the language school, keeping them supplied with materials and also developing materials that we could send out to our units with the forces that were doing the fighting. We had to go to the point of reproducing books that I've mentioned before, dictionaries, glossaries. And we made a deal, I think it was with the University of Michigan to use its press. What we did was take the books that we had and with this fairly new photo-printing technique that had been developed, these books were put out. The whole business was put out by the University. They did a very fine job of it. As a matter of fact, the reproductions were a hell of a lot easier and better to read than the originals in many cases, because the type was bigger and so on and so forth.

So that's the way that thing was done, and these packs were made up. As I said, later on, when I was in Australia, all I had to do was send back word here, send me so many packets of translators' material, and it would come, a packaged job. Hindmarsh rode herd on that, and Shaw was his assistant. Shaw having the Japanese language capability was constantly shuttling backwards and forwards to Boulder, and Hindmarsh had to go out every once in a while to mollify the Professor of Naval Science and Tactics, because we had these rather unmilitary people out there. A fellow named Leo Welsh. But it worked out pretty good. All those Boulder Boys - they called them all Boulder Boys - as I have indicated the first two or three classes were from the University of California and Harvard, but they got to be known later on as the Boulder Boys. They weren't as good, obviously, as a man who'd studied in Japan three years, but within their limitations and all things considered, they did a superb job and they filled a need. In some of this Intelligence business you need volume, numbers of people, among other things. Some were better than others, and we had a lot of them. Rex Reid who was out there in Australia with me, was one of these fellows. Then there was a fellow, Stratton, who now is a Congressman, he was another one. We had several others, the Bartlett boys. They went to school and tried to learn to read and write, but they were older. Sam Bartlett was a civil servant up in Massachusetts. His brother, Don, is now a professor at Dartmouth, and there's still another one. These were all older men, but they had gone through the school to brush up on their Japanese language competence, and they were very good because, for instance, both Don and Sam had grown up to at least late teenhood in rather isolated sections of Japan, in other words, where they had to be thrown with the Japanese community. They were sons of missionaries in little stations down on the inland sea, up in Hokkaido, and so on, and the result is that they had the colloquial knowledge of the language which a lot of the rest of the boys didn't have, and a feeling for the psychology. As I've mentioned before, a knowledge of folk lore which is very useful in talking with people to elicit information, people such as prisoners of war. They're scared to death anyway, in most cases. They were invaluable.

I just use that as an example, but the other boys I don't think were quite up to doing things on that basis because their education and knowledge of the Japanese language was a little bit more mechanical, and necessarily so.

Q: You put little cadres of these men on ships, too, didn't you?

Adm. M.: That's right. Of course, I didn't do that. We did in places there during the war later on. Rochefort in Pearl Harbor originated the idea that when a task force commander would go to sea one of these linguistically qualified people would be put on his staff, one or two, and sometimes, three. At first they were very effective. Later on, their effectiveness deteriorated, not because of any want of ability in them, but because the Japanese got smart enough to quit using plain language radio. But at one time, in the early stages of the war, you take a fellow like Biard, Lieutenant, (j.g.), who was one of the people we trained in Japan, he was on Admiral Fletcher's staff there at the Battle of the Coral Sea, he could tune in on the voice radio and hear the chitter chatter between the Japanese aviators. He could say, well, you've got an air attack coming in and it's coming in from there. That's pretty good information! And you could pick it up merely by listening to the aviators talk to each other on their radios and so on.

Of course, our people did the same thing. They jabbered their heads off, too, when they got in the air. Maybe the Japanese were listening to them. We kept trying to tell them to pipe down without too much luck, and the Japanese were having the same difficulty.

Q: Kind of a nervous reaction!

Adm. M.: They all talked when they got up there. How's the wind coming for you? My alto pressure's going down, and so on. All those things are information of no particular value, but when you start getting this volume and it starts increasing, you know the attack is coming in. That's about the size of it, and they were very useful, very successful. But by the time we got up to Leyte Gulf in 1944, I reckon it was, that type of thing was really of no use because the Japanese had gotten wise enough to use a fairly simple code, but a code takes time to break down. But I did insist when we went there that Admiral Kinkaid have such a group on board. I just wanted to keep the old man covered, that was all! You can't afford to leave that kind of thing undone.

Also we used the men in Australia and New Guinea and so on. We sent these fellows up with the Army troops in combat. The Army never did have enough of them. They depended more on Nisei people. Well, the difficulty out in the Southwest Pacific was that most of our troops were white boys and they weren't having any truck with any yellow people fooling around, even if they did talk American. By and large, you couldn't use any number of these Niseis, all capable men. There was no question about their loyalty, but, after all, they looked just like the Japanese and you put them up and try to mix them in with an outfit like the 42nd Infantry Division, boys from Montana, and they just as soon shoot one of these guys as another. You just couldn't use them, at least not in the quantities required. So we did have these boys that had been trained in Boulder, these Intelligence fellows, and we sent them up and attached them to Army divisions and so on, to do the preliminary interrogation of any prisoners, reading documents that came to hand, and so on. The Generals of the divisions they were attached to were, as far as I know, uniformly loud in their praises. They kept hanging medals on them. The Army medal procedure was a little bit more generous than the Navy's, and these fellows liked to go up there because they got a medal every time they went into action with the troops. But they did do quite a bit of good, and the Army Air Corps people were all very appreciative of the help these fellows gave.

Of course, out there, it was a different situation than it was in the Central Pacific. The forces that Admiral Nimitz commanded immediately, the tactical forces. There we were in constant contact from the first day that I got there with some land element of the Japanese forces and sea elements. In other words, the traffic in so-called barges, motorized sampans, or something that came down and kept the troops supplied, the Japanese troops along the north coast of New Guinea and along down as far as Milne Bay and other places. It was all done by this more or less coastal traffic. To intercept that was the work of the PT boats and so on, and you had to have these people. They were very effective. At least, the people in command said they were effective, and I think they were.

I'm afraid we've strayed a little bit off, because we did set up these schools and got the first ones operating interestingly enough in September of 1941 and this was before the war. I think I've covered the Japanese-language school aspect, but we were up to our ears in that thing and all during the war we kept that going.

Q: It was largely your motivation, wasn't it, originally that got all of that going?

Adm. M.: Yes, that's right. I'm not trying to take any great amount of credit. It was as plain as the nose on your face that you had to have people who could talk the Japanese language if you were going to fight them, so that's what we did.

There's one other rather interesting thing. Before we go too much into the argument between war plans and ONI, which got pretty acrimonious during 1941, we did do one other thing that is of interest. The then director of Naval Intelligence, Admiral Alan G. Kirk, at that time Captain Kirk.

Q: He was only there for a year, wasn't he?

Adm. M.: Less than that. Alan G. Kirk had been naval attache in London and he came to ONI where he took over about the 1st of March and he left about the 1st of November. He was a very brilliant man and I had known him...

Q: But he hated the duty.

Adm. M.: No, I don't think...

Q: That's what he told me. He didn't want to be there.

Adm. M.: Well, I know, and that is understandable, and I think people have forgotten. It wasn't a question of hating the duty, but anybody with any prescience knew that ONI had its neck stuck out from the start. You were prohibited from doing certain things and the effort to make the machinery work was very great. Alan Kirk said that he didn't like the job and I don't think he did, but he didn't like it primarily for this reason. Alan Kirk had been Naval Attache in London for four years, and that was fine. When he went to London, Alan Kirk had thought that he had had in his big ship or command. As a quite senior commander he had been given command of one of our light cruisers, and at that time the sine qua non of being selected as a seagoing officer to flag rank was to have had a so-called big-ship command. In other words, an aircraft carrier or a battleship or a cruiser. The light cruisers were put in that category. To increase the flow of promotion the Navy Department had put senior commanders in command of some of these ships. In other words, people who had been selected for captain but hadn't made their numbers yet. Well, Alan Kirk figured that he had had his big ship command in and when he came back to be director of ONI he very soon found out that the people that were likely to compose any Selection Board that he would appear before took a dim view of an officer of his rank and experience that hadn't been to sea for four years and had had no destroyer squadron or comparable command. So Alan Kirk immediately started getting himself lined up for a destroyer squadron, which he went to, and was duly selected to Rear Admiral and so on up. You know the rest of his career. He was a very bright fellow and he backed me up in my viewpoint that the war with Japan was coming. We didn't know when, but it was coming. It was getting more pressing all the time, and as early as July of 1941, he sent for me and we sat down and talked.

He said, "Mac, how many language students do we have in Tokyo?" I said, twelve, and he said, "Don't you think it's time we got them to hell out of there?" And I said, "Yes, Sir, I do." I sent a memorandum out there that we ought to pull them out because they were getting more and more police harassment, they didn't have diplomatic privileges. In other words, they were gone.

Q: And they'd be lost to you anyway.

Adm. M.: That's right. So he said, "Let's get them back." So we sent a dispatch out to Tokyo. I went back and took a look at the list of people, and of the 12, or maybe 14, people that we had out there, two of them had been in Japan less than six months, that is, in the course, and obviously had no linguistic competence. So we took the rest of them and the most experienced, that is, the ones that had been longest in the course in Japan - the course was three years - about three or four of them we instructed the Naval Attache to send at once to the Commander-in-Chief of the Asiatic Fleet to bolster his intelligence operations, thinking, of course, that he would put them to work in the code and signal place down there at Corregidor. There were about a half a dozen, as I recollect, who were ordered to report to the Commandant of the Fourteenth Naval District in Hawaii under the guise of continuing their studies in Japanese at the University of Oahu, and instructions were sent to the Commandant of the Fourteenth Naval District, at that time Admiral Block, to make these people available to the Commander-in-Chief of the Fleet, who at that time was Admiral Kimmel.

Rochefort, who was running the codes and signal business, in other words the Communications Intelligence Center there at Ewa, moved then to a building within the confines of the Navy Yard at Pearl Harbor to be closer to the Commander-in-Chief and so on. And these people were promptly put to work by him. That was the nucleus of the corps and they were very capable. Every man that had a Japanese language capability that we could scrape up was sent to the Fleet either Asiatic or Pacific. We scraped people off of active duty commanding destroyers and other places and funneled them out as fast as I could get them out to Hawaii. For instance, General Lasswell, at that time a major of Marines, I snatched him out of a Marine regiment some place. He didn't like it. And we got a fellow named Finnegan who was on the staff as flag secretary to Rear Admiral Bagley. Finnegan rather liked it. He'd been in that business before and knew what it was about. I don't think we pleased his Admiral too much. In other words, we were scraping the barrel.

Anywhere we could lay our hands on the Japanese language oriented person, we were getting him out of his job and putting him down in Cavite, or the Hawaiian Islands. We deliberately went shy in our group here in ONI. In other words, we figured that the need was going to be out there and we had to get them out there, which we did.

The Japanese government, one way and another, did quite a bit to try to block the exit of these people from Japan, and by this time - which would be in late July of 1941 - we were almost in a state of undeclared war with Japan. We had embargoed oil and the merchant ships weren't running ships' schedules. Air transportation as we know it today was virtually nonexistent. None of our planes, anyway, went into Japan. The Clippers, as they called them, ended up the line there either in Manila or Hong Kong, and they flew once a week or every other week or something of that sort. It took almost as much as ship time to get out there. The ships went direct. Finally by August, I think it was, we started making this effort by mid-July to get them out of Japan - and by early August the last one was out.

Q: How did the Japs try to delay their departure? They were American citizens.

Adm. M.: They were American citizens, that is right, but they also had the question of how much money did they have in Japanese banks and, things being tight, they had to have an exit visa. The Japanese had put in a visa system. You not only had to have a visa on your passport when you went in, you had to have another chop when you went out. There are all kinds of ways that you can delay the issue. Visas are just one technique. There are others. Do you owe anybody any money in the country, and so on...

Q: Yes, all these little annoyances.

Adm. M.: Little, that's right. Little bureaucratic annoyances. And we can do the same thing upon occasion. But theirs was a much more centralized bureaucracy than ours was then. It was rather easy to manipulate. In other words, the national police force was immensely powerful. There's no local police, as such, in Japan. It's the national police. Police, it's true, operate in cities and in the countryside, but it's all run by what you would call the Department of the Interior - a European type agency.

We did get them out and got them distributed, and they proved very useful. I didn't think that Admiral Hart and his Intelligence officer, Commander Mason, made all the suitable use of these people they should have. For instance, one of the senior men, a fellow named Wilson, instead of being used for his Japanese capabilities was made executive officer of a destroyer. Of course, we didn't know that. And the destroyer was sunk by the Japanese and Wilson was scooped up as a prisoner and spent the war in a prison camp in Japan. I just use that as an example. Another fellow named Jordan who came out with the gunboats from the Yangtze Patrol, was made no use of in his language capabilities. He was later a prisoner and died at that Cabanatuan prison camp in the Philippines. There was another fellow named Pyzick, who was one of the Intelligence Officers with the Fourth Marines most, evacuated out of Shanghai and apparently either they couldn't shake him loose or he was overlooked or something.

But I thought on the whole very effective use was made of these people. Most of them had been in Japan about two years, some not quite that long, but they were all useful in some degree out there in the Central Pacific with the Fleet. Later on, after I got to Australia, I was fortunate enough to be able to grab on to one for my own set-up there and there were two or three others sent out who ended up in the Communication Intelligence Center down at Melbourne. That Melbourne outfit, so far as the American contingent was concerned, was composed of people who had been evacuated out of Corregidor. We took special pains when it looked like that place was going to fall to get those people out and they were given priority and pulled out by submarine down to Australia, first to Perth and then across to Melbourne, where the Australian Navy had set up a small Communications Intelligence unit headed by a retired Royal Navy commander, and they merged forces.

So that's about it along there.

McCollum #7 - 301

Interview No. 7 with Rear Admiral Arthur H. McCollum, U. S. Navy
(Retired)

Place: His apartment in McLean, Virginia

Date: Wednesday morning, 17 February 1971

Subject: Biography

By: John T. Mason, Jr.

Q: Admiral, it's good to see you. I've been looking forward to this chapter today, which is a continuation of your period of duty in ONI prior to the outbreak of war with the Japanese, and I think you were planning to talk today about War Plans and ONI.

Adm. M.: Yes. The War Plans Division in the early autumn of 1940 got a new chief in the person of then-Captain R. K. Turner.

Q: A very dynamic chief!

Adm. M.: A very capable man. The director of Naval Intelligence at that time was Rear Admiral Walter S. Anderson. Shortly after Turner became head of War Plans; Naval Intelligence - I think partly at the suggestion of Admiral Turner - set up a new periodical called the Fortnightly Summary. It had a longer title than that, but it was a short, bi-weekly magazine having to do mostly with operational type intelligence, what was going to happen or what we thought was going to happen. The first of those was issued on the 1st of December of 1940, and they came out every two weeks thereafter for about a year or two, then somehow or another petered out. I don't know why.

Q: Got too busy with the war!

Adm. M.: Well, they may have. On the other hand, one of the difficulties with that, as with everything else as far as the Far East Section of ONI was concerned, our interest was in the Pacific. We were located in Washington. It took a long time for any information to get to us from the Far East by mail. Of course, radio was quicker, but that did offer certain difficulties. To get a periodical of this sort out and get it back out into the Pacific area where it would be at all timely was almost impossible. There was very little air mail, or at least not in bulk to handle this sort of stuff, so it took four or five days by train across the country, then to get out, for instance to Pearl Harbor, it was another five to seven days by ship. So that by the time this thing got out there any news value it had was pretty well gone. Its timeliness had disappeared.

Q: What was its classification?

Adm. M.: It was classified confidential. In certain circumstances it was classified "Secret." That also would offer more difficulties if it was secret. But I think it was usually "confidential." Occasionally it would be marked "Secret" and if that was the case, it was supposed to go only by officer courier which was very difficult to manage. Actually, the content, I thought, was pretty good. At least it was widely read around the Navy Department, and about the middle of December 1940, or shortly thereafter, Admiral Anderson was detached as Director of ONI and ordered to the Pacific Fleet to take command of the battleships. He never did fleet up to the third star. That job had, up until that time, carried three stars with it, but there was a reorganization of the forces afloat more or less in the works at that time, and the battleship command - Anderson got the command all right, but he never got the third star. That went somewhere else, I don't know where. Possibly to the aircraft carriers.

Admiral Anderson had done me the honor to invite me to be a member of his staff as his Operations Officer, which was the Number two spot on the staff. The Chief of Staff was #1 and the Operations Officer #2. I was quite junior for that job, judging by the people that had had it before, and naturally I was very much flattered and I thought that was fine, but the Admiral said he was going to leave right away and that I would have to stay for three weeks or so in ONI till the new man got things running. About that time Captain Kirk was back from London and he was very much impressed with what the British called the COIC, Combined Operations and Intelligence Center system, and he suggested that some such arrangement as that be put up within the precincts of the Navy Department. That was enthusiastically received, and in early January of 1941 there was a conference held presided over by Rear Admiral Ingersoll, who at that time was the Assistant Chief of Naval Operations. They got a new man to set this thing up, a Captain Leighton, who had been selected for flag rank. He was selected to get this thing in operation. I don't think he wanted the job particularly and he was very much in a fog as to what was required.

Anyhow, at this conference, each Section within ONI had a person designated to make sure that Leighton and his outfit got the necessary Intelligence to make the situation work. Our own forces operations they would get from the Operations Division, which at that time was called Ship Movements, so that they could combine the two. Ship

Movements, of course, was a section within the Office of the Chief of Naval Operations and was the staff division designated to issue operating orders and so on to the forces afloat and to keep track of their locations and movements. What they were doing, and so on. War plans also came into it very much. Turner was getting more and more into everything, which was very fine. When they designated me to be the Far East liaison with this outfit, I made the mistake of saying, "Well, now, you'd better designate someone else because I'm under orders to go." And Admiral Ingersoll looked up quickly and said, "You are? Well, we'll stop that right now." He picked up the telephone in my presence and called the Bureau of Navigation and said, "Cancel McCollum's orders." Well, what the hell could I do!

Anyhow, I think it well at this time to review certain things that happened. As you know, Admiral Richardson was relieved of Command of the Fleet. Admiral Kimmel was chosen as his successor. Richardson, you understand, had been Commander-in-Chief of the U. S. Fleet. Kimmel was never that. Kimmel was Commander-in-Chief of the Pacific Fleet, and, theoretically, if various elements of the United States Fleet which now under the new set up was considered to comprise the Atlantic Fleet, the Pacific Fleet, and the Asiatic Fleet, if all three of them ever got together, the Commander-in-Chief of the Pacific Fleet would be designated as Commander-in-Chief of the whole works, but the chances of anything like that ever happening were most remote. So the title and the function of the Commander-in-Chief, U. S. Fleet, virtually disappeared. The new organization went into effect about the 1st of February 1941. That's about the time that Kimmel assumed command.

I had to write Admiral Anderson that I had pleaded with Admiral Ingersoll to let me go. I would much have preferred to go to sea, particularly with Anderson whom I knew I could get along with very well indeed, but I couldn't get shaken loose.

Q: Who, then, was DNI?

Adm. M.: Jules James, who had been the assistant DNI, filled in because it was then known that Captain Kirk who, at that time was still the Naval Attache in London was coming as soon as he could get relieved over there. He was coming back here and was going to assume the job of DNI. There was a rank difficulty there because Jules James was senior to Alan Kirk by about a year. Jules, I believe, was commissioned in 1908, and Kirk I believe was 1909 or thereabouts. So as much as Jules James liked Kirk and so on, he just didn't think he should serve under a person junior to him, so it was known that he was going to leave within a reasonable time after Kirk took over.

Both Kimmel and Kirk were, I understand, personal selections for their respective jobs of the Secretary of the Navy, Mr. Knox. Mr. Knox was very much impressed with Admiral Kimmel on one of his trips out to the Hawaiian Islands - now this is what I've been told, it's hearsay, I don't know; and he was very much impressed and taken with Admiral Kirk who, as you know, has a very engaging personality. I don't think he had very much regard for Admiral Anderson because Admiral Anderson was rather outspoken and rather blunt, and Mr. Knox didn't like too much outspokenness or too much bluntness.

Q: He preferred to be outspoken himself!

Adm. M.: That's right. He wanted to do all the roaring and not be roared at by anybody. That was his personality. He was a very charming person, but that was his personality.

I realized all along that these fortnightly summaries were very useful things and so on, but they wouldn't carry the news out into the Pacific very rapidly, so we had for a long time, almost weekly, sent out a sort of appreciation of the situation. That went out by radio, so that it was in the hands of the Commander-in-Chief of the Fleet, and the Commander-in-Chief, Asiatic, almost at once. So it did have a timeliness that the other lacked.

Q: And that was always secret material, was it?

Adm. M.: Not necessarily secret material. Most of these kind of things went out under a "Confidential" label because "Secret" before the war was very little used. Theoretically, a secret dispatch or a dispatch encoded in a secret system was not to be held or copied by anyone. It was shown to people and then other people ran off with it somewhere. So the result is that very few people used the "Secret" label. But right after the war started anything that wasn't marked "Secret" you just threw in the wastebasket to start with, and a lot of the secret stuff you did the same way, but at that time Confidential was still a pretty high security rating and it was used rather sparingly, but these things did go out "Confidential" and they could be retained when they were encoded in a Confidential code system. "Confidential" meant largely not that the material itself was so confidential but that the opinions expressed in there should be encoded in a confidential system to give them a little bit of security from general reading by everybody.

I think it might be well for a moment here to review the pertinent parts of the Naval Intelligence Manual of that time. Now, these are revisions valid as it existed in January 1941. They've had several revisions since then. This was a Confidential publication called ONI 19, and I think two or three articles in there are quite pertinent and with your permission I'd like to read:

"Article 105E. Technical information is not evaluated by the Naval Intelligence Division except in some cases as to reliability of source. Evaluation of purely technical matter is entirely a function of the Technical Bureaus.

"Article 107B. The value of intelligence depends on its reaching the person that can use it in time to serve its purpose.

"Article 201A. Foreign Intelligence. The collection of all classes of pertinent information concerning foreign countries, especially that affecting naval and maritime matters, with particular attention to the strength, disposition, and probable intentions of possible enemy naval forces."

Here, you see the evaluation of probable enemy intent is very definitely a function of the Naval Intelligence Division. To get the technical aspect of it working, I think it was in the autumn of 1940, each Technical Bureau was directed by orders of the Secretary of the Navy to set up an Intelligence Liaison Section. They all agreed on paper, but they didn't do a darned thing about it and it never did function to amount to anything. In other words, before that, when you routed an intelligence report, which was customary in those days, it circulated around through the various departments, and it might lay for weeks or months at a time in one or another because nobody had time to pick it up and look at it, initial it, and pass it on. But this did give you one point to send it to, and you could call the fellow up. Boscoe Wright, later a Rear Admiral, for instance, was the man designated by the Bureau of Ordnance, as ONI liaison. He gave you a telephone number and that was the fellow to call, and these were the people to evaluate technical information, for instance, on a Japanese gun or torpedo or something, and presumably that person had been following the development of that weapon or whatever it was in that particular country. You can't just pick it up and come in cold from being the torpedo officer on one of our destroyers, see something about a Japanese torpedo, and say, oh ho, and pass it on. You can't evaluate it without some background. And, of course, that was never provided. So, to that extent, this business of evaluating technical information by the technical bureaus was a bunch of bunk. The only time it got evaluated was when Mike Schuyler would come rushing down from the Bureau of Ordnance with his hair on end because he figured that somebody had found out about our influence fuses, because it had been offered for sale by a Frenchman who said he'd invented it out in French Indochina. The Frenchman had stumbled on the principle of it and he did have a workable solution, but then the Bureau of Ordnance didn't know what to do. I didn't even know that we had such a thing, but of course we did, and that's what set them on edge. Here was a guy way out in French Indochina offering just about their pet secret for sale to them! The principle, as you know, is quite simple and once one understands the principle, you can devise some technique to make it work.

So, the point is this, that the evaluation here of probable enemy intent is a function of ONI.

As a result of that, we had in the Far East Section weekly and sometimes at more frequent intervals sent out what we thought was going to happen, the location, strength and movements and so on of the Japanese Fleet, political developments within Japan, what had transpired and so on. Well, in early February of 1941, following our usual custom, without more ado I sent out a dispatch forecasting a move of the Japanese into French Indochina. Their forces seemed to me to be so disposed, and it didn't make too much difference, they had the capability certainly of doing it. Their troops were then massed in the vicinity of Canton which isn't very far away, and I just figured they were ready to move. And, here, about the 3rd or 4th of February I was sent for and was told that hereafter I -- along with the others in ONI were instructed that hereafter War Plans would do all of the evaluating of probable enemy intent and that we had to be particularly careful that the Director of War Plans in person got all of the pertinent information. Now, he was a very busy man and here he was going to do that, not only for the Far East, but, my goodness, for the British, the Germans, and everybody else.

Well, obviously, he was soon bogged down with this kind of business, so he organized what amounted to an Intelligence Section within his Division of about three officers. They all were fine people, nice fellows, but they had no prior knowledge of Intelligence at all, and what would happen is that these fellows would come into your office and spend two or three hours of your time so that they would be sure that they got all the dope, and they would carry the word to

Turner, and first thing you know, they were cranking out little publications for distribution within the Navy Department. It was a rather futile business because it was time-consuming in the first place, you had to brief these fellows and then they'd bring out their grist and bring it back to you for checking. So it was just a very onerous job.

Q: Just a duplication.

Adm. M.: Duplication completely. I commenced to wonder why this had taken place, so I did a little snooping on my own and found that about the same time that my dispatch had gone out predicting an invasion of French Indochina to take place within a month or so, Turner had issued, without any knowledge of ONI at all, a prognostication that the Japanese were going to invade Siberia! And he continued in that view, on what basis I don't know. At one time I think I made him rather angry when I suggested that maybe he was privy to some intelligence that I certainly didn't have. Anyhow, he was convinced that the Japanese were going to invade Siberia. So I finally went to Charley Wellborn, who was the Administrative Aide to the CNO, a friend of mine, and I said, "Charley, what is all this business about?" and he said, "Well, I'll tell you, maybe you'd better go and see the Admiral," meaning Admiral Stark. Admiral Stark said he realized that it was a function of ONI to talk about intentions, it was in the manual, and all that, but he thought that in the interests of coordination, it ought to be coordinated, and that Turner was the man to do the coordinating.

Well, of course, that didn't make any sense because once you start a coordinating job you've got your hand on the gullet, you've got a stranglehold, and that's exactly what happened. Another thing, they had a complex on secrecy around there, which was all very well but it tended to make people so secretive that they didn't tell anybody what was going on, so ONI was put in the unenviable position of having stuff going out about enemy intentions and what-have-you that they didn't know about at all. Any orders to our own forces we were not told about in ONI because we were considered probably not too discreet - I don't know. Anyhow, these things were going on and the only way you found out about it was to have a private pipeline to some of these places, which is not a good way to do. But that was the situation, and I brought this up to Admiral Ingersoll, and Ingersoll said, well, he knew that in the Army the Military Intelligence Division did the evaluating, but the Navy didn't do it that way. In the Navy, War Plans always did it. I said, "Admiral, if that's the case, how about issuing an order in writing amending that part of the ONI manual?" He said, "Get the hell out of here. A verbal order is enough." By this decision, ONI was put on the spot, saying in effect, all right, if there's anything wrong with the evaluation, you guys did it, and you guys and not War Plans must take the onus. That's what it amounted to. It was a very unenviable spot.

Q: What was the role of the DNI in this picture?

Adm. M.: The DNI was fighting to try to maintain the integrity of ONI, but was losing out. Every time he'd go to bat, he'd strike out on it. The idea was of course - Admiral James was very definite in his views and didn't hesitate to express them, but he was just turned down every time. He himself went up to Admiral Ingersoll and asked for this revision and Admiral Ingersoll said, no, he didn't see any necessity to revise that. James's position was that it was a rather important thing to change and certainly it should be put out in writing so that it would be a matter of record. Well, neither Ingersoll nor Stark agreed with that, and Turner apparently didn't agree with it because he continued to crank out these evaluations. Even when the Japanese did invade Indochina which, I think, happened on the 15th of March 1941 - on the same day Turner was still saying that they were going to invade Siberia. It just got to be an impossible situation.

Q: Was it largely due to the fact that you had a strong personality there who had connections?

Adm. M.: Well, you had a strong personality, you know, when Kirk took over as DNI in about one month, and Kirk certainly wasn't any weak sister. He immediately went to bat and he and Turner were on the mat all the time. Kirk with one point of view saying, all right, if you want to do it, then you send it out, but I won't okay it. That went on in May of 1941. In the Fortnightly Summary there was a note - of course, the Fortnightly Summary was cooked up in my Section so far as the Far East was concerned - Kirk had written in his own handwriting, "In my view, the Japs will jump and pretty soon." And scrawled in handwriting on this copy that I have in Turner's handwriting and initialed by him, RKT, is, "I don't think the Japs are going to jump now or ever." I don't know what was his basis for this opinion, the aggression was there all the time. The Japanese pressure was moving to the south. And I think it's very interesting that finally, with the constant pressure being predicted for an attack in Manchuria, we got a very interesting dispatch on the 25th of June 1941 from the Commander-in-Chief, Asiatic Fleet, "The following is my analysis of available information (mainly diplomatic intercepts): If Japan starts new war in immediate future it will be against Russia. Success in the advance against Russia will be necessary before Japan makes advance to south. However, I continue on the assumption that the next Japanese coup will be in this direction," that's in the south. This is Admiral Hart talking now, presumably with the consent of his intelligence officer, "Does your analysis agree with mine?"

I drew up an analysis and submitted it through channels as was required, and how in the world it got by I don't know. It did get by. Turner added something as he usually did. This went out on the 25th of June in answer to Admiral Hart: "Your 23 15 25 (that was the dispatch number of Admiral Hart's dispatch) Invite your attention to the following circumstances, (a) a defensive rather than an offensive deployment is indicated by the strength and disposition of the Kwantung Army. Detachments of aircraft from that army made some time ago have not been replaced. Considering the strength and disposition of the Russian forces, Kwantung Army would require considerable reinforcement before it could undertake an offensive. In view of the offensive deployment of Japanese army and planes in Central China and the combined operations now under way in the vicinity of Wenchow, it is questionable whether reinforcements are immediately available - that means reinforcements for the Kwantung Army. The present deployment of the Japanese Navy is normal for eventualities southward rather than northward. Preparations for future action in Indochina are indicated by recent deployments in that region. Collapse of the western republic of the USSR would not necessarily undermine the political and military integrity of the Siberian Republic, in view of the semi-autonomous organization of the union. (b) A still fluid political condition is indicated by all recent reports from Tokyo. Consider your analysis not now justified in view of these factors."

Q: And that went out under whose signature?

Adm. M.: Well, it went out under ONI chop but it was also initialed by war plans. Turner added this to it, "But this does not rule it out as an eventuality. Advise careful and continuous evaluation of the information from all possible sources." Well, what the hell else do you do?

Q: If you're alert!

Adm. M.: Turner added "My analysis is that the Japs have not reached any definite decision and will continue an opportunistic policy." A perfectly meaningless codicil to the preceding, but we did get the other out.

Q: Was there any indication that Hart bought that?

Adm. M.: Yes. He came back. That was the end of June 1941. On the 3rd of July. So about five days later Turner sent this - I hadn't seen it before it went out: "Information from numerous sources leads unmistakably to the deduction that the Japanese government has determined upon its future policy, and that this policy is supported by all principal Japanese political and military groups. Policy probably involves war in near future. While an advance against the British and Dutch cannot be definitely ruled out [that was down in Singapore and the Dutch East Indies, of course] CNO is of the opinion that Japanese activity in the south will for the present be confined to seizure and development of naval army and air bases. Russian neutrality pact will be abrogated and major military effort will be against Russian maritime provinces probably toward the end of July, though attack might be deferred until after collapse of European Russia."

Now, the situation in the Far East in five days had not changed at all, but the Germans had attacked the Russians. As you know, the attack came about the 1st of July. Admiral Turner was completely bemused by the fact that the Germans had attacked and he freely predicted the collapse of Russia in Europe almost momentarily. And this is the reason for his change, but you see, again, the thinking within the Navy Department tied Japan to the tail of the German kite, which never was the case. The Japanese never considered themselves as a satellite to anybody. But the constant feeling was that you looked at the situation in Europe and you expected the Japanese to react to the European situation, and so far as the Japanese were concerned, they could have cared less. They had the opportunity in the south or wherever it was and they were prepared to exploit that opportunity, regardless. The Germans didn't want the Japanese to get involved, you know. They wanted to keep the Japanese out. They did their best, but the Japanese weren't about to buy that. That was one reason the Japanese Ambassador in Germany was relieved. He was at that time General Oshima. Later on, Oshima was sent back as Ambassador, but at that time he was a Lieutenant General and the Ambassador to Germany. He overstressed the German point of view and thereby displeased the people in authority in Tokyo, so he was pulled out, to be sent back after the war with us had started, or maybe just before. Anyhow, when the Tojo cabinet came in, Oshima went back as ambassador to Germany.

Q: And I suppose it can be said that we were Europe-oriented ourselves and didn't think in terms of an independent action in the Pacific.

Adm. M.: That's right, and the thing that I had to struggle against constantly and never could seem to get across was that the Japanese were not conditioning their policy on anything that the British or the Germans did in Europe. If a situation arose in Europe that would definitely tie up the powers in settled action that would preclude the possibility of their reacting against the Japanese, then the Japanese were prepared to exploit the situation. But they by no means conditioned anything that they were going to do on what necessarily was going on in Europe, except as it might help them. In other words, they weren't helping the Germans. If the Germans got fighting with the English and so on and there developed a situation that was useful to the Japanese, the Japanese would exploit it. It was just as simple as that. And of course the same thing goes for Russia.

You see, few people realized that the Russian Far East Republic, as it was called, was virtually an independent nation, for many years under the rule of the redoubtable Field Marshal Blucher, who was so powerful that Stalin hesitated to liquidate him. He eventually was liquidated, but at that time he was still pretty much the top dog, and his army was his army. It was the Far Eastern Army, and he didn't take any pains to let anybody forget it. And, as I have indicated before somewhere, it was in pretty good shape. It defeated a Japanese in division strength in, I think, 1939 up at Nomonhan. Continuing with the dispatch now:

"All Japanese vessels in U. S. Atlantic ports have been ordered to be West of Panama by August the 1st." This was, of course, a reaction to our embargo on oil and so on, which was being put into effect at that time. There wasn't any point in having Japanese merchant ships floating around over here when they couldn't pick up any cargo anywhere.

"Movement of Japanese-flag shipping from Japan is being suspended," that is movement West. That's the information that we had.

"Under stringent secrecy inform Army commanders and all ambassadors, British," and so on. Those were actually delivery instructions. This was prepared by Op-12 which is War Plans, and was released by Admiral Stark, and I append this copy.

Q: And this was directed again to Admiral Hart?

Adm. M.: Not to Admiral Hart, no. This was directed to Commander-in-Chief, Asiatic Fleet, Commander-in-Chief, Pacific Fleet, Commander-in-Chief, Atlantic Fleet, Commandant, Fifteenth Naval District;

SPENAVO, which was the Special Naval Observer in London, and so on. There is no evidence that ONI ever saw this dispatch before it went out. There's no signature, no initials, on it anywhere. Normally, it should have been under the coordination theory, if Admiral Turner prepared the dispatch and it's indicated in the dispatch that he did, or his division did, it should have been presented to ONI for a chop, unless it was something that had to do with the administration of ONI people and so on, which we'll come to later on.

There are two or three other dispatches along the same vein there. As I say, Turner had the theory that Russia was going to fold up, cave in. He figured that the Japanese would plunge into Siberia, on what basis I don't know. I mean there wasn't any intelligence that I had or certainly any information available to me that, to my mind, indicated any move toward Siberia at all. The movements were all to the south. You see, as I explained to you before, we had an observation network along the China coast which was specifically charged with the observation of Japanese movements.

The Japanese, of course, had to more or less use the ports of China to embark and disembark troops, supplies, and so on. So you could put in, as was done, a group of observers in a port like Shanghai, for instance, and it was virtually impossible for the Japanese to make any considerable movement into or out of Shanghai without it being observed, and it was observed and it was reported. In other words, the so-and-so division was loaded into such-and-such a transport, they were wearing tropical uniforms, the tanks were camouflaged in green splotches, which again is not the white of cold Siberia, and so on and so on. I mean it was information from actual visual sightings coming to us in that kind of detail. Of course, what the Japanese did was that these ships went and they moved from there to Formosa. Well, you don't train men in Formosa for getting ready to fight in Siberia; as far as I know. Formosa is semitropical and usually pretty hot. Yet we constantly got this Siberian uproar. Turner wasn't alone. The Chinese agreed for purposes of their own. I was always very skeptical of any information that was supposedly vouchsafed to us by the Chiang Kai-shek government. I always looked tentatively - maybe wrongly - suspicious with "What do these guys want out of us? Why are they giving us this? What is their purpose?" For some reason or other, we were flooded with reports from Chiang Kai-shek that the Japanese could be expected to attack Siberia. How he could know that, I don't know, but they said well, he's got a way. Well, you understand the government was in Chungking at that time which is one hell of a long way from the Siberian border, that is, thinking in terms of the maritime provinces of Manchuria. Nevertheless, these things were predicted and I just don't know why, but I do know that it was one source of information supposedly that was very hot and good as coming from the Chinese. I always thought that maybe it was an echo of our own stuff here. You know, in this intelligence business, you tend to echo each other.

Q: What was the British position? Was it also in terms of Manchuria?

Adm. M.: No. The British at this time were very much occupied with the war in Europe and they were not thinking too much in terms of the Far East at all. They were thinking in terms of Singapore and Singapore was the Gibraltar of the East and they were quite at ease with it. The British had set up a Far Eastern Intelligence Center in Singapore. Sir George Sansom, I think, was the head of it. He wrote a number of very fine books on Japan. He was a qualified Japanese linguist and a good one. When I knew him in Tokyo in the late 1920s he was Commercial Counselor of the British Embassy there.

So you had the conflict. The thing is that the only difference so far as the Far East was concerned, going back to reading the dispatch that I was able to get sent out without too much emasculation or addition on the 25th of June - there was no difference in the basic situation in the Far East between then and this dispatch that was sent out on the 3rd of July by Turner. There was no movement, nothing, to indicate any change.

The War Plans Division would prepare a dispatch and send it out without reference to or even consideration by ONI at all. These dispatches would frequently be released either by Admiral Ingersoll or by Admiral Stark, presumably assuming that ONI had been consulted, but neglecting to look to see if there was the initial of the DNI on it. The result is that you had a situation which left Intelligence without any information as to what our own government was doing, and we frequently picked it up only as a result of decoding Japanese diplomatic cyphers, which is a ridiculous situation. Here, on the 25th of July, for instance, the War Plans prepared a dispatch, perfectly properly so, but again ONI was not told. Everybody else was told about it apparently. The following is a joint dispatch from the U. S. Army chief of staff and the chief of naval operations.

Q: Sent to whom?

Adm. M.: Well, it is "Addressed to the commander-in-chief, Pacific, Commander-in-Chief, Asiatic, Commander-in-Chief, Atlantic, Com 15, SPENAVO," and that's it:

"Appropriate addressee, please deliver copies to the commanding generals of Philippines, Hawaii, and Caribbean Defense Command, and also to General Cheney in London. You are herewith advised that on July the 26th at 1400 GCT the United States will impose economic sanctions against Japan. It is expected that these sanctions will embargo all trade between Japan and the United States subject to modification through the medium of a license system for certain materials. Import licenses may be granted for raw silk. It is anticipated that export licenses will be granted for certain grades of petroleum products, cotton, and possibly some other material. Japanese funds and assets in the United States will be frozen except that they may be moved if licenses are granted for such movement. It is not expected that the Japanese merchant ships in ports of the United States will be seized at this time. U.S.-flag merchant vessels will at present be ordered to depart from or not to enter ports controlled by the Japanese." In other words, we suspended all our merchant shipping to Japan. "CNO and Chief of Staff (Army) do not anticipate immediate hostile reaction by Japan through the use of military means, but you are furnished this information in order that you may take appropriate precautionary measures against any possible eventuality." What are you going to do? Be ready to shoot in all directions at once? "Action is being initiated by the United States Army to call the Philippine Army into active service at an early date. Except for immediate Army and Navy subordinates, the contents of this dispatch are to be kept secret. SPENAVO London inform Chief of Naval Staff but warn him against disclosure."

In other words, it's almost impossible to start any evaluating of intelligence on what is going to happen unless you have some knowledge of what we are doing. I picked this up later on, but it was a fait accompli before I knew it, which is all right. I had no way to change it. Certainly the people should have been advised in this business, but you can't go prognosticating actions about the Japanese or wondering why the hell they're suspending the sailing of their own ships till you find out that we've suspended ours. In other words, these things are all done on a reciprocal basis. The United States quits sending their merchant ships to Japan, Japan quits sending their merchant ships to us. It works that way in practically every case. And to say that the guy who has the job of trying to figure things out can't be told what we're doing is pretty ridiculous, but that is the situation that existed. You had a constant conflict between Turner and Kirk and, later on, between Wilkinson and Turner, and Turner was in practically every case - maybe rightly so - supported by his boss, the CNO, and by Admiral Ingersoll, who was Assistant CNO.

The thing is that it's perfectly proper and not unusual for an Admiral to prefer the advice of certain individuals on his staff, presumably people that he served with before and had confidence in their views and so on regardless, you might say, of the staff line and so on. That was done. But one of the amazing things to me is the frequency with which the War Plans people were called on for all sorts of advice outside the competence of the War Plans Division.

In the Navy Department Turner, in the Pacific Fleet Sock MacMorris who was War Plans Officer out there and was constantly queried by Admiral Kimmel as to what he thought the Japanese were going to do. Well, of course, the man that was supposed, presumably, to tell him that or keep him advised of that would have been Layton, who was his Intelligence Officer. Yet MacMorris didn't hesitate to issue his opinion as to what was going to happen with, as far as I know, no basis for it at all.

Q: Doesn't this all reflect the standing of ONI prior to World War II?

Adm. M.: Well, I don't know just what you mean by that.

Q: I mean the fact that...

Adm. M.: Why, no, I don't think so. ONI had - heavens, I'm talking about the days when Puleston, for instance, was Director of Naval Intelligence. The CNOs, both Standley and Standley's relief, Admiral Leahy, relied on ONI. I know. I was Intelligence officer on the staff of Admiral Hepburn, Commander-in-Chief of the Fleet, and we were in constant communication back and forward between, for instance, Admiral Leahy when we had the famous Christmas of 1937 mobilization out there when the Panay was sunk. We got word from Admiral Leahy who was Chief of Naval Operations at the time. He said Naval Intelligence estimates and so on, you will do so and so. The job of an intelligence officer is inherently that of a race-track tout. He brings information up to the Admiral and says well, now, I think this and I think that, put your money on this horse here. Well, you see, if he wins, the guy pats himself on his chest and says how smart a guy I am. He never gives that tout any credit. But if he loses, that skunk told him wrong.

Q: Still the fact does remain that ONI and all the Intelligence agencies existing prior to World War II didn't have the stature which they achieved afterwards. We see our intelligence set-up today and how important it is, the whole picture, but prior to World War II...

Adm. M.: Well, I don't know that anybody else had any - I mean, who else had any greater stature? Certainly not the Communications Division. They were looked on purely as a technical service. War Plans when it was sticking to war plans had no greater emphasis. And you must realize also that the Ships' Movements Division, which was traditionally an admiral-maker, at that time was headed by Brainard who in that position was made a Vice Admiral. They (Ship Movements) were left more in the dark as to what in heck was going on than ONI was. Their opinion was never asked. I remember one morning Brainard came in so damned mad he could hardly talk. He found that all this that he was supposed to be looking at, monitoring, the movements of our own ships was being ordered from some sources without his knowledge at all. Yet he was the guy responsible for knowing where these ships were. Movements of ships actually were ordered and that emanated from War Plans. We had nothing to do with it. His hair was standing on end - what little he had. So that ONI by no means was alone. There had grown up in the office of the Chief of Naval Operations a coterie of about three or four officers - in other words, there was Stark, of course, the head of it, and Ingersoll and Turner. They were sort of a triumvirate. Turner would bring in the ideas and these guys would execute them, frequently without reference to anyone else on the staff, on any staff level at all, any staffing, as we would say, of the matter. ONI, for instance, was in no worse fix than Ship Movements.

Communications was a little bit better off because, obviously, these things were sent out by Communications, and the result is that most communications people read the mail. They're not supposed to read it, but they did, and the result is that they were somewhat better informed, but not because they'd been asked even in matters that affected them. They knew because it had to go out and be coded, over the radio, and so on. So it was only through that, you might say, bootleg system that they got it. You did have that situation repeatedly. In hearings before the Congress it has become very apparent that there was no lack of effort, because these were all very able men. They just felt that these things were so secret that they didn't dare discuss them. Anyway, you'd hear, for instance, Admiral Stark will testify, or did testify, down at the hearings. Why, yes, we had a conference on the subject. Well, who were the conferees? They were Stark, Ingersoll, and Turner. That was the conference. That's all right. It doesn't make any difference, but I don't think that ONI, as far as I could judge, suffered any more than the rest of them did.

I think people have forgotten that, because, you see, in the first place the Navy Department was set up on the basis of a technical service, and there was only one technical department, actually, excluding the Marine Corps, that was staffed or under the direction of what you might call line officers, and that was the Bureau of Ordnance. The Bureau of Ships, as it was later called, was at that time the Bureau of Construction and Repair. The head of that bureau was an officer of the Naval Construction Corps. The Bureau of Engineering, as it was called, that had to do with the engineering, the materials and engines of ships and so on, was, theoretically, under a line officer but actually an engineer specialist. In other words, he was an engineering duty only officer.

Q: BuSanda?

Adm. M.: Well, the Bureau of Supplies and Accounts - that was, of course, a supply officer. The Bureau of Medicine and Surgery. The other line department would be the Bureau of Navigation, which was later known as the Bureau of Personnel. So the only staff you had was the staff of the CNO, and you had various divisions within that staff who maintained close liaison with the technical bureaus. At one time Charlie Lockwood because he was a submariner was the head of an outfit called the Materiels Section, within CNO to maintain touch with the technical bureaus and keep them abreast of materiel developments abroad and so on.

You have repeated several times ONI's reputation was at a low ebb. I don't think it was at a bit lower ebb than some of these others. Within the staff of the CNO he had the Communications division which was, theoretically anyway, a Communications Service and it did very much the same thing in its way as ONI did. It provided a communications service for the Chief of Naval Operations' office. It also operated the Naval Communications system, shore-based radio stations and so on, throughout the United States and wherever we had them abroad, very much like ONI ran an Intelligence Service, but we also were supposedly the intelligence arm of the Chief of Naval Operations. War Plans was supposed to do war planning. Later on, there was organized within the CNO's staff what they called a Materiel Division, which was headed for a while by Captain Hooper, later on by Admiral Robinson, that coordinated the functions of the various technical bureaus so they didn't get messed up in their orders to the factories and so on. They needed that kind of a regulating agency.

Q: War Plans at this time also organized a chart room, did they not, and gave a report to the President, and ONI was invited to be a part of that?

Adm. M.: No. That chart room - that's this thing that was set up under Layton. It was a chart room with buttons to move around for ships and locations, and so on, but they got so bemused with different shapes of buttons for different kinds of ships that they couldn't see the woods for the trees. But that was a room. It was set up across from the offices of the Chief of Naval Operations, and supposedly access to it was very limited - the Chief himself and certain of his officers. I went in. As I told you, I was supposed to be the contact man from ONI, so I would go in to make sure that as far as the Far East was concerned they had as much information as I did. Then people started thinking that the room was too open, too many people saw it and that kind of thing, so they tended to pull back a little bit. Particularly the communications people were worried that something might give away the code-breaking business. Ridiculous, in my opinion, but nevertheless they held to it.

Then, of course, I had to have some kind of a basis for studying Japanese ship locations. I had a little chart room in the sense that I had charts of the Pacific stuck up showing where the Jap fleet was and that sort of thing. We had to keep some kind of a system of that sort. My function was not duplication, but to make sure that the central chart room had my two bits' worth on it. I think the British Desk did something similar to that, and later on, of course, they had a regular proliferation of these chart rooms. After the war started, there was one Admiral Turner had in his own office and this other thing sort of fell by the wayside. After Admiral King came he turned that thing into his own Intelligence Section, which was headed, as you know, by George Dyer. But that didn't take place until well into 1942.

So that is your conflict. War Plans versus ONI. It existed and it continued to exist right up until the war broke. In 1941 there were all kinds of things that I found out later on - the war warning dispatch of the 27th of November - all that sort of business went out and we in ONI were in the dark.

Q: This without regard to ONI?

Adm. M.: That's right. You see ONI was also prohibited from drawing any conclusions from information at all. That was solely a function of War Plans. We could only send information out, without the approval of War Plans, in case it was nothing but pure facts. So you'd get a dispatch like this: "Sent to Commandant, Sixteenth

McCollum #7 - 329

Naval District, Commander-in-Chief, Asiatic Fleet, Commander-in-Chief, Pacific Fleet" - this was on the 3rd of December 1941 - "Highly reliable information has been received that categoric and urgent instructions were sent yesterday to Japanese diplomatic and consular posts at Hong Kong, Singapore, Batavia, Manila, Washington, and London, to destroy most of their codes at once and to burn all other important, confidential, and secret documents."

Now, we were inhibited from saying, "Invite your attention that this is a prelude to war." We couldn't say that, but this was a fact, so we could issue that, which we did.

[Note: In my discussion of a conflict of views between the War Plans and Intelligence divisions of the staff of the Chief of Naval Operations, I may have over-stressed that ONI and its successive Directors took umbrage at the War Plans Division being assigned the duty of estimating enemy intentions. This was part of it, of course. No staff division enjoys having its assigned duties handed over to another staff division. It implies incompetency and lack of trust by the Commanding Admiral, in this case Admiral Stark. It is not unusual in my experience on naval staffs to find that the Admiral prefers the advice of one or more of his staff assistants over others regardless of staff cognizance. In these instances, however, estimates, orders and instructions issued under the imprimatur of the Admiral are usually made known before issuance to the cognizant staff division.

[Here we have quite a different situation. The Navy Regulations, The Organization of the Office of the Chief of Naval Operations and the Office of Naval Intelligence Manual (approved by the Chief of

Naval Operations) all placed the responsibility for estimating "enemy" intentions upon ONI -- Why not then change the appropriate instructions when this function was transferred to War Plans? Neither Admiral Stark nor his Assistant Rear Admiral Ingersoll was willing to do so.

[This was the point our successive Directors James, Kirk, Wilkinson were trying to make. They had no luck. This put ONI in the unenviable position of being blamed for anything that went wrong in the estimates without the benefit of any knowledge whatsoever of what estimates were being sent to our major Commanders-in-Chief. By this device ONI was put on the spot whereas War Plans sheltered itself under the anonymity of the CNO originator numbers. It was this responsibility without due consultation that our ONI Directors were protesting against.

[In other words if War Plans was now making the estimates why not say so? Neither Stark or INgersoll have had anything to say on this subject.]

I had been away, as you know, in England from August to October 1941 and it was while I was in England - I had had this concept for some time - that we ought to set up an Intelligence Center in the Pacific and probably in the Asiatic to serve the needs of the Commanders-in-Chief in those areas. The British had that set-up and I was very much interested in seeing how it operated. For instance, Admiral Sir Andrew Cunningham, who was Commander-in-Chief of the British Mediterranean Fleet, had his intelligence center located in Alexandria and it operated very effectively, or it seemed to me that it did. They more or less patterned themselves after the combined operations intelligence center that existed in London to serve Admiral Sir Dudley Pound, who was the chief of naval staff, and, as I say, Admiral Cuningham had one out in Alexandria. They had branches in other places to serve the Commander-in-Chief, Asiatic Fleet, originally at Hong Kong, but it was moved almost at once to Singapore because Hong Kong was never considered secure. They served a function there and it seemed to me we ought to have something like that of our own.

So when I came back from London I suggested the set-up of such a thing and it was enthusiastically received. Admiral Struble, who at that time was the plans man for ONI - ONI had a plan section - and I were designated to design one of these things, which we did. Knowing the dislike of most of our flag officers for large staffs, we deliberately undermanned the center, but the one that we designed for the Pacific, for instance, I think had a staffing limit of 119 people, mostly officers.

Q: Where was this, Cavite?

Adm. M.: No. This was to be the first one - Cavite already had something working fairly well. You see, the Asiatic Fleet wasn't much of a fleet. You had one cruiser - maybe two, I think there was a light cruiser out there at that time - and one squadron of destroyers, four-pipers, plus about 6 submarines, and that was it. The rest of them were a bunch of junk. The Houston, I believe, was the flagship at that time. The Marblehead was the light cruiser. That was an increase because before that they hadn't had that. You had a destroyer tender which was the merchant ship Blackhawk which had been tender out there ever since I can remember, and they had a lot of curiosities - a ship called the Abarenda with a top speed of seven knots. I think she'd been confiscated from the Spanish during the Spanish-American War.

Q: They had the Lanakai also.

Adm. M.: I didn't know about that. The only relatively modern ship was the flagship, the Houston. The Houston and the Augusta used to alternate in that job. Now, the point is that you came right up here to the outbreak of war with ONI constantly sending out information which we did, but I saw no action. I got considerably worried because I hadn't seen any warning dispatches going out to anybody, so in the latter part of November I sat down and drafted a memorandum about what had been going on in the Far East, and I presented that memorandum - I took it up to the Director of Naval Intelligence, Admiral Wilkinson, and he took it down to Admiral Stark. Admiral Stark called a conference of his principal flag officers, and I went over what the Japanese had done in preparation for war, step by step, outlined it and so on, and the question was deliberately asked whether the Pacific Fleet and the Asiatic Fleet had been warned and it was answered in the affirmative, they had been warned and they had been ordered to take every step necessary to be ready for war.

Q: This was asked of the group by Wilkinson, was it?

Adm. M.: No, I asked the question and it was backed up by Wilkinson, and Turner, Ingersoll, and Stark repeatedly assured both Wilkinson and me that adequate and ample warnings had gone out. We hadn't seen any. Now, for instance, there's a war warning dispatch but I hadn't seen it, but I had to back up this information. I had drafted another dispatch and they said it was unnecessary to send it because of the others. Finally, I raised so much sand in Turner's office that he showed me the dispatch - the war warning. That was the first I'd seen of it. This was the 1st of December. This war warning dispatch, as you know, went out on the 27th of November. So here we're talking about four or five days later. By this time, you understand, we had established out in the Far East a Naval Attache in Siam, at Bangkok, and we had a Naval Observer in Batavia. We had a Naval Observer at Sandakan, a town on the Makassar Strait, we had a Naval Observer at Medan, which is in Sumatra, which is on the Strait of Malacca. We had a Naval Observer posted at Hanoi who was under cover as a consular agent. We had suggested to the Commanding General in the Philippines the establishment of a shipping observation network and offered to man it, and we were politely turned down and told that if they were going to do anything of that sort MacArthur was perfectly capable of setting up his own system, or words to that effect.

You had a conflict there because with the supposedly impending liberation of the Philippines, making them an independent nation. The Army had for many years said that the Philippines were untenable from the defense point of view, and were very loath to put any more men in the forces in the Philippines. MacArthur started with his usual flamboyance - now, understand that I'm a very great partisan of MacArthur - he started just plastering the War Department with his view that the Philippines could be held indefinitely, that the Philippine Army which he had been training for five years was a fine fighting outfit and ready to go, and so on. So along about in the summer of 1941 it had an effect. The War Department actually came around to the view that with the addition of a few planes out there, the Philippines could be held indefinitely, just like MacArthur said. So you had a different strategic thinking taking place. MacArthur didn't need any navy out there - although the Navy did make plans at one time to bolster the Asiatic Fleet by two divisions of cruisers or something of that sort, until Admiral King started pulling everything into the Atlantic. But you see, we then had a problem on our hands, and on the 3rd of December ONI issued instructions to the Naval Attaches at Tokyo, Peking, the Assistant Naval Attache at Shanghai, the Naval Attache at Bangkok, to destroy all of their codes and cyphers and all secret and confidential material whatsoever, and be prepared to be taken over, and that when this had been accomplished to send us a code word. The word, as I remember it, was Gobbledygook. I got the chop of the Director of Naval Intelligence on it, and went down and personally saw that this message was sent. All messages, under instructions from ONI, relating to the Far East were relayed via or through or to both the Commanders-in-Chief of the Asiatic Fleet and of the Pacific Fleet, both going and coming. I had the confirmation in my hands that this had been accomplished by the 5th of December, which was a Friday, I believe.

Q: Must have been Friday.

McCollum #7 - 335

Adm. M.: Well, it was the 5th anyway. This Gobbledygook came bouncing from all over the world on this business. Major Williams at Shanghai was ordered to get out and to get out at once and take up his war position, which was down there near Foochow. Well, Williams figured he could disguise himself as a Chinaman. I don't know how he figured a blond could do it, but he tried it. And the result is that he was captured. He was the only man we lost. He was captured by the Japanese and put in that Bridgehouse jail at Shanghai where he spent about a year - he and his sergeant. Of course, we'd expected the Naval Attache at Tokyo to be interned along with the Embassy staff and that of course was Smith-Hutton, the Attache, and a fellow named Stone who was the Assistant. The yeoman there was a fellow named Wagner. Maybe Wagner hadn't but the rest of them had diplomatic immunity. And we expected the Naval Attache in Siam to be interned. You remember that, at that time, Siam was supposedly pro-Japanese and they had a very clever general who was the head of the government, Pibul, I think his name was. He very cleverly sat on the fence, first one side and then the other, but we didn't have any illusions but that the embassy would be sequestered because Siam technically went to war with us. Nobody paid too much attention to it, except the people who were put in the jug.

So these things did go out, but it was accomplished with some difficulty, and that about tidies up the business of the war between War Plans and ONI. But I repeat that I don't believe that the Intelligence position in this discussion was in any worse position than, for instance, Ships' Movements and a number of others. Traditionally, the director of Ships' Movements division was considered to be the premier staff division chief within the office of the Chief of Naval Operations. That followed the usual set-up in there. For instance, on a fleet staff such as I served on - and I use this as a typical example - you have a Chief of Staff and you have an Operations Officer who, in every case, is the next senior on the staff to the Chief of Staff. Then, the rest of them are more or less technical people. You have the Flag Secretary and the Flag Lieutenant, which in later years was a sort of social aide to the Admiral, but of course originally he'd been a communications man, the flag hoist boy. Then you have a rather large Communications Division headed by the Fleet Communications Officer, and so on. And you have that pretty much duplicated here, and almost invariably the Director of the Ships' Movements division, while he was in that job, would in almost every case be selected for flag rank. Kimmel had had the job at one time, Taffender, who was Chief of Staff to Admiral Richardson, had the job at one time.

The same was true of ONI. I served in ONI off and on or knew about it from 1922 on, and there were only two officers that were directors of ONI that failed to make flag rank, only two. And that means - the job usually only lasted a couple of years, but some of them had more tenure than that. The thing is that the naval staffs never were clearly visualized by naval people. I keep going back to the Army because they had adopted the German system, or whatever system, this 1, 2, 3 business, which the Navy came to during the war. But at that time they weren't, and every time the command would change, a new Commander-in-Chief would come and throw away the old staff book and write up a new staff manual. It was almost typical. But there wasn't a clear-cut understanding within the Navy as to how these staffs were supposed to function, and there was a stumbling through and over the fences from one place to another with a certain amount of consequent confusion.

The one objection that the Navy always raised to the Army system was that it was too rigid, too stereotyped, it wasn't flexible enough. Well, that may have been so. I don't know, but that was the reason that they didn't want one. They wanted one that was flexible, so it could be changed around.

Q: They had inflexible characteristics, too!

Adm. M.: Yes, that's right.

Q: Would you tell me about your trip to London?

Adm. M.: Yes.

Q: Who manned your office while you were abroad?

Adm. M.: The next senior in line was at that time Major Boone of the Marines. He was head of the China branch in the Section. Lieutenant Commander Watts was head of the Japanese Section, and ably assisted by Hindmarsh, then a lieutenant I believe, was more or less office coordinator. And of course these people were all assisted by their civilian specialists. In the case of Watts, he had John Clark there and one or two others. Boone had Emmanuel Larson and a couple of others, and so on. That was it.

I never quite understood why I was selected to go. Of course, by this time Kirk was Director of Naval Intelligence.

Q: And who was in London? Paul Bastedo?

Adm. M.: No. Bastedo was over there, but the man in London was Charlie Lockwood. Charlie Lockwood relieved Kirk as Naval Attache in London. At least, he was there when I got there. I first met Lockwood out in the Asiatic Fleet many years ago and later on when he was commanding one of the V-boats (submarines). He was, as you know, a submarine officer, also a very good officer on any score.

To go back a little bit, in May, I think it was, of 1941 Vice Admiral Godfrey, who was the British Director of Naval Intelligence, I've forgotten his first name, but anyway he was a "Sir" as most British Naval officers of that rank are, visited ONI in Washington. He brought over with him, curiously enough, a man that has become very very famous since then. He was a Commander in the wavy-navy, they called it, in other words a Reserve Commander named Ian Fleming. They and one or two others visited Washington and were shown the works - taken around to anything in ONI and down into the Communications Intelligence set-ups and so on and so forth. Then, of course, following custom, the British were pressuring us to return their visit. So there was a return visit arranged and there were four of us selected to go. Why, I don't know, one was a British Marine officer named Archie Wrangham. The new head of Foreign Intelligence of ONI, and a very fine officer, too, a full Captain Sherwood Picking was the head of the mission. Then, the assistant head of the British desk, Walter Chappell, and me.

Q: The head of Foreign Intelligence was Bode at that time, was it not?

Adm. M.: Bode had just been relieved. This chap was Captain Sherwood Picking.

Q: You set off for London. What was your objective?

Adm. M.: To return the visit of the British DNI. In other words, they'd made a call so we were returning their call.

Q: Yes, but other than that was there something specific you were looking for?

Adm. M.: Well, Captain Picking who was head of Foreign Intelligence supposedly had the data on what we were supposed to do, and I was supposed to assist and see how they handled matters in the Far East and that sort of thing, and pick up anything else I could. But my instructions were very vague. We had a Captain who had the full instructions. I had just been promoted to Commander as of July of that year. Then we had a chap Walter Chappell, who was a Reserve officer and a very nice fellow, and this Archie Wrangham, a British Marine Major, and I don't know how he got himself on an American mission, but he did. The British you know are great for liaison and he was a liaison. Anyway, at that time, to fly to England was a very chancy business, and the Army Air Forces had set up a flight route that went up to Newfoundland, then across to Iceland, and from there to an airfield in the north of Scotland called Prestwick. It was strictly an austere type of flight...

Q: And fairly uncertain, wasn't it?

Adm. M.: It was very uncertain. The planes were not heated and we tried for a couple of weeks around Washington here to get a definite priority on these planes. It was useless to go up and try to hop a ride with them without a priority. Anyhow, it developed that we could only get priority for two of the four of us, and the quicker and more immediate way to go was selected by Captain Picking and Archie Wrangham, this liaison character. They took the Army Air Force plane. Chappell and I after some rustling around finally managed to get seats on a Clipper. At that time the clippers were flying boats, as you know. They went from New York and hopped down to Bermuda, then from there to Horta in the Azores, and from there on to Lisbon. So Chappell and I, feeling very sorry for ourselves, were on this clipper and we had, frankly, an amazing voyage over there. We were held up overnight in Bermuda. We hadn't expected to be held up there. It was rather uncomfortable but we were put up at Pan American's expense at a hotel there overnight because the waves were too high at Horta for this plane to land. That seemed to be the key thing. You had to wait for the seas to quiet down sufficiently to land. Finally, after a day or two extra there, we managed to get to Horta, and there it was repeated again. We had to wait there because the waves were too high to take off. So we waited another night and finally did land at Lisbon, an amazing place, just full of spies or so they said. Portugal was neutral.

Q: A place of intrigue!

Adm. M.: Yes. My goodness, I didn't know where to go so we immediately went out to the Naval Attache's, a fellow named Post. We hadn't had a naval attache there before, but the idea of expanding these observation places throughout the world – a fellow named Charlie Post, who had resigned from the Navy and had been recalled and put on active duty as Naval Attache – he put us up out at the Palacio Hotel at Estoril. Of course, Estoril is a European type spa, you know, centered around a big gambling casino, and so on. It was the damnedest thing in the world. You'd sit in the bar at the Palacio Hotel in the afternoon, and someone would nudge you and say, see that guy, he's a German spy; you see that woman over there, she's the mistress of the prime minister of Spain. You know, for a country boy from Alabama that was a most intriguing atmosphere!

Anyhow, after a day or two at Estoril we managed to get setas on a KLM plane – that's a Dutch outfit – a single-engine job, and flew to England.

Q: Across the Bay of Biscay!

Adm. M.: Yes. We flew to England in it and we landed at Bristol just about dark. England at that time in the dark was certainly not a good place to be. It was the most harassing kind of a place. Chappell and I finally managed to get on a train to London. We arrived at London about eight o'clock at night to find the Naval Attache's office shut up tight and nobody knew where Charlie Lockwood was nor could we find out and we couldn't stumble around London in the black-out indefinitely. We were supposed to have had reservations made for us at the Connaught Hotel. Well, Chappell and I went to the Connaught. We got nowhere. They'd never heard of us. Apparently we didn't have the proper letters of introduction. Next day it developed that they had heard of us but by this time a taxi-man took pity on me and I holed up at a place called the Bristol. I think every British town has a Bristol Hotel. Chappell used his banking connections and was put up at the Carlton, the best. I know I was very much impressed with the Carlton. It was the first time I'd ever seen it. They had steam-heated towel racks - pretty good idea. You'd hang a wet towel on it and it dried out nice and fluffy for you. It was all right. I don't know how they regulated the temperature of the steam.

The next day we went around and we finally found Lockwood in his office and reported to him, only to be told that our two friends, Archie Wrangham and Captain Picking, had died in a crack-up of their plane coming into Prestwick. They'd hit a mountain and killed everybody on board, including our people. It hit Charlie Lockwood very hard because Captain Picking and he had been very, very close friends, in addition to being great admirers of each other, and he could never quite get over it. Then, to cap it off, I got a dispatch from ONI, you're the next senior, go ahead and carry out your instructions. I had no instructions. The instructions were all in the hands of the guy that was killed, if there had been any instructions. I just hadn't the foggiest idea of what to do. So Chappell and I fiddled around.

We looked into the DNI set-up there, the Division of Naval Intelligence. They were very cordial indeed, and I met some very delightful fellows. The head of the Asiatic Section there was a fellow named Steve Barry who was a retired officer recalled to active duty, and two or three other people of the same ilk. All of these people were retired and had been recalled to active duty. The bulk of DNI were that kind of people. The war had been going on and every available line officer would be shunted to sea, with a few exceptions, so their places were being taken by other people who were perfectly adequate. Steve Barry, for instance, later on was the Intelligence Officer for the Naval component of Mountbatten's Navy out in the Indian Ocean.

Q: In Ceylon?

Adm. M.: Yes, but originally it wasn't based on Ceylon, it was based some place on the African coast called Killendini and moved to Ceylon later on. I also met a fellow who came in very handy later on named Lamplough. He was a Marine lieutenant colonel, and he ended up, I believe, as Mountbatten's head of intelligence after he moved to Ceylon. He relieved Steve Barry. Steve wasn't too well. An awfully nice fellow. We met all these people.

Q: Was Lockwood and his crew holed up in Room 49?

Adm. M.: I don't remember the room number, but he probably was.

Q: You know the book on British intelligence - Room 49?

Adm. M.: I may have seen it, I don't know. Like everything British, you know, you get the impression that it's not very well organized, that it's rather diffused, but it does work - that's the main thing, and after spending some time with Steve Barry I realized I wasn't getting anywhere. They weren't doing any more than just keeping posted on these so-called country monographs. In other words, they weren't really an active intelligence outfit at all. They'd get the dope and...

Q: They were the library!

Adm. M.: They were the library, more or less, and that's about what they were doing. You had a small coterie of people up around Godfrey who were doing the estimating of what was going to happen and so on and so forth, including this Ian Fleming who was very much interested at that time - why, I don't know, why DNI were doing that - issuing propaganda. In other words, they were fooling the Germans, so they would issue these fantastic things which they expected the Germans to believe, and Ian with his wonderful imagination was the guy who wrote them, and he did a damned good job, too. He had me to lunch one day at the St. James Club and I was duly impressed. I understood later on that the St. James is one of the most exclusive clubs in London. I don't know, but anyhow he was a nice fellow. He was personally very nice and very agreeable and tried to be as helpful as he could. But it became quite evident that certain elements of the intelligence function which I knew that they had were not being disclosed to us, principally the degree of success that they were having or had had with breaking the Japanese codes and cyphers. Of course, that had been shown to Godfrey while he was here in Washington. I finally approached Admiral Godfrey about it and he said, "Well, you know, McCollum, that's a very difficult thing to do because we don't control that. I couldn't possibly offer anything of that sort because I really don't have any control over it." I said, "Well, Admiral, who does?" and he said, "Damned if I know," which of course was ridiculous. He said he didn't control it but it did exist. Somebody controlled it, obviously.

I was pretty disgusted. I was sitting around having dinner with

Frank Watkins, who was on the naval staff there, at the Senior Club in London, and after dinner a rather nice looking but elderly - at least older than I was - fellow came and sat down, wearing the uniform of a lieutenant commander in the Navy, our Navy. We sat and chatted around and Frank said, "Well, Mac, how are you making out?" I said, "Well, I'm getting the usual god-damned British run-around. I've got to sit down and drink tea with these people for a couple of weeks, I reckon, before I get to know them really. I mean they approach rather slowly." This older man spoke up.. His name was Paul Hammond, incidentally, and he and I got to be very good friends later on.

Q: A New York banker!

Adm. M.: I didn't know who Paul Hammond was. I had no idea who he was. He said, "Well, Commander, perhaps I can help you." I said, "I'd be grateful for help from anybody," but I didn't think there was much to be done. I thought it was just a matter of time. Well, Sir, I had made it a point never to go down to the Admiralty before about 9:30 in the morning because that gave people time. They were open all night.. People were sleeping on cots and so on in their offices, that's true, but they actually, just like our Navy Department, more or less started to function along about 9:00 in the morning and the boys needed about half an hour to read over their latest dope and get their meetings and so on out of the way. So I never got down there before about 9:30 or a quarter of ten.

Well, on this day I walked into Admiral Godfrey's outer office and the Admiral came bouncing out and said, "McCollum, where in hell have you been?" I said, "Well, I've been at my hotel, Admiral." He said, "Well, you know, the Chief of the Naval Staff wants to see you at once." "See Me?" "Yes, get up there," he called a guy and said, "Take him up."

I went up there and went in and in the outer office - and as you know, in the British Navy, the flag secretaries to flag officers are invariably paymaster branch people. So here was a very fine-looking and a very nice Paymaster Captain sitting at the desk, in a small office, and he said, "The Admiral will see you at once." I was wondering what in hell I'd done wrong. Fleet Admiral Sir Dudley Pound looked up at me and said "How are you making out?" I said, "Fine, Admiral," and he said, "The hell you are. My friend Paul Hammond tells me that Godfrey and his gang are holding out on you. I want you to know that there's nothing that's going to be held out and I've just instructed Godfrey to take his hair down and get off this secretive kick and give you the works." -- or words to that effect

Q: So you had talked with Paul Hammond?

Adm. M.: I met him there, but I didn't know who the hell he was. I had no idea. Apparently, Paul was an old yachting companion of Dudley Pound. Paul was quite a yachtsman, I found out later on. He sailed in the King of Spain races and that kind of business. I think he belonged to the Sewanhaka Yacht Club out on Long Island. He took me sailing when I was up in New York after the war. I learned one thing, keep your damned trap shut. The most innocuous-seeming guy may have powerful friends around.

But anyhow it was helpful, because from then on they went through a lot of secret hocus-pocus, but I did get a pretty good idea of what they were doing. You see, that kind of thing, code analysis, in England had been handled technically by a private corporation. The people who sponsored it and had the control of it was the Foreign Office. The Army, and the Air Force, Navy, all contributed money and people into this common pot. Theoretically, as a great many other thing were, it was a private, non-government corporation. I don't know how it was set up under British law. In other words, in theory, it was not a government endeavor at all. Actually, it was controlled and the taps turned on and off by the Foreign Office and had been for centuries. The working elements were scattered out in various places out in the country. A lot of that stuff was done in the university towns, near university towns, Cambridge or Oxford. Rather pleasant.

Q: So you went to all those places?

Adm. M.: I went to a number of them. I did go to Oxford and was very much impressed. They were putting out these Isis papers, more or less area studies, sort of pre-invasion of places and so on. That was being done by a staff of Dons, College Professors, anyway, there at Oxford at this particular time. Maybe the other Isis papers or other works were being done in other places, I don't know.

We had a very pleasant relationship over there, and one thing that I did learn in addition to this business of setting up these Intelligence Centers which I had known about vaguely before, and saw how it worked and how the information was channeled to the COIC there at naval headquarters in London from both Alexandria and

Singapore. I was quite impressed.

Another thing that I discovered was something that I hadn't thought about before, is that they had a naval architect and a staff of two or three people within the DNI itself, and the minute any information on a ship came in - a cruiser, we'll say - these fellows started putting that information down and trying to fit it in to a naval architect's drawing of that ship. And it would be amazing how you could take bits of seemingly unrelated data and by the process of trying to synthesize it into a drawing start making sense out of it.

Q: This was an early form of a computer, wasn't it?

Adm. M.: Yes, well, you brought it in and put it on a drawing, so when you got through you had a drawing of a warship, along with the turrets and all the rest of it, your profile, and side, and so on. And it was very good. So when I got back to Washington I put that idea in. By this time the director of ONI was Rear Admiral Wilkinson and he was enthusiastic about it. We picked up Sam Smiley out of your division...

Q: He was on the German Desk.

Adm. M.: Well, Sam, I found out, was a ship-model nut.

Q: He loved them. There wasn't anything he didn't know about ships.

Adm. M.: So we set up an office there with Sam to do this kind of thing, and I understand they were quite successful at it. We had done it after a fashion by these Japanese models that I mentioned, that we had made over here. But it was amazing how you could fit that in, you know. Much earlier I had had an example of that back in the late 1920s when I was Assistant Naval Attache in Tokyo. We acquired what purported to be a drawing of a new Japanese cruiser, and we got it, quite frankly, through the Italian Naval Attache who obviously had bought it. Our Naval Attaches were under strict orders not to buy any information because they were afraid they'd get compromised. That didn't seem to inhibit our Italian friend, but he was worried because he couldn't speak or read Japanese himself and he didn't dare put this kind of information in the hands of his translator who, as in every other Naval Attache's office, was a Japanese national. He'd heard that I could read this stuff so in exchange for my translation into English which he would then convert into Italian, he would let us make copies of this thing. I had the job of doing it of course, so I made copies of it, and you know this old printing system where you take something and put a blue piece of paper on it and hold it to the sun, or something of the sort, and the lines come out. Well, that's the way it was done, and wash it out in the bath tub. And the more I looked at this darned thing, the more I commenced to doubt its authenticity. Of course, in profile, it all looked fine, turrets here, two stacks there, the mast, and so on. I looked at this thing and finally I got the plan drawing, looked at this plan drawing, and I all of a sudden realized that these were three-gun turrets. The Japanese, to my knowledge, had never had a three-gun turret. The only people stupid enough to have such a turret were the Americans. We did have three-gun turrets. The British continued to stick with two-gun turrets, but we Americans had three-gun turrets, and so far as I knew we were the only maritime power that had three-gun turrets.

So we duly copied this thing off and said it was supposedly a model of a Japanese cruiser and gave its name, I've forgotten what it was, but said that in studying this thing the Naval Attache's office was very dubious that it was, in fact, a Japanese ship of any kind, but was under the impression that it was probably a copy of the plans of one of our own new cruisers. After two or three weeks we got the word back that our surmise was correct!

Q: Tell me, the British were cooperating greatly in interchange of information, were they doing it on the level of the code-breaking? Did they share their knowledge, their progress?

Adm. M.: Yes, they did. As a matter of fact, in the first place we were very, very much ahead of them in relation to Japanese things. The British, I don't know why, were very slow about Japan and I got a very poor impression as to the validity of a lot of their information in relation to Japan and the Japanese Navy.

Q: Could it have been their proximity to Germany?

Adm. M.: Yes, partly that. In other words, they were preoccupied and had been for years with Germany, but I had always thought that they were very effective in the Far East. But their intelligence about Japan was inferior. There isn't any question about it. We were way to hell and gone ahead of them in knowledge of the Japanese Navy and so on and so forth. For instance, you know the Japanese built a class of cruiser, the Furutaka class. There were three or four ships of that class, Furutaka, Kako, etc. I don't know whether

McCollum #7 - 351

Furutaka was the class name or not, but there were four cruisers. When the Japanese, you know, along with everyone else, put down a ship - this was still going by the so-called London Naval Treaty - a light cruiser carried no more than a 6-inch gun and a heavy cruiser carried no more than an 8-inch gun - so you all of a sudden had a class of cruiser - it wasn't the Furutaka, I forget which one, with guns stuck all over the place, and they were 6-inch guns which classed them although they were of a tonnage...

Q: They were light cruisers.

Adm. M.: They were light cruisers, but their tonnage was bigger, pretty close to 10,000 tons, as long as they stayed just under 10,000 and carried no bigger than a 6-inch gun, all right. Well, we in ONI had found out that, sure, they were carrying 6-inch guns now but the mountings and so on were all set inside of the turrets of these ships to be converted to 8-inch guns. But, of course, they couldn't convert as long as they were bound by the treaty. Of course, the difference in addition to the additional weight of metal an 8-inch shell as you know the old rule-of-thumb formula you cube the thing and divide by two or something like that, and you get the weight of the shell. An 8-inch shell weighs approximately 250 pounds as against a 6-inch shell which weighs about 105 pounds. I may be off on the weights, but that's approximate. And, of course, the range for an 8-inch gun is a few thousand yards greater than that of a 6-inch gun. And our information all pointed to the fact that these cruisers were so designed that as soon as the London Naval Treaty expired, which it did in 1936, regardless of all this nonsense about whether it's a light cruiser or a heavy cruiser, disappeared, and you then said, OK, they could put in the 8-inch guns and those were the guns that were shooting at us in the Solomons a little bit later on. We had said so all along in ONI. The British took great exception to it, in spite of Sir Oscar Parks who was the editor of Jane's Fighting Ships at that time, they were saying that the Japanese would never do a thing of that sort. Our information was all to that effect, but the British were sticking with it, that these were 6-inch guns and that was it so far as they were concerned.

They had their drawbacks, the same as we did. In other words, they weren't quite flexible-minded enough in some respects. Their technical people were just as hard-headed and adamant as our own, but I didn't get a good impression of their information on the Japanese Navy, or for that matter on basic Japanese capability. Their data and information on Japanese shipbuilding capacity, which is essential in some respects, was woefully missing. Somebody had forgotten that one of the most important civilian ship yards in Japan was located in Nagasaki, and there were big carriers building down there. Mitsubishi at Nagasaki built them. Of course, by this time, Nagasaki was an out-of-the-way sort of a port, people didn't go there very much any more, and it never was much more than a coaling port. And of course their Navy yard at Sasebo, which is on the Japan sea coast on the island of Kyushu is not easily accessible. It's a beautiful place, its location physically, and a very capable Navy yard indeed. Their data dated back to about 1881. Well, it was worthless. It's difficult in that mountainous country such as Japan is, to build graving docks because it requires a lot of blasting out of very hard rock. Once you get them built, they're wonderful. They're hard to destroy. But the building is costly. They can't just take bulldozers and scoop out the sand and put cofferdams and so on around there to keep them tight, like we can in a good many places. Puget Sound is an example of a yard that was not easy to build because it sits on rather rocky ground, as you know, and that rock is hard and had to be blasted out. In the old days blasting techniques hadn't been too well developed for that sort of work. But they just didn't have it, in my opinion, and I reported that when I came back. Admiral Godfrey asked me what I thought of it and I told him that I thought that in some respects we were better than they were and would be very glad to put our data at their disposal. He said, sure, "I know that. When you get back we'll a arrange that. I'll take care of the arrangements." Was it with Dewar? Who was the naval attache here at that time?

Q: There were so many of them.

Adm. M.: Well, they did, they rotated through. I've forgotten. Anyhow, we were to give it to the British naval attache over here and he would pick it up from there, and anything we wanted in return... So we established a very good working interchange on an exchange basis.

McCollum #8 - 354

Interview No. 8 with Rear Admiral Arthur H. McCollum, U. S. Navy
(Retired)

Place: McLean, Virginia

Date: Wednesday morning, 3 March 1971

Subject: Biography

By: John T. Mason, Jr.

Q: Last time you talked about an Intelligence Center which you observed that the British had set up and you were intrigued with it and its effectiveness. You reported it to Washington and the idea was that we would duplicate it in a sense in our own service. Tell me about that.

Adm. M.: The British Admiralty, much more so than our Navy Department, ran the war tactically as well as strategically. The Commander-in-Chief of the Home Station, for instance, took his tactical orders as we would call it, from the Admiralty; and the Admiralty had set up a center which they called a Combined Operations and Intelligence Center, COIC, and in that center they had an officer of the rank of commander or above from the operations side, who was assisted by an officer of slightly lesser rank from the intelligence side. The Intelligence man's job was to filter and evaluate on the spot, immediately, intelligence that came in of a tactical nature, and these fellows were empowered in the name of the Chief of the Naval Staff, Admiral Sir Dudley Pound, to issue tactical orders to the Commander-in-Chief of the Home Fleet. Now, that was the center in London. They had such a center with more elaboration, actually, set up in either Port Said or Alexandria, I've forgotten which -

I rather think it must have been Alexandria. And the function of that center was to render an intelligence service and to coordinate an Intelligence Service and Tactical Operations service for the Commander-in-Chief of the Mediterranean Fleet, who, at that time, was Admiral Sir Andrew Cunningham. That center also engaged in a certain amount of espionage. They had an element that did espionage and also sent in reconnaissance probes to develop information, in other words, they ran intelligence operations to develop information of certain places that were of interest to the CinC. But the function of that center was primarily to serve an Intelligence function for the Commander-in-Chief of the Mediterranean Fleet, and it was under his orders. In other words, he or his staff would say, now look, we need more information on this area. This was the outfit that went out and got it, or developed it. They also were tied in, I understand, with the code-breaking set-up in London in some form. I don't know just how. In other words, the information that was available in London was available in Alexandria and that also was digested and was available immediately to the Commander-in-Chief of the Mediterranean Fleet.

Now, originally, there had been a rudimentary set-up of that sort at Hong Kong. Some time before the Japanese entered the war, that center was removed to Singapore, and one of the most prominent members of that center was a man whom I had known well in Tokyo, Sir George Sansom. Sir George Sansom was a Japanese linguist. When I knew him in Tokyo in 1928-29, he was the Commercial Counselor of the British Embassy, he has subsequently written several books, one a history of Japan, a Cultural History of Japan, he called it, and it was very, very good. He's a very able person and also a very nice man. I did not know, except by reputation, any of the officers in it, but the purpose of that center at Singapore was to service the Commander-in-Chief of the China Station. And, again, you have a set-up in which you have essentially an intelligence function, both operations necessary to gain information and so on, but again directly under and subject to the command and direction of the British Commander-in-Chief on the station. At that time, he was, I believe, Vice Admiral Sir Geoffrey Layton. I later got to know him very well - when I say very well, I mean as much as a fairly junior Captain can know a man who's a full admiral, when my ship was lying at Portsmouth after the war, because he was Commander-in-Chief at Portsmouth. He had served on the China Station. I was very much impressed with the British COIC set-up because I had said some years before that what we needed was to establish such an outfit.

Now, to do intelligence as we had to do in those days we had to assemble and read over - somebody in an intelligence organization, or some group, must read over, or at least look at and make some kind of an evaluation of every scrap of information that comes in, if it's only to look at it and say, this is worthless and throw it in the waste basket, or file it for future reference, and so on. It takes a considerable staff of people to do it, because you get these rumors and everything else flowing in and so on, but some kind of a digestive apparatus has to be set up , and it can't be small.

I had urged some such set-up as that because I had been convinced since some years ago that if we had taken the Far East Section of ONI, for instance, and established it in San Francisco and let us send radio messages back to Washington, we probably would have been more listened to.

In Washington, so far as the Far East was concerned, the Far Eastern Section of ONI was trying its best to fulfill, you might say, that intelligence center function for the Chief of Naval Operations. We did set up a thing of that sort. It took a while to do it and get approval, and Admiral Struble, at that time a Captain, was the plans officer of ONI, a very brilliant man. He came to me and said he didn't know too much about it, so he and I got together and we devised what we thought would be a suitable table of organization, to use an Army term. In other words, a staff setup with sections and so on for an Intelligence Center to serve the Commander-in-Chief of the Pacific Fleet. That was our main fleet out in the Pacific opposing the Japanese. The Asiatic Fleet was in the process of disintegration. We were able to devise a thing of that sort, and after much study came up with an organization and in March of 1942 I was sent out to Pearl Harbor to discuss the subject with Admiral Nimitz and his staff and to see if we could persuade the Admiral to set up such a center, and we did.

We had planned originally to fly to Pearl, but it was pretty impossible. Flying in those days was just sporadic...

Q: That was a flying boat, wasn't it?

Adm. M.: A flying boat. Martin's flying boats, they were, and they were run by Pan Am under contract, I suppose. Places on them were very hard to get, and you only had about two flights a week out of San Francisco for Hawaii, and they frequently would get to a point of no return and come back because they were running out of gas, and so on.

There was an Army officer and an Army Air Force officer to go with me because we were anxious to bring in the intelligence function into a joint sort of a thing, where we would have Army and Air Force participation. And we did. A Colonel named Pettigrew - Moses Pettigrew - who was the deputy head of the Far East Section of MID, Bratton was the head of it. Mose was his deputy or assistant, and an Army Air Force officer who was a very nice fellow but knew nothing of intelligence, he was a crack pilot, but an older man named Ted Koenig, went with us.

We finally took a transport out of San Francisco and it took us five days at sea to get to Pearl Harbor, part of it because of what they thought was the necessity of zigzagging part of the time, which, of course, doesn't let you go as far, you lose distance and time, but we finally arrived safely. I had not known Admiral Nimitz before except by sight, but most of the higher officers on his staff I had known in one way or another. I had served with them. At that time, his chief of staff was Rear Admiral Milo Draemel and Milo Draemel had been captain of the Pennsylvania the fleet flagship and also, for a brief period of time, was Operations Officer of the Fleet when I was his assistant at the time when Admiral Hepburn was Commander-in-Chief. Bill Fechteler, who had been pulled off of something, I had known well. Later on Fechteler was Chief of Naval Operations. And so on. Walter DeLany, Admiral DeLany, was Fleet Operations Officer and he had also been Kimmel's Operations Officer, so you had the remnants of Kimmel's staff, or some of the remnants of Kimmel's staff, all over the place. Nimitz was at this time in the process of slowly replacing, rebuilding, and regrouping his staff because there had been a psychological trauma on the part of some of these people, naturally, that had been serving under Kimmel and were there when the attack on Pearl Harbor was made. Nimitz apparently realized this and he was trying to restore confidence, which he did. He was very much occupied because, you understand, by the time we got there this was getting along towards late April or early May and practically all of the available forces in the Pacific that Nimitz had at his command were down in the South Pacific, where under Rear Admiral F. J. Fletcher, I believe it was, they engaged in the Battle of the Coral Sea on 4 - 8 May 1942, wasn't it?

Q: Yes.

Adm. M.: They were very much engrossed with that situation, and of course you had Rochefort and his Communications Intelligence organization which he had, in a large measure, improvised. Some of these people, for instance, were bandsmen from the fleet band, that is, the Commander-in-Chief's band. We figured we didn't need any horn-tooting but they could read and do a certain amount of research work. But it was growing and he had a lot of fellows there with him. He had, of course, these language officers that I've mentioned and he had several top-flight cryptologists. I mentioned one fellow named Dyer, another one named Ham Wright. Those two were excellent; among the top. They had another fellow named Hockins who was very good at what they called traffic analysis. I just mention these names because they were the tops, and their whole attention was concentrated on trying to do something about the Japanese naval codes other than the one rather innocuous one sort of like what we might call a service cipher.

Then, of course, the Fleet Intelligence officer was a fellow named Eddie Layton, and Layton depended for his information very heavily on this communication intelligence. He was a very brilliant man, but he hadn't thought too far ahead in the sense of area intelligence. He had considered himself primarily as the Intelligence Officer on the staff of the Commander-in-Chief of the Fleet and, as such, any information that came in to him, he would try to interpret and pass it on to the Plans Officer or to the Operations Officer, as the case may be, and probably to the Admiral himself, on occasion.

Q: He saw himself as an activist!

Adm. M.: Well, I wouldn't say an activist because - of course, he had a difficult situation, but I mean he hadn't thought far enough ahead in the sense of developing some outfit to go out and actually procure information and, if necessary, to suggest operations designed to develop information. It takes that kind of thing.

I did get in to see Admiral Nimitz. He was, as usual, very gracious and as friendly as he could be, and after I'd been there about a week....

Q: Was he receptive to your idea?

Adm. M.: I didn't present the idea at this time. I let it percolate up. I talked to Admiral Draemel about it and so on. What I was there for was to see if we could coordinate the intelligence and so on and so forth.

Finally, one day, much to my amazement, Admiral Nimitz sent for me. He sat down and he was very much at ease, and he said, "Well, young fellow, what have you done around here?" I said, "I've done this and looked into that and so on and so forth. I've tried to get the Army Air Forces to think in terms of sending out search planes that would be capable of doing it" - of course, we didn't direct anything of that sort, but after all they had to have some kind of search and reconnaissance from there. They couldn't depend entirely on the flying boats of which the Navy had very few. The trouble with the Army Air Forces, as I've mentioned before, was that at that time their training in navigation or aerial navigation was inferior, particularly in their fighter planes, they weren't equipped with the stuff that is necessary to get back to home base. If they flew out of sight of land, they were lost, broadly speaking. They just hadn't thought in those terms. So something had to be done about that and we did talk to both the Bomber Commander and the Fighter Commander, and also to General Tinker who was Commander of the Army Air Forces in the Hawaiian area. He was later lost on a bombing mission where he had no business going, in my opinion, right around the Battle of Midway. After all, he was a Major General and it would seem to me his function should have been back at his headquarters. Anyhow, the old pilot, you know, just couldn't stand it. There's an airfield named for him - Tinker Field, I think it is, in Oklahoma. He was a very fine man and someone said he was either whole or part Indian. Anyway, he was known as Indian Joe Tinker.

Q: What was Nimitz' reaction?

Adm. M.: Nimitz' reaction after I talked to him, he said, "I've heard that you've been talking around about an Intelligence Center for the Pacific Ocean Area. Tell me about it." Well, I told him about it and explained how we'd set it up and how we thought it would work. We had the package in mind and were only waiting for his go-ahead to send it in and so on and so forth. He said, "Sounds pretty good. How many people is this going to take?" I said, "Well, Admiral, we have tried to keep the original establishment down to a minimum."

Q: You knew this was his watchword?

Adm. M.: We knew it was not only his but every officer, every admiral in the Navy, was "agin" big staffs. They just couldn't seem to realize that they were fighting a campaign now, and they continued to think in terms of relatively small tactical staffs. He said, "How many would it take?" And I said, "We've figured and trimmed every corner, Admiral, and it takes about 120." With that, he rocked back in his swivel chair, and let out a roar you could hear all over the place, laughing. And he said, "McCollum, how in the world am I ever going to get 120 people of this kind of a thing on board my flagship, the Pennsylvania." I finally said, "Well, Admiral, that's not the concept." I didn't dare tell him that in my judgment he would never go to sea on the Pennsylvania, but I said, "The concept is this. This outfit will be set up here at your base for you, and when you go to sea on the Pennsylvania a select group, such as you select, four or five, will be sent with you on the Pennsylvania, but this organization will be feeding them the information and evaluated data right to them and to your staff."

"That makes a little more sense," he said. "O.K. Go out and discuss it with Layton and Lynn McCormick (McCormick being the Plans Officer) and DeLany, if you want to, and get it fixed up."

So we went into a discussion of about three days on this subject, and Lynd McCormick, the new War Plans Officer, more or less sharing the discussion, and we finally came to an agreement...

Q: Did McCormick and Layton go with the idea?

Adm. M.: Layton, curiously, was rabidly opposed to it, at that time. he never did quite accept it.

Q: Why was he opposed to it?

Adm. M.: I don't know. But, you see, Layton continued to serve throughout the war as the Intelligence Officer of the Pacific Fleet Staff. In other words, he was the Staff Intelligence. And later on he came to draw his intelligence from the Intelligence Center for the Pacific Ocean area. After the thing grew and grew and grew, the Intelligence Center of the POA, as they called it, Pacific Ocean Area. Nimitz was the Area Commander and also the Fleet Intelligence Officer of the Fleet Commander, but a lot of his information and also a lot of things that had to do with the tremendous number of maps and so on that were necessary for an amphibious operation were all cranked out by this Intelligence Center. A fellow named Joe Twitty, a colonel of Engineers - I'd known him in Japan, he was a Japanese student on the Army side, a brilliant fellow and very agreeable. The Army promptly promoted him - what the Navy would call a spot promotion - from lieutenant colonel to brigadier general, and he was then put in command, you might say, of the Intelligence Center for the Pacific Ocean Area. He did an excellent job. There you had the code-breaking and everything else joined in one, but the initial outfit of about 100 to 120 people was sent out under the man designated to head it up, Hillenkoetter. Hillenkoetter was later made head of the Central Intelligence Agency after the war. Hillenkoetter didn't like the job, I don't think he ever wanted it.

Q: Did you have trouble assembling that number of people for the intelligence duty?

Adm. M.: No, there wasn't any trouble there, because most of them were Reserves and they didn't know what they were getting into exactly, but it sounded good. Our main difficulty was in getting, you might say, a regular officer who could get easy entree into the Commander-in-Chief's staff and have sufficient rank to carry some weight with his opinions and so on, and who was a pretty good administrator. The rest of it, these eager beavers could do the job on their own pretty well. And you also had a nucleus, as I've said, in the Communications Intelligence set-up which was running under Rochefort there. So we had a ready-made set-up to start with in certain respects, and it only remained to set it up in these divisions of screening the intelligence, putting out the reports, and that sort of thing as was necessary.

Q: And Hillenkoetter became the man?

Adm. M.: Yes. Hillenkoetter was what they called the officer in charge of Pacific Ocean Area Intelligence Center.

Q: Had you known him before?

Adm. M.: Slightly, yes. He was Assistant Naval Attache in France when I was over in the Mediterranean commanding the Jacob Jones in 1938-39. I'd known him slightly at the Naval Academy. He was among the top graduates, scholastically, in the class ahead of me at the Naval ACademy, class of 1920, and I had known him there slightly. Intellectually, he was a very clever person. He did not want to be in intelligence during the war and took steps to get out. So we were fortunate in being able to pick up a fellow named Bill Goggins who was also of the same class. Bill had been executive officer on the Marblehead, I think it was, in the Java Sea and had been badly wounded and burned and so on in action. He was hospitalized for some time but he had now come back to duty. Bill's naval specialty, other than being a line officer, was Communications, so he was a logical choice. He was a very steady-going, down-to-earth kind of a fellow, and when Hillenkoetter pulled out Goggins...

Q: How long was Hillenkoetter there?

Adm. M.: About four months.

Q: Oh, just to get it going.

Adm. M.: Yes. In other words, he was spending, actually - and this is no derogation of Hillenkoetter - he was pulling all the strings he could to get to heck out of there. He didn't like the set-up, apparently, and after about four months in the center he took command of a destroyer tender, I think it was, called the Dixie and spent about six months out in the Solomon Islands area. Then came back here and I don't know what happened to him the rest of the war. Next time I saw him was in 1945 when he was on duty in the Bureau of Naval Personnel and getting ready to take command of the Missouri.

Q: How did Joe Rochefort take to this?

Adm. M.: Joe Rochefort welcomed it. He said it was just exactly what we needed, we've got to get it out here, but we just can't seem to get this thing off the ground, because we've got to get this thing going. I'll fit right in with this anywhere you want me, and that was fine. Of course, it worked that way. In other words, Joe just took his whole organization lock, stock, and barrel, the code-breaking, the attack on Japanese communications, under the direction of Rochefort immediately became a part of the Intelligence Center. There was no ill-feeling, nothing but the greatest of cooperation and so on, on Rochefort's part.

Q: Layton and Rochefort cooperated greatly from the beginning as...

Adm. M.: Well, they had a very close personal relationship, and I think in some ways, looking back on it, I think it may have militated against it. You see, Layton and Rochefort had gotten acquainted with each other, so far as I know, when they came out to Japan on the same ship, in 1929.

Q: Yes, they had. This was the basis.

Adm. M.: Yes, that's right. Eddie Layton was a bachelor. Rochefort arrived out there with his delightful wife, Fay, and their little boy was about five or six years old, I reckon, Joe, Jr., and for a while Layton was taken in as a sort of paying guest with the Rocheforts. In other words, Fay was a sort of house mother, and off and on since then they had seen each other and known each other, but there was sometimes a professional difference of opinion. Joe was very hesitant to go around the corner or to bypass Layton in any way, and Layton was a fairly junior Lieutenant Commander at the time. He had initially - and I'm speaking of the time on Kimmel's staff - Layton apparently had not established any real close relationships with the Admiral himself and was a little bit hesitant about bypassing or going around such people as Captain McMorris, for instance, the Plans Officer. So that, in a sense, Rochefort was a little bit inhibited. Now, that's an opinion, purely and simply, but you did have that inhibition and it wasn't until Rochefort realized that Layton probably, for one reason or another, didn't have the entree that he, Joe, thought he should have, that Joe took it upon himself to go directly to people like Admiral Nimitz and Nimitz' Chief of Staff.

Q: I think their relationship probably was helpful in the sense that Rochefort felt that he necessarily should interpret some of the material he got, and this, of course, was contrary to existing standards, wasn't it?

Adm. M.: It's hard to say, Dr. Mason, where recipients come in interpretation. Just like any other form of intelligence, you get something in a code, that comes in and it has to be related to something else, and frequently the fellow that's doing the code-breaking has to have a good deal of what we call collateral information in order to break the code. So you do have right there, at that point, a certain degree of evaluation. You can't have it otherwise.

Q: You can't avoid it.

Adm. M.: No, you can't avoid it.

Q: Nor should you avoid it.

Adm. M.: No, nor should you. Particularly the translator and the code-breaker should feel perfectly free to say, "I think this," or "I think that," and then if you don't you can always discuss it with him and come to some other conclusion, if it's indicated. Now that is particularly true, of course, in the realm of traffic analysis. All of a sudden, the ships' call signs change, or part of them change. What does it mean? You can't sit up in an ivory tower over here and say, it means so-and-so. These fellows who are actively listening in on this thing, even down to the radioman who picked it up, all have an idea on the subject and lots of times their ideas are the best source of evaluation you can get. The same is true of radio bearings, for instance, compass bearings, or whatever you call it. All those have to be interpreted. How far away is the darned thing? Is it bouncing off ionosphere or what? Those things frequently change.

And, another thing. Every radio operator has, as you know, what is termed, I believe, in the business a hand. In other words, after you've listened to a fellow for a while, just like a telephone voice, you know it's Joe Zilch sending - that's his hand. I'm not a radioman at all, but they tell me that it's almost as distinctive as a signature. The guy doesn't have to say who he is. For instance, if a radioman is transferred from this ship to some other ship and starts using another call sign, you immediately know that he's been transferred. It may mean something, it may mean nothing, but that incidental intelligence, or evaluation, if you will, comes from those sources, and just as with other sources, you have to evaluate it as to whether this is likely or not likely or probable, based on all of the data that comes in to you. You get a bombastic report from a Japanese Captain, for instance, that he's sunk umpteen ships. Well, is it true or isn't it true? Who are we to say it isn't true? The Captain is reporting to his Admiral that he's sunk all these ships and so on, well, sometimes you can even look out of the window and see it's a damned lie because the ship is lying right there at the pier.

You have to do a certain amount of that, but this all is part of the evaluation process and I don't know that you can have a separate group set apart to do nothing but evaluate, because you can't. They have to be themselves in rather close touch with where the information comes from and how it comes.

Much later on in the war, two or three months before the Battle of Leyte Gulf, we had been successful in setting up a coast-watching station on the island of Mindoro and I had gleefully reported to the Admiral that we had it there. The island of Mindoro is that place that sits on the most important passage from the China Sea into the

Mindinao Sea, and the most important passage there is the Apo East Pass. We had these people set up and we had a very fine officer in command, but he was a little bit of an eager beaver and it was almost impossible to control those people from a far away place. I had warned him thoroughly that he must train his people and screen them and so on. And the day after I gleefully reported to the Admiral that we had it covered, we got this message: "One hundred Japanese battleships sailing down the Apo East Pass."

Well, Kinkaid almost fell out of his chair laughing! He said, "McCollum, what in the hell is all this?" And I said, "Let me look into it." But you know those kind of people we had to use, a lot of them were semi-savages and they couldn't count very good, and to those people anything that carried a rifle even, was a battleship. The Japanese, at that time, had these little sailing bankas up and down there - they had groups of them that they would send out on occasion - and when the guy counted up to ten or three and there were more than that, he just picked out a number and somebody sent it.

So, you have to have that kind of evaluation somewhere. You just can't take some of these things at face value. You've got to have some knowledge of where and under what circumstances that information is being sent. That applied also to this set-up here - I'm getting way ahead of the story...

Q: Well, how long did you spend in Pearl in the development of this center?

Adm. M.: About two weeks. It was merely selling the idea and making sure that everyone was happy, and making sure that they had a place to go, and talking to the Commandant of the District to be sure that he would set up the physical office space necessary.

Q: Was that Admiral Bloch?

Adm. M.: Bloch, yes. He was very receptive and also a very fine man whom I had known some time back. When I say I knew all these fellows, you understand, they were very senior people and I was quite junior, so I wasn't very chummy with people like that, never expected to be, but I did know them. I had a great admiration for Admiral Bloch. I'd known him when he was Commander of the Battle Fleet and also known him when he was Chief of the Bureau of Ordnance. He was a very unflappable type of person and very competent, in my judgment. He said, well, we've got this and we'll put the pieces together and get it ready for your people all the way. He had even lists such as desks, typewriters, and the electric current that would be required, and so on, in such a set-up. He went right ahead and when the first of them arrived in about a month, or later, everything was set for them. They moved right in.

Q: How wonderful!

Adm. M.: There's always the business of getting settled down and finding out who's who and where the other guy lived around the corner, and so on and so forth. But that's the way it is.

Q: Did you have a chance to see Nimitz again before you left?

Adm. M.: Oh, yes. I called on the Admiral just before I left, of course, and expressed my appreciation for his cordiality and also to tell him good-bye. You had to do that, you know.

Q: And was he glad that the job was all...

Adm. M.: Well, he said, "Well, McCollum, we're going to give it a whirl and I hope it works. It sounds like a good idea and I hope it works." He also gave me a letter and a picture to bring back to Mrs. Nimitz and tell her that "I'm too busy to write too often, but otherwise I'm fine," and that sort of thing. So when I got back to Washington, one of the first things I did was call on Mrs. Nimitz. It was the first time I'd ever had the privilege of meeting her. She was living in an apartment. I don't know where it was. It was up here off Connecticut Avenue. She was a very charming person, and the Admiral was personally very warm to me, as I understand he was to everyone. As I say, I had not known him before. I knew who he was by sight because most of the time that I'd been in Washington before that he'd been chief of the Bureau of Navigation, and I'd see him from time to time.

That more or less set that up, and that outfit grew to amazing proportions. Later on in the war, they had several thousand people in that thing. And with General Twitty presiding over it...

Q: By that time, Nimitz had gotten used to it.

Adm. M.: Not only that, he depended on it - well, he depended on it through Layton, usually, but that didn't prevent the General from coming in. This was part of the POA joint staff which was then in the process of being rigged up, some Navy, some Army, some air people, and so on. Out in Australia where I served later on under the supreme command of General MacArthur - MacArthur never had such a staff. He called it a joint staff, but it was in no sense joint. It was a typical Army staff. All of the head staff positions in there - for instance, G-1, G-2, G-3, chief of staff, and so on, were all Army officers. He did have attached mainly as liaison three or four rather unhappy naval people. He needed that to put a little window-dressing around and make it look like a joint staff. I've always thought that.

But, for instance, General MacArthur's - talking strictly intelligence now - General MacArthur's G-2 was, when I arrived there, a Colonel Willoughby and almost immediately after I arrived in Australia - this would be in the fall of 1942 - was promoted to Brigadier General. General MacArthur insisted on having direct contact with the Intelligence Chiefs of the three services. Now, you see, General MacArthur's concept of his organization was basically in three groups. In other words, you had Ground Forces, Air Forces, and Naval Forces. The Ground Forces were commanded by an Australian general, General Sir Thomas Blamey. His intelligence chief was a brigadier, also an Australian. That was the ground forces. Then you had the air forces' intelligence which was headed up usually by an Australian Air Commodore. For a long time it was Air Commodore Hewitt. He left briefly and came back. A very nice fellow. And they had developed, after the British fashion, one of these air-plot things and they put it to very good use.

Now, of course, the air forces - all of them, the Allied Air Forces - were under the command of an American officer who, at that time, was Lieutenant General George Kenney. And the Allied Naval

Forces were under the command of an American admiral. When I arrived in Australia, it was Vice Admiral Carpender. So any other people who were on the GHQ staff was a typical Army set-up. In other words, you had your 1, 2, 3, and so on down the line, and interspersed in there, as a sprinkling, there was - for instance, General Willoughby had a naval airman attached to his G-2 group for a while and he was usually very unhappy. He'd be more or less called in to okay this without having seen it. None of them liked it and they took steps to get out as soon as they could, unfortunately. But that was the set-up.

Nimitz was in the process of differentiating two things. One was his Naval Command, which was the Fleet. And the other one was the Joint Command, which was Army, Navy, and Air. I never have known exactly how the whole thing resolved. But from the Intelligence point of view, right up to the end of the war, General Twitty was the commanding officer - or the officer in charge - of the Intelligence Center for the Pacific Ocean Area, and that embraced all of this outfit. They sent their data in to Layton, and Layton had access back and forth and that, in turn, stemmed up to Nimitz. And when Nimitz did go to sea, as he did later on, from Pearl Harbor to Saipan...

Q: He did go there, yes.

Adm. M.: It doesn't make too much difference. Anyhow to the Mariana Islands.

Q: Well, he set up his headquarters in Guam.

Adm. M.: Layton went along with selected officers from this outfit. Rochefort also initiated, about this time, a system of supplying linguistically qualified officers to the staffs of task force commanders, notably Admiral Halsey, and equipped them with a staff of radio people and so on, and their job was to listen in on the spot to Japanese radio communications, to see what they could glean and what they could interpret. And at first, as I've remarked, they were very successful. Later on, when the Japanese got a little smart, like we got a little smart, too, their utility deteriorated, because the security of communications improved to the point that by the time they could break down some codes and get them translated and look around, from a tactical point of view, it was too late for any help. But they were useful and gave the Admiral a feeling of confidence. Admiral Halsey was very loud in his praise of the young man sent to him and he insisted on taking him with him wherever he went. He was a very fine officer.

Later on, I followed the same thing out in the Philippines. In other words, we had officers who had spent a long time in training in the geography and the culture and the history of these places. Of course, our problem was quite different there. We had the coast-watcher service. We were in immediate contact with the enemy. We were the only element in the Navy all during the early part of the war that had almost daily personal combat contact with the enemy. As a result, we had a great list of stuff that came in that it was almost impossible to digest. A commander coming in on a rotation basis as ships went there, coming in with a force of, we'll say, a cruiser division and a destroyer squadron moving into the Bismarck

Sea area or the Coral Sea area, it was strange to him. Sure, he'd read the geography books and so on, but here was a guy we'd put on his staff who said, all right, we've got a small army installation over here, and this information is coming from there, and in my judgment it means so and so, or, in my judgment, it means nothing. After the Battle of Leyte, I had several of these flag officers who came over to me - hunted me up on Admiral Kinkaid's flagship - and said, "You know, that young man you sent over there, when can I get hold of him again? He's invaluable." Well, he was invaluable as long as you could keep him within the scope of the area in which he knew something. But, if you took that same young man, we'll say, out of the Mindinao Sea or the Coral Sea, or something like that, and shifted him up the line to the Marianas, he was just another guy in a blue suit up there, because he didn't have the background, and that's what it takes in that kind of business. But that outfit did function very well.

Later on in the war, I was just amazed. Of course, as I have intimated, Joe Twitty was an engineer officer of the Army. He was a West Pointer - I've forgotten what his class was, probably around 1926 or 1927 - and, as you know, in the Army at that time, maybe now, the group that's responsible for mapping combat maps and all that sort of thing are the engineers. So one of the first steps that Joe Twitty took after he took command of the Intelligence Center, P.O.A. was to set up a map bureau, and the enormous number of maps and so on that are necessary, or thought to be necessary, for an amphibious attack were produced right there in the printing plant of the Intelligence Center, POA, and cranked out by the hundreds,

Note: by accident page 377 has been omitted in the original effort at pagination...p. 378 follows on page. 376.

little ones, big ones, with the elevation and so on. We did somewhat the same thing out there in Australia. Of course, later on, as the art of aerial photography developed and we learned to be able to triangulate things, optical things on maps, and so forth, as the photograph would come in to us, we could even locate Jap gun positions and stuff like that, and the likely size of the guns that were there - amazing. So that sets up the Pacific Ocean Area, and after about two weeks in Pearl Harbor, where we were greeted with a great deal of cordiality all the way around, the three of us, Pettigrew, Koenig, and myself came back, and we came back the same way we had gone. No, we didn't, we flew back.

Q: Were you going back to the Far East desk?

Adm. M.: Yes. When we landed in San Francisco, why, I got the news about the break-up which I think we've gone into of the Japanese-language school at the University of California at Berkeley. I think we've covered all that before.

Q: Yes, you have.

Adm. M.: After two or three days around San Francisco which were rather futilely spent, I did, without telling anybody, sneak off down to Los Angeles to make a visit to my mother-in-law, who was living there with her younger daughter, and I spent about one day there. Mother Benninghoff was feeling very, very lonely at the time and I hope I pepped up her morale a little bit. Dr. Benninghoff, as you know, was a minister and he would more or less supply a pulpit in various places, but his real love was back in the midwest and the east, so he was first at a little school in Missouri and so on. Mother Benninghoff was trying to get him to come and stay in Los Angeles, but that didn't suit the old gentleman. But I did go and spend about two days down there visitng with Mrs. Benninghoff and her younger daughter whose husband had been captured by the Japanese and was incarcerated in French Indochina. He was one of the head accountants of the Standard Vacuum Corporation, which was a Standard Oil operation out in the Far East. His name was Dennis.

From there I came directly back. I was amazed, I came on an Army plane and flew to places that I'd never heard of before, Phoenix and Olathe, Kansas, back to Washington. As I told you, then we started trying to reconstitute the Japanese-language school, which was eventually put at Boulder. We've gone into that, I think. Now I think, maybe, we should swing back to talking about what happened in and around the Far East Section of ONI shortly after I got back from London.

Q: All right.

Adm. M.: When I left ONI Captain Kirk was the Director, and I left on 25 August 1941. Chapelle and I got to London in quite good time. The Clipper took us from New York to Lisbon and from Lisbon we went to Bristol and from Britsol by train to London. I spent about two weeks in London, then rather than travel by ship coming back, we took the Dutch plane back to Lisbon. There we got hung up for the better part of three weeks, and it was a very touchy thing because the season for flying from Lisbon to the Azores by Clipper theoretically expired in October because of the winds and the North

Atlantic storms and so on. So we were hung up in Lisbon, or actually Estoril, where we were staying, for the better part of three weeks because of the unavailability of any plane space to sit in. We finally did get away from there and we eventually landed at New York. We came through Bermuda and I took the opportunity while we were there to go and call on Admiral Jules James, who had been the Assistant Director of ONI when I had gone there and was in the process of setting up and commanding the American Naval Base at Bermuda.

I then got back to Washington and by the time I got back Admiral Wilkinson was the director and Captain Kirk had disappeared to sea. Admiral Wilkinson, whom I hadn't known at all before, was very kind and very pleasant to me. At this time somebody had fleeted up and filled in as head of foreign intelligence. I believe it was Moore.

Q: Sam Moore, wasn't it?

Adm. M.: Well, they called him S. N. Moore - Nobre Moore. He was lost, you know, with his ship at Guadalcanal. He was an awfully nice fellow whom Captain Wilkinson had picked up when trying to get ONI direct access, you might say, to the CNO without being throttled at every turn by the director of war plans and was having some small success.

When I got back I found that this fortnightly summary which I have mentioned before, a paper sort of thing, an intelligence digest, had been swung around under the dictation of Captain Turner, the Director of War Plans - into half-way projecting an attack on

Siberia by the Japanese. I took two or three days to look the situation over and I couldn't see any change in it at all, so far as the direction of the major thrust to be expected by the Japanese. So the next one of these things went out, the Siberian fairy tale was thrown out of the window. It didn't sit too well, but we managed to get it through. You had that constant contest, and then the ukase came down that we could not send out any - we mustn't make evaluations of the intelligence, we could only report facts. In other words, the Japs are burning codes, that's a fact. We couldn't say burning codes means - is one of the preludes to war, that's opinion or evaluation. So it was a very difficult situation in which to operate, and we were frequently not told anything. Anyhow, it seemed to me that the situation - this would be in October now of 1941, to be precise, I think it was about the 11th of October. I went to Captain Wilkinson and I said, "Look, this thing in my view is getting more and more serious and I would like your permission to put my section on a twenty-four-hour watch basis. I want to have either myself, Lieutenant Commander Watts, or Major Boone, in that office day and night. In other words, we slept down there, so that we were in constant touch with anything that was coming in.

At that time there had been set up within the Navy Department what they called a Command Watch, and that was where it should have been set up, in the Division of Ship Movements, which is the operating arm of the staff of the CNO, at that time headed by Admiral Brainard. At that spot you had immediate telephonic contact with the Chief of Naval Operations and the Assistant Chief, who was Admiral Ingersoll, and with Admiral Turner, the Director of War

Plans, and so on. This was just telephoned through the switchboard, not a private line, so that it was open to listening in on under certain conditions. Anyhow, the function of the so-called command duty officer was to take immediate operational action in the name of the Chief of Naval Operations, should the necessity arise. Naturally, being where we were located and so on, our immediate preoccupation was with the Atlantic. The war was pretty hot at that time in the Atlantic. Admiral King was trying to help set up things in Iceland, and so on. A German battleship would get loose and all hell would break loose.

I was taken off of that watch in order to be able to function in this ONI thing. I couldn't do both, because these command duty officers would go down there and a cot was made up and they slept right there in the office. They came in at, say, five or six o'clock in the afternoon and they spent the night there, and they were relieved about seven or seven-thirty in the morning when the regular staff came to work. So I was taken off that list so that we could set up practically the same thing in my section in ONI. To use a naval term, we went on a heel-and-toe watch. There was myself, Watts, and Boone, always with an assistant or two along to help. When the day's work was over, usually around four o'clock, whoever had the watch stayed there until six o'clock the next morning, when we came back to work. If it was a holiday, you stayed right on. That explains why I personally was down there on Sunday morning, December 7th. Watts had the night before, which was Saturday, and I came in and relieved him about seven-thirty. At that time, I lived in Arlington and in the driving of those days it was less than a ten-minute drive by car from where I lived to Main Navy. Watts lived only two or three blocks further away. Boone lived in an apartment here in town. So, none of us were physically more than ten minutes' drive from the Navy Department, which is an item that has sometimes been lost sight of.

Anyway, so far as the Far East Section of ONI was concerned, we went on an approximation of a war footing with watches and immediate attention to things, in about the middle of October or the first of November 1941. And that's the condition we were in when the attack on Pearl Harbor took place, and that's why we were able to send out our messages when we did. In other words, when we got the message, a code message, broken code, diplomatic code by the Japanese Foreign Office ordering their offices in London, Paris, and all over to burn their codes and confidential papers.

Q: When did that happen?

Adm. M.: That happened about the 3rd or 4th of December. I've got a message which we sent out. We not only did that but we - as soon as we got this - I got hold of domestic intelligence and I said, "I think you people ought to put a special watch on the Japanese Embassy to see if this is actually taking place." They did, and, sure enough, found them toting papers out and putting them in an incinerator and then burning them. So we not only had the code order, but we saw it being carried out. Let me get that paper for you.

Q: The dispatch that ONI sent out?

Adm. M.: Correct.

Q: After getting the intelligence from the Japanese diplomatic code that they were burning papers.

Adm. M.: Not only that, but actual observation at such places as the consulate general in New York and the embassy here in Washington. We didn't have time to get the reports on the observations, if any, from the consulate general in San Francisco.

This is a multiple-address dispatch and it was sent on the 3rd of December 1941 at 1850, Greenwich Civil Time, which would mean about five hours earlier than that here in Washington.

This goes to the Commandant of the 16th Naval District, Commander-in-Chief, Asiatic Fleet, Commander-in-Chief of the Pacific Fleet, and the Commandant of the 14th Naval District. The 14th District, of course, is the Hawaiian Islands, and the 16th is the Philippines. It says:

> "Highly reliable information has been received that categoric and urgent instructions were sent yesterday to Japanese diplomatic and consular posts at Hong Kong, Singapore, Batavia, Manila, Washington, and London to destroy most of their codes at once and to burn all other important, confidential, and secret documents."

That dispatch was sent - released - by Wilkinson. There's no indication on the copy that I have that it was shown to anyone else before release. There is an indication that a copy of the dispatch went to War Plans, it was shown to Op-20G, which is the intelligence communications set-up here, to the Naval Aide, CNO file, 28 file, in other words to all the files. This is on the face of the original dispatch.

At the same time, ONI sent out orders to all of our places abroad that we thought might be gobbled up by the Japanese, to destroy their codes and ciphers, confidential papers, and so on, and report by dispatch when this had been accomplished.

Q: That was the gobbledygook?

Adm. M.: That was the gobbledygook. We made it a standard practice with everything that was sent out of that nature also went to the CinC Pacific and Asiatic, whether you may call it an information dispatch or an action dispatch, they all basically, from a common sense point of view, were the same thing. Under the communications system as it existed, theoretically, in most cases, unless someone had to do something about it quite definitely, you sent it "action" to one guy and "information" to all the rest of them. All of them were equally capable of taking action. The reason I mention it is there had been some argument that in certain cases, Admiral Kimmel only had an information dispatch. From a practical point of view, I can assure you that it doesn't make a damned bit of difference. You sent it "action" Commander-in-Chief, Asiatic, "info" Commander-in-Chief Pacific, Com 14, and so on. It's just a mechanical gadget, you might say.

So, that went out, and, at the same time, ONI issued orders for the Naval Attaches - you see, some time before that, as I think I mentioned to you, ONI in the foreign intelligence aspect had undergone some slight modification. Before that, the colonies, one might call them, or the possessions of the various powers in the area - in other words, India belonged to England, so the man who handled

India was the British desk; the Dutch East Indies belonged to Holland, so the man who handled the Dutch East Indies was the Dutch desk; and so on, around. Same with Australia. That was British. Sometime before that, there had been set up in ONI what they called a strategic area, and the Far Eastern desk was made responsible for the strategic coordination of anything in the Indian Ocean and India and all these places. Australia and New Zealand, which we had never considered part of our bailiwick at all. But we worked, of course, v very closely with what we called the country desks, and there was no friction at all, I can assure you. These guys were only too glad to cooperate and anything that I would suggest, particularly people like your boss, Captain Heard, or Nobre Moore, who was head I think of the Dutch and German desk or something like that at the time, they were glad to help us. It was a most cordial relationship. There wasn't any friction whatsoever, as might have been expected. That put us on the spot, so we suggested observer posts - Captain Kirk started it. We set up what we called Naval Observer Posts and we manned them with retired officers that we could get and with, in certain cases, Reserve officers. So, you see, in addition, they were supposed to be under some kind of a cover, shipping adviser to the Consul, for instance. This was the fellow named Abbot who was sent down to Batavia, which I believe nowadays they call Bandung, and there was a Consul there, so he was there as the shipping adviser to the Consul, but his function was to pick up information and report back and forward to us. We had another one at Medan in Sumatra. We had quite an establishment. We had a full captain down in Singapore who was liaison with the British, a fellow named Creighton, whom

I'd relieved in two jobs before. He had a couple of assistants. We had these shipping advisers, another one was at Sandakan, a fellow named Murphy. And we'd established a naval attache's office in Siam.

Of course, as I explained before, on the China coast we had a kind of a mess in certain ways. Basically, the Naval Attache's office was in Peking. For diplomatic reasons, the State Department did not want to pull out of Peking. Peking of course, hadn't been the capital of China for some time. Chiang kai-Chek's capital originally was in Nanking. He never did move to Peking. Nevertheless, we had certain treaty rights or juridical rights or something like that, and we had, of course, the comforting presence of a battalion of American Marines, a battalion of Royal Marines, or something of that sort. Apparently none of the European powers, and I include the Americans, wished to pull out - you might say, evacuate Peking.

At this time we had in Peking the Naval Attache, who was Major McHugh of the Marines and he was in Chungking. An Assistant Naval Attache, also a Marine major, Gregon Williams, was in Shanghai, and there was sort of a rearguard, a housekeeper type of fellow, in Peking - I've forgotten what his name was - just someone to keep the fiction of an office open there.

So, on the 3rd of December 1941, the same time as we got word the Japanese were burning their codes and ciphers, we sent this message out to all of these posts - Tokyo, Peking, Shanghai, the naval observers at these other places, and so on - to burn all of their stuff because, we didn't say so, but obviously war was coming - and when they got through and didn't have anything more to report they sent this code word, gobbledygook, or whatever it was. I took that and went to Safford who was responsible for the code security and code-destruction messages, and so on and so forth, and showed it to him, and got his advice on how to set it up from a strictly communications point of view. He's the one who suggested the "gobbledygook." I never took to it. I don't like the word, anyway. But that's neither here nor there.

Anyhow, these messages did go out, and they went out on the 3rd of December and, of course, like all these others, they went information to Commander-in-Chief, Pacific, Commander-in-Chief, Asiatic, Commandant, 14th Naval District, Commandant, 16th Naval District, and so on. In other words, the top American naval commander in the area affected knew, or should have known, that our own people had been more or less directed to batten down and get ready for hostilities, that's what it amounted to.

Q: Did they ever signify that fact, that they knew this?

Adm. M.: That who knew this? The high commanders said nothing. To show how important we thought this thing was, we directed all these various addressees to burn their codes and ciphers to relay the acknowledgement that this thing had actually been done through this same chain of command, or what have you. I had the answer in my hand in the Navy Department on the 5th of December 1941.

Q: Did Admiral Stark react in any way to this message going out?

Adm. M.: I don't know. I don't know whether he ever saw it or not. He should have seen it. But when this thing happened my staff had gotten to worrying, gosh, how about war in those places? I said, well, my friend, that's your responsibility. We can't touch that.

The naval governor out there, you know, how about Samoa? And how about this outfit out in - that's building a seaplane base out in Wake? We had the reports of compliance from all - I had it in my hands in the Navy Department on the 5th, which was Friday.

Q: Was Safford far enough advanced with his efforts with the naval code to usbstantiate this information?

Adm. M.: No. Up until then we had, as I say, one naval code as far as I know. It might have been two. But they were of minor security category. So important things would not be sent out by the Japanese or any other command in a code of that relatively low security. I mean code security, you understand. Safford got to worrying about it, so he then cooked up a message and sent it to the governor of Guam and to Wake Island and to the Commander-in-Chief of the Pacific Fleet and to a place called Johnson Island where they were putting up some kind of a base, and so on and so forth, along the same lines.

Q: Was this under the Chief of Naval Communications?

Adm. M.: Sure, Safford was under the Chief of Naval Communications. He apparently got the okay of Admiral Noyes, who was the chief of Naval Communications at that time. There were also some instructions to the Commander-in-Chief of the Fleet, Admiral Kimmel, in the instruction that was sent out by Safford in relation to codes and ciphers, what we should do with them under certain circumstances, and how we could continue to communicate, the technical details.

But the fact remains that by the 5th of December 1941 ONI and Communications had directed the destruction of our own codes and ciphers in certain exposed places. ONI went one step further. We ordered Major Williams to get out of Shanghai and go to his war post, which, incidentally, was in the mountains behind Foochow. The only thing that wasn't obeyed explicitly was that Williams thought that he could outwit the Japanese by another day and he stayed and they grabbed him, which was unfortunate for Williams and for us.

Q: What about your observers in a place like Sandakan? Were they ordered to leave?

Adm. M.: No. They could go back in the bush or something, if they wanted to, but their codes were gone but they could communicate other ways. In other words, they were warned the Japs were coming. Murphy was killed, it seems to me, or died of malaria or something. At that time, I thought he was too old and shouldn't have been sent, but that's neither here nor there. We were scraping the - I don't mean any adverse comment on Commander Murphy's capabilities because he was a very capable person so far as I know, but age was creeping up on him.

Q: You said that one of the recipients for this message that went out on the 3rd was the naval aide. Was there any reaction there?

Adm. M.: I don't know. We had made it a point on these kind of important messages to keep the Naval Aide to the President, who in those days was still somewhat of a personal naval adviser to the President, informed. At this time he was Captain - later Rear Admiral - Beardall, and he was our pipeline for this kind of stuff to the President. I mean the pipeline for ilk such as me. Admiral

Stark had no hesitancy - I've seen him do it - in picking up the telephone and talking directly to the President in the White House, or to the Secretary of War or to General Marshall and so on. After all, you know, 17th and Constitution was only about three blocks from the White House, and Admiral Beardall had an office in the Navy Department. He also had an office in the White House complex, at that time, I think, in the West Wing of the White House itself. He kept an assistant in each office. He didn't have any official title, he was just an assistant to Captain Beardall. But Beardall himself would take this stuff and, presumably, would take it over and discuss it with the President and I don't know who else.

Anyhow, our pipeline for such as me or such as Wilkinson was laid down to be through the Aide to the President. That did not preclude us, of course, from going directly to Admiral Stark and saying we think so and so, and Admiral Stark or Admiral Ingersoll, either one of them, would take action. The interesting thing is that in all this, so far as I know, neither Communications nor ONI ever got an order to do anything about our codes and ciphers from anybody up the chain of command, other than our immediate bosses. In other words, Admiral Turner, Admiral Ingersoll, Admiral Stark, maybe they saw all these things going and said, well, everything's going all right, there's no necessity for us to put in our piece, which is all right, but I mean the initiative came from Intelligence and Communications.

Q: One would have thought there'd have been some reaction, though, because it was such a drastic thing. It indicated something impending.

Adm. M.: Well, you know, on the 1st of December I had written this paper that I've referred to several times and all were agreed that it was impending, and I pointed out that the Japanese Navy, the merchant marine, the country was on a war footing and so on and so forth, the fleets were forming to go here, there, and yonder, task forces were being organized, and so on, right down the line.

Q: There was no reaction from SecNav, either?

Adm. M.: If I remember rightly, at that time, Mr. Knox may not have been in town. He might have been away. I don't know.

Q: What about the Secretary of State?

Adm. M.: Well, what we depended on there was Captain Schuirman later a Director of Naval Intelligence, but at that itme, the Director of the Central Division of the Office of the Chief of Naval Operations. The central division was a thing that was set up - to go back in history a little bit - by Admiral Pratt when he was Chief of Naval Operations back in the early 1930s, to bring in a lot of extraneous things that the Chief of Naval Operations should have been interested in and to act as what the Army would call a secretariat of the general staff. Schuirman was, I think, one of the ablest officers in our service. Anyhow, he was designated as the official liaison between the Office of the Chief of Naval Operations and the Secretary of State, and daily he would come down to my office or send for me and we could go over what we thought, and he would take this stuff over and talk to one of three people in the Department of State, either the Secretary himself, Mr. Hull, the Under Secretary,

Mr. Welles, Dr. Hornbeck, who had the title of Political Advisor.

Q: The Far Eastern Desk?

Adm. M.: No, he didn't have the Far East. He'd been promoted, he'd gone up the line. He was a special adviser or something like that in the State Department. The man who technically headed the Far Eastern Division of the State Department was a fellow named Max Hamilton, who had for many years been Dr. Hornbeck's assistant. Dr. Hornbeck, when I first knew him, was the head of the Far Eastern Division. Hamilton was his assistant. A fellow named McKay was the Number Three in there. These were under the State Department organization and the type of personnel they had at that time. These were under the State Department organization and the type of personnel they had at that time. These three fellows and a number of assistants were what they called State Department officers, in contradistinction to Foreign Service officers, because of the special expertise required for the Far East, there was an adjunct in that office manned by Foreign Service officers. At this particular time, I believe Gene Dooman was the head of this little group and a fellow named Cabot Covette was his assistant. Both of them were qualified in the Japanese language, and they had a couple of assistants around, too. They also had access to Dr. Hornbeck or to the Secretary or the Under Secretary. On two or three occasions, Schuirman would ask me to go over with him to the State Department to make sure that the impact of what he was going to say was understood, and if he didn't get it right I would be there to nudge him or something. On those occasions, I did see the Secretary, Mr. Hull, and I got a very high opinion of him. Of course, who am I to say I had an opinion of the Secretary, but I thought he was very level-headed. Mr. Welles seldom said anything at these conferences, although he was always present. Dr. Hornbeck was quite free with his advice and usually very good. Usually he was backed up by Mr. Dooman. Mr. Dooman has been Counsellor of Embassy - I reckon Cabot Cavelle was his assistant, because Gene Dooman was Counsellor of Embassy in Tokyo.

So, you had a set-up in which there was provision made for this thing to go over. ONI had also set up another system in order to make sure that information that came in to the Department of State, if it was at all pertinent and so on, would get to the Navy Department. We set up another liaison fellow named S. A. D. Hunter. Do you remember Dr. Hunter?

Q: Oh, yes, of course, I remember Sam Hunter.

Adm. M.: He had been in the consular service at one time and was an associate professor or something I believe at Georgetown, and he was a Naval Reserve officer and put on active duty, and because of his knowledge and personal contact with so many people in the State Department that was his job. So every morning, Sam would go over to the State Department and the State Department had set up a special office for him headed by a man named Wilson, who was a very senior Foreign Service officer. In other words, he was a contact officer. Sam would come in my office to pick up what was necessary, and he'd trot over to the State Department with it. Even though they were that close together, by the time you got through the paper mills in each place it was very easy for a delay of two or three days in the process of getting untangled from the necessity of checking it in and checking it out and routing it, and a-1 the paper work folderol that goes on with that.

So Sam was able to come back with any hot dope, so to speak, directly, or take any hot dope over and present it to this Mr. Wilson. In other words, there was every effort made to mesh in an interplay of information, not that it existed but to make sure that the time element in transit would be cut down.

Q: Why, then, in your opinion, did this system fail on this occasion when war was imminent?

Adm. M.: Well, I think this, Dr. Mason. It was generally agreed that war was imminent...

Q: I mean this specific notice that things were pending, why did it fail to make its impact?

Adm. M.: Because we had expected war at any time. I mean any time within the next two weeks. What people confuse with it, is that we didn't know and did not find out that the commencement of war would entail an attack on Pearl Harbor. It might. It might entail an attack on Manila, as it did. And it might entail an attack in other places. In other words, there was no (what we have come to term now) hard intelligence that Pearl Harbor, as such, would be subject to an attack at the outbreak of the war. It should have been understood. It seems to me that anybody sitting out in a place where he's outside of support of something can expect an attack on the outbreak of war. Admiral Kimmel and Admiral Hart had been warned at least on three occasions throughout the summer of 1941 that it was the Japanese and the German custom to attack without warning, frequently on a holiday, and so on and so on. It's very difficult to know what else could have been done. It did have an impact but what were you going to do? As far as I know, the State Department sent no specific instructions to our Ambassador to Japan, Mr. Grew, as to what he should do, nor did they send any instructions to their Ambassador to China, who, at that time was, I believe, Nelson Johnson. And they had a minister in Bangkok, and I heard from "Red" Thomas, who was our naval attache there, that the minister knew nothing of all this business, it all came as a surprise. We had a Consulate General in Shanghai which was almost on a par with the Embassy because it was one of the most important posts in the Far East. Another one in Hong Kong, and a guy in Tientsin. And, so far as I know, the State Department did not send any instructions to these people at all. They may have. I don't know.

Q: Later on, in one of the various and sundry investigations of Pearl Harbor, did all of this come out?

Adm. M.: Well, the matter of the sending out of the messages, the one that I've quoted here that we sent out, as far as the naval side of it, did come out because it was included in my testimony before the Joint Investigating Committee. The State Department, by and large, didn't figure too much in that investigation. The investigation was narrowed in scope to why the attack on Pearl Harbor and so on. The broader investigation as to what happened and what was done all over the Far East, so to speak, never entered into the scope of the investigation. The investigation was kept on the basis of why Pearl Harbor, and that is something else again.

There were a great many people who didn't realize that the Japanese were a competent fighting machine, or refused to realize it. That's even a better term, because obviously from 1931 on, as far as the continent of Asia was concerned, the Japanese Army went any damned place it pleased. The Japanese Navy did the same thing. There was no reason to suppose they weren't competent to deal with everything over there when they wanted to deal with it. The Japanese intelligence service was pretty stupid in some ways, but they were were rather good in others. General Doi, for instance, the spy chief in Manchuria - he was quite good. As a matter of fact, like the Japanese always did, they always like to tack on a British name - they'd say Togo, for instance, is the Nelson of Japan. So Doi was called the Lawrence of Manchuria and he was expected to raise the Mongols and stuff like that. He was quite a guy. I knew him slightly.

The Joint Congressional Investigating Committee which was held in 1945 to 1946 had its perspective narrowed mainly to the Army and the Navy and Pearl Harbor. For instance, it did not investigate the ramifications of the broader things that occurred in the Asiatic sphere, particularly the actions of the State Department, the Navy Department, the War Department in relation to all of their outlying responsibilities. So that in that sense you did have an investigation which, probably very rightly, was narrowed down to a point. None of these other factors that we were discussing, what instructions were sent to the Ambassador, to China, the Ambassador to Japan, and so on, by the State Department ever appeared.

Q: What were you called upon as a witness to supply?

Adm. M.: What the Far Eastern Section of ONI was doing about all this.

Q: What did you tell them? Essentially what you've told me?

Adm. M.: Pretty much. It's a matter of record. I must say that the Committee were very kind to me in many ways. I was, at that time, commanding a cruiser, a new one, which was in the process of undergoing what we call shake-down training at Guantanamo. Our crew had been pretty well decimated attendant to the peace move in this country, and my executive officer, Commander Chew, was left in command. We had expected the <u>Helena</u>, after her period of training to go on to the Panama Canal and out into the Pacific. Admiral Fechteler, who was then commanding the cruisers and battleships of the Atlantic Fleet, called me up on the telephone from Norfolk and said, "How quickly can you get your ship up to Boston? Can your exec take her up there?" I said, yes, the exec could take her up there, he was a very competent officer, but I said, "Admiral, you must realize that in the current state that we're in there, that would mean that he'd have to be on the bridge twenty-four hours a day, because there are no other officers in the ship, with one or two exceptions, who could possibly take over the command, because we've been watered down." So he said, "Well, Mac, how quickly can you shake yourself loose from that Congressional Investigation and get back to Guantanamo, so you can take your ship to Boston?" I said I didn't know but I would do my best to see if I can get away. So, I did. I made a plea through the then-counsel for the committee who was Seth

Richardson, I think, who had been a former assistant attorney general, and Mr. Kauffman, who was his assistant, very smart people. I said, "Look, I'm faced with this situation. I have this command and I've been sitting here now in attendance with the committee for about two months and have not been calledon yet. Would it be possible to get me called on and then excuse me." And they did. They very graciously did that. So I was called on and I did testify in early January of 1946. I was excused by Senator Barkley, the chairman, with the approval of all of them.

But they had all sorts of funny things coming in. I remember Senator Ferguson coming down and he showed me - and he said, "Now, look, this thing looks like a definite clue to the attack on Pearl Harbor." And I said, "Why do you say that?" He showed me a Japanese five-sen piece, which was the equivalent to our nickel and, of course, it was draped with Japanese characters, and one of the characters did look like our figure "7" and it was in fact the Japanese figure "7", but like all coins the "7" related to a date. It was the time the thing was stamped, which was the seventh year of Taisho. He said, "This is proof, isn't it? I mean that these guys had been planning this thing" - the seventh year of Taisho would be about 1919 or somewhere like that.

Well, I mean, you had all these kind of wild rumors going around. I don't know whether that's legalistic or loyalistic, or whatever it is, but the thing was to try to make his attitude, of course, he was in the opposition, he was a Republican, to show that the stupid executive branch of the government knew all these things for ten or fifteen years and didn't act. And here was proof positive by this Japanese nickel!

Q: You also were called to testify at the Roberts' inquiry, weren't you?

Adm. M.: No, I did not testify there.

Q: Were you called by Admiral Hart?

Adm. M.: Yes, I was.

Q: And what did he ask you for?

Adm. M.: Well, he asked me for very much the things you're asking me for, and I told him just like I'm telling you.

Q: And his investigation came shortly after he returned?

Adm. M.: Yes. I don't know when that was, but that must have been - I think the balloon went up there in the Far East... When did Hart leave the ABDA command, so-called?

Q: He left as soon as he could.

Adm. M.: Yes, and I don't blame him. It seems to me that it must have been March or April 1942 before Admiral Hart got back.

Q: That was it exactly, yes.

Adm. M.: That would be my thinking, and I did talk to him, and I did not appear before the court of inquiry that was later on held, I believe at Pearl Harbor, or the Army court of inquiry, also at Pearl Harbor. I did not appear before any of those bodies. At that time, frankly, we were very busy fighting the Japs down there in the southwest Pacific. Admiral Kinkaid, who was my admiral at the time, just said that until this thing settled down a little bit McCollum couldn't be spared.

Q: When you were called upon to testify, say, before the Joint Congressional Committee, did you have to have the approval of the Judge Advocate General?

Adm. M.: No, not at all. I was warned that I shouldn't discuss the techniques and so on relating to code-breaking. The Judge Advocate General at the time was a fellow named Colclough, who was a classmate of mine, and he said that at the direction of Admiral King he'd have to give me this warning. When I was ordered down here to appear before this thing, or seemed to be about to appear, I was ordered down from New York to talk with the chief of staff of the Atlantic Fleet, at that time Commodore Oscar Smith, and he handed me a paper, a secret document that had been issued by ComInch warning everybody of the penalty of being hung at the yard arm, not to discuss anything attendant upon code-breaking or anything of that sort. He said he just wanted to make sure that I knew about it. Then I came on down to Washington. Then went back to Boston and took my ship down to Guantanamo and when I was ordered up from there I came up to Washington to testify.

Q: Did the committee in any way try to question you in that area?

Adm. M.: No, they did not.

Q: They also were aware...

Adm. M.: I presume so. They did not touch on that aspect at all, as I remember. The files, however, are filled voluminously with translations of Japanese diplomatic dispatches marked "Navy Translations," "Army Translations," "Code Descriptions," and they have all of these things in the files. Actually, the files were open and there wasn't any necessity for questioning the likes of me on them. They were, as I said before, very generous in their whole attitude as far as I personally was concerned.

Mr. Kauffman, who was the assistant to Mr. Richardson, handled my examination, I suppose you'd call it. All he did was to put me on the stand, ask a few preliminary questions, and then throw me to the dogs, or the wolves or whatever you want to call them, which was all right. The peculiar part of that thing is that in that investigation the man who was originally to be the chief counsel of the committee, Mitchell, had thrown up his hands in disgust at the way this thing was going to be run and had quit. He had been Attorney General of the United States.

Q: Mitchell, yes.

Adm. M.: Yes, he happened to have the same name as the present attorney general, I understand he was a very highly thought-of legal mind. He went through about a month of this business, threw up his hands in hopeless disgust, I've been told, at the general tenor of this thing and had got out. It was at that time that Mr. Richardson took over as chief counsel.

Well, I think that takes us up to December 7th, except for the things that went on on Sunday morning, and I think, maybe, we ought to leave it for the next time to get into that.

McCollum #9 - 403

Interview No. 9 with Rear Admiral Arthur H. McCollum, U. S. Navy
(Retired)

Place: McLean, Virginia

Date: Wednesday morning, 17 March 1971

Subject: Biography

By: John T. Mason, Jr.

Q: Admiral, today you intended to begin with an account of that fateful day, the 7th of December 1941. You happened to have the watch duty in ONI on that occasion.

Adm. M.: I think, to reach back a little bit, you will remember that we had set up about a month before that a constant, twenty-four-hour watch by the Far East Section of Naval Intelligence. As I remarked before somewhere, there were three of us. I was the head of the division, or the Section. Lieutenant Commander Watts was the head of the Japanese Section, or subsection, and Major Boone was head of the China section and the rest of it. One of the three of us, all of us regular officers, was on duty in the Far East Section of ONI. In other words, when we quit for the afternoon around four or five o'clock one would stay on and slept in the office. He was immediately available. In that stance it was not an ONI watch, it was the Far East Section watch so that we would be immediately available to Kramer and his staff of translators and to the decoders and so on, in case they needed help. I'm sure you understand that in the process of decoding or trying to decode an encrypted message it's frequently very helpful to have collateral information, background, where did this take place, and things of that sort. The whole business of the conditions under which things occurred is sometime very, very helpful to the people who are making an effort to unlock the secrets of the code.

Q: It makes it more intelligible.

Adm. M.: They've got to have it or else they don't know what they're hitting for. It's like clues in a crossword puzzle. You've got to be able to know what the clue means, then that helps you get the puzzle, and so on. So it's been explained to me.

I knew, of course, that the thirteen parts - you remember, on Saturday night in our date here the 6th, I think it well to note that the dates are the 7th in East longitude, that is where Japan lies, one day ahead. In other words, the 7th here was the 8th there. Therefore, the 6th here was the 7th there. Some people have been confused because they haven't realized that. The Japanese, for instance, always speak of the attack on Pearl Harbor having taken place on the 8th of December, which it was from their point of view. As you know, the Japanese Navy did all of their time evaluations on Tokyo time, regardless of where it was, whether it was in India, which was in a different time zone, and so on. Curiously, with the war in the Pacific where it was, the island time, or the "I" zone, which is the Tokyo time zone, minus eight, I reckon we would call it, applied pretty well. They were never more than an hour off one way or the other, but it is worthwhile noting that.

I knew that the thirteen parts were coming in. As a matter of fact, when I left the office on Saturday I knew they were coming in and Kramer was staying on on duty and the translators weren't necessary because this particular note came in in English. It did not have to be translated, but they were translating other stuff and so on, and the fine people that we had working down there, both the cryptologists and the others, stayed on. These people, a good many of them, were civil servants and they did stay. They didn't get any extra pay for it and so on. We didn't have the money to pay them but they stayed on on their own because of their sense of duty, that's what it amounted to. It was very gratifying to get that sort of response which wasn't, I'm sad to say, true in other areas sometimes.

I knew that the thirteen parts were coming in. I stayed on in the office for a while and Kramer came to see us from time to time and I knew that the thirteenth part was coming in, but I finally left; and sometime on the night of the sixth at my home in Alexandria Kramer called me and said rather cryptically that it had come in and he was going to make his rounds, and he briefly discussed over the telephone what he meant by "his rounds," who he was going to see and to whom he was delivering the booklet with the thirteenth part in it. Sometime around midnight he called me again at my home to tell me that he had made delivery but he had not been able to reach Admiral Stark, but he had made the other deliveries pretty much and he was all through and was going home to catch a good sleep for a little while, which he did.

I was taking over from the watch to be on duty all day on Sunday in the Far East Section of ONI. I don't mean to say that I was alone. I had an assistant with me, John Clark, as I remember it, who was one of our very fine civilian analysts, we called them. He knew Japanese and so on, he was a very, very fine man. So I came down as usual, Navy fashion, to go on watch with the changing of the clocks. I came down to the Navy Department and got there about 7:30 a.m. After chatting with Watts for a little while, Kramer came on in and brought up the thirteenth part and we read it together. Then Watts went home to get breakfast.

Q: Will you talk a little about the thirteenth part?

Adm. M.: Well, I don't know. It's hard to recollect. It's all listed of course in the Congressional Inquiry and so on. As you started out, as is not unusual in diplomatic dispatches, it starts out on a fairly low key and builds up and the thirteenth part was building up to a climax which was coming in the fourteenth part, which they said was coming, and at the end of the thirteenth part it was very significant, we thought, there came a sort of thank-you message from the Foreign Office. This was in Japanese, not English, and it was thanking the ambassadors for their work and so on and so forth and telling them, well, it's too bad, but we didn't make it this time but it wasn't due to any lack of effort on your part, or words to that effect. That seemed rather odd. The thirteenth part came on through with the fourteenth to follow.

Shortly after I got in the office Admiral Wilkinson, the Director of Naval Intelligence came into the office and the minute I heard that he was there, I took the whole set of dispatches and went down and discussed the situation with him. We thought it was very important to make sure that Admiral Stark knew about this, so Admiral Wilkinson called Admiral Stark's quarters at the Naval Observatory and found that the Admiral was on his way down to the Navy Department at that time. So I went up and asked the Admiral's orderly, a Marine corporal I believe, the minute Admiral Stark came in the office to give me a ring so that we'd be up there. Around nine o'clock we got word from the orderly that the Admiral was in his office, and Admiral Wilkinson and I went up to see him and showed him the thirteen-part message and discussed the whole situation with him.

Around ten o'clock or maybe a little bit before Kramer came in with the fourteenth part. That was the end. In other words, diplomatic relations were being broken. The fourteenth part was the final. In other words, in spite of everything, you people have wronged us and so on, summing up the case and breaking off diplomatic relations.

Q: This was from the Tokyo Foreign Office?

Adm. M.: From the Tokyo Foreign Office and the Ambassadors here were directed to present the aide-memoire, I believe they call it, or the note in exactly the words it came in. In other words, the Foreign Office did not wish the Ambassador here to add anything or change one line or dot. That's why it came in English. They didn't want to take a chance on these people here trying to calm it down or polish it up. So the note itself came on in English precisely as it was to be presented. In the fourteenth part they said instructions on the timing of the presentation would follow. Well, the fourteenth part was coming in and Kramer hot-footed it over to the White House along with Admiral Beardall, who was the President's Naval Aide, and tried to get it to the President, which they did or someone did, and also to Mr. Hull, the Secretary of the Navy, and so on.

I continued to haunt Admiral Stark's outer office. You know, the office of the Chief of Naval Operations - I mean the actual office that he occupied, suite of rooms - consisted of two or three rooms, and you came into his center room and normally Smedberg, the Admiral's personal aide, or flag lieutenant some people call him, although that wasn't the term used, and a Mrs. Hull who was the confidential secretary to the Chief of Naval Operations occupied the big center room and there were a couple of chairs in there where people sat around. In other words, it was an ante room. As you came in the center door Admiral Stark's office was off to the right and off to the left was a small office occupied by Charlie Wellborn, who was the Admiral's Administrative Aide, and then the office of the Assistant Chief of Naval Operations, who at that time was Admiral Ingersoll. So that was the office layout.

Kramer came in about 10:30 and he said, "We have the final - we've got the instructions for delivery," and it repeated over and over that it must be delivered to Mr. Hull at precisely one o'clock Washington time - it was *your* time. Kramer and I thought about it for a minute and said let's see what the times are. You know, in the Far East Section of ONI, as I've said before, whenever we got anything that had to be worked on a time basis we always thought in terms of the three or four time zones. In other words, Washington time, Hawaiian time, Manila time, and so on, and of course we knew and we had sighted and had under observation the Japanese task force heading west in the Indian Ocean. In other words, heading for the Kra Peninsula where they landed, again on the 7th of December,

Washington time, and we were concerned with that, so on the wall of the outer office there of Admiral Stark there was a time-zone chart, you've seen them, blue, light blue, and pink, with the zones, and we quickly looked it over and said, all right, here it is one o'clock would be 7:30 a.m. Hawaiian time roughly, it would be sometime later in Manila - I forget offhand what the time was, but we figured it out, and it would be just about dawn at Kota Baru which is on the Kra Peninsula. And, of course, that would be the ideal time, as we then thought, to create a surprise amphibious landing.

Q: And that's where you were focusing the main attack?

Adm. M.: Well, we had accounted for, both by radio intelligence and confirmed by actual sighting, what ships were involved - we had identified them as the task force that we had originally thought was coming from the Second Fleet and under the command of the Commander-in-Chief of the Second Fleet. I'm not too sure who he was now, but anyhow it obviously was an amphibious force covered by a very strong and powerful naval striking force. We knew, of course, that the British had two battleships out there, the Prince of Wales and Renoun, and they knew they were coming because we had been telling them and they had picked it up. In other words, the trailing of this fleet moving westward in the Indian Ocean had been picked up and followed. We had picked them up from Hainan Island all the way down the French Indochina coast, and out the corner there, Cape St. Jacques; and the British took over the trailing of them from us. They were distantly trailed by flying boats, also some surface ships staying pretty well out of sight. We still had not accounted for the rest of the fleet. They were thought by Communications Intelligence to be in the Japanese home islands. The fact is that we nor they - I say we, but about the only information that we had on the movement or the location of the Japanese fleet at that time came from Communications Intelligence, because as long as they hung around Japan we had no way of checking by actual visual observation. Right there, off the China coast, we did. I've explained that before. But in Japan proper the security had gone so very, very tight that it was virtually impossible to check it in time to be of any value. In other words, one had to see it and then be able to get it out and report it, and it was reported - we had people to do that kind of thing - but we couldn't get it out possibly in time because radio transmissions from Japan was out of the question, except for government sources. Radio, of course, in those days was nowhere near what it is now. Cables you couldn't send because there was a heavy censorship on them. I don't care who you were you couldn't send them without the approval of the government. So there was a blanket on all communications. The best you could hope for was that you might be able to smuggle a letter out through the censorship to, say, Shanghai. The Japanese were still running their ships between Nagasaki and Shanghai. It was an express service by very fast passenger ships the Shanghai Maru and the Nagasaki Maru which alternated and made a trip once or twice a week or something of that sort. That was about the only connection, the only way you could get mail out of Japan and into Shanghai was by these two ships because all foreign ships, American ships particularly, had disappeared.

We figured this time out and it was taken in to Admiral Stark and I sent an orderly down to get Admiral Wilkinson, who came in promptly to Admiral Stark's office. We both went in there and talked about the message and pointed out the time and what it was - the time elements in it. Admiral Stark understood right away and he didn't seem to be very much perturbed. Admiral Wilkinson asked again, it was almost monotonous, whether the Pacific Fleet had been alerted. Admiral Stark said, yes, they had, and Captain, later Admiral, Schuirman, who was the head of the Central Division, came in and out, and we were in and out of Admiral Stark's office and the outer office most of the time. I mean not any formal conference, but everyone of those who were there were coming in. Admiral Turner had not arrived and, as far as I knew, didn't plan to come, but I understand that Admiral Stark called him at his home and asked him to come down, apparently on another matter. I don't know.

Admiral Turner showed about eleven o'clock in the morning. At this time we asked again whether the Pacific Fleet had been warned and I believe Admiral Wilkinson suggested to Admiral Stark that he pick up the telephone and call Admiral Kimmel, and I thought he was going to do it, but apparently he changed his mind and tried to get through to the White House and was told the President wasn't available. About eleven o'clock apparently the office of General Marshall called up and talked to the Admiral, and the Admiral - Admiral Stark - and Admiral Stark said, no, he didn't think any further warning was necessary, that they'd had ample warning and he couldn't see it would do any good, and then he talked a little while and called back on the phone and apparently got the Chief of Staff of the Army and said, add on to your message a "tell Navy" -

Q: This was a message to General Short?

Adm. M.: That's right. Of course, Bratten was running in and out between his office and my office and Admiral Stark's office. He was like a crazy man. They couldn't locate Marshall, they couldn't seem to find him. Nobody knew where he was. He was alleged to be out riding somewhere, but no one seemed to know where the General rode, and of course a lot of the accounts that you read have him riding in Rock Creek Park, which is completely ridiculous. Actually, where he was - you know, at that time, the Virginia shore of the Potomac down past where the Pentagon now stands was an experimental farm. It was country and it was a small step to bring a horse down from Fort Myer stables and ride these country trails in Arlington. At that time, Arlington was half-rural, anyway, and that's where, I understand, he did ride, but no one seemed to be able to catch him. His horse was too fast - I don't know!

Anyhow, he got down as near as I can figure out, around eleven o'clock, this thing was sent out, and Bratten came back and said that it was going out that way. Admiral Noyes had come in by that time and he said to Admiral Stark, "Why don't they let us send it? I know I can send it and we'll have a definite confirmation in less than twenty minutes." Well, of course, Admiral Stark said, no, we would let it be handled by the Army. I got the impression - and this is purely an opinion - that you know they had had a regrouping of, you might say, responsibilities for the joint action Army and Navy group, and that had been approved and gone into effect a little bit before. This time the defense of the Hawaiian Islands was placed as an Army responsibility, and I got the impression then that Admiral

Stark was bending over backwards to let the Army exercise their prerogative. The Army wanted it for a long time and it had never been definitely settled. The Navy was just as glad it was settled. It was an Army responsibility, the defense of the islands and the defense of the naval base, and that was fine. In other words, the fleet based there went in and out and operated offensively. The fleet itself was not a part of the Hawaiian defenses, although as long as they were there and had a certain amount of artillery mounted they would participate in any defense that came up and so on.

So that was Sunday morning and about eleven o'clock on Sunday the general feeling in the office was that everything had been done and all preparations had been made to minimize any damage that would be resulting. It was realized that with a surprise attack coming, if it did come, anywhere - Manila or anywhere else - that we were going to have to take it on the chin. The problem acutally was one for people such as Admiral Kimmel and Admiral Hart to hope that they could minimize the extent of the blow, the extent of the damages. I don't know that Admiral Kimmel ever seemed to clearly understand that feature of it. He must have. Certainly Admiral Hart did, judging by his actions and writing subsequently, and that's why he withdrew from Manila when it became evident that the Army antiaircraft couldn't begin to cope with the Japanese planes. You see, the Army at that time used roughly a 3-inch antiaircraft gun and its ceiling was about 12,000 feet. Well, all the Japanese planes had to do was to come over at 14,000, 2,000 feet above the ceiling, and they couldn't be hit by any possible shells and dropped their loads, which they did. The Navy antiaircraft gun at that time was something different again. That was a 5-inch, 38 caliber, and that had a ceiling of something well over 20,000 feet. In those days you didn't bomb very accurately from 20,000 feet. At 10,000 to 12,000 feet you were pretty accurate.

Well, the feeling in the office of the Chief of Naval Operations was that we've done everything we can and it's now just in the hands of the Gods. We were keeping very close to the State Department to see what was going on, see if we could help in any way, and what had happened is that Mr. Hull had refused to see the Japanese Ambassador at one o'clock. They asked for a one o'clock appointment and they were very insistent that it be at one o'clock. Mr. Hull and the rest of them said, well, we know something's going to happen at one o'clock, so don't let's play at one o'clock, let's say we'll see them at two or three and see what happens.

Q: You say ambassadors, in the plural?

Adm. M.: There were two.

Q: Who? Karuso and ?

Adm. M.: Admiral Nomura was the Ambassador and Mr. Karuso had been sent over, you know, to assist Ambassador Nomura. Karuso was a career diplomat. I knew him when he was in a much lower grade in the foreign service. His wife was an American, and he had for a long time been Consul or Consul General in Chicago, and his wife was a native of Chicago. He had had a very wide diplomatic experience, both in South American and Europe. His last job in Europe was as Ambassador to Belgium and he handled the signing of certain treaties or had attended as the Chief Japanese plenipotentiary to handle treaties between Germany and Japan, leading to their agreement on certain things, anti-comintern pact and so on.

Nomura, of course, was a man of tremendous prestige in Navy circles, but he was not a professional diplomat, which Karuso was. That's why Karuso was sent over here. For one thing, they felt that maybe Nomura in his dotage was a little bit too pro-American to be real tough and they sent this man over who was a career man to toughen it up.

Q: And a very brilliant man, wasn't he?

Adm. M.: I don't know about that, but I presume so because he went right to the top in the Japanese diplomatic service.

Q: At that time, he certainly had that reputation.

Adm. M.: Yes, he had that reputation in the Japanese diplomatic service. I had known him in Japan when he was on duty in the Japanese Foreign Office in 1923, I reckon, or somewhere in there.

Q: So they failed in their mission to see the Secretary at one o'clock?

Adm. M.: That is right, but in spite of the fact that they had been told repeatedly and flatly that they couldn't see the Secretary, or he wouldn't see them, at one o'clock, they hopped into a car and came down there and were in the State Department at one o'clock. In other words, they were apparently going to try to force their way in. That is where they were when word came through that the attack had taken place. I understand that Mr. Hull did see them about two o'clock, whereupon he castigated them unmercifully, I think, and fired them out of there. So that is about what happened in Washington.

Of course, the Navy Department went into mobilization. Everybody dug out their uniforms. We were all in civilian clothes up to that time.

Q: Was the Secretary present in the morning?

Adm. M.: No, not in Stark's office. He came in after word of the attack had come through, which he had apparently received while he was in conference over in the State Department. I believe they had a conference going on there between Mr. Hull, Mr. Welles, Mr. Stimson, and Mr. Knox. I believe so. That seems to be historically fairly correct.

Q: Admiral, in later years, from any intelligence that was gleaned from the Japanese, had they anticipated that the task force to land on the Kra Peninsula would act as a kind of a decoy to us and throw us off?

Adm. M.: No, no, I think the whole tendency had been for us to look on the Japanese attack on Pearl Harbor as the main event. The main event was the attack on the Kra Peninsula. The operation at Pearl Harbor was purely a covering operation to immobilize the American Fleet, which was the only possible thing that could have interfered with the operation against the Kra Peninsula. If Japan was going to continue in the war at all, she had to have access to the raw materials in that region and in the Dutch East Indies. That was the main effort. The principal effort was there. The other one was purely a covering operation, and even if it was partially successful it might throw that fleet off balance. That was the concept. In other words, the main effort was on the Kra Peninsula, and that's the reason - people say, "Well, why didn't they destroy the oil and the gas storage, then they couldn't have done anything?" The answer is because they didn't want to destroy the oil and the gas. What they wanted to do and did do was to immobilize the mobile units of the United States fleet. They didn't want to destroy the others because Yamamoto was not quite as shortsighted as that. He expected within six months or less to move in on the Hawaiian Islands and take the darned place, if he could get the fleet immobilized, which he tried to do, and was foiled at the Battle of Midway in June of 1942. The whole pattern fits in that way. Why destroy the Navy yards, why destroy the oil storage, when my people will take them anyway and we can use them?

The concept that the attack on Pearl Harbor was the main scheme does not fall into place. If you look at the strategic picture, and they did, the drive was to take the raw material sources of the Dutch East Indies - because you see they went from Malaya and so on. Their object in going there was to try to neutralize the Singapore base. The minute that was accomplished, the minute General Yamashita and his army was landed on that continent and started working down the Malay Peninsula toward Singapore, that more or less immobilized Singapore, particularly after the Prince of Wales and the Renown were sunk - or the Repulse, the British had almost no fleet then What little they had was based on Ceylon at a place called Kilindini. The Japanese forces immediately went in. In other words, the same fellow, Nagumo, who commanded the attack on Pearl Harbor, that task force, virtually that same task force within a month of that attack debouched into the Indian Ocean and scattered the British and raided all the way to Ceylon, covering the operation of the amphibious drive against Java. That was what was done. Then from Java they took it step by step. Java was oil-rich, Sumatra was oil-rich; the demolitions of the oil people were ineffective to a great extent. They were not well carried out. Someone had to - everyone would be trying to, "You blow yours up. We'll just remove a few pieces of pipe," and that sort of thing.

Q: In other words, the Dutch were reluctant to do it?

Adm. M.: Not only the Dutch were reluctant. The British were just as bad. For instance, there's a very fine oil field in North Borneo called the Miri Field where the oil comes out of the ground and almost without refining you can run it right in the ship. That was a shallow-well field as far as oil wells are concerned, and the technique of destruction was to remove sections of pipe and hide them in the jungle. At Miri, which was also the name of the port, the ships that came in there to oil, like tankers and so on, to carry the oil somewhere else, did just about what they had to do at Aden. For instance, they moored and a pipeline was floated out to them and they took the oil in the roadstead, you know. It's not a harbor.

So, that's about what happened here on Sunday morning, December the 7th. We all stayed down there and people came rushing into the Department from all places. Of course, Japanese ships, once the word was out, were reported all over everywhere, particularly off the

West Coast - a Japanese submarine came in there and threw a few shells at a place called San Luis Obispo on the California coast and one or two other places. Japanese planes were seen all over everywhere. Actually, within a couple of days of the attack on Pearl Harbor, the antiaircraft batteries ringing the city of Los Angeles were firing for about three hours at what they claimed was an air attack, but it wasn't. And so you had all kinds of phantom reports coming in, which is not unusual, but it got to the point -

Q: It was a kind of a panicky thing?

Adm. M.: Yes, it was a panicky thing and all kinds of curious people were picking up dispatches and firing them back out to the fleet. The air was full of stuff. Within a week, we had one very distinguished officer - how he got in the act I don't know, he was heading the convoy system in the Atlantic - was picking up messages and sending them to Admiral King and sending them all over to everyone else. One of these things, I remember, was constantly talking about Japanese submarines or something off, about 700 or 800 miles west of Seattle or Portland, up in the northwest. We hunted that spot over and over again and had seaplanes out but couldn't find a thing. We finally identified the signals and due to some of the vagaries, the peculiarities of radio transmission they were the call letters definitely identified as belonging to a Japanese submarine which we knew from sight was operating off of the coast of Java. You have that. I don't know, they call it a skip distance or something. It hits the heavy side of the air and bounces back or something. You do get that phenomenon from time to time. It took almost a week before the Chief of Naval Operations could assert himself and say, now, look here, enough is enough. All these kind of things are going to be screened through the Office of Naval Intelligence. Nobody is going to send any messages out to Admiral Kimmel or anybody else on this thing unless it's screened through O.N.I.

Curiously, the War Plans Chief was noncommittal. So from then on we just put a stop to this wild-eyed alerting everybody all over creation. But it took about a week to get it through.

Q: How quickly did we determine what had happened at Pearl?

Adm. M.: Oh, we had that right away. We know now, we didn't know then, and radio intelligence, communications intelligence, we had it in the Navy Department consistently. We placed the carriers, of which there were six, in home waters. We knew that they had been there much too long and we couldn't account for the fact that none of the big carriers had been seen in the task forces operating in the south and we were very dubious as to the location of them. The minute the attack was made by merely counting - there were two small carriers down with the southern force, the Hosho and something else, I forget what, the Ryujo possibly. They were small and fairly slow. The big fast carriers were not there. There were three to six they had. One was the Shokaku class, which were new and there were either five or six. Then the Kaga and the Kako. They were originally like our Saratoga and Lexington were converted. The Japanese had laid them down as battle cruisers and their conversion took place along in the 1923 or 1924 period. We knew that they were there and following the pattern we also figured that they had their usual accompaniment or two, and possibly four, of the fast battleships. The Japanese battleships, the big-gun ships, were in two categories. You might say the battleship proper and what had originally been laid down as battle cruisers, that was when the battle cruisers were popular - that would be the Kongo, the Kirishima, the Hiei, and the Haruna. The Kongo was built in England around 1914 or so. They were originally a group of four, 27-knot battle cruisers. They mounted, of course, the big guns, 14-inch guns, and they were nearly always with this task force, the air task force grouping. YOu had the carriers, of course, with their destroyer screen, then you had two or three fast 8-inch gun cruisers, the new ones, and this group of anywhere from two to four of the fast battleships because they could keep pace with the carriers and provide a backlog for defense in case they were attacked.

Q: And the Japanese battle cruisers were similar to the Repulse and the Renown, were they?

Adm. M.: Well, they had been modernized several times.

Q: And their one difference from a battleship was their speed and also the fact that they had armor protection?

Adm. M.: That's right. They were originally coal-burners, of course. They had been converted to oil and they had been modernized. In other words, they'd been rebuilt two or three times over the years so that they were very formidable ships having a speed of probably around 30 knots, instead of their original 27 because of more power in the engine due to oil and new boilers, that sort of business, new boiler design and so on, which give you more horsepower. You can increase the speed of such a ship to only a certain limit because then you start getting in trouble because the underwater hull isn't designed to get through the water that fast, originally. There are certain limitations that get imposed unless you build the entire ship over again, which I don't think was done. That was a combination the Japanese had used and we knew it right away. As a matter of fact, we sent a message out to Admiral Kimmel and told him exactly what we thought he'd been hit with. I don't think he knew. There's no evidence that they knew. They did pick up a couple of planes that had crashed and identified them as coming from such and such a ship. There weren't too many of them in those days and some of them were pretty badly smashed. There was no real systematic effort to get it.

The trouble is that out there at Pearl Harbor the opinion seemed to be, that is Admiral Kimmel and his staff always insisted that the attack was coming from the southwest, in other words, from the direction of the mandated islands. There was a Japanese force knocking around the mandated islands, mostly a decoy force, I suppose you'd call it. But the attack here came in from, as we all know now and knew then here in Washington that it came in from just where it did come in - from the north. Everything we had came from there. I think we've gone into the fact that that area up there was practically devoid of shipping. Normally for the Pacific compared with the Atlantic the shipping is fairly sparse anyway - that is, merchant shipping I'm speaking of. It had been practically denuded of that because of the embargoes that we'd put in and the Japanese had put in. Normally there would be two or three or maybe a dozen American and Japanese merchant ships cruising that area. That's a compromise between the great-circle course from the West Coast to Japan and the longer more salubrious course by the Hawaiian Islands. Of course, the other one comes up pretty close to the Aleutians and it's just like the great-circle course in the Atlantic. It stretches into an area of very heavy storms and heavy weather, so that the travel lanes usually hit a compromise. In other words, they went so far on the great-circle course and flattened it out on the rhumb line, Mercator course, and then took the great circle where it dips towards Japan - that is, on the Mercator charts it dips - and picked it up and went on in that way. So normally that area would have had a number of ships in it and of course ships that would be going from the Hawaiian Islands to go to Japan would more or less head up into that general direction. But at this time there was nothing. The first effort to find the force that was mounted by the Pacific Fleet, I remember, was a search to the southwest. Then it was determined that they were coming in from the north - almost due north as a matter of fact. They swung the search around in that direction but by this time it was pretty late. I mean the planes didn't have anything to search for.

We had two carrier task forces out, very much the same set-up that the Japanese had. In other words, we had a couple of carriers with attendant destroyer screen covered by two to four heavy cruisers, that was all we had so that's what you had. Halsey was at sea with a task force of that kind. He was down there toward Johnson Island, which is down in the southwest, on a resupply mission. Halsey was supposed to be doing something about Wake Island or something of that sort. You have a peculiar coincidence. YOu know, Admiral Kimmel had had a scheme at this one time. In other words, he had divided up his heavy ships and others into groups of three with the idea that two of the groups would be constantly cruising at sea and the other group would come in and spend maybe a week in port replenishing and so on. Then when it got ready to go to sea, why, it went to sea and another group took its place. It's not a bad scheme.

Just before December the 7th they were drilling constantly out there. In my judgment it was too much. They were drilling so much everybody was drill-crazy. A couple of the battleships had been in collision. There was not a great deal of damage done. That, of course, I didn't know, that is, at the time. They were pulled in along with the group that was supposed to be regrouping, and these came from different groupings, which only left one battleship to cruise round by itself. They were holding a board of investigation or a court of inquiry as to the collision, and that was why these ships were in there. So it was one circumstance after another, so you could almost say that some uncanny almighty hand had his finger in that thing.

Q: Was it not true also that the system of reconnaissance planes going out had been curtailed somewhat?

Adm. M.: It had to be. You see, you had this problem. The Army Air Force there which was commanded by a very fine man called General Tinker. He was a Major General in the Air Force and he had a typical Air Force set-up copied from the British. In other words, you had a Bomber Command and a Fighter Command and so on. Well, the Bomber Command were the only planes with any long range at all. Their navigational training was very skimpy, and the fighters had no navigation equipment at all, or very little, and they were a strictly short-range outfit. They couldn't fly more than fifteen miles out from Hawaii because if they lost sight of the Islands they couldn't find their way back. That is a fact. Actually the fighters did a wonderful job, the ones that weren't destroyed. A couple of them weren't. They were hidden out somewhere by the initiative of their pilots, and they did quite a bit of slaughter.

Q: My remark was about Navy reconnaissance flights.

Adm. M.: The only planes the Navy had to do any reconnaissance at all were the flying boats, PBYs we called them. Later on, the Australians called them Catalinas, I think. They had various names but those were the only ones that were long range. Most of those planes were not metal, a good many of them were still fabric-covered. They could only fly so often and they had to come in to be repaired and rehabilitated, so to speak. The base there for those planes was too full. We had Ford Island which was in the middle of Pearl Harbor. That was normally not a seaplane base, although seaplanes did sometimes operate from there. The seaplane base was up at Kaneohe up beyond Waikiki beach, which is almost directly across the island from Pearl Harbor. Of course, the Japanese worked over that place, too. So you had very few uninjured aircraft anywhere, so the only planes that could have done anything of that sort were carrier-based and they were on the carriers.

Q: I was told that Admiral Richardson when he was still there had inaugurated a systematic reconnaissance plan and that this plan had been somewhat curtailed after he left the command.

Adm. M.: Yes, I think that's true. I frankly don't have any first-hand knowledge of that and I just don't know, but it's indicated that it had been done and part of that is due to the fact that Admiral Kimmel did not have at his disposal the quantities of aircraft and ships and so on that Admiral Richardson had had at one point. I think you have to recollect that there was a carrier task force and destroyer squadron almost at the Panama Canal ready to go through the canal and come into the Atlantic. They were turned around and sent back out after the attack on Pearl Harbor, but that shows you. The pressure, you see, was on the Atlantic.

Q: I was going to ask you, Admiral, has it been determined, has it been pinpointed, the actual difficulty, the reason why we were subjected to a surprise attack?

Adm. M.: Well, I think when one thinks in terms of a surprise attack one has to think in terms of the frame of mind. It's almost impossible to keep a Navy task force or any other group of ships or a regiment of men on the constant qui vive all the time. The point comes where the human machine will not take it any more.

Q: It becomes commonplace!

Adm. M.: It becomes commonplace and you can't be charging around, you can't keep your people at general quarters all the time. That was the mistake we made in the early stages of the war. We had, you remember, in every ship one, two, three conditions of readiness. Condition One was general quarters, full battle stations and man the engineers force and everybody else. Condition Two is supposed to be watch and watch. In other words, half the batteries, half the offensive armament, half the engineers, the others are sleeping and so on. You can only keep that up for a relatively short time, a couple or three days and the human machine starts wearing out. Condition Three is, of course, you might say, the peacetime cruising formation. You have a watch in four. That's when the people run ship. The officer of the deck and so on and so forth, the officers in the engineroom, and a great many sailors are not employed in that situation, except in shining brass work or working on the upkeep of various things.

It's almost impossible to keep up, and even in the war zone later on, we found out you couldn't do it. Now, one of the reasons - this is getting ahead of the story again - I've always felt one of the reasons that we got completely walloped at the first Battle of Savo Island in August of 1942 was the fact that those fellows had been standing watch and watch for weeks and they were mentally and physically pooped out. That was all. It was pointed out as early as 1933 we had gone down when Admiral Schofield, Commander-in-Chief of the fleet, and we deliberately tried this thing out to see how long it would take. When we staggered into the Gulf of Panama, Admiral Schofield said, "I did this, gentlemen, purely and simply to try to convince the Navy Department that it's highly unrealistic to try to keep people at battle stations the way we've been doing here for a week. All of you people and the crew, they're completely fagged out. We just can't do it, so we've got to be more realistic."

During the war, later on, of course, so what you did, you did get more realistic. You divided up your ship into groups of three and the people on board the ships, and you didn't send them to general quarters, you didn't man full battle stations for an air attack or anything of that sort, only part of it went. So that if you had to go into battle you had your people rested up. Not enough attention was paid to that kind of thing. It took people of the lieutenant class, for instance, like I was in 1933 and a good many others - you know, we were lieutenants an awful long time, as my wife keeps throwing up at me. She said at one time she didn't think they had anything but lieutenants in the Navy, and she was just about right. The thing is that we took it on the chin. We could see the effects on our men. A watch and division officer on a big ship was in touch with his men. He had to be, and that was one of the things that I enjoyed most. Unfortunately, when you went up the pole a little bit you lost that intimate touch with the enlisted personnel, as you were designed to do because then you were dealing with the officers and through them with the enlisted personnel. But it was very illuminating to watch these kids trying to take it. Some of them were only sixteen years old and they just couldn't keep awake, that went for your battle lookouts and so on. You had these people peering through night glasses all night long and, my goodness, along about four o'clock in the morning they couldn't see anything if it was thrown at them. You just cannot keep a force constantly alerted.

Later on in the war as we moved, for instance, toward re-entry into the Philippines at Leyte Gulf and so on as is well known our base was at Hollandia, the harbor was Hollandia, the naval headquarters was some ten or fifteen miles inland. We didn't do anything of that even when we had this big amphibious armada on the way under the command of Admiral Kinkaid moving toward Leyte Gulf we didn't keep people at battle stations. The fleet flagship was the Wasatch, which was one of these new-fangled command ships. In other words, she was a converted - I don't know whether she was built originally as that or not - it's just a question of how far you can go.

Q: Indeed, then, that was a factor and you intimated off the tape recorder that also the authorities in Pearl were not truly convinced that an attack on the Hawaiian Islands was coming.

Adm. M.: Well, first of all, going back a ways, shortly after Admiral Kimmel relieved Admiral Richardson, he was constantly concerned about the fact that he was losing the reconnaissance type of aircraft and ships on which possibly a warning of attack would come. At that time he was completely bemused that the attack was probably building up or could be building up in the mandated islands - that's Truk and those kind of places, and I think it was in February of 1941 I drafted a letter to him which was signed by Admiral Stark, in which I told him that at this time the Japanese did not plan an attack in the foreseeable future. Of course, this was in February of 1941, and as a matter of fact, going back to 1941, right at that time there was a very sensible easing of the diplomatic tension between the United States and Japan. Ambassador Admiral Nomura had recently arrived in Washington as Japanese Ambassador. From reading the Japanese diplomatic codes, his plan was to try to tread water and ease the situation, which he was doing. In other words, there was a definite lessening of tensions, and it just didn't seem possible at that time that the Japanese contemplated an attack anywhere. And, of course, the foreseeable future - how far does one foresee the future? Maybe two weeks or a month or what-have-you, and the situation can change and it did change. It changed radically. Yet Kimmel in his defense brings up this, that he was told in February 1941 that they weren't going to attack, and that's what he bases it on. Since that time, of course, he had been told repeatedly that an attack might come most any time and would come presumably on a Sunday or a holiday. We didn't know where it was coming from, and I repeat again that there was no intelligence that certainly I had, and as far as I've been able to read and judge, that Captain Layton had out there - he was Kimmel's intelligence officer - as to the possibility of an attack on Pearl Harbor.

Now, you take people like Admiral McMorris, who was the war plans officer on Admiral Kimmel's staff, he's quoted in the reports as telling Admiral Kimmel flatly that the Japanese simply weren't going to attack. You had the same feeling in Washington. In spite of the fact that the Japanese were moving steadily southward into French Indochina, which they went into in a big way in March, I think it was, of 1941. Here in May of 1941 they came to the grand conclusion that the war was going to be fought in the Atlantic. So all the emphasis was on the Atlantic and at the very time that the Japanese were building up their build-up in the south, apparently that was completely disregarded. Now, I'm speaking of the people on the General Board. Admiral Greenslade is one that I have in mind. I don't know whether they got their orders from the White House or what-have-you. Anyhow the decision was made somewhere around May of 1941 that if there was going to be a war as far as the United States was concerned, it would be in the Atlantic and we could forget about the

Pacific, or that was a corollary. Of course, that was not my view at all, because I naturally, forgetting about the Pacific or making it of lesser importance, deflated my ego a little bit, but the fact is that you could go round here, and I did, and talked to people like Commodore Dudley Knox and some others and said, look here, we're underestimating these people.

Again, we go back to what you and I have discussed before - the preoccupation of our people who are mostly of European origin with things in Europe. That's wehre the pull is, and of course the persecution of the Jews in Germany by Hitler was tearing things up politically in this country because of the large Jewish minority and politically very vocal minority. So, you had the whole accent, well, we'll forget about the Japs. They can take some of these silly places down there. And of course nobody here that I could find out seemed to realize that the very reason for the greatness of some of these European countries, such as Great Britain or Holland and so on, depended on the fact that they owned these very valuable colonies. That's why you had the Governor General of the Dutch East Indies, as we called them, was a man of rank and prestige superior to the prime minister of Holland. The Queen of Holland was also the Queen of the N.E.I. and actually the N.E.I. was the source of a great deal of the wealth that the Dutch had, as were places like India and South Africa, the African colonies, and so on, and the dominions, Australia and New Zealand. France had her colonies and so on in Africa, none of them as lucrative as the British ones, but a great deal of the economic force of the European nations, with the exception of Germany which·was stripped during World War I of these appurtenances, was attributable to this. Well, if they started losing all this, the thing in Europe logically folded up on itself. You couldn't seem to get a reading of that here. Everyone had their eyes fixed in that direction, on the terrific drama that was taking place in Europe - and those are the only words that you can use to express it.

So there was a tendency to disregard it. In other words, it was unfortunate that we had this damned nuisance of the Japanese. We just would have to let them fiddle, they couldn't do much harm anyway, so let them play. I'm trying to re-create a frame of mind. Of course, Admiral Kimmel was faced, as I say, with a very difficult situation. Our personnel problem has never been good. I just got a paper here by Admiral Zumwalt that talks with horror of the fact that only about a third of our enlisted men re-enlist. Well, that's nothing new. I was a division officer on the West Virginia back in 1930 to 1933. I had a division of eighty-five to ninety men, and of that eighty-five to ninety men only about six of them were re-enlistees. The rest of them were doing their first four years. Now I say that, I had - I could almost count off my fingers petty officers there. I had a first class petty officer who had a couple of hashmarks - you could line them up and see - if they didn't have any hash marks, which is, you know, a service mark. So it's not unusual this situation, and of course this was at a time when the Depression was biting and some of them did re-enlist. We always had one of these odd characters in every division, a fellow who refused to take promotion. He had been promoted and for some reason or other he had been demoted. He got to be a seaman first class and that's what he wanted to be and nothing else. He was petty officer material, a fine figure.

As a matter of fact, he occupied a petty officer's billet in the battle station of the turret but you have that. You always have in the American Navy ever since I've known it an acute personnel problem. You have a heavy turnover of the personnel.

When you get a ship that's on a wartime footing, you've got these fellows and you don't have the turnover. Any turn-over you have comes from natural causes or battle casualties or sicknesses and that sort of thing which you have to replace. But you do have that. It must be always a problem to a man like Kimmel and that's why he seemed to be completely bemused by the need for training, and he was training, training, training. Well, you can train people and we did the same thing in the earlier days. I go back to my service in the battleships in the thirties. In 1933, it was very rugged and you were so busy training that you didn't have time to think hardly of other things, and you do get into that frame of mind. I've been in it and I think maybe that had something to do with it. But in some ways, you - the Navy lost about 3,000 men killed, mostly drowned in that Pearl Harbor attack. I didn't know that at the time, of course, but those seem to be accepted figures. I don't think anyone will ever know exactly how many. But I think 3,000 is probably a pretty fair estimate, and aside from those it is in a sense rather providential that the ships were in Pearl Harbor because, you know, those big battleships only had a foot or two of water under their bottoms and that's about as far as they sunk. Of course, they settled a little bit in the mud later on. But had they been out and been hit - and had they been, for instance, cruising up there in the north where this task force came from, and had been hit by that outfit, once those ships were lost they'd have been lost with all hands because your depths up there are, what, a thousand fathoms or something on that order? Maybe not that much but it's pretty deep water. Every one of those heavy ships with the exception of possibly the Oklahoma and the Arizona which blew up, apparently a bomb hit or an armor-piercing projectile hit in one of the magazines and blew her up, that's the Arizona. And I don't think the Oklahoma ever got back, I don't think they ever turned her over, her keel was turned over and she capsized at her moorings. She was opened up for inspection, which she shouldn't have been. She should have had her watertight compartments closed off, as most of the rest of them did, but she was one of the ships that had been involved in this collision deal and she was getting ready for this board of inquiry to come down on her, and they had to open up and air out these spaces so that people could go down and see what damage had been done by the collision. At least, that's the story you get.

So you've got a number of factors there. I don't think - I never have thought - that the staff of Admiral Kimmel was sufficiently alerted and the other staffs as well, to the fact that war might come. A very good friend of mine, for instance, who served on Admiral Anderson's staff, and Admiral Anderson, as you know commanded the battleships, he was the staff gunnery officer, and they'd come in from a couple of weeks out on this training business and he was concerned of the ammunition supply. So he made sure in his function as gunnery officer on the staff that the antiaircraft ammunition was in order and so on and available. But then what does the guy do? On Saturday night he goes to the Moana Hotel, which is across the island from Pearl Harbor to relax. I don't blame him for that. I mean the ships get pretty hot sitting there in port, so he went there, but the result is that when the attack came, here was this guy rushing back and it was fifteen to twenty miles to Pearl Harbor. Yet he says, heavens, if we had know nall this kind of thing, why it never would have happened. That's a frame of mind again.

Q: Did the Army command share this attitude that an attack wasn't a feasible thing?

Adm. M.: Well, they shouldn't have because obviously - you know the Army in the Hawaiian Islands considering the resources that the Army had was very well found. They had an Army on there of about 25,000 or 30,000 men, which is quite heavy. That's more than we had anywhere else. I don't think we had that many people in the continental United States even, and these were all seasoned troops. I use the word "seasoned" meaning that they - very few of them had ever engaged in any battle but they had been thoroughly trained and were good t troops. The Army blew hot and cold on it, and that again depended somewhat on the personality of the Commanding General. The man who immediately preceded General Short, I think his name was Heron - General Heron, who was very realistic about it and he kept his people right on their toes all the time. But, you see, one of the dangers riding through all this thing all the way through is that you must not alarm the civil population. Almost every one of Marshall's dispatches said, do this but in such a way that you can't alarm anyone. In a place like Hawaii, how are you going to do it? You're going to have everyone running around with tanks and none of the people are going to know it! It's sheer nonsense. You're talking through your hat. You can't go on a full alert in a place like Honolulu - heck, the island is only about twenty-five or thirty miles round - maybe more, I don't know, but it's a relatively small place and it's full of people, and if you start moving out your garrison people and putting them in the pineapple fields all around there, somebody's going to know it, and if they disappear from the streets of Honolulu on a normal liberty night and the bars are doing no business, somebody's going to know it. You can't keep them from it. So it borders on the ridiculous to talk of doing these things in such a way that you're not going to alarm the folks. Surely you're going to alarm some people because they're not making the money they feel entitled to for one thing, and so on and so forth. It comes round in a vicious circle. You can't go and do these things without it being pretty well known to the populace.

If we had a system such as the Japanese had in what they called their fortified areas - in other words, each naval base struck a radius with a set of dividers on a map of thirty miles radius and put a ring around it and make - evacuate it. There were civilians in those areas, such as Yokuska, for instance, Kure and Sasebo, and so on, but each one of those people had an identity card and had to be checked. You couldn't come in or out of those zones without having a ticket. And that way newspaper men nor anybody else could come in. If we had had such a system as that, which is completely foreign to our way of running things and I personally wouldn't like to see it, but nevertheless it's almost impossible under our governmental set-up and the tenor of our people to keep these kinds of things from being unknown to the general populace. When you speak in these grand terms of do it this way and do it that way, but don't tell anybody, don't let them know, you're just hitting a pipe dream. It cannot be done, as far as I know. I don't like to use those terms because I've often said I don't like that word, I think anything can be done and it can, but we're not willing to pay the price.

You know that in Pearl Harbor itself, the fishing rights in Pearl Harbor were reserved to the territorial government by treaty that the then Hawaiian Islands made with us. So that any Hawaiian or any resident of Hawaii was free to come in and out of Pearl Harbor and go fishing all he wanted to in the place. It was specifically reserved to them. Japanese fishermen? Sure they came in there. These so-called fellows who were supposed to be spying on our fleet, they went fishing right in Pearl Harbor. That's the kind of stuff you had. When the Army tried to put up that radar they got into a fight with the Interior Department because they were doing things to the ecology out there, I think we call it now. We didn't know that word in those days. But that was the reason they couldn't put it in and they were having an awful fight, and they couldn't get the radar. It was more or less a rudimentary radar they had at that time but it couldn't be stuck up to get a range unless you went high up on the mountain and that meant cutting a road through there and so on, and that spoiled the pastoral grandeur of it and I suppose sent the iwa birds, or whatever they are, into a tizzy, so you had a fight on and Interior wasn't about to budge on these things.

Those are just some of the problems that come up. I feel this way about it. I don't think that General Short, from what I have read and know, appreciated the problem. His G-2, Colonel Fielder, and also his assistant, a fellow named Bicknell, were completely hipped on the idea that there was going to be an uprising among the Japanese population, persons of Japanese nativity or kindred in the islands

Q: In Hawaii?

Adm. M.: In Hawaii, yes. In the Hawaiian Islands, and it was a complete bugbear that bemused the Army command. That same situation that we've already talked about. In my opinion, General DeWitt on the West Coast went off the deep end in relation to the Nisei and had the same idea. Of course there were many more people of Japanese ancestry on the Hawaiian Islands - I've forgotten the figures now - but in all of the western United States, that includes Washington, Oregon, California, and slopping over a little bit into the border states, I doubt that there were as many as a total of 100,000 people of Japanese ancestry of one sort or another, either immigrants or subjects or second generation and so on. While in Hawaii, of course, on the island of Oahu alone there were supposed to be 40,000. Those were the figures that were bandied around. So that security and safety of this military installation and so on certainly lay very heavily on the minds of any Commanding General out there, and I will say this - you will note from reading the record that when General Marshall sent a message about a week or so prior to the attack on Pearl Harbor to General Short to go on a limited alert out there, General Short did come right back to General Marshall and outline exactly what he was doing, that he was planning an alert against sabotage. In other words, he told him and of course there was no reaction from the War

Department. In other words, he did just exactly what I was always trained to do in the Navy - you get an order from an admiral, well you face the situation and you're quite confident that there is a situation that was not foreseen at the time the order was issued. What do you do? You're not in touch with him. You can send a message saying "unless otherwise directed, I'm going to do so and so," which may or may not be what he wants done - and if he doesn't want you to do it, then he comes back and tells you, no, don't you do that, do something else.

I've done that repeatedly and that's exactly in my judgment - I don't know whether the Army works that way or not, but that's exactly what General Short was doing. He received these orders, he'd go on a limited alert, don't alarm the civilian population, and do so and so forth for a defense against attack, well he didn't say what, so he said all right, the most likely attack is an uprising in the civil population, so let's fix it so that we'll be hurt the least, and that's sabotage. Antisabotage alert, and he came right back to the Chief of Staff of the Army and told him exactly what he was doing, what kind of alert he was going on.

Again, one of the confusions that arose out there and still arises is, as I have mentioned before, that the Navy has these conditions of readiness, one, two, and three, of which three is the most relaxed. The Army also had what they called conditions 1, 2, and 3, but that was just opposite. No. 1 was the most relaxed and No. 3 was the all-out! And the people on Kimmel's staff didn't know that, apparently. They made no effort. They went over to find out what condition of alert the Army was in and came back and said "Condition

3," or "Condition 1," something of that sort. It's amazing, it's just amazing that the operations staff and so on didn't know what condition of readiness that meant in Army terms. It was perfectly proper for the Army to use any numbers they wanted, but at least we ought to be capable of translating it into our language - and that's about all it comes to.

You have these same things - I remember later on in the war we got into one of the biggest hassles with the air people out there in Brisbane along with our operations officer. We were talking about making a reconnaissance from New Guinea up into the direction of the Marshall Islands, and Cruizen, who was the Operations Officer, and I sat down and we did our map work and went down and found that the Army air staff, presumably working from the same charts, had come down with a completely different set of figures. Come to find out that we were talking - and it didn't occur to us until we got into a terrific row and started to cool off a little bit and Cruizen looked at me and said, "You know, Mac, we were two of the biggest damned fools I know of." What those guys were talking about were statute miles and we were talking about geographic miles! Sure enough that's what it was. The Army air force at that time had been trained and they worked - and the Army did, on the statute mile - 5,280 feet. The Navy, of course, worked on the basis of the knot, or the sea mile, roughly 6,020 feet, or thereabouts, which is quite a difference when you're talking in terms of 800 to 1,000 of these units, and it can make the difference between whether a plane can do it or whether it can't do it. So you have those little things that came up here, and I think there was a measure of that then, but, of course, I can't see

McCollum #9 - 441

that there was much excuse for that in the case of Hawaii. My goodness, Pearl Harbor's one place and Army headquarters are not over a mile away at Schofield Barracks or in that vicinity. They had a sort of underground command post there that they'd dug into the mountainside. It's not very far, and this business of going out and playing golf with each other I didn't think much of that. I don't think that had got anything to do with it. That's been used a great deal as a sign that their relations were good and so on. I don't think it necessarily followed. Because two fellows go out and play golf together about once a month and netiher one of them is a particularly good golfer that they're going to get along too well together professionally. That's something else.

I just think you had a frame of mind, as I have said before. I know that I'm fatalistic, but you had so many factors that seemed to fall into place, you almost have a feeling that some kind of an over-all intelligence just willed these things.

Now we get back to Admiral Nagumo, who was the Task Force Commander of this outfit. We know now, which we didn't know then, that this plan to attack was devised by a special staff set up by Admiral Yamamoto. A fellow named Genda, who was then a Commander, and a flying officer, who has since stayed on as a Japanese officer. He retired two or three years ago. He was then a Commander and was more or less given the job to assemble a staff to plan this attack. The plan was generally approved tentatively by Admiral Yamamoto, Commander-in-Chief of the Fleet, in May or June of 1941. Special exercises were held, down in the island of Kyushu, using Kogoshima Bay, which in a sense is similar in shape and so on to Pearl Harbor.

Q: Then in May it became the foreseeable future?

Adm. M.: Well, we didn't know that. Of course, none of this, you understand, had been approved up the line. Again I repeat people have overstressed the power of Yamamoto. Yamamoto was undoubtedly a man of strong will and he had a terrific following among the more - the younger officers, the more radical group, but you understand the man who made the decision in the Japanese Navy for anything of this sort at all would be the Chief of the Naval General Staff, at that time Admiral Osami Nagano. Nagano had been naval attache here in Washington, he'd been chief of the intelligence division, he commanded the Japanese training squadron, he'd been Commander-in-Chief of the Fleet, President of the War College, President of the Japanese line academy at Etajima, and so on. In other words, he was probably one of the outstanding Japanese naval officers. I knew him and I've always had the greatest of respect for his mental acuity.

Yamamoto as Commander-in-Chief of the Fleet couldn't make a move of this sort without the approval of the Naval General Staff. So what he had to do, and did do, was he came back after he found out that these things could be feasible and lobbied it through the Naval General Staff. It was originally not approved by the Naval General Staff and later only tentatively in October of 1941. So, you see, by doing this, what Yamamoto had done, whether he realized it or not, he may have or may not - I don't know, he had completely reversed the strategic concept on which the Japanese Navy was built. As I said before, the Japanese Navy was built primarily to fight in waters contiguous to their home territory of one sort or another, not to make any overseas long-range thing like coming over to the West Coast of the United States. In other words, that's what you call the strategic defensive but the tactical offensive. That was the idea - those hit and run and night attacks and so on, which they were very good at, but when he decided to go in and strike here, then he was overreaching that sort of thing. In other words, he was overreaching the physical capacity of certain of his ships. Now, what he did do was he sent, in November of 1941, Nagumo his six carriers and a couple of battleships and cruisers and so on up to a place that's given various names, up in the Kurile Islands, I've been there. Some accounts call it Tankan Bay. I've always known it as Hitokappu. It's the same place, the same thing. You see the difficulty there with those names, a good many of those names are not basically Japanese names. They are Japanese transliterations or Japanese renditions of names that are Ainu in origin or Aleut and so on. When I was up there in 1924, we had the same thing over and over again.

Well, they stayed up there and on station for about a month before they were ordered to move, and even then they were ordered to move out, make a rendezvous with the oilers at such and such a place, and if they ran into any shipping to turn around and come back, not to go ahead. Under no circumstances was the attack to be made until the word came through to attack. That word was by arrangement of a private code between Admiral Yamamoto, Commander-in-Chief of the Fleet, and Vice Admiral Nagumo, the Commander of the Striking Force. That was a private code between them, not a Navy code that might be broken and so on. Nii taka yama nobore! This is the Japanese emphatic - the verb "to climb" and Nobore is the emphatic form of this verb. So the attack was not to be made until they got this private code phrase. So the order to attack came just two days before the attack developed. Nagumo had not said anything. He had apparently made contact, he refueled, he was still under strict radio silence and so on. Radio silence was not broken until after the attack took place.

So you have that picture. As a matter of fact, it is said that Admiral Yamamoto was so afraid of some word of this leaking out some way or another, and that's the reason he got these carriers off up there so early. He practically put them in quarantine up at this place. It's a very sparsely settled area up there. There are almost no natives left. They'd been killed off first by the Russians, then by the Japanese and so on and so forth, and the only time that any life goes on up there is in the fishing season when the fishing fleet comes up and lives and works out of a fishing camp, so that you had practically a place where nobody could see anything of what was going on. And it was from that point that they sailed for the attack.

Now, this is partly reconstructed from reading and so on, you realize, but it is also said, as I started to say, that Admiral Yamamoto was so intent on running this decoy that he actually gave special liberty to the fleet down at Yokuska, Kure, and those places and sent the sailors into Tokyo and Kobe and Yosaka where they could be seen. The place was full of sailors on shore leave and so on. In other words, everything is calm and orderly and nothing unusual is going on.

Index

to Series of Interviews

with

Rear Admiral A. H. McCollum
U. S. Navy (Retired)

Volume I

Amphibious Landings (1930): practices conducted from USS WEST
   VIRGINIA, 134-136

Anderson, Adm. E. A. - CinC, Asiatic Fleet (1923): arrival at
   Tokyo in flagship HURON to render aid to earthquake victims,
   49, 53

Anderson, VADM Walter S.: Director of ONI in 1939, 269, 276, 302-303

USS ARGONNE, transport: trip to Manila, 31-33; McCollum tranships
   in Manila for Japan, 34-35

USS ARKANSAS, BB: first tour of duty on her, 26-27; personnel problems
   in post war era, 27-28

Beardall, RADM John R.: 390-391

Bennehoff, RADM O. R.: Captain of S-11, 83-84

Blamey, Gen. Sir Thomas: Australian Commander of ground forces
   in the MacArthur command, 373

Bloch, Adm. Claude C.: Commander of 14th Naval District (1942) -
   helpful in setting up COIC unit at Pearl Harbor, 370-371

Blucher, General (once known as Galitzin): Russian General in Far
   East - defeats Japanese Division (1940) at Nomonhan, 268

Bode, Captain Howard (Ping): head of Foreign Intelligence, ONI,
   1939-40, 269

Boone, Col. R. A., USMC: head of China Section, Far East desk, 403

Brainard, VADM Roland M.: head of Ship Movements (1941), 324, 381

British Intelligence Centers: 329-330

British Naval Intelligence: ONI delegation to London (1941) for
   purpose of making survey, 343-347; British methods of data
   gathering on naval ships adopted by ONI, 348; lack of current
   intelligence on Japanese Navy, 351-352; working exchange between
   British and ONI established, 353

Bristol, Adm. Mark L.: CinC Asiatic Fleet (1928) - senior foreign naval representative at Accession of Emperor Hirohito, 91-94

Bureau of Ordnance: concern about security of data on influence fuses, 308

Burnet, Col. Charles: military attache in Tokyo, 88

Chappell, Cdr. Walter, USNR: assistant head of British Desk, ONI (1941), member of delegation to Lond, 1941, 338-341

Chart Rooms: first set up by RADM Layton in CNO corridor - limited access, 327; ONI Far East sets up one, 328; others follow, 328

Chiang Kai-chek: 319

SS CHICHIBU MAKU: Japanese passenger liner - escorted into San Pedro harbor by DDs of the Fleet, 202

Choshu Clan: relationship with Japanese Navy, 99-100; Hirohito marries a member of this clan, 101

Clark, John: Analyst with Japanese desk, ONI, 258, 405

CNO: organizational set-up in 1941, 325-327

Coco Solo, Panama: base for SS Division VIII (O Class), 81

COIC (Combined Operations and Intelligence Center): 303; instigated in U.S. by Adm. Kirk and inspired by British practice, 303-304; British system used as model for unit set up for CinCPacFleet, 354; 357; McCollum confers with Adm. Nimitz (March, 1942) about setting up such a unit, 357-360; 370; 373; 375; system of attaching especially qualified linguists and intelligence officers to serve on staff of Task Force Commanders, 375-376

Colclough, VADM Oswald S.: as Judge Advocate General, warns McCollum not to discuss code breaking before Joint Congressional Committee investigating Pearl Harbor, 401

USS CONNECTICUT, BB: on midshipman cruise (1920, 22-24; loses her
　　propeller on run to Cuba, 23; armament, 24

Courts, Cdr. George M.: N.A. in Tokyo (1928), 86; illness and
　　attendant difficulty, 87, 160

Cunningham, Adm. Sir Andrew: CinC, Med Fleet (1941), 329; 355

Davis, Hartwell C.: Assistant Naval Attache in Tokyo (1921), 38-39

Denby, James: Third Secretary at U. S. Embassy, Tokyo, 48-49

DeWitt, Lt. Gen. John L.: Commanding General (1942) Western Defense
　　Command, issues order putting Nisei in concentration camps, 287

Direction Finding: inaccurate as a means of locating a ship, 279-280

District Intelligence Office, San Pedro, Calif.: 166; care of Confidential Documents stolen from fleet units and getting into hands of Japanese Intelligence, 166-176; other cases, 177-186; comments on the contributions of Reserve Intelligence Officers, 186-187

Dooman, Gene: Japanese speaking official at U. S. Embassy in Tokyo, 41, 43, 46; in 1941 on duty, Far Eastern Section of State Department, 230; 393-394

Draemel, RADM Milo: Chief of Staff to Admiral Nimitz (1942), 358, 360

Economic Sanctions: U. S. imposes Economic Sanctions on Japan – despatch of July 26, 1941, 321-322

Elliessief, Dr.: head of Oriental studies at Harvard (1941), 280, 283; creates difficulty for ONI in teaching of Japanese course, 284

Emperor Hirohito: 56, 58-59

SS EXOCHORDA: Export Line vessel in Marseilles harbor at outbreak of war – 1940, 241

Far East Desk, ONI: See entries under ONI.

Ferguson, Homer, U. S. Senator: member of Joint Congressional Investigating Committee on Pearl Harbor, 399

Fleming, Cdr. Ian, RNR: visits ONI in May, 1941, 338

<u>Fortnightly Summary</u> - of international situation: publication of ONI in 1940, 263, 301; difficulties with its publication, 302-303; 306; radio version for immediate delivery to Fleet, 306-307; 312; 380-381

Frost, Cdr. H. H.: Captain of DD JOHN D. FORD (1924), 61

FURUTAKA, Japanese cruiser: constructed in 1930, 350-351

Genda, General Minoru: assembled staff under direction of Adm. Yamamoto to plan Pearl Harbor attack, 441

Ghormley, VADM Robert L.: operations officer on staff of Adm. Hepburn, 197, 204

GOBBLEDYGOOK: Code Word to indicate burning of code books in various naval attache offices had been accomplished - in accordance with order of Dec. 3, 1941, 334-335; 383, 388

Godfrey, VADM John Henry: head of British Naval Intelligence, visits ONI in May, 1941, 338; asks U.S. delegation return visit, 338; not helpful in supplying U.S. delegation with kind of intelligence they were seeking in London, 1941, 344; Paul Hammond interceded with Adm. Sir Dudley Pound and got results, 345-346

Greenslade, VADM John W.: Commandant, 12th Naval District, 1942, 287

Hamilton, Max: Duty Far Eastern Division, U. S. State Department, 230

Hammond, Paul: American banker, assisted ONI delegation in getting data from British, 345-347

Hart, Admiral Thomas C.: fails to use Japanese language capabilities of ex-student from Tokyo, 299; his analysis of probable Japanese actions (1941), 313-314, 317; conducted inquiry on Pearl Harbor - McCollum testifies, 400; Hart understood pre-war problem for defense of Manila - inadequate army anti-aircraft defense, 413-414

Heard, Capt. Wm. A.: takes command of SS Div. VIII at Coco Solo, 82; 386

USS HELENA: McCollum serves as her skipper - on shakedown cruise to Guantanamo, when McCollum summoned to hearings before Joint Congressional Investigating Committee on Pearl Harbor, 398

Hepburn, Adm. Arthur J.: 108-109; succeeds Adm. Reeves as Commander, U.S. Fleet, McCollum becomes his Fleet Intelligence Officer, 196-197; becomes Commander, 12th Naval District in 1938, 201; just before Christmas, 1937, in response to message from CNO puts fleet in state of readiness, 201; the "Christmas War," 202; incident involving Japanese passenger liner, 202; (1936) as Commander, PacFleet tried to restructure War Games to no avail, 163-164; 209

Hillenkoetter, VADM R. H.: sent out from Washington to head COIC unit at Pearl Harbor (1942), 364-366

Hindmarsh, Dr. Albert E. (Captain, USNR): on Far East Desk, ONI, 259-260; language symposium at Cornell U (1941), 280-281; through him ONI makes agreement to start courses in Japanese at Harvard and Berkeley, 282-284, 290

Hittokappu Bay (Tankan Bay), Kuriles: station for USS Pope (1924 expedition), departure point for Pearl Harbor striking force in 1941, 60; 443

Hopkins, Captain A. A. (USNR): headed special investigative force in sheriff's office, Los Angeles County, 167, 186; credited with organizing Naval Districts into Zone Intelligence Areas, 194-195

Hornbeck, Dr. Stanley: Head of Far Eastern Division, U. S. State Department, 230-231; political adviser to Secretary of State, 393

USS HOUSTON, flagship of Asiatic Fleet, 1941: 331-332

Hulings, LCDR Garnet: assigned to Tokyo as Assistant Naval Attache, 34, 39, 53, 112-113

Hull, The Hon. Cordell: Secretary of State (1942), 393-394; refuses Japanese Ambassadors request to see him at 1 p.m. on Dec. 7, 1941, 414-415

Hunter, Dr. S. A. D.: ONI liaison officer with Department of State, 394-395

USS HURON, BB: flagship of CinC Asiatic (1923), steams to Tokyo to help with aftermath of earthquake, 49, 53-55

Ingersoll, Adm. Royal E.: Assistant CNO (Jan. 1941), orders COIC established, 303; refuses request to amend ONI manual, 311; 320, 322, 324, 331

ISIS Papers: special studies put out by British Naval Intelligence in WW II, 347

USS JACOB JONES, DD: 1938, McCollum takes command in Atlantic, 211; strawberry festival cruise, 212; SS target practice off New London, 214-215; President's Cup Regatta, 214-215; European-Mediterranean cruise, 215-240

James, VADM Jules: takes over as DNI - interim between VADM Anderson and ADM Kirk, 305; tries to get ONI manual amended, 311-312

Japanese-American Citizens League: group based on West Coast and helpful to U.S., 189

Japanese Army-Navy rivalry: see entries on Satsuma Clan and Choshu Clan, also 101-106

Japanese customs and characteristics, social attitudes: 54-56; practice of adopting a family name (Yoshi), 57, 66-67; Accession Ceremonies at Kyoto, 90; method of dating historical events, 89-90; naval events after Accession rites, 92-93; paying formal calls, 92-94; discourse on customs and particularly as found on west coast of Japan prior to WW II, 188

Japanese Earthquake, 1923: 49-53; McCollum acts as liaison between Fleet Admiral and the Embassy, 52-53

Japanese Language Kits: 253-254

Japanese Language Officers for Staff of TF Commanders: useful procedure in early part of war, 291-292; McCollum insists on such a group for Adm. Kinkaid, 292-294

Japanese Language School: ONI started in 1941 at Harvard and Berkeley, 282-283; phased out at Harvard - continued at Berkeley, 285; action of U. S. Army in putting Nisei in concentration camps, 286 ff; language school moved by McCollum to U. of Colorado at Boulder, 288-289; teaching materials, etc., 289-290; 294

Japanese language students in Tokyo - 1941: Adm. Kirk, DNI has them recalled in July, 296 ff; Japanese authorities try to block exit, 298

Japanese Language study: unstructured methods employed with young naval officers, 40-43; some students prove too old to undertake the task, 70-71; Navy interest in program (1924) - but it remained unstructured, 71; selection process for students go into effect in 1928, 72

Japanese Language Symposium: at Cornell University (1941), 281-282

Japanese Merchant Ship Movements: Capt. Puleson sets up section in ONI (1934) - State Dept. refuses to cooperate for lack of money, 248-249; U. S. Vice Consul in Kobe gives ONI monthly summary of Japanese merchant shipbuilding in Kobe area, 250, 252

Japanese Naval Academies: N.A. visit, 116-117; rafts used for target practice had silhouette of MISSISSIPPI Class BB, 117-118

Japanese Naval Air Training: 115; making tour of inspection - air stations and facilities, 115-116

Japanese Naval Ships: ONI prepares recognition manuals (1941), 252-253

Japanese Navy - intelligence gathering on: 106-108; difficulty in obtaining data on shipbuilding, 112-113; Japanese care in covering aircraft production, 114-115

Japanese Navy Command Structure: 97-98; relationship to Cabinet and Premier, 98-99; history and background of Naval Command relationship with Army Command, 99-100; Choshu clan takes over Army at time of civil war (1867-8) and Satsuma clan takes over Navy, 100

Japanese Observance of Treaty Commitments: 153-155; case of MUSASHI and YAMATO, 155-156

Japanese on West Coast of U.S. - characteristics: 102-103

Japanese speaking U. S. citizens: ONI prepares lists in 1941, 255-256; use for which they were intended, 256

Japanese Torpedoes: 146-147; ONI pre-WW II reports downgraded by BuOrd, 147-148

Japanese War Strategy - initial attack on Pearl Harbor and the Kra Peninsula, 416-418

USS JOHN D. FORD, DD: stationed in Kuriles (1924) to assist Army A/F in around the world flight, 60, 68

Johnson, VAdm. Alfred W.: Director of ONI, 1928, 86

Joint Congressional Investigating Committee, Pearl Harbor (1945-1946): 394-395; concentrated hearings largely on Army and Navy, McCollum's testimony, 398-399; McCollum warned by Navy not to discuss techniques of code breaking before Committee, 401-402

Jones, VAdm. H. P.: 23

Kato, Adm. Kanji (Hirohara): CinC, Japanese Fleet (1928), flagship BBNAGATO, 92, 96

Kenney, General George C.: Allied Air Forces Commander under General MacArthur, 373

USS KENTUCKY, BB: on midshipman cruise (1919), 21

Kimmel, RADM Husband E.: CinC, PacFleet, 304-305; DNI suggests that CNO telephone him in Hawaii on morning of December 7 (Washington time), 411; his staff convinced the Japanese attack had come from the SW and the Mandated Islands, 422; lacked planes for reconnaissance at Pearl Harbor, 425-426; letter from CNO Stark in Feb. 1941 stated that Washington did not see a Japanese attack in the "foreseeable future" - this apparently effected Kimmel's thinking in the matter, 429-430, 433

Kirk, Admiral Alan G.: Director of Naval Intelligence, 1941, 294-296; recall Japanese language students training in Tokyo, 1941, they are assigned fleet duty, 296-297; 305; his disagreement with Adm. Kelly Turner, 312

Knox, The Hon. Frank: Secretary of the Navy, 305-306

Kobayashi, Masashi: (1933) N.A. in Washington, D. C., 156-157; attempts to use long-range camera at fleet review in New York harbor (1934), 159-160

Kogoshima Bay: area of special Japanese fleet exercises to determine feasibility of plans for Pearl Harbor attack, 441

Kra Peninsula: focal point of Japanese amphibious landing on December 7, 1941, 408-409; McCollum states Pearl Harbor was covering operation to guarantee success of Kra landings, 416

Kramer, Captain Alwin D.: Head of Japanese desk in ONI (1939), 250, 262, 269, 275; decoding section of Far East Desk, 405-406; delivers copy of Japanese diplomatic message on morning of Dec. 7, 1941 to Adm. Beardall at White House, 407-408

Kurile Islands: expedition to meet U. S. Army Air Force flight around the world (1924), 59; preparations in the Islands with Japanese consent, 59-67

Kurusu, Saburo: Special Japanese Ambassador - sent to Washington in 1941, 414-415

Kyoto: site of Accession Ceremonies of Emperor, 90

Lackey, RAdm. H. E. (1938): in command of squadron 40-T with flag in OMAHA, 222

Laffin, Captain Tom: President of Laffin and Sons, ship chandlers in Japan (1924) - also chief poacher for sea otters in Kurile Islands, 61-63

Larson, Emmanual: analyst with China desk, ONI, 258

Layton, RAdm. Edwin T.: PacFleet Intelligence Officer (1942), 360; opposed to establishment of COIC for PacFleet, 363-364; relationship with Captain Rochefort, 366-367

Layton, VAdm. Sir Geoffrey: British CinC (1941), China Station, 356

Lockwood, Adm. Charles: N.A. in London, succeeds Adm. Kirk, 338; 342-343

MacArthur, General Douglas: promotes with War Dept., his idea that Philippines could be defended indefinitely, 333-334; his intelligence Staff, 373-374

MacVeagh, The Hon. Charles: Ambassador to Japan, 88-89

USS MARBLEHEAD: 332

Marshall, General George C.: his aides unable to locate him on morning of December 7, 1941, 411-412; they wanted confirmation of the message prepared for General Short in Hawaii, 412

Mashbir, Colonel Sidney: U. S. Army Japanese language study in Tokyo, 42, 48

Mason, RAdm. Redfield: (1940), Fleet Intelligence Officer, Asiatic Fleet, 264

McCollum, RAdm. A. H.: vital statistics, 1-6; early life in Japan, early education, 6, 11-13; death of father, 11-12; mother finds employment, 12; early loss of facility with Japanese language, 33; meets future wife in Japan, becomes engaged, 70, 73; marries (1925), 74, 81; to Japan as Assistant N.A., 85 (1928); difficulties because of this assignment, 85-86; son is born in California, 121-122

McLaren, Cdr. John: in command of DD POPE for Kurile expedition, 63; later in charge of Japanese Desk in ONI, 74, 80

McMorris, VAdm. Charles H. (Sock): 323

Melville, Edward: Counselor to Embassy, Tokyo (1928), 88, 91

Miri: location of British oil field in North Borneo, 418

USS MISSISSIPPI, BB: goes aground on departure from Pearl Harbor (1936), 204-205

Miyazaki, Lt. Cdr. Toshio: student at Stanford U. involved in spy case in San Pedro area, 171-174; 185

Moore, Major Charles: Japanese language expert in War Department (1941), 281-282

Moore, Captain Samuel Nobre: head of Foreign Intelligence, ONI in 1941, 380

Moses, Capt. Stanford E.: Captain of the ARKANSAS (1921), 29; arranged for McCollum to be assigned as an Assistant Attache in Tokyo, 30-31

Mukden, Manchuria: incident involving Japanese Consulate General, 276

Nagano, Adm. Osami: in command of Japanese training squadron that put in at Panama, later Chief of Japanese General Naval Staff, 83; 442

Naganuma: Japanese instructor who developed an efficient method for teaching U. S. students in Tokyo, 254; the Naval TOKUHON, 255

Nagasaki, Japan: place of RAdm. McCollum's birth, 1-2

Nagumo, VAdm.: Japanese Task Force Commander who made attack on Pearl Harbor, 418, 441

Naragansett Pier: visit of DD JACOB JONES, 1938, 212

National euphoria: discussion of national state of mind in 1941, focused on conflict with Germany, and neglect of a possible Japanese war, 429-435; problems of Army in Hawaii, operating under the stricture that general populace must not be alarmed, 435-436; problem of Nisei and possible sabotage, 438-439; confusion on Adm. Kimmel's staff as it pertained to conditions and readiness in Army, 439-440

Naval Academy: appointment secured through Senator Bankhead, 14-15; education at Academy, 16-17; summer cruises, 19-25

Naval Communications: 273-274; by-passed by War Plans but fared better than ONI and Ship Movements, 325; follows ONI in ordering burning of codes (Dec. 1941), 389-390.

Naval Intelligence Manual: quotations from, pertaining to evaluation of materials, 307; McCollum asks VCNO to amend rules if War Plans takes over task of evaluation, 311

U. S. Naval Observers: in 1941 stationed at Bangkok, Batavia, Sandakan, Medan, Hanoi, 333

Naval TOKUHON: the Japanese reader developed by Naganuma for use with U. S. Naval students, 255

Navy Fleet Bases in Pacific: (1930s) Adm. Reeves' interest in upgrading Pearl Harbor as fleet base, 203-204; 205

Navy Personnel Problems: 126 ff; 136-137; example of Asiatic Fleet units consistently winning competition honors because crews did not rotate frequently, 138

Navy War Games: as played in 1930s in the Fleet and at Naval War College, 163-165; simulated dawn attack on Pearl Harbor (1937), 164; 206-207

Nimitz, Fleet Admiral Chester: 357; his staff at Pearl Harbor (March, 1942), 358; gives his approval to COIC center, 361-362; 371-372

Nojiri: summer resort in Japan, 69-70

Nomura, Adm. Kichisaburo: Japanese Ambassador to Washington, named in 1940, 414-415; his commission, 429

Noyes, VAdm. Leigh: Director of Naval Communications, 274

Ogan, Capt. Joseph Vance: Naval Attache in Tokyo, relieves Cdr. Courts, 110, 116, 161

Okura, Baron: 56-58

USS OMAHA: flagship of Sq. 40-T, 222

ONI (Office of Naval Intelligence): description of its functions in 1925, 75-76; intelligence gathering, 77-78; obligations on diplomatic circuit, 78-79; McCollum's first tour of duty, 80; ONI in 1933, 139-140; Far East Section, 140-142; interest in Japanese warship pictures, etc., and Japanese language kits, 142-143; use of ONI by other sections of Navy, 145-146; tendency of technical bureaus to downgrade reports on Japanese Ordnance, 147-150; our tendency to suspect Japanese - differences in approach, 154-155; cooperation of Japanese N.A. in Washington, 156-157; exchange of hydrographic information even after outbreak of hostilities, 156-157; difficulty in getting qualified Japanese language men to serve as N.A. in Tokyo, 161-162; McCollum returns to head Far East Desk, 1939, 245 ff; organization of Far Eastern desk in that period, 245-246, 251; recognition manuals of Japanese ships updated, 252-253; Japanese language translators kits, 253-254; development of Far East Desk, 256-258; stepped up program for disseminating intelligence to fleets, 261-263; reorganization of China Observation network, 263-264; Public Relations problems, lack of understanding in U.S. of Japanese and their ability, 264-265; ONI sends Lt. Steve Juricka, Asst. N.A. for Air, Tokyo, around Department - and country - to talk about Japanese prowess in the air, 266; difficulty with U. S. reporters in Japan, inadequacy with language, 269; implacable attitude of U. S. missionaries in China towards anything Japanese, 267; Kramer heads translating section, Far East desk, 273; cooperation with Naval Communications, 273-274; tendency of ONI officials to accept information in Japanese diplomatic despatches, 275-277; Far East Desk maintains a plot of Japanese Fleet units, 279; Far East Desk sets up Japanese language training course at Berkeley and Harvard, 283-284; Harvard phased out, 285; July 1941 Adm. Kirk (DNI) instigates recall of Navy language students in Tokyo, 296; struggle with War Plans over evaluation of probable enemy intent, 309-312; Far East desk continues to maintain point that Japanese plans, actions not predicated on lead of Germany, 315; Germans didn't want Japanese to get involved, 316; Turner despatch of July 3, 1941, possible Japanese action in Manchuria, 314-319; McCollum attitude towards intelligence emanating from Chiang-kai-chek headquarters, 319; ONI not notified of Economic Sanctions levied against Japan, 321-322; references to Command reliance on ONI prior to WW II, 323; conflict with War Plans, 328; ONI prohibited from drawing conclusions based on intelligence at hand, 328-329; See Note added by McCollum on ONI-War Plans Conflict, 330-331, also 335-336; further discussion of evaluation of material, on part of recipient, 367-370, 381; ONI sends despatch (Dec. 3, 1941) to advise that Japanese Foreign Office had ordered burning of codes and documents, wording of this despatch, 383-384; ONI asks N.A.s in precarious positions to burn codes, 385, 387, 390; lack of reaction by CNO, SecNav, etc., 390-392; more on Foreign

Desks structure in F Section of ONI, 385-387; 24-hour watch set up on Far East desk about one month before Pearl Harbor Day, 413-414; Japanese Foreign Office message that was decoded in 14 parts, 404-405; discussion of time factors in Japanese despatches, 408-411; difficulty in getting any intelligence data out of Japan in period just before December 7, 409-410

USS ORION, Collier: tows BB CONNECTICUT, 23

O-7: McCollum becomes captain, description of ship, 82

Paramushiro: northernmost of Kurile Islands, station for DD JOHN D. FORD at time of Army A/F around-the-world flight, 60, 63

Pearl Harbor Day in Navy Department: 406 ff; rumors and disorder, 418-419; advises Kimmel about Japanese units thought to have participated in P.H. attack, 422

USS PENNSYLVANIA, BB: flagship of Admiral Nimitz, 362

Picking, Captain Sherwood: head of Foreign Intelligence, ONI (1941) succeeding Capt. H. Bode, heads delegation to London, 338-339; killed in landing at Prestwick, Scotland, 342

USS POPE, DD: stationed in Kuriles (1924) to assist Army A/F in around the world flight, 60, 68

Pound, Adm. Sir Dudley: Chief of British Naval Staff, 329

SS PRESIDENT McKINLEY: 86

Puleston, Capt. Wm. D.: changes he effected in ONI in 1934, 247; coast watcher service, 247-248; world-wide system of Japanese merchant ship movements, 248-249; develops idea of having ONI serve the fleet in outlying areas, a weekly appreciation of situation in Far East prepared and mailed from ONI, 251

Redesdale, Lord (Mitford): 46

Redman, RAdm. John: author of plan for quarterly schedules for fleets, 209-210

Reeves, Adm. Joseph Mason: (1935) as CinC, U.S. Fleet, 166; request assignment of McCollum to his staff, 169; recollections of Reeves as Fleet Commander, 190-191; stresses need for ship maintenance and repair facility at Pearl Harbor, 203-204

Richardson, Adm. James O.: 304

Richardson, Seth: Counsel for Joint Congressional Investigating Committee (1945-46), 398

Rochefort, Captain Joseph: suggests to Adm. Reeves that McCollum handle the spy problem in San Pedro area, 168-169; Reeves sends him to negotiate with San Pedro officials, 192; with change of command (Reeves to Hepburn) Rochefort changes jobs with McCollum, 196; originated idea of putting a Japanese language-qualified man on staff of task force commander, 291-292; receives some of language students at Ewa, 297; Intelligence organization at Pearl Harbor, 359; highly approved of COIC set-up for Admiral Nimitz, 366

Rockport, Mass.: visit of the Jacob Jones, 1938, 212

Rogers, Captain F. F.: first Japanese language qualified Naval Attache U. S. sends to Tokyo, 160-161

Ryan, Lt (jg) Thomas Clark, Jr.: meets McCollum in Manila, 35-36; assigned to Embassy in Tokyo, 36-38; wins Congressional Medal of Honor for rescue work at time of earthquake, (1923), 51-52

Safford, Capt. Lawrence F.: 278; gives help with strategic message, 387-389

Sansom, Sir George: 320; prominent member of British COIC unit at Singapore, 355-356

Satsuma Clan: relationship with Japanese Navy, 99-100

S-11: McCollum becomes Executive on S-11, 83-84; takes command, 84

S-51: 81

Schuirmann, RAdm. Roscoe E.: Director of Central Division, CNO (1941), 392-393

Sebald, Capt. Wm. Joseph, USNR: Japanese experience and background, 269-261; works for ONI, 272

Shaw, Glen: Japanese language expert hired by Far East desk, 260-261; 290

Ship Movements Division: 208; Redman plan for running fleets on quarterly schedule, 209-210

Ship Movements: Division is by-passed by War Plans, 324-325

Short, Major General Walter C.: 425; involved with problem of Japanese population in Hawaiian Islands before Pearl Harbor attack, 437-438; advises General Marshall of his steps to prevent sabotage, 438-439

Singapore: British establish Far East Intelligence Center there with Sir George Sansom, 319-320; British naval forces based at Singapore destroyed by Japanese air attack, 417-418

Smiley, Sam: detailed by Adm. Wilkinson (DNI, 1941) to set up enemy ship design unit for facilitating identification, 348; 349-350

Spear, Dr. (Captain) Raymond: Medical Director, U.S. Naval Hospital in Yokohama, 47; confines McCollum as language study to hospital for six weeks to save on living expenses, 48

Stark, Adm. Harold R.: CNO (1941), 310, 312, 320, 322; member of triumvirate comprising Ingersol and Turner, 324-325; 331; Adm. Stark personally affirms (late Nov., 1941) that PacFleet and

Asiatic Fleet had been warned of Japanese preparations and ordered to take every step necessary to be ready for war, 332-333; 388; 391; Wilkinson and McCollum discuss Japanese diplomatic message with him on morning of Dec. 7, 1941, 406-408; 410-411; DNI suggests that he telephone Adm. Kimmel at time of discussion, 411; Stark apparently restrained from telephoning by recent agreement by which Army was in charge of defense of Hawaiian Islands, 412-413

SS STEEL ARROW: merchantman undergoing repairs in Kawasaki shipbuilding yard, Kobe, 113

St. Nazaire: French port visited by DD JACOB JONES just prior to outbreak of WW II, 235-236

Suzuki, Adm. Kantaro: Japanese Chief of Naval General Staff, later Grand Chamberlain to the Emperor, 110-111

Takamatsu, Prince: his visit to U. S. eventual source of Japanese spy story in Los Angeles area, 179

Tankan Bay: see entry under Hittokappu Bay, same place.

Technical Evaluation of Intelligence reports: done by Bureaus (1941) for ONI, 307-308

Tinker, Major General Joe (Indian): Commander of Army Air Forces (1942) in Hawaii, 361; 424; lack of planes for reconnaissance work, 425

Tokugawa Shogunate, history of its destruction: 99-100

SS Training School, New London, Conn.: 73-74

Turner, Adm. Richmond Kelly: (1940) new chief of War Plans, Navy Dept., 301; his prognosis for Japanese actions, 1941 - disagreement with Adm. Kirk and McCollum, 311-312; Tendency to tie

Japanese actions to German efforts, 315; despatch of July 3, 1941 giving reasons for probable Japanese move towards Manchuria, 314-318; further discussion, 319, 324

Twitty, Brig. Gen. Joe: Army puts him in charge of their intelligence center for POA (1942), 364

Tyrwhitt, VAdm. Sir Reginald: R.N. hero of WW I, in command of cruisers at Accession ceremonies for Emperor Hirohito, 92, 96

U. S. Army Command, in Hawaii (1941): problems faced before Pearl Harbor attack, 435-436; fear of an uprising among Japanese population on the Islands, 438-439

U. S. Diplomatic Representatives abroad: comments on, 228-230

Villefranche: Mediterranean port - served as land base (1938) for Squadron 40-T, 222, 224-225

Walne, Dr. Florence: University of California, Japanese language director (1941), 280; enthusiastic about Japanese language training course undertaken by ONI in 1941 at Harvard and Berkeley, 282-283

War Plans, Office of CNO: R. K. Turner becomes chief (1940), 301; takes over from ONI task of evaluating probable enemy intent, 309-311; McCollum asks that ONI manual be amended to give evaluating authority to War Plans and not ONI, 311; procedure for sending dispatch without reference to ONI, 320 (1941); economic sanctions against Japan - prepared by War Plans and not submitted or routed to ONI, 321-322; ONI feels War Plans called on for advice outside their competence, 322-323; takes on some of duties of Ship Movements, 324, 328; See Note added to transcript by McCollum on War Plans-ONI controversy, 330-331, 335-336; reaction to Pearl Harbor news, 420

War Warning Despatch: November 27, 1941, 332-333

Watch fatigue: discussion of subject, experiment of Adm. Schofield in 1933 and its bearing on Pearl Harbor surprise attack, 426-429

Watson, Capt. Edward H.: Naval Attache in Tokyo (1921), 38, 40

Watts, Lt. Cdr. Ethelbert: Head of Japanese Section, Far East Desk, 403, 406

Wellborn, VAdm. Charles: 150-151

Wells, The Hon. Sumner: Under Secretary of State (1941), 392, 394

USS WEST VIRGINIA, BB: (1930) McCollum given command of a gun turret, 121; description of ship characteristics, 122-124; discourse on award of Navy E for fleet competition, 125-127; use of personnel, 128-130; practice for amphibious landings, 134-136; re-enlistment problems, 432

Wilkinson, VAdm. Theodore S.: has conference with Adm. Stark and staff on Far East portents, Stark affirms appropriate commanders had been warned and ordered to be prepared for war, 332-333; McCollum asks permission from him on Oct. 11, 1941 to put Far East Desk on a 24-hour watch basis, 381-382; made aware of Japanese diplomatic messages before hostilities, 406; present with CNO when decoded Japanese diplomatic messages are read to him - suggests Adm. Stark telephone Adm. Kimmel in Hawaii, 411

Williams, Major Gregon (USMC): N.A. in Shanghai, ordered on Dec. 4 to his war post, 390

Willoughby, Major General Charles A.: Chief Intelligence Officer for General MacArthur, 373

WW II - War clouds over Europe, 1939: 234-242

Wrangham, Major Archie, RM: British marine named member of ONI

-21-

delegation to England (1941), 339-340; lost his life in plane crash at Prestwick, Scotland, 342; 379-380

Wynd, The Rev. Wm.: American missionary with whom McCollum stayed in Tokyo, 37-38, 49, 52

Yamaguchi, Tamon: Japanese Naval Attache, Washington, D.C. - ordered home because of spying activities, 158

Yamamoto, Fleet Admiral I.: Japanese CinC, 417; sets up temporary staff to plan attack on Pearl Harbor, 441; engages in special exercises to determine feasibility of the Genda Plan, 441; approval of plan by high command comes in Oct. 1941, 442; completely reverses strategic concept upon which Japanese navy had been built, 442-443; sends Adm. Nagumo and his carriers in November, 1941 to the Kurile Islands - practically in quarantine, 442-443; private code with Adm. Nagumo to launch expedition against P.H., 443; gives special liberty to fleet units at Yokuska, Kure, etc., to complete cover for Task Force foray to Pearl Harbor, 444

Yamashita, General: Japanese General who landed army on Kra Peninsula, Dec. 7, 1941, 417

Zacharias, RAdm. E. M.: Assistant to N.A. in Tokyo (1921), 38; takes McCollum in tow and prepares him for life in Tokyo, 39, 46; invites McCollum to share housing, 48; 87; his quarrel with N.A., 87-88; U. S. Ambassador has him recalled from Japan to end feud with N.A., 89; wanted to attend Accession Ceremonies as U. S. representative, 90-91

In reply refer to Initials
and No.

Op-16-F-2

NAVY DEPARTMENT
OFFICE OF THE CHIEF OF NAVAL OPERATIONS
WASHINGTON 25, D.C.

December 1, 1941

Memorandum for the Director

1. Attached hereto is a resume of the outstanding military, naval and political moves made by Japan during the past two months. No effort is made to draw conclusions in each instance but a view of the general situation would indicate that the principal preparatory effort has been directed by the Japanese looking towards, first: an eventual control or occupation of Thailand followed almost immediately by an attack against British possessions, possibly Burma and Singapore.

A. H. McCollum

Distribution:
Copy No. 1 and 2 - DNI
Copy No. 3 - Op-16-F
Copy No. 4,5,6,7, - File

Memorandum for the Director

ARMY PREPARATIONS
December 1, 1941

Starting about 1 October and continuing until about the middle of November the Japanese shipped out of the port of Shanghai alone a large quantity of military supplies. Vessels carrying this equipment were seen headed south or southwest. The equipment consisted of all sorts of military stores and equipment, a large number of landing boats being particularly noted. Other especially noteworthy items consisted of a considerable number of tanks and trucks, quite a few of which were camouflaged green; considerable railroad equipment, particularly locomotives and rolling stock. While a few troops were taken out at this time these ships principally carried equipment. Starting about 15 November the character of the shipments underwent a marked change. From 15 to 21 November large transports took out of Shanghai alone some 24,000 fully equipped veteran troops, while an additional 50,000 were reported as being withdrawn from North China reputedly destined for Formosa. From 21 to 26 November 20,000 troops were landed at Saigon and 4,000 at Haiphong which with the 6,000 troops already there were sent South to Saigon and Cambodia by rail. All wharves and docks at Haiphong and Saigon are reported crowded with Japanese transports unloading supplies and men. It is estimated that the following Japanese troops are now in French Indo-China ready and equipped for action.

(a) South and Central Indo-China   70,000
(b) Northern Indo-China   25,000

The landing of reinforcements continues and additional troops and supplies are undoubtedly available on nearby Hainan Island and more distant Formosa.

NAVAL PREPARATIONS

Starting about 1 October and continuing through November extensive naval preparations have been made. The following are the high points of this preparation.

(a) All possible ships have been recalled to Japan for a quick docking and repair check up that has now been completed.

(b) Some additional naval aircraft strength has been sent to the Japanese Mandate Islands area.

(c) An air and surface patrol was established on a line between the Marshall Islands and the Gilberts. Guam was placed under air and submarine observation.

(d) The CinC 2nd. Fleet organized two task groups, both rather loosely knit organizations; group No.1 to operate in the South China area and group No. 2 to operate in the Mandate Islands area. This organization is about finished and the CinC of the 2nd., Fleet expects to be in Southern Formosa by about 3 or 4 December.

(e) The CinC of the Combined Air Force has just completed an inspection of all outlying naval air groups, particularly those in the Mandates, South China and Formosa.

(f) Many merchant vessels have recently been taken over by the Navy and at least three of these have been equipped as antiaircraft ships.

POLITICAL PREPARATIONS - 1 October - 30 Nov.

Japanese residents particularly women and children have been evacuated from

    (a) British India and Singapore
    (b) Netherlands East Indies
    (c) Philippine Islands
    (d) Hongkong
    (e) Australia
    (f) Many Japanese residents have recently withdrawn from the United States, Canada and South America.

Preparations have been made to shift the center of the War Intelligence and Espionage net covering the Americas from Washington to Rio de Janeiro, Brazil. Japanese Embassy at Rio de Janeiro has been equipped with short wave radio transmitter.

Great stress has been laid on establishment of espionage net in Thailand and Singapore as follows:

    (a) Japanese consulate at Singora is manned by 4 Army Intelligence Officers.
    (b) A consulate has been established at the northern railhead of Chiengmai.
    (c) Army communication personnel and equipment is present at Singora, Bangkok and Chiengmai.
    (d) Four Army and Navy officers under assumed names have been sent to the Embassy at Bangkok. The Ambassador has received instructions not to interfere with the work of these men.
    (e) A chain of drug stores manned by Intelligence agents is in process of establishment.
    (f) Japanese Army doctors under assumed names are in the hospital at Bangkok.
    (g) At the end of November 60,000 Bhats were sent in gold to the Ambassador at Bangkok with instructions to hold it for emergency Intelligence use.
    (h) At least two sabotage agents have been sent into Singapore

In French Indo-China the Japanese military has taken over many police functions. Many Chinese and Annamese are being summarily arrested. At the end of November Japanese Ambassador Yoshizawa queried his government as to whether he and his staff should take over the governmental functions of French Indo-China or continue to function through the front of the French Government General.

The Consul General at Shanghai has informed his government that all preparations are complete for taking over all physical property in China belonging to British, Americans and other enemy nationals

The Army General Staff sent urgent requests for information for U.S. and Dutch troop and plane strengths and dispositions in the Philippines and Netherlands East Indies.

Special Ambassador Kurusu sent to the United States to conduct negotiations with the United States.

The Saturday Review
25 West 45th Street
New York 36, N.Y.

June 7, 1954

Dear Admiral McCollum:

It was to be expected, I suppose, that your review of "The Final Secret of Pearl Harbor" would provoke some responses from readers. I enclose a carbon copy of one received in this morning's mail, from a prominent Boston lawyer.

Our thought is that we should publish it, at least in shortened form, on our Letters to the Editor page. Naturally, we'd like to publish a reply from you at the same time. Doubtless, you will be able to dispose of the points Mr. Montgomery raises in short order.

Sincerely,

Raymond Walters, Jr.
Raymond Walters, Jr.

RW/mg

Admiral A. H. McCollum, USN
3522 Third Street
North Arlington, Virginia

Robert H. Montgomery
30 Federal Street
Boston, Massachusetts

Editor, The Saturday Review
25 West 45th Street
New York 36, New York

Dear Sir:

It is hard to believe that Admiral McCullom is the author of your review "The Final Secret of Pearl Harbor."

McCullom in 1941 was stationed in Washington as head of Far Eastern Section, Naval Intelligence. We had broken the Japanese codes and were day by day decoding and translating all their diplomatic messages. McCullom was one of seven on the Navy Department Distribution list who received a copy of every message. Short and Kimmel in Hawaii had no decoding machine and Washington sent them no copy of digest or messages.

At the time of Pearl Harbor McCullom was in a position to know and did know how inadequate and misleading was the information available or made available to Short and Kimmel and did his best to supplement and correct what they were receiving.

On December 1, 1941 he prepared a memorandum digest of the Japanese situation which he considered should be sent the Naval Command in Hawaii. This was discussed by Admiral Stark, his principal advisers, and Commander McCullom himself. Admiral Stark decided not to send it.

On December 4th McCullom tried again. This time he drafted a proposed dispatch summarizing the United States-Japanese situation for transmission to the Commander-in-Chief of the Pacific Fleet, which contained the phrase "War between Japan and the United States is imminent."

Admiral Turner showed him the "war warning" dispatch of November 27th, upon which so much reliance was placed in the review, and asked whether he still thought his message was necessary. McCullom said he did, but the message was never sent.

If his advice had been followed and the information he wished sent had been sent and had been supplemented by a day to day report of later developments, the raid on Pearl Harbor would not have been a surprise and might never have occurred.

Why this officer who made these honorable and intelligent efforts to save our fleet should not refer to them in a review of Admiral Theobald's book is as inexplicable as his failure to mention the strange events and omissions of December 6 and December 7.

It would be easy to answer the arguments made in the review but too long for a letter. The book itself is the best answer.

Robert H. Montgomery

THE CALAMITOUS 7th

"The Final Secret of Pearl Harbor", by Rear Admiral R. A. Theobald USN (Ret.) (Devin-Adair. 202 pp $3.50), argues the thesis, in lawyer's-brief fashion, that F. D. Roosevelt deliberately goaded Japan into World War II. Below it is reviewed by Rear Admiral A. H. McCullom, USN (Ret.), who at the time of Pearl Harbor was head of the Far Eastern Division of Naval Intelligence.

By A. H. McCollum

The "author's introduction" to Rear Admiral R. A. Theobald's "The Final Secret of Pearl Harbor" is the key to the tenor of his book. In it, Admiral Theobald states: "The normal sequence of deductive reasoning is discarded in favor of the order used in a legal presentation. The case is stated at the outset, and the evidence is marshalled and discussed." Thus the author, with commendable candor, gives due notice that he is out to prove a case and in consequence will present only those facts and his own deductions therefrom that tend to support that case.

Admiral Theobald's thesis is the somewhat overworked and stale one that the consummately clever and adroit Franklin Delano Roosevelt, then President of the United States, deliberately goaded Japan into war as a means of insuring United States entry into the European war on the side of the British. In order to achieve his purpose - so the argument runs - the President connived with the highest civil and military officials in the government in Washington and, presumably, with high military and naval commanders in the remoter reaches of the Pacific to induce Japan to start the war by a surprise attack on Pearl Harbor. The plot went even farther: Admiral Kimmel and General Short, the American commanders in the Hawaiian area, and their forces were carefully prepared and deliberately tricked into slaughter as a human sacrifice that was thought necessary to arouse the American people.

In the development of his thesis, Admiral Theobald seems to disregard or dismiss as worthless much of the testimony of practically every high official, civil or military, then in the government, and perhaps as important, that of high naval commands in the Far East. Moreover, he appears to have drawn some rather unusual conclusions from his data. He makes much of the efforts of the United States to deter Japan from further armed aggressions in Asia in 1940 and 1941 and interprets these diplomatic moves as conclusive evidence of a goading of Japan into war. Other students and observers of events, then and now, are generally of the view that these same moves were but a logical expression of American foreign policy at least as old as John Hay and his Open Door Policy, emphasized so far as Japan was concerned, by President Theodore Roosevelt's despatch of the American fleet to the Pacific and thence around the world in 1907.

Throughout the book Admiral Theobald constantly stresses the thought that if the Hawaiian commanders had been given all the information available to Washington and (he says) to Admiral Hart, commander of the American Asiatic Fleet, particularly that obtained from reading the broken Japanese diplomatic codes, different and presumably effective steps would have been taken to prevent surprise. This oft-repeated claim for superior perspicacity on the part of the Hawaiian commands over all other commands in the Pacific and in Washington is hardly borne out by what the Hawaiian commands did do on the basis of the very considerable information that they did have and in response to specific orders from Washington. On November 27, 1941, the Navy Department sent the following warning and instructions to the commanders of the Pacific and Asiatic fleets:

> THIS DISPATCH IS TO BE CONSIDERED A WAR WARNING. NEGOTIATIONS WITH JAPAN LOOKING TOWARD STABILIZATION OF CONDITIONS IN THE PACIFIC HAVE CEASED AND AN AGGRESSIVE MOVE BY JAPAN IS EXPECTED WITHIN THE NEXT FEW DAYS. THE NUMBER AND EQUIPMENT OF JAPANESE TROOPS AND THE ORGANIZATION OF NAVAL TASK FORCES INDICATES AN AMPHIBIOUS EXPEDITION AGAINST EITHER THE PHILIPPINES THAI OR KRA PENINSULA OR POSSIBLY BORNEO. EXECUTE AN APPROPRIATE DEFENSIVE DEPLOYMENT PREPARATORY TO CARRYING OUT TASKS ASSIGNED IN WPL 46. INFORM DISTRICT AND ARMY AUTHORITIES .....

Admiral Theobald characterizes this dispatch as adequate and effective for Admiral Hart, commanding the Asiatic Fleet, but totally inadequate and confusing to Admiral Kimmel. Of this same dispatch and a parallel one sent by the War Department to the Army commands, the distinguished historians William L. Langer and S. Everett Gleason in their book "The Undeclared War 1940-1941," have this to say: "These warnings would have appeared to have been adequate and clear ....." Admiral Kimmel's response to the order to deploy was to concentrate a major part of his fleet in the anchorage at Pearl Harbor.

It seems unfortunate that Admiral Theobald should have chosen to devote his very considerable talents to the assemblage of such a miscellany of partial facts and innuendo. Its lack of balanced objectivity of judgement, and its ignoring of most of the relevant facts and data that do not gibe with the author's predetermined thesis render the book of dubious value.

NOTE: As published in the Saturday Review of 29 May 1954

A REPLY FROM THE ADMIRAL

It is quite evident that Mr. Montgomery disagrees with my review of Admiral Theobald's book, but his reasons for so doing are, as he intimates, probably too many for detailing in a letter. In any event, he does not state them. He limits himself to expressing surprise that one such as myself, who tried repeatedly to get more information (or at least an expression of his views) to our Pacific commanders and failed, could have written such a review.

Mr. Montgomery has been most kind in summarizing my efforts (as they appear in the record of the Joint Congressional Committee investigating Pearl Harbor) to get more information and considered opinion before our Pacific commanders, including Admiral Kimmel. It has always been my view that intelligence should err, if err it must, on the side of giving too much rather than too little information. I have also felt that it is the function of Naval Intelligence at whatever level to give to the commanders concerned its considered opinion of what the enemy may do or may not do as developed from the best information at hand. The command in Washington, quite obviously, did not agree with my views. I may add that this was not particularly novel either before or after Pearl Harbor and later on. I have often felt that the extremes of secrecy imposed on the use of "Magic" as well as certain other intelligence, before, during, and after Pearl Harbor, often tended to make this valuable information useless in practice.

To get back to the point however, it seems to me to be the function of the reviewer of a book to:

(a) State as briefly as may be consistent with clarity and fairness, the principal theme of the book.

(b) Express an opinion as to how well or how poorly the author has developed or supported his theme.

(c) In the light of (a) and (b) above, and in a work of this nature, take one or two major arguments of the book and subject them to critical appraisal.

I believe that in my review I stated the theme of Admiral Theobald's book accurately and fairly. More briefly restated it was:

(a) The President of the United States deliberately goaded Japan into war as a means of insuring United States entry into the European war on the side of the British.

(b) To this end he had the active or tacit connivance of the highest officials, both civil and military, in the government and in the remoter Pacific commands.

(c) The Hawaiian commanders were deliberately tricked into error leading to catastrophe, by calculated denial of information in order that by their sacrifice the American people might be adequately aroused.

I find the evidence set forth in the book in support of these theses unconvincing when considered in the light of all the facts developed by the several Pearl Harbor investigating bodies and in the light of our historical position, right or wrong, in the international politics of the Pacific basin. It seems to me that reasonable appraisal of the developed facts, as well as an appraisal of the character of the men themselves, does not warrant any such charge as that Roosevelt, Hull, Stimson, Knox, Stark, Marshall, Hart, MacArthur, and others wilfully connived at the destruction of our principal combat force in the Pacific. While I, personally, would like to believe that our Hawaiian commanders might have done differently if they had been given additional information, I suggest that, except in the crystal clear light of hindsight, what they might or might not have done remains in the realm of conjecture. The developed facts seem to indicate that, despite the very considerable information that they did have, they did not take a tactical posture for adequate reconnaissance and defense.

It was not my purpose to analyze or discuss the Pearl Harbor affair in detail, but only to review Admiral Theobald's book fairly and objectively. This, I believe, I have done. His argument depends very largely for support on his own deductions from data carefully selected by him for the purpose -- as he quite candidly admits -- of proving a predetermined conclusion. The book can, therefore, offer little of appeal or value to the serious student in search of objective analysis.

A. H. McCollum

Arlington, Virginia

NOTE: Published in July 3rd 1954 issue of the Saturday Review

LAW OFFICES
FREEMAN, FOX & FIECHTER
TWELVE SOUTH TWELFTH STREET
PHILADELPHIA 7
WALNUT 2-3446

PAUL FREEMAN
WILLIAM LOGAN FOX
FREDERICK C. FIECHTER, JR.

June 29, 1954

Admiral A. H. McCullom
Care of "The Saturday Review"
25 West 45th Street
New York 36, New York

Dear Admiral McCullom:

I read your review of Admiral Theobald's Book with no little satisfaction, for it is a frightful thought that some 3,000 of our men were needlessly killed and our Pacific Fleet almost wholly destroyed to bring to fruition President Roosevelt's determination to take part in the Second War. However, that is Admiral Theobald's own deduction, and doubtless is quite wrong. But there is a preliminary matter which is even more important and which is:- Has Admiral Theobald misstated any fact--whether accidentally or purposefully? Certainly you yourself were in a position at that very time to know more than he of the true facts and of all the facts.

And for that reason I venture to ask you certain questions in the hope that you will be so generous as to answer them, and excuse my trespass on your kindness.

1. From your knowledge of matters, did you detect any misstatement of fact in Admiral Theobald's Book?

2. In your review, you speak of his assembling "partial" facts and innuendo. By the word "partial" do you mean that only some of the facts were given and others equally important purposely omitted, or do you mean that he relied on facts--though they supported his "partial" (and not impartial) deductions? For a fact, if it be a fact, is not "partial." It may be amplified or explained by other facts, but in, of and by itself it can be neither "partial" nor impartial.

3. The Admiral states that for some years prior to 1940 our Navy had concluded (a) that the Philippines could not be defended successfully against an attack by Japan, and (b) that in the event of a War, Japan would certainly strike at Pearl Harbor (or at the Canal). Is this statement accurate?

4. If the previous statement be correct, then why was a Magic machine sent to the Philippines and not to Pearl Harbor--if only one could be spared, and who was responsible

Admiral A. H. McCullom - 2   June 29, 1954

for that decision? Furthermore, since one can conclude that our forces in the Philippines had a Magic machine one wonders why the information obtained there was not communicated to Pearl Harbor. Do you know anything on this point?

      5. I have read the Report of the Navy Commission on Pearl Harbor which concludes with the terrible stricture on Admiral Stark--that never again should he be entrusted with a position requiring the exercise of superior judgment. Do you know whether at that hearing these Magic telegrams were in evidence? From a reading of their Report I gather not, but I should like to know. This seems to me most important.

      6. Certainly the President was advised promptly of the information contained in the Japanese telegrams. Did either the Secretary of War or the Secretary of the Navy know of their contents each day as they were decoded, and if not, do you know when they first learned of them? Besides the President, Admiral Stark, General Marshall and you yourself, do you know who else each day and day by day knew their contents?

      7. Your answer to Mr. Robert H. Montgomery does not deny that you urged that Admiral Kimmel be given full information. If you did so--and I am certain from your own letter that you did--were you given any reason or any excuse for the failure to follow your very sane suggestion, and if you were, what was it?

      8. My information is that Admiral Kimmel has never been granted what he has so frequently demanded, i.e. that he be court-martialed. Can there be any reasonable doubt in your mind that such a court would have found him guilty of the grossest neglect and given him a dishonorable discharge, had he been sent the data you yourself prepared (and urged that it be sent on to him) and thereafter followed the course he did in fact follow?

      To me the basic question is not what conclusion Admiral Theobald comes to, for (given the _facts_, and all the facts) each intelligent person must draw his own conclusion.

      As I said at the beginning, it is not a pleasing thought that the President (in effect) purposely arranged matters so that the two local Commanders were deprived of information which they should have had, but that is a deduction and the more important thing is to know whether what Admiral Theobald's book states as facts _are_ facts, and what if any vital fact he has failed to state. That is my purpose in asking you to be so kind if you will as to let me have the answers to my questions, for if his "facts" are wrong his deduction is worthless.

      Very respectfully yours,

PF:C

3522 3rd., Street North
Arlington 1, Virginia
13 July 1954

Mr. Paul Freeman
12 South 12th Street
Philadelphia 7, Pennsylvania

My dear Mr. Freeman:

I have delayed somewhat in replying to your very thoughtful letter of June 29th referring to my review of Admiral Theobald's book. May I say at the outset that your questions and remarks are very much to the point and are most moving. Before essaying a discussion therefore, I thought it but due you that I refresh my mind from the official record.

I do not know that I can answer your queries in the one, two, three order in which you have posed them. I shall however, try to discuss each of the points you have raised in the hope of clarifying what has, in many respects, become a most confusing matter.

I am grateful for your scholarly dissertation on what constitutes a fact. I thoroughly agree with you that a single fact cannot be partial or impartial. It is an entity and stands solely on its own merit. In my use of the adjective "partial" to qualify the plural noun "facts", I thought I was following the definition of "partial" set forth in Webster's New Unabridged Dictionary which defines the adjective "partial" as:- of, pertaining to, or affecting a part only; not total or entire.---- Very likely a more precise term for me to have used would have been "a part of the facts".

I have not made a point by point check of the facts that Admiral Theobald presents in his book. I feel sure however, that the Admiral would not present anything as a fact that he did not believe to be one. I suggest that what we are concerned with here, is not an assemblage of isolated facts but rather a series of episodes that are difficult of appraisal unless <u>all</u> of the <u>then known</u> facts as well as the temper of the times is taken into consideration.

Admiral Theobald's statement cited by you, to the effect that the Philippines could not be held is, I think, a fair appraisal of Naval opinion, shared generally by most thinking Naval Officers (and there were some who did think), prior to about 1938 or 1939; and by many even after those dates. It might be well to recall that in 1922, the United States entered into a treaty for the limitation of armaments with a number of nations including Japan. This treaty limited the number and size of certain important categories of naval vessels that could be possessed by each of the signatory powers. Another, and most important item so far as the United States was concerned, provision was the stipulation that prohibited the United States from improving, modernizing or increasing the garrisons of Naval or army bases in United States possessions west of the 180th meridian. By this means United States interests and possessions in the Far East were put in pawn to the Japanese and the United States Navy was rendered incapable of early offensive action in the Orient.

This treaty was hailed in this country as a great accomplishment for peace; and the then Administration and the then Secretary of State received much popular acclaim for the negotiation of this masterful implement of peace. Many senior naval officers of the time were rather outspoken in their criticism of this treaty but were effectively silenced by the

Administration then in power and by popular clamor. I think that from 1922 onward for some years, it was generally conceded in Naval circles that we could not hold the Philippines nor quickly regain them in case of Japanese attack. The Japanese abrogated this treaty in late 1934 and the abrogation became effective two years later in 1936. The U.S. Congress however, repeatedly refused to appropriate any considerable amount of money for building up defenses or Naval establishments in Guam or the Philippines.

On the other hand, General MacArthur, having at first as one of his principal aides our present President, General Eisenhower, went to the Philippines in 1934 or 1935 for the avowed purpose of building a Philippine Army as a bulwark for the defense of the independence of those islands then scheduled for 1946. By 1938, and certainly by late 1939, when I assumed the duty of Chief of the Far East Section of O.N.I., reports from General MacArthur justified the belief that, even if the whole of the Philippines could not be held, at all events, an important enclave centering around Corregidor could be held for several years; if not indefinitely. Many individual officers of the War and Navy Departments were dubious of these claims. Nevertheless, the Navy Department, accepting the War Department's appraisal resulting from General MacArthur's reports, went ahead to acquire underground space in Corregidor and to place in operation therein an Intelligence facility. An important element of this Intelligence facility was a Communication Intelligence set-up and the effort right up to 1941 was to build up this organization at the expense, if necessary, of other Communication Intelligence groups. Assuming that the base could be held, as was consistently reported right up to the evacuation of Manila on 2 January 1942, the advantage of a functioning Communication Intelligence organization in the Philippines is obvious.

Regarding Admiral Theobald's statement that in case of war it was generally believed that the Japanese would strike at Pearl Harbor or the Panama Canal; this is again, I believe, a fair appraisal of Naval opinion. So far as I know this opinion was not based on any specific information but derived as a result of consideration of the strategic geography of the United States. I am sure that such a possibility was constantly in the minds of the Commanders in Chief of our Fleet from 1935 to 1938.----I knew the views of Admiral Reeves Commander in Chief in 1935 rather well; and served on the Staff of his successor Admiral Hepburn from 1936 to 1938. What could be more obvious than that in the event of war, the Japs would promptly attack our most important base in the Pacific within reach, Pearl Harbor; or would try to destroy the Panama Canal in order to impede the movement of our naval forces and sea-borne logistic elements from the Atlantic to the Pacific?

I think that in the foregoing discussion I may perhaps, have indicated why a "magic machine" was sent to the Philippines rather than to Pearl Harbor. The decision on this would have been taken in accordance with approved policy by the Director of Naval Communications, who had general cognizance over these matters.

Our forces in the Philippines and in the Far East in general, were instructed to send copies of their Intelligence reports to the Commander in Chief Pacific Fleet, which they did. To lend added emphasis to this point, some three weeks to a month before the attack on Pearl Harbor, Admiral Hart was specifically ordered to send reports and estimates of Japanese naval movements and intentions direct to Admiral Kimmel as well as to the Navy Department. This was done, at my insistence, on the basis that Hart was closest to happenings and was in the best position to evaluate quickly.

Referring to your item 5; I presume that you refer to the proceedings, findings and opinions of the Naval Court of Inquiry, convened sometime in 1944, on the Pearl Harbor affair. A Naval Court of Inquiry is, or was at that time before the so called uniform Military Code, a legal body of competent jurisdiction somewhat analogous to a Grand Jury in Civil legal proceedure. The members of this Court were three distinguished Admirals, retired shortly before the war viz:- Admiral Orin G. Murfin, Admiral Edward C Kalbfus and Vice Admiral Adolphus Andrews. This Court arrived at a long series of findings of fact and a somewhat less lengthy set of opinions. This Court found that there were no grounds for preferring charges for trial by General Court Martial of any officer concerned. In other words, and in civil parlance (forgive me if I err), there was no true bill. In the 2nd. endorsement on the record of this Court and dated 1 December 1944, the then Commander in Chief and Chief of Naval Operations, Admiral E. J. King, comments in paragraph 6 as follows:- "The derelictions on the part of Admiral Stark and Admiral Kimmel were faults of ommission rather than faults of commission. In the case in question they indicate lack of the superior judgement necessary for exercising command commensurate with their rank and assigned duties rather than culpable inefficiency". In paragraph 7 he states:- "Since trial by General Court Martial is not warranted by the evidence adduced, appropriate administrative action would appear to be the relegation of both these officers to positions in which lack of superior judgement may not result in future errors".

The Secretary of the Navy, Mr. Forrestal, was not entirely satisfied with the findings and opinions of the Court of Inquiry and the recommendations thereon of the Commander in Chief and Chief of Naval Operations; mainly because neither Rear Admiral T. S. Wilkinson, Director of Naval Intelligence at the time of the Pearl Harbor attack, nor I had been able to testify before the Court. The two of us were separately engaged in important operations against the enemy and our immediate Commanders informed the Navy Department that we could not be spared at that time to go back to Pearl Harbor to testify before the Court. The two Commanders to whom I refer were Admiral Halsey, in the case of Wilkinson, and Admiral Kinkaid, in my own case. Neither of these two officers was in or around the Navy Department at the time of Pearl Harbor. Subsequently the Secretary of the Navy directed Admiral H. Kent Hewitt to investigate the Pearl Harbor matter primarily for the purpose of developing what Admiral Wilkinson and I had to say on the matter. Finally under date of 13 August 1945, Mr. Forrestal agreed with Admiral King's endorsement of 1944 and stated:- "Accordingly I direct (a) Rear Husband E. Kimmel USN (Ret.) shall not hold any position in the United States Navy which requires exercise of superior judgement. (b) Admiral Harold R. Stark USN (Ret.) shall not hold any position in the United States Navy which requires exercise of superior judgement."

As one reads Admiral King's endorsement in its entirety, there are descernable certain political over-tones of the times. The Secretary of the Navy, as was to be expected of a political appointee, was more circumspect.

He waited about one year plus one investigation before committing himself. I understand that Admiral Stark has since received a retraction of their statements from Admiral King and the Secretary of the Navy.

I think that on the whole, certain other things should be understood.

Mr Knox, the Secretary of the Navy at the time of the attack on Pearl Harbor, was relatively new in the position. He was a prominent Republican politician, having been that party's nominee for the Vice Presidency in 1936. He was also one of Teddy Roosevelt's Rough Riders of 1898. All in all he was a grand man but hardly attuned to the subtleties of Pacific basin politics and grand strategy. In December 1940 Admiral Richardson, the then Commander in Chief of the Fleet, had come to Washington for the avowed purpose of protesting to the President the fixation of his fleet at Pearl Harbor, and its depletion of reconnaissance elements such as destroyers and aircraft carriers for service in the Atlantic. Admiral King, then commanding in the Atlantic, had a constantly growing problem of more and more area to patrol and he quite properly insisted that his forces be augmented as his responsibilities were increased by government policy. The only way in which the ships and trained crews necessary for the Atlantic could be obtained, was by further withdrawals from the Pacific Fleet. The types of ships most needed for patrolling in the Atlantic were precisely those types essential to tactical reconnaissance around the core of a fleet at sea or around a fleet anchorage containing a fleet, viz:- aircraft carriers, cruisers and destroyers. Richardson's point was, that either the withdrawals from the Pacific Fleet must be stopped or the bulk of the Fleet should be withdrawn from its exposed position in the Hawaiian Islands. Admiral Kimmel, then commanding the Cruisers of the Fleet, concurred in this view. Mr. Knox, in his review of the situation, is said to have felt that Admiral Richardson did not have a sufficiently belligerent attitude. In any event Richardson was relieved of his command rather abruptly and Kimmel substituted in late January or early February of 1941. Therefore, when Kimmel accepted the job of Commander in Chief he must have realized that his strategic base was fixed at Pearl Harbor by politics and that he could expect further depletion of his aircraft carrier and destroyer strength for service in the Atlantic under Admiral King.

With all this in view and the further consideration that there was a very considerable mass of information, independant of "magic" sources, available to Admiral Kimmel all pointing to the increasing imminence of hostilities; and that he had been specifically given a "war warning", he still did not assume an adequate tactical posture for the security of his force. In the final analysis a commander, faced with the possibility of an attack on his forces, must depend for ultimate security upon a system of physical reconnaissance and local counter attack. From a technical point of view I do not think there can be serious cavil with Kimmel's decision to bring his fleet under the defenses of Pearl Harbor. It would seem however, that before entrusting the safety of his entire fleet to those defenses it would have been entirely proper for him to have determined for himself the state of efficiency and alertness of those defenses. The recorded testimony indicates that he did not do this. It should be noted here that the defense of Pearl Harbor was the responsibility of the Army and the then Army Air Force. It was their almost total failure in time of need that resulted in the slaughter of 3,000 sailors, and the immobilization of our sole offensive arm in the Pacific.

I think that I can answer two other of your questions rather quickly. The Secretary of War and the Secretary of the Navy when they were in Washington, as they usually were, were advised just as promptly as was the President of the information contained in the Japanese telegrams. Admiral Theobald's book contains a list of the regular recipients of "magic".

I am sorry that I have inflicted this long drawn out discussion on you; but simple answers cannot be given to the searching questions you have posed. I have tried to give you a careful and considered appraisal as I think that I sense from your letter that you are interested in an objective appraisal. Might I suggest that in the view of the historian the political direction of our government was not entirely guiltless for the debacle of Pearl Harbor as well as for the "Death march of the Bataan survivors". I make bold to say that this Republic of ours has been exceptionally well served by its professional military and naval people. They have consistently eschewed domestic politics to their personal detriment, and have freely offered their lives for the maintenance of policies that, in the field of foreign affairs, has, at times, seemed to take but small cognizance of the hard facts. Our wars have been won, thank goodness, by the superb courage and ability of our citizen forces, as is proper in a Republic. Nevertheless, it is heart rending for a professional to have to send this fine human material into combat, partially unprepared as we have had to do, because of the previous lack of appreciation on the part of our people of the requirements for national survival on our own terms.

Sincerely yours,

A. H. McCollum

LAW OFFICES

FREEMAN, FOX & FIECHTER
TWELVE SOUTH TWELFTH STREET
PHILADELPHIA 7
WALNUT 2-3446

PAUL FREEMAN
WILLIAM LOGAN FOX
FREDERICK C. FIECHTER, JR.

August 2, 1954

Admiral A.H. McCollum,
3522 Third Street,
Arlington 1, Virginia

Dear Admiral McCollum:

My delay in acknowledging your letter of July 13th has been solely because I have been away on vacation. And, now that I have it, I feel most apologetic for having put you to so much trouble. Almost I would have preferred that you had tossed my letter into your scrap-basket. You have been most courteous, and I thank you sincerely.

My real difficulty is just this:- Was anyone to blame for Pearl Harbor? Perhaps Admiral Kimmel and General Short were not so vigilant as they might have been, but was Washington not really more at fault - and all things considered it seems to me that there is much weight to Admiral Theobald's theory.

To speak candidly, were I in the position of either General Marshall or Admiral Stark, I would welcome the book, for then the only fault one can lay at their doorsteps is that they did as they were bid by the only one who could "bid" them. And that fits in so well with the whole picture that reason and logic make the conclusion almost inevitable. What happened prior to 1940 seems (to me at least) rather immaterial, so far as concerns Pearl Harbor, for I am convinced that Roosevelt was determined to have this Country enter the war - if not by the front door then through Japan. And because of the temper of the people anything other than a serious attack by her upon us would not have availed him.

I send you an article by Admiral Beatty. In view of the facts set forth in your letter and in the book itself, I think it quite impotent. Would you mind returning it in the enclosed envelope please?

Well, we killed and maimed hundreds of thousands of our young men and spent hundreds of billions of dollars to destroy Germany and Japan - and now are striving to build them up again. The folly of his creatures must astonish even God Himself.

Thank you again and most sincerely.

Cordially yours,

PF:k   (over)

It seems to me that much of the objection to the book is due to the author's implication that there was a "conspiracy." The word has ugly connotations which cause resentment. The Navy and the Army heads may or may not have suspected the purpose of their Chief, who surely would not have disclosed fully what was in his mind, but they were in no position to voice effective objections.

3522 3rd., Street North
Arlington 1, Virginia
14 August 1954

Mr. Paul Freeman
Freeman, Fox & Fiechter
12 South 12th Street
Philadelphia 7, Pennsylvania

My dear Mr. Freeman:

Thank you for your letter of 2 August 1954. I am also enclosing herewith the article by Admiral Beatty which you sent me. He is a very pleasant person.

May I disagree with you that what happened before 1940 was of no moment? To my mind, the whole psychological and political atmosphere of what went on in the Pacific in 1941 was but a logical development of our policies and politics for the 20 to 40 years before that time. It has never been my claim that Washington was faultless in the Pearl Harbor affair. In fact my sworn testimony indicates otherwise. Nevertheless the appaling lack of tactical preparedness of the people on the spot at the time, of whom Admiral Theobald was one, still leaves me aghast. I say this in the light of one who was acting Fleet Operations Officer in December of 1937 at the time of the Panay incident.

To my mind one of the fatal errors of our diplomacy over the last thirty years has been our penchant for considering things Oriental as adjuncts to things European. Even so great a man as General Marshall made this mistake. Certainly since 1925 when the forcefulness of the Gun Boat policy in some of the Orient was shown to be invalid we still continued to think of the Orient in terms of European spheres of influence.

When you say that President Roosevelt wanted to get us into the European war by the front door if possible, by Japan if necessary, it seems to me that you disregard all Japanese evidence. Before about 1932 or 1933 it was possible for us to have made an accomodation with Japan. After about 1935 such an accomodation was no longer possible. When Admiral Yamamoto boasted that he would have breakfast in the White House --- He meant it---. Few of us still realize how our own apparent softness and pacifism lead the Japanese leaders to conclude that they could have their will with us with impunity. Not the least of their arguments was the refusal of President Hoover to support his Secretary of State, Stimsom, in stopping Japanese aggression in Manchuria in 1932.

Today we are witnissing an even more disagreeable and ominous debacle in Asia. We have settled a Korean war on shameful terms because we did not have the nerve to push it to an adequate conclusion. We tried to support the sorry French in Indo-China with our Mr. Dulles given the go by at Geneva. So far as the last two years are concerned our record in the Orient has been one of shameful capitulation. How far are we willing to go or how far can we go in hinging a policy upon the whims of the decadent European national entities without regard to the realities of the Orient

Sincerely

A. H. McCollum

www.ingramcontent.com/pod-product-compliance
Lightning Source LLC
Chambersburg PA
CBHW080627170426
43209CB00007B/1526